THE SONG OF THE HAWK

Also by John Chilton

Sidney Bechet : The Wizard of Jazz

Who's Who of Jazz : Storyville to Swing Street

Billie's Blues : A Survey of Billie Holiday's Career 1933–59

Stomp Off, Let's Go! : The Story of Bob Crosby's Bob Cats & Big Band

Teach Yourself Jazz

McKinney's Music : A Bio-discography of McKinney's Cotton Pickers

A Jazz Nursery : The Story of the Jenkins' Orphanage Band

Louis : The Louis Armstrong Story (with Max Jones)

THE SONG OF THE HAWK

The Life and Recordings of Coleman Hawkins

JOHN CHILTON

Quartet Books
London New York

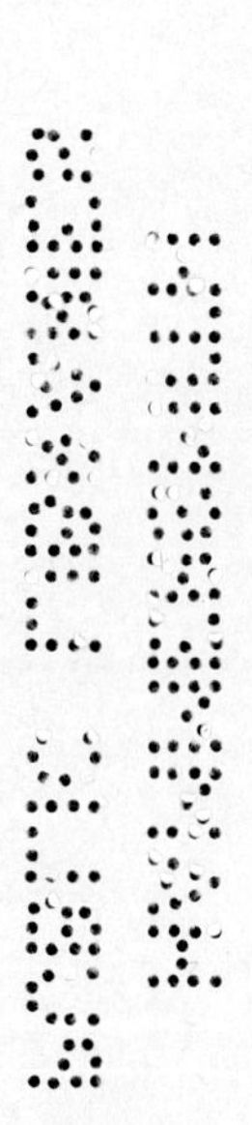

First published by Quartet Books Limited 1990
A member of the Namara Group
27/29 Goodge Street, London W1P 1FD

British Library Cataloguing in Publication Data
Chilton, John, *1932–*
The song of the hawk : the life and recordings of
Coleman Hawkins.
1. Jazz. Hawkins, Coleman – Biographies
I. Title
785.42′092′4

ISBN 0-7043-2737-6

Typeset by AKM Associates (UK) Ltd, Southall, London
Printed and bound in Great Britain by
BPCC Hazell Books Ltd
Member of BPCC Ltd, Aylesbury

For my brothers
Tom and Ron

Acknowledgements

Special thanks for their help to: Jeff Atterton, Leslie Diamond, Pete Felleman, Ron Geesin, Eddie Locke, Earl Okin, Brian Peerless, Arthur Pilkington, Johnny Simmen, and to the following: Dan Morgenstern, Institute of Jazz Studies, Rutger's, New Jersey, USA; Herman Openneer, Netherlands National Jazzarchief; Arnvid Meyer, the Danish Jazz Center; Jacqueline Lewin, Saint Joseph Museum, USA; Kansas City Historical Society, Topeka, USA; State of Missouri Department of Health; State of Kansas Department of Health.

Grateful thanks for their assistance to: George Avakian, Paul Bacon, Josephine Beaton, Max Bennett, Ed Berger, Ira Berger, Johs Bergh, Michael Berniker, Eddie Bert, Albert Bettonville, Stanley Black, Gunter Boas, Claude Bosseray, Michael Brooks, Eric Brown, Bob Burns, Garvin Bushell, Billy Butterfield, Thelma Carpenter, Benny Carter, George Chisholm, Buck Clayton, Peter Clayton, Al Cohn, Derek Coller, Graham Colombé, Eddie Cook, Gerald Crossman, Joe Crossman, Stanley Dance, Dave Dexter, Ed Dibble, Bill Dillard, Kenny Drew, Frank Driggs, Herman Dykstra, Roy Eldridge, Nancy Miller Elliott, W.A. Eschauzier, Leonard Feather, John Featherstone, Tommy Flanagan, Slim Gaillard, Joyce Gordon-Walker, Bob Graf, David Griffiths, Roland Hanna, Barry Harris, Cees Hartwig, Rene Hawkins, J.C. Heard, Alan Henderson, Hamilton Henderson, Nat Hentoff, Milt and Mona Hinton, Morris Hodara, Franz Hoffman, Julian Holland, Major Holley, Peter Ind, Victor Ingelveldt, Illinois Jacquet, John Jarvis, Norman Jenkinson, Jerry Jerome, Max and Betty Jones, Larry Kart, Catherine Kent, Pete King, Joe Knight, Peter Kok, Ben Kraaijenbrink, Guy Lafitte, Hans Langeweg, Stan Levey, Robert Levin, Harris Lewine, Herbert Lewis, Harry Lim, Thomas Lindsey, Lawrence Lucie, Jaap Lüdeke, Prentice McCarey, George Masso, Tony Middleton, Eddie Miller, Francis Mitchell, James Moody, Michael Morgenstern, Billy Munn, New Orleans Jazz Archive (Tulane University),

George Nicholas, Cecil Norman, Peter den Otter, Remo Palmier, Alfredo Papo, Jimmy Parsons, Vincent Pelotte, Bernhard Peritz, Robert Pernet, Michael Pointon, Jake Porter, Lewis Porter, Annie de Reuver, Larry Ridley, Peter Robinson, Martin Roman, Howard Rye, Saint Joseph Musicians' Association, Trevor Salter, Phil Schaap (Station WKCR), Victor Schonfield, Ronnie Scott, Tony Scott, Alyn Shipton, Edward Sims, Jimmy Skidmore, Louis Stephenson, Roy Stevens, Jessie Stone, F.D. Streep, Mike Sutcliffe, Buddy Tate, Mev Taylor, Bob Thiele, Marcel Thielemans, Mark Tucker, Peter Vacher, Andy Van Der Geest, Lou Van Rees, J.A. Van Tilburg, Gerry Vejmola, Françoise Venet, Bryn Venus, Steve Voce, Selwyn Warner, Al Washington, Oliver Weston, John Whitehorn, Jeff Williams, Johnny Williams, Val Wilmer, Fred 'Tiny' Winters, Laurie Wright, Ann Xhofleer-Palier, Les Zacheis.

Contents

'As a person, Coleman Hawkins is an enigma to many people. Quiet, reserved, cynical, worldly, he is enormously different from the portrait of the average jazz musician'

Down Beat magazine,
20 October 1950.

1
Missouri Breaks

Almost all of the men who pioneered jazz were unschooled musicians. The formal tuition that Louis Armstrong, Sidney Bechet and Jelly Roll Morton received was little more than a demonstration of how to produce music on an instrument. Subsequently these young men blended hard work with inborn genius, gradually acquiring formidable musical techniques, in the process using their growing skills to express themselves via revolutionary improvisations.

In the rapidly changing economic conditions of the early twentieth century, however, new opportunities allowed many young black musicians the chance to benefit from thorough musical coaching. Only a few years separated these young performers from the men who had virtually originated jazz, but during that brief period an army of youthful black musicians emerged whose parents were able, and willing, to pay for their offspring to study.

Among this second wave of jazzmen was a musician whose studies embraced every facet of music. He was as well-versed in the classics as in popular tunes, but his destiny lay in granting form and beauty to the art of improvising jazz. His name was Coleman Hawkins, and his successes led him to be recognized ever after as 'the father of the tenor saxophone'.

Unlike Armstrong, Bechet and Morton, Hawkins was not from New Orleans, Louisiana. He was born in Saint Joseph, Missouri, in 1904. It's tempting to think that this sprawling city on the east bend of the Missouri River was an unlikely spot for a jazz almighty to be born so early in the music's history, but by the time Hawkins was in his teens the music that had first flourished in New Orleans was establishing itself in a great number of places throughout America.

St Joe, as Hawkin's home city is often called, burst through the 100,000 population mark at about the time that Hawkins was born. Being large and fairly prosperous (mainly through its various stockyard enterprises), the city was able to support a wide spectrum of musical entertainment, so there can be little doubt that the sound of embryo jazz reached Hawkins during his childhood. Ragtime was still being played in the city and blues songs from the Southern states continued to float into its busy port, carried by the voices of black itinerant workers.

Hawkins was always vague about his early musical influences. In a recorded interview he said, 'First jazz I heard? I was just a little kid, yes, I heard jazz right then. These places like down Second Street, which was like the real Tenderloin, more or less, that's where they used to have the jazz bands playing all night.'[1] On another occasion he said, 'Why, I heard saxophones on record when I was just a little kid. There was one trio with a tenor sax; that was about the earliest music I can remember.'[2]

But throughout his life Hawkins was rarely at ease when being questioned about his early years, and never once, in countless interviews, threw any direct light on the exact sounds that had charmed him towards jazz. His usual answer when cornered on the subject of his original inspirations was simply to say that he listened to every sort of music during his childhood. This was the truth. Both his mother (a pianist and organist) and his father adored all forms of music and Hawkins grew up developing the catholic tastes that stayed with him for the rest of his life. His father, William Hawkins, was not much of a musician; Coleman said later, 'My father could play one piece on the piano. That was one of them funny pieces he made up.'[3] But his parents were eager that their young son should begin playing the piano, so his keyboard studies began when he was five years old.

As a young child, Coleman practised conscientiously on the piano, also playing the cello from an early age, but neither the keyboard nor the sound of the strings brought him any deep satisfaction and somehow he developed the fixed idea that he wanted to play the saxophone. The yearning grew and manifested itself in a stream of oblique hints to his parents.

The doting couple decided that their only child (their first born, a daughter,* had died in 1903 at the age of two) should have his wish; they bought him a C-melody saxophone. Hawkins said that the instrument was

* Local Registrar 157 (Division of Health of Missouri) recorded the birth of a female child to William Hawkins and Edna Cordelia Coleman Hawkins on 8 March 1901. This document became the basis for a mistaken belief that Coleman Randolph Hawkins was born in 1901.

given to him as a present on his ninth birthday: 'My father used to say that the instrument was as large as me.'[4] It was a remarkably young age to begin playing the saxophone, particularly in an era when the instrument had not achieved the popularity it would later gain. Also it might have been more suitable for a boy to have started on a saxophone with smaller dimensions than the C-melody (an alto or a soprano, perhaps), but even at nine years of age Coleman's frame had begun to fill out. He said, 'I think I stopped growing by the time I was twelve, I didn't get any taller.'[5] On another occasion he commented, 'I don't think I was ever a child.'[6]

Late in life Hawkins became mysterious about his place of birth, and touchy about giving the date on which he was born. In 1956 he said he was born at sea, while his mother and father were returning from Europe: 'On the Atlantic Ocean, on a boat. To me it's hard to say actually where my real birth would be.'[7] The truth was not quite as romantic. Coleman Randolph Hawkins was born on 21 November 1904 at 1713 Angelique in the Buchanan District of Saint Joseph, Missouri; he was delivered by Dr Preston Edwards. Coleman's parents, William and Cordelia, lived at 1713 Angelique with Cordelia's parents, Mr and Mrs Coleman. Cordelia's maiden name (Coleman) became the infant's first name. At the time of the birth, Coleman Hawkins's mother (who was always known as Cordelia, even though she had been christened Edna Cordelia) was in her late twenties, and his father was then thirty-two. Both parents had been born in Missouri: William in St Joseph and Cordelia in Plattsburg.[8]

William Hawkins was in regular employment, which meant Cordelia did not have to go out to work to supplement the family income. She was able to stay home and raise the new infant. When Coleman was twelve his father joined the American Electrical Company in St Joseph as an assistant packer, remaining with that organization for the rest of his life. To help pay for Coleman's musical tuition William also worked as a part-time janitor at the Dollinger Building in St Joseph.

Cordelia's father, Thomas Coleman, was a janitor at nearby Christ Church; his position there allowed Cordelia access to a piano and an organ. She became a proficient musician and played for church services and social gatherings. Apparently her grandfather (who according to Coleman was born in Rouen, France) also played the organ. Hawkins rarely spoke about his lineage, but late in life he occasionally mentioned that his grandmother had given shelter to the famous Missouri outlaw, Jesse James. Hawkins grew up surrounded by mythology about Jesse James, as did most of the youngsters in St Joseph, where in 1882 (on 13th and Lafayette) the notorious outlaw had been shot dead.

Cordelia Hawkins was most anxious that her son become a fine cellist, and insisted that he practise for at least two hours a day. Hawkins resented this and showed a preference for playing the piano, but when the new saxophone arrived both the piano and the cello were relegated down the list of his interests. He never needed to be cajoled or even reminded about practising the saxophone and spent every spare moment playing musical exercises on it.

In 1934, while Hawkins was touring Scotland, he told Mev Taylor in Edinburgh,

> My mother recognized that I had a keen ear for music, so she got a cello for me. After some tuition she realized that I wasn't practising as much as she thought that I should. She started putting me in a hut we had in the backyard so that she made sure I got on with my practise. Eventually, when I got that saxophone, instead of having to lock me up in the shed she had to interrupt me to tell me it was meal times.[9]

Coleman Hawkins was taught cello by a local musician, known as 'Professor' Pennell. A Mr Streep, who worked at a local music store, took a close interest in Coleman's progress on the saxophone, but it was not until the youngster visited the store to try out a new mouthpiece that the salesman realized just how talented the boy was. A local musician named Ted (or Tad) Clark overheard Hawkins trying out the mouthpiece and called into the store. Clark, who acted as a part-time agent in providing bands to play at local functions, asked the youngster if he could read music. Coleman's answer was a quizzical 'yes'; having learnt to read music as an infant, before he ever came to grips with the printed word, he was surprised that the question had been asked at all.

The upshot of the meeting in the music store was that Coleman played his first paid engagement on saxophone, working with a pick-up group at a local dance. The group consisted of old and young musicians, but the most junior was at least three years older than Hawkins, who was then about twelve years of age. Word quickly spread about the precocious talent of the young saxophonist and he was offered many local engagements. He also played at school dances, so his teachers were well aware of his musical prowess, their only regret being that Coleman never left himself enough time to develop his skills as an essay writer.

Hawkins recalled the school dances:

> These early ones we played used piano, drums and myself. Once there was a boy that I played with out in Topeka who couldn't play in anything but F sharp (i.e. playing mostly on the black notes of the piano). Every piece he played was in F sharp, so naturally I learnt how to play in my G sharp on the tenor. That was good for me . . . it gave me an early start on transposition and composition and all that stuff when I was going to school.[10]

This snippet about those early days highlights a curious pattern in Hawkin's reminiscences, one that he was prone to repeat. It concerned the sort of saxophone that he first began playing. Three musicians (Garvin Bushell, Jesse Stone and Freddy Skerritt) independently saw and heard Hawkins play in his formative years and all said that he was playing a C-melody saxophone, which is slightly smaller (and pitched a tone higher) than the B-flat tenor sax. In the 1910s and early 1920s the C-melody model was more common than the tenor; it was the first type of saxophone to be available on the Sears Roebuck mail-order catalogue. Its supposed advantage was that it was a non-transposing instrument, allowing a performer to play direct from piano music or from a violin part, whereas a tenor saxophonist needed to transpose a tone up from the so-called 'concert' pitch.

For some reason Hawkins deliberately altered his personal history (even throwing in the anecdote about the pianist's limitations) to stress that his early days were on tenor sax. Why did he do this? Perhaps he did not want his own trail-blazing to be compared with the pioneering of the white saxophonist, Frank Trumbauer, who remained a C-melody specialist all his working life. Although Trumbauer (a few years older than Hawkins) also grew up in Missouri (in St Louis) there is no evidence whatsoever to suggest that Hawkins had ever heard (or even heard of) Trumbauer during those early years. Certainly their work was totally different, both stylistically and tonally.

The real reason for Hawk's deception was probably more mundane. He always liked to be in the vanguard of fashion and was well aware that the vogue for C-melody saxes was notably brief. To be linked in any way with anything out-moded would have been too painful for him to contemplate. He was also morbidly concerned with age at the time he gave his Topeka reminiscences and knew that the early ownership of a C-melody sax would have tied him to a decade that he chose not to remember. In any case, his readjustments of fact do not alter his tremendous achievements in shaping the role of the saxophone in jazz.

Coleman's parents were extremely proud of their child's musical progress, and they could see that he had set his heart on making music his career. Cordelia Hawkins made no attempt to dissuade her son from his ambition even though music was not then a highly regarded profession among devout churchgoers. But Coleman revealed early wisdom in not concentrating on the cello (as his mother wanted him to do); at that time no black musician was considered to be worthy of a place in any of the main American symphony orchestras, racial bigotry preventing them from even auditioning for a vacancy. As a consequence, no matter what brilliance Hawkins might have achieved on cello he would not have been appropriately rewarded.

Racial segregation was part of everyday life in Saint Joseph at this time, so Coleman's parents decided to send their son to further his general education at the Industrial and Educational Institute in Topeka, the state capital of Kansas (some eighty miles south west of Saint Joseph). The institute, which had been organized in 1895, admitted only black pupils. So Coleman temporarily left the homestead to study in Topeka; his mother, determined that her son should make a good impression at the institute, insisted that he took only his cello there, not his saxophone.

Hawkins's skill on the cello soon gained him invitations to take part in musical evenings with local players; some of these musicians were students from the Washburn College in Topeka. Hawk's technique and theoretical knowledge was comparable to that of these occasional colleagues, but he must have envied them the advantages that they had enjoyed. Years later Coleman claimed to have been a student at Washburn, but the present Dean of Arts and Sciences, Dr Robert L. Burns, could find no record of this. This does not rule out the possibility that the young man studied privately with one of the Washburn tutors, or that he attended (without graduation) an academy that coached pre-Washburn students.

During this period Hawkins teamed up with pianist Jesse Stone, who later became a noted bandleader and composer. Stone recalls:

> Four of us young musicians joined together to play engagements around Atchison, Kansas. Myself on piano, Jess Ogden on drums, George Bell on violin and Coleman Hawkins on the cello. But having two stringed instruments in the line-up didn't work when we played dances – the cello wasn't suitable for this sort of work – so Coleman began doubling on C-melody sax with us, and that was fine. He was still a student at the Topeka Institute, which was about forty-five miles from Atchison. Our band played all around the area, including Saint Joseph, mostly for black audiences; it was very seldom that any white people came along. Coleman was a bit younger than I was (I was born in 1901); he was a very studious young man. He'd had

> a lot of formal training on the cello but I got the impression that he was mainly self-taught on the saxophone. Coleman Hawkins was one of three good young sax players from St Joseph; I think they all pulled one another along. One of the others was Elmer Birch, a cousin of mine who later worked in animal husbandry, and the third was Henry Martin, who played music professionally for a while. All three were about the same age.[11]

Hawkins gradually outshone his two hometown rivals but his reputation ran level with another young saxophonist, Paul Evans (nicknamed 'Stump' because of his diminutive height), who was gradually making a name for himself in the Missouri and Kansas territories. Evans, born in Lawrence, Kansas, a month before Hawkins, was a prodigy who had been taught by his father, Clarence Evans. Unlike Hawkins, he chose to specialize on the alto saxophone. Alvin Dahlene, a resident of Kansas City in those years, remembered the rivalry that existed between those who said Hawkins was the better player and those who supported Evans. Curiously Hawkins said that he never heard Evans in person, even though St Joseph is only eighty miles north east of Lawrence, Kansas. But Evans soon moved to Chicago, and died young.

Hawkins was always at pains to correct those who credited him with being the first jazz saxophonist, pointing out that 'Stump' Evans was his contemporary. In turn, Evans had the highest respect for Hawkins's achievements. In the 1920s, when trombonist Preston Jackson complimented Evans (in Chicago) on the way he played the saxophone, Evans told him, 'Wait until you hear Coleman Hawkins.'[12] Speaking of his early days, Hawkins told writer Leonard Feather, 'Nobody paid saxophone any mind, the good ones couldn't improvise too much and some of the fellows used to play with those little bitty mouthpieces just like clarinet mouthpieces; I always used a hard reed and developed an open mouthpiece.'[13]

During the Topeka Institute vacation periods Hawkins often worked in Kansas City, playing in theatre orchestras on cello and saxophone, sometimes augmenting a visiting unit. By this time recordings made by the Original Dixieland Jazz Band had reached most parts of America, including Missouri, but Hawkins didn't identify with that style of music at all. His dislike of the ODJB's music was not on racial grounds, since as a schoolboy he had listened with pleasure to Ted Lewis and Sophie Tucker performing at local theatres, but the sound of a dixieland ensemble never appealed to him. He said years later, 'All that dixieland sounds alike to me,'[14] and on another occasion he wrote that he had always disliked rough musical sounds of any sort. Even so, he admitted that he enjoyed hearing the work of the local pianists when he was a young man: 'I used to hear piano in every place. It was more like boogie-woogie, I guess, a kind of mix-up. Very good.'[15]

A golden age for black performers was about to begin. At the forefront of this development was the singer Mamie Smith, whose August 1920 recording of 'Crazy Blues' became a nationwide success. Mamie is often described as a blues singer, but she did not specialize in the blues. She sang all types of popular material, but the fact that her main successes on record were based on songs described as 'blues' naturally caused her to feature a good deal of similar material in her stage repertoire. Her OKeh recording of 'Crazy Blues' is generally acknowledged to be the first commercially successful recording by a black popular artist; its sales figures (said to have topped a million within five months of issue) inspired many recording companies to begin issuing work by other black performers.

Mamie Smith's success on recordings meant that audiences throughout the USA were anxious to see the new star in person. Theatrical touring was nothing new to Mamie; she had worked regularly on stage since becoming part of a white act known as the Four Dancing Mitchels at the age of ten. Born in the South, she settled in Harlem in 1913 and sang in various shows and cabarets. While appearing in *Maid in Harlem*, she was spotted by the black entrepreneur and composer, Perry Bradford, who arranged for her to make her first recordings.

Backed by her own Original Jazz Hounds, Mamie played successful dates in New York and Philadelphia before accepting work further afield, but the freelance musicians who worked with Mamie on her early recordings and local bookings (including the eminent cornettist Johnny Dunn) didn't want to go on tour. Mamie began using pick-up bands, but dissatisfied theatre managers soon demanded that she toured with the same class of musicians that she used on her recordings. After a disgruntled tour of the Midwest, Mamie returned to New York and persuaded the ace trumpeter Bubber Miley to join her group permanently. She also secured the services of a fine young reed player, Garvin Bushell.

Together with trombonist Cecil Carpenter, pianist Charles Summers and a violinist and drummer, this new version of the Jazz Hounds played a series of theatre dates with Mamie in Pennsylvania and Ohio en route to the Avenue Theatre in Chicago, where they played an eight-day residency beginning on 21 May 1921. The entourage eventually moved on to Kansas City to play at the 12th Street Theatre. Like many other burlesque halls, this venue usually closed for the summer months, but it was not shuttered up and could be hired by touring troupes, or by local promoters. Thus Mamie Smith was engaged to play at the theatre for a week, hired by a local agent to present her own show, complete with various supporting acts, including a comedian and a magician; Mamie came on stage for the second half of the production.

Garvin Bushell, recalling this engagement, said,

> In Kansas City we had to play the first half of the two-hour show in the orchestra pit, accompanying various acts. It was decided to augment the band and someone recommended that we hire a young local musician, who turned out to be Coleman Hawkins. So the first time I ever heard Coleman was at a morning rehearsal at the theatre. He was outstanding, ahead of anything I'd ever heard. He read everything at sight without any mistakes; his sight reading and musicianship was faultless even at that young age. He was playing a C-melody saxophone and it was obvious that he had total command of it. As far as his personality went, well you could say he was a cocky youngster who realized he was head and shoulders above anyone of his age, anywhere. But he was a very knowledgeable young man, highly intelligent, with none of the common ways that some touring musicians had.[16]

Hawkins wasn't in the least overawed by the situation he encountered and played the written and improvised parts of the show with such skill that he made a highly favourable impression on all of Mamie Smith's musicians, and on the star of the show herself. Mamie, and her manager, realized that the young prodigy would greatly enhance the stage show, so they asked if he would be interested in joining the troupe permanently. He was non-committal and said he would have to discuss it with his family.

The group were due to move on to Tulsa, Oklahoma, but a recent race riot there caused them to change their plans. As a stop-gap date, Mamie Smith's group played a hastily arranged dance in Hawkins's hometown, St Joseph. Hawkins played with the band on this date, and, after it was finished Mamie and a deputation from the band (including Garvin Bushell) visited the Hawkins home. His mother and father were out of town visiting relatives, so Mamie Smith asked Coleman's grandmother (who was looking after him temporarily) for permission to let the youngster join the show permanently. The grandmother said (according to Bushell), 'No, he's only a baby; he's only fifteen,' though Coleman was actually sixteen by this time.

So Coleman remained behind when the troupe moved on. When Cordelia Hawkins returned home she was in total agreement with her mother's sentiments; Coleman was bitterly disappointed but respectfully abided by the family decision. He returned, somewhat restlessly, to his studies in Topeka and continued working on band dates with Jesse Stone. Happily for Coleman, however, the Mamie Smith show again visited Kansas City to play dates at the Gillies Theatre during the first week of April 1922. Neither Mamie nor her manager had forgotten the young saxophonist and they again visited the Hawkins household and offered to take Coleman with them.

To forestall any homesickness, Mamie Smith offered places in the travelling show to all four members of Jesse Stone's group. Stone and drummer Jess Ogden declined the offer, but violinist George Bell accepted. The fact that Coleman would have 'hometown' company (Bell was also from St Joseph) may have swayed Cordelia Hawkins, but she was also disapprovingly aware that Coleman had become heavily involved with a local girl and this may have affected her decision. Whatever the reason, Cordelia Hawkins agreed that her young son could join the troupe, providing that Mamie Smith agreed to act as a legal guardian. The singer readily agreed to this stipulation and Hawkins packed his bags (as did George Bell) to move off with the group for their next engagement, a return residency (in April 1922) at the Avenue Theatre, Chicago.

In the 1950s, when Hawkins was prone to mischievously lopping years off his age, he said that he was twelve when he heard King Oliver and Louis Armstrong playing together in Chicago. But in 1916 neither Oliver nor Armstrong had yet left New Orleans, and Louis was still in Louisiana in April 1922 (Oliver had by this time been in Chicago, but in April 1922 he was working in California). Hawk's claim to have heard these two giants playing together was thus probably another example of what he laughingly described as 'kidding'.

During his early dates in Chicago with Mamie Smith, Hawkins met up with a local musician, Albert 'Happy' Caldwell, who recalled: 'He was crazy about my clarinet style and asked me, "Say, why don't you come and join us?" You know he learned cello there in Chicago, at Chicago University. He studied there in Chicago.'[17] These details of further studies may have been created by more of Hawk's 'leg-pulling', although it is conceivable that he attended 'refresher' lessons while in Chicago. Caldwell eventually joined Mamie Smith, but by that time Hawkins had left the group.

In Mamie Smith's show Hawkins was immediately given billing as 'Saxophone Boy', and as such was singled out for special mention by the *Chicago Defender* newspaper. By this time Garvin Bushell had left the troupe, as had Bubber Miley. The personnel of the Jazz Hounds in April 1922 was George Bell (violin), Charles Matson (piano), George Mullen (cornet) Bob Fuller (clarinet), Curtis Mosby (drums), Cecil Carpenter (trombone) and Coleman Hawkins (saxophone and cello).

For the first few months of his stay with Mamie Smith's company Hawkins doubled on cello. Musician Freddy Skerritt clearly recalled Hawk playing cello and C-melody sax during this period. It's likely that Coleman's mother insisted that her son take his cello on tour, since she was always more interested in his progress on it than she was in his saxophone playing. Soon after Coleman left home, a young erstwhile saxophonist, Walter 'Foots' Thomas, temporarily lodged at the Hawkins household while visiting St Joseph as a member of a touring basketball team. Thomas had begun playing the sax and was well aware of Coleman's reputation, though to his great surprise Mrs Hawkins seemed much prouder of her son's achievements on the cello.[18]

After Chicago, Mamie's group played dates in Cleveland, Ohio, in late April 1922, then doing what the *Chicago Defender* called 'a grasshopper to New York for recordings'. This meant that the troupe did the long journey from Ohio to New York by rail so that Mamie Smith could record more titles for the OKeh company. So, early in May 1922, Coleman Hawkins made his recording debut on 'Mean Daddy Blues'. His role, on C-melody sax, is a prominent one: he takes the lead for part of the introduction and establishes the melody link to Mamie's vocal entry. Mamie sings the strong, attractive tune with genuine spirit. She was a highly competent vaudeville vocalist but she was not a blues singer, a point underlined by Garvin Bushell's comments: 'Mamie Smith wasn't a real blues singer like Bessie Smith. She didn't get in between the tones the way Bessie did. Mamie was what we called a shouter. But the white people called it blues!'[19]

Hawk's main task in the early stages of 'Mean Daddy Blues' consists of reinforcing the melody, often doubling the same note that Mamie Smith is singing, but he is not tied to that tactic and during gaps in the vocal phrasing he embellishes brief fill-ins. Later he drops into the lower register and slap-tongues an elementary counterpoint, but neither the fill-ins nor the backing phrases resemble an accomplished jazz performance. Almost every saxophonist performing popular music during this era created notes by emphatically slapping the tongue against the reed fixed in the mouthpiece. The staccato notes that ensued were emphasized dramatically in a way that precluded the creation of smooth-flowing, swinging phrasing. In the early stages of his career Hawkins was just as guilty as the rest in producing the clipped slap-tongue sound that is now employed only for comic effect.

On record, the overall effect of Mamie Smith's group is that of a burlesque-hall orchestra doing its best to superimpose a 'raggy' feel to a popular song. Their performance has none of the elegance or organization of ragtime, nor any of the excitement generated by jazz rhythms. Most of the band's phrasing has a stiff, even-note feel which negates the sort of swing that was soon to be a feature of recordings by King Oliver's Creole Jazz Band.

The coda of 'Mean Daddy Blues' contains the first sample of Hawkin's work as a soloist. He plays his brief, one-bar phrase with confidence, but no one could have forecast, on this evidence, that he would become a sensational jazz improviser. 'Dem Knock Out Blues' again demonstrates Hawkins's eminence within the group. He takes the melody throughout a twelve-bar interlude, offering fleeting clues within the final bars of this section that he was attempting to get to grips with the revolutionary concepts of jazz phrasing. 'Mean Daddy' and 'Dem Knock Out' were both good popular tunes, but neither was a blues; they were simply described as such on the record label (as were hundreds of songs in the 1920s) to add novelty appeal.

On 'Lonesome Mama' Hawkins plays a less active role behind the vocalist's phrasing, but makes up for it by dominating the twenty-four-bar instrumental interlude; he plays a solo break during this section and again in the final bars of the performance. Hawkins is just as prominent in the twenty-bar instrumental section of 'New Orleans', tonguing his notes with a force that virtually propels him into the lead during an every-man-for-himself ensemble.

Hawkins's entry into the profession of popular music was almost at the top rung of the ladder. Mamie Smith's tours drew vast crowds, initially because record buyers were curious to see her in person, but her artistry and the lively backing music usually resulted in return bookings on the various theatre circuits. One chain of halls, managed by the Theatre Owners' Booking Association, was spoken of as the TOBA circuit, the abbreviation soon dubbed Tough on Black Asses or, more genteelly, Tough on Black Artists. Only a few of the theatres that employed Mamie Smith's troupe showed an unrestrictive attitude toward black customers; most often the show worked to segregated houses where black patrons were permitted to sit only in the top balcony.

At the height of her fame Mamie Smith was able to command a thousand dollars a week for a booking at the Lafayette Theatre in Harlem. On tour her fees were even higher. In Philadelphia she was paid 1,500 dollars a week and for a single night's booking at Billy Sunday's Tabernacle in Norfolk, Virginia she was paid 2,000 dollars. An early newspaper report said, 'Theatres begged dates from the heavy-hipped, deep-voiced blues shouter.'

Coleman Hawkins's share of the singer's income was a salary of fifty dollars a week, with extra money for recordings. Garvin Bushell, recalling the cost of living at that time, said, 'You could get a hotel for a dollar a night, and a good meal only cost fifty cents.' So the money was good, but in terms of the experience that Hawkins was gaining the job was worth a fortune. He learnt a good deal about stagecraft and developed the knack of projecting his tone right to the back of a vast theatre, an important skill in this pre-microphone age. He also got to know how to improvise his way out of any emergency that occurred while the band were accompanying the various acts that formed the first part of Mamie's touring show. His reading was faultless and he seemed able to play by ear in any key.

After Hawk's recording debut (for which he was paid thirty dollars) the group left New York for another round of touring. At the New Douglass Theatre in Baltimore, Hawkins was listed as a featured artist. The show did sensational business at the New Douglass and after playing for a week at the Howard Theatre in Washington, DC the troupe returned to Baltimore for another booking, this time for two weeks. The cast, which included the variety acts of Brown and Brown, Wells and Wells and the Norfolk Jazz Four, played to almost 19,000 people during their first week back at the New Douglass.

Joseph Jones provided the *Chicago Defender* with a report of proceedings:

> Wells and Wells, trapeze artists, started off the Mamie Smith Revue. Coleman Hawkins, saxophone king, was in the deuce spot and made 'em like it. An outburst of jazz from behind the lowered drop warned us that Mamie Smith's Jazz Hounds were ready to put in an appearance. As the curtain was slowly raised the Jazz Hounds – Charles Matson, pianist; George Mullen, cornettist; Cecil Carpenter, trombonist; George Bell, violinist; Coleman Hawkins, saxophonist and Curtis Moseley [sic], drummer – poured forth some wicked jazz in the form of 'Bugle Blues'. When this finished they struck up the 'Arkansas Blues'. The flowered drop parted in the middle and there stood Mamie Smith in a beautiful dress of blue, iridescent, with yellow

> flowers, plumed headdress and gold slippers. She came down the stage chirping the 'Arkansas Blues' with the Hounds all around her. She sang her next number, 'Daddy', in a beautiful silver dress with silver fringes at the sides and her third and last number, 'There's Only One Man', in a beautiful solid-gold cloth trimmed with rhinestones. The Hounds rendered some very jazzy numbers between Mamie's songs.[20]

For the group's second week at the New Douglass Theatre some of the accompanying acts were changed and yodler Charles Anderson joined the show. The *Chicago Defender* of 3 June 1922 reported that the second week's booking was even more successful than the first. Unfortunately the huge inflow of cash proved too much of a temptation for the manager of the theatre and the *Chicago Defender* was forced to report the sad news that he had 'flown the coup with the dough'.

The manager's defection introduced Hawkins to one of the hazards of the touring life. It was a lesson he remembered for all of his professional days, and he did his utmost to avoid a repetition of the experience. His insistence on pre-payments or cash settlements, and his carefulness with money, caused him to gain the reputation of being an avaricious skinflint, but because he hadn't saved any money during his first weeks with Mamie he actually went hungry through the manager's defection. It was a sensation for which his comfortable upbringing had not prepared him and as a result he never forgot it.

The loss of two weeks' earnings encouraged Mamie Smith and her manager to supervise their own box-office affairs by travelling with their own complete show, hiring theatres and collecting all the admission money direct from the customers. At various times Mamie's company featured every sort of vaudeville artist, including the gargantuan Baby Jim, who only had to waddle on stage to convulse an audience. Another star was 'the world's smallest woman', billed as 'Princess Wee Wee'. The band had to accompany all the acts, whatever their shape or size. Mamie soon decided to drop the Jazz Hounds billing, and began publicizing her show as Mamie Smith and Her All Jazz Review, this later becoming her Syncopated Revue and, later still, her Gang.

At most times Mamie Smith had a kindly disposition, but she also had a quick temper and a streak of unreasoning jealousy. Most of the musicians who worked with her weighed up the odds and steered clear even of attempting a romantic attachment with her. Mamie's husband, William (who died in 1928) didn't tour with the show, which allowed the singer to indulge in a long – and sometimes violent – affair with her manager, Ocey

Wilson (whom she later married). But Ocey, like Mamie, could be violently jealous and he often made the singer wear veils off-stage so that no one would be tempted by her attractive face. Mamie stood this imposition for a while, before she forced Ocey to revoke his instructions by brandishing a pistol at him.

As the baby of Mamie Smith's band Hawkins naturally attracted a lot of attention, particularly from the young girls who formed the show's chorus line. Coleman responded by developing a line of confident, charming patter that appealed to a good many young females both in and out of the theatrical world. The elegance that later became part of his lifestyle was gradually developing but he was not, in those days, a model of smartness. The young man was so busy playing, rehearsing, charming the girls and revelling that he had little time to keep up with his laundry, resulting in his band colleagues giving him the unflattering nickname 'Greasy'.[21]

Some of Mamie's musicians found the volatile atmosphere of the troupe unappealing and stayed with the group only briefly. The singer herself once admitted that it would take a detective to keep up with the comings and goings of musicians who worked with her,[22] but Hawkins, perhaps because he had no previous touring experience to compare his situation with, settled in without flinching and became one of the group's more durable fixtures.

In June 1922 the entourage returned to New York, where Mamie had bought a luxury house on West 133rd Street. Singer and band did some local theatre work and private engagements, and they also played a sporadic residency at a cabaret called The Garden of Joy, built on a vast jutting rock situated on 7th Avenue at 140th Street. The stay in New York also allowed the troupe to resume recordings. No drastic change of musical policy had occurred but there are indications on the OKeh sessions from the summer of 1922 that more attention was being paid to harmonizing various background figures. Hawkins is not quite as prominent as he was on his debut session. The instrumental interludes are generally briefer, but the most important development concerned Hawkins's choice of instrument, for during that summer he made the change from C-melody to the B-flat tenor saxophone. At about this time, too, he phased out the cello, choosing occasionally to amuse himself by playing a written cello part on his tenor sax.

Incongruous though the suggestion may seem, Mamie Smith's performance on the recording of 'Mamie Smith Blues' is reminiscent of the white singer Sophie Tucker's early work, both in delivery and enunciation. The song itself is a curious autobiographical meander, containing the bizarre advice: 'Don't be blue. Lots of girls wish they were Mamie Smith too.' The band increase the tempo for their sixteen-bar instrumental, breaking into a stiff-kneed trot (punctuated by the clackings of woodblocks) that makes them sound more like a pit band than ever. 'Alabama Blues' is another indifferent song. The band are prominent only during the introduction and a two-bar interlude but they continually provide a series of artless musical backdrops. Within this morass of sound, however, Hawkins begins to shape his phrases effectively and to season them with judiciously placed blue notes.

Mamie is at her most vivacious on 'Got to Cool My Doggies Now', on which Hawkins chose to play the baritone saxophone, booming out notes below the range of a tenor saxophone with power and confidence. An alto saxophone plays a roving role and a ubiquitous violin saws out some squeaky musical patterns. There is no instrumental section in 'You Can Have Him', but the background figures show that Hawkins had reverted to playing tenor sax (after his brief sojourn on baritone).

It might be imagined that Mamie Smith was deliberately thwarting the development of jazz inspiration within her backing group, not wishing for too much favourable light to fall on her accompanists – but the three instrumentals that the band recorded (without Mamie) are as stilted as ever. 'These Longing For You Blues' resembles the sort of brief overture that small theatre ensembles used to play before it was time for the curtain to rise and this is probably what the piece's function was in the band's repertoire. The trumpet and trombone are allocated brief heraldic solo interludes, which provide a merciful respite from the hurdy-gurdy-like sound of the ensembles. Hawkins muffs his two-bar break by gurgling his notes and the harmonized duet between the alto and tenor saxes has a near-comic quaveriness. The alto-sax player changes swiftly to clarinet for a final 'hot' chorus, but the choppy rhythms keep everyone tightly harnessed.

'Stuttering' is not quite as bad as the title implies, in that there are no deliberately reiterated effects. After a brisk ensemble Hawkins and an alto saxist (whose playing is no less jazzy than Hawk's) share a duet. The trumpeter (who possesses a strong, clean tone) and the trombonist then play a highly syncopated chorus that benefits from a loosely phrased obbligato from Hawkins. The saxes share some parallel harmonies then the altoist again picks up his clarinet for a wild, disjointed finale, during which the pianist pounds the keyboard, the banjoist tremoloes for all he is worth and the drummer hits at everything in sight. Hawkins takes the lead initially on 'Strut Your Material' then steps back to answer the trumpeter's melody line, which is adroitly phrased, the same player (Johnny Dunn?) also revealing good technique in a double-time break. Here Hawk's backing phrases have an impressive panache; a feeling of inexorable continuity was beginning to grace his work.

The musical quality of the three instrumentals is not deplorable, since the participants play reasonably in tune and keep the tempo steady; the correct harmonies are also (for the most part) faithfully observed. The dismaying aspect of the band's performance is that they were failing to include the exciting innovations that jazz was offering. Mamie Smith's group were by no means alone in revealing this deficiency. During this era, hundreds of small bands were slow to grasp the importance of the musical revolution that was at hand. It was only when formidable jazz soloists (most of them from Louisiana) made their impact in person that the New York-based musicians began to change their approach.

Mamie Smith excelled at performing light-hearted songs such as 'Wish That I Could' and she had a gift for interpreting quasi-dramatic pieces such as 'Sighin' Around with the Blues', but on both of these recordings the band continue to plod along their previous path, despite the addition of a second trumpeter. However, on 'That Da Da Strain' the musicians seem to be genuinely trying, not too successfully, to develop the rapport and the inflections of a jazz band. Hawkins's two-bar break is intentionally 'corny', being a deliberate farmyard imitation, but elsewhere on the three numbers, recorded in August and September 1922, he continually displays his growing flexibility.

Bubber Miley temporarily rejoined Mamie Smith's band for dates in the New York area, but when the troupe left for a wide-ranging vaudeville tour on the Loew's Theatre circuit his place was taken by another young ace trumpeter, Joe Smith, who later featured on recordings with Mamie's namesake, Bessie Smith (the two singers were not related to each other, or to the young trumpeter). Joe Smith, who came from a family of brass players, had a mellow way of playing that added to the band's appeal, but Hawkins was still the most consistently featured musician in the stage performances. The October 1922 tour itinerary took the troupe into Canada, where they played Loew's Theatres in Toronto, Montreal and Ottawa. After working for a week at each of these venues the package wended its way south by working at Loew's State Theatre in Buffalo, New

York (for a week beginning on 30 October) and at Loew's Metropolitan in Brooklyn from 6 to 11 November 1922.

On their return to New York City the band recorded six numbers during December 1922 and January 1923. Mamie is featured throughout 'I Ain't Gonna Give Nobody None of this Jelly Roll', singing two choruses and the seldom-heard verse. Because all of these early sides were recorded acoustically (non-electrically) it's virtually impossible to dissect the instrumentation, but it sounds as though a soprano sax is present. On 'Don't Mess with Me' a clarinettist (inspired by Ted Lewis) is prominent in the ensembles. The tune is a sixteen-bar, minor-key composition that later formed the basis of songs like 'My Daddy Rocks Me'. An alto sax is present alongside Hawkins, but the narrow frequency range makes the violin sound like a swanee whistle.

Mamie is at her most soubrette-ish on 'Mean Man', the trombonist blows some fruity glissandos and Hawkins shows that his tone in the higher register was filling out nicely. The band begin to gel very effectively on 'The Darktown Flappers' Ball', with Joe Smith's voluptuous sound making itself clearly heard in the instrumental interlude, which is graced by his superbly constructed two-bar break. The trumpeter is equally impressive on 'You've Got to See Mama Every Night'. Hawkins is featured on 'I'm Gonna Get You', playing a twenty-two-bar solo that keeps closely in touch with the melody. Slap-tonguing is still evident in most of his phrases, and his vibrato is still unruly, but even so it is clear that he is pioneering a new way of playing the saxophone.

Hawkins had arrived at his own style without apparently being heavily influenced by anyone in particular. Looking back, he said, 'I guess it's true that I introduced a new style, a new way of playing tenor. I had a much heavier tongue, for one thing, than most of the others, and their tone was kind of thin.'[23] But woe betide anyone in later years who questioned Hawkins about recordings from this early part of his career. His peremptory retort to any enquiry about the Mamie Smith sides was: 'Who wants to know?'[24]

Early in 1923 the Mamie Smith package again left New York, this time to play a long strong of engagements that gradually took them over to California where they became part of a Fanchon and Marco review called *Struttin' Along*, which included comedian Eddie 'Rochester' Anderson (later to gain fame with Jack Benny), singer-dancer Carolyn Snowden and a young newcomer to vaudeville, Ivie Anderson, then a dancer, but later to join Duke Ellington as a singer. The band's drummer Curtis Mosby had been replaced by Lutice 'Cutie' Perkins, and pianist Harvey Brooks had been appointed musical director of the group, which now consisted of Hawkins, Joe Smith, George Bell, Cecil Carpenter, Bob Fuller, Perkins and Brooks.

The show played various theatres in the West, including bookings in Seattle, Washington, Oakland and Long Beach, California. They also visited Tia-Juana. Cornettist Jake Porter has vivid childhood memories of the animated part that Hawkins played in the show during their dates in Oakland: 'It seemed as though he was wrestling with his horn on stage.'[25] Trombonist Clyde Bernhardt, recalling this period, spoke of Hawkins lying on his back and playing the saxophone during Mamie's show (pre-dating, by some thirty years, the horizontal performances of rock-and-roll saxists).

Hawkins apparently didn't care for the excessive showmanship that he was asked to project, but this wasn't the reason he quit Mamie Smith's show. He realized that he had learnt about all he could concerning life on the theatrical circuit, and it was time to move on. In June 1923 Mamie, and some of her troupe, went to see boxer Jack Dempsey training at a camp in Montana. That outing seems to have been part of a post-tour vacation, for by then Hawkins and Joe Smith (both restless for Manhattan) had decided to make their own way back to New York.

Some of Hawk's first gigs were at the Garden of Joy, the Harlem cabaret where he had occasionally worked with Mamie Smith. The management there had noticed that the clientele liked his playing, so they welcomed him back with open arms. Two of Hawk's colleagues there in the early summer of 1923 were pianist Ginger Young and trumpeter Charlie Gaines, who remembered the place as 'a wild spot'.[26]

Garvin Bushell, who had been out on tour with Ethel Waters and with a Modern Cocktail after leaving Mamie Smith, recalled his reunion with Hawkins,

> I went up to the Garden of Joy one night and who should be sitting on the bandstand but Coleman. I said, 'I thought your grandmother wouldn't let you come'.
>
> He said, 'Well, the girl that I've been fooling with, grandmother didn't like her family so to get me out of town she let me come to New York'.[27]

Bushell stressed that Hawkins's playing was having a sensational effect on the listeners:

New York had never heard anything like him. He didn't, as was the custom then, play the saxophone like a trumpet or clarinet. He was also running changes then, because he'd studied the piano as a youngster. As for soul, he had soul, but it was less on the blues side. He had a lot of finesse.[28]

2
The Young Star in New York

Having settled in New York, Coleman Hawkins had no cause to experience even the merest ripple of anxiety about his professional future. Well-paid gigs flowed in and he worked as often as he wanted to throughout the summer of 1923. Engagements were even plentiful enough for him to quit the Garden of Joy.

He played regularly in an orchestra led by violinist Ralph 'Shrimp' Jones at the Club Bamville (199th Street and 7th Avenue) and also worked at the Renaissance Casino in a band fronted by alto saxophonist Cecil Smith. Pianist Louis Hooper was in that group and retained a vivid memory both of Hawkins's impressive talents and of the dreadful state of his silver-plated tenor saxophone; the instrument was 'unclean' and covered with elastic bands, doing the duty of long-broken springs. But Hawk was clearly able to play supremely well on this dilapidated horn for he was soon offered the opportunity to work in a prestigious band led by Wilbur Sweatman.

While Hawkins was working with Sweatman he was heard by pianist Fletcher Henderson. Henderson, then in his mid-twenties, had abandoned graduate work in chemistry to concentrate on music. By 1923, 'Smack' (as he had been nicknamed) was beginning to establish himself as a bandleader, composer and publisher, and was also being booked regularly to play on gramophone recordings. Henderson began employing Hawkins in the bands he assembled for these recordings and the young saxophonist soon proved that he was ideally suited, both in temperament and talent, for this skilled freelance work. At first his role was a subsidiary one but on the band's accompaniment for Edna Hick's vocal 'You've Got Everything' Hawkins can be heard playing confident and apt fill-ins behind the vocalist.

On the following day (9 August 1923) Fletcher Henderson's Orchestra recorded an instrumental version of 'Dicty Blues', on which Hawkins is allocated two solos. The main feature of the arrangement is a series of chimes which the band echo before moving into a standard blues sequence. Hawkins takes a flamboyant solo, accompanied by figures played by the cornet and trombone. After a bridge passage he sounds equally assured in the new key. The solos do not contain any harmonically 'daring' notes – there are a few sixths, sevenths and ninths – but most of the phrases are built on the notes of a triad. Neither are there signs of outstanding rhythmic ingenuity; almost all of the patterns are unsyncopated two and four-bar phrases. Yet the solos radiate the musical presence that was to be a mainstay of Hawk's performances throughout his career. The notes are all cleanly articulated and the phrases delivered without a trace of hesitancy.

Certain trademark patterns of Hawkins's work in the 1920s make themselves obvious, particularly the arpeggic runs consisting of a series of eighth notes (what Gunther Schuller called Hawk's 'up and down delineations of chords')[1] but everything is harmonically correct. At this stage of his career (and for years afterwards) Hawkins rarely attempted any startlingly different variations if called upon to record a second or a third take. On whim he occasionally improvised steadfastly for each succeeding take, but mostly he chose to make only small embellishments on the shape of his solo. This was a deliberate plan, as he made clear in one of his first interviews when he said, 'the repetition is not so much memory as method'.[2] On two takes of the August 1923 version of 'Dicty Blues' the contours of Hawk's phrases are almost identical, even when there are changes in his note selection. The results are not great jazz, the phrasing and articulations are still too stiff, but the solos offer an augury of the young man's future status.

On 'Dicty Blues', Hawk's performance is infinitely superior to that of Don Redman, whose clarinet playing here has only period charm. It is an example of the 'gaspipe' style, an onomatapoeic description of the shrill sounds and jerky phrasing that many dance-band clarinettists adopted in the 1920s. Hawkins himself was still guilty of using slap-tongued phrasing, but he was trying hard to eliminate this obstruction to his progress. It was a dramatic change because it had been his main method of creating notes since he had begun playing the saxophone years before. The smoothing-out process took Hawkins a long time, and on the three versions of 'Dicty Blues' that Henderson recorded in as many months it is only just possible to hear that a transition is under way.

The record-buying craze was gathering pace and several labels were eager to market the sounds of Henderson's orchestra, but the leader wisely refused to sign an exclusive contract with any of them and was thus able to record the same tune for rival companies. In the case of 'Dicty Blues' the first was for Vocalion, the second for Columbia and the third (issued as by the Seven Brown Babies) for the Ajax label. Sometimes Henderson's subsequent versions were very similar to the original, but this wasn't so with 'Dicty Blues', a change of tempo and a reshuffling of the solo order gave each company's issue a discernible difference.

During the last months of 1923 the band made dozens of recordings, many of them instrumentals. Hawkins played a prominent part in most of these, and in September his skills gained him special mention on the record label, a fairly unusual accolade in those days. On the record itself, a vocal by Rosa Henderson entitled 'It Won't be Long Now', Hawkins plays an unflurried thirty-two-bar chorus. It doesn't contain any wild flights of daring improvisation but it is artistically phrased, and considering that Hawk was still in his teens he displayed remarkable poise.

But the growing technical mastery didn't encourage Hawkins to be more diligent in the care of his saxophone. Black composer Tom Delaney (who wrote 'Jazz Me Blues' and other popular songs) recalled seeing Hawkins soon after he'd begun working with Henderson: 'The first appearance of his cheap, battered sax was greeted with shrieks of laughter.' Delaney said to Henderson, 'You don't mean that this boy is going to play that thing?' Henderson apparently just smiled and said, 'Wait – he's good.'[3]

Fletcher Henderson's pick-up band had little chance to develop its own identity, the style of its arrangements (and sometimes its instrumentation) being continually altered to suit the commercial requirements of the various record companies who hired it. On one session the band might sound like a sleek dance band, while on an adjoining date it could work up steam as it moved into waters already navigated by King Oliver's Creole Jazz Band.

At that time, Henderson's reliability and the effectiveness of his musicians kept him in demand with recording companies, but decades later, when the work of his earliest bands was analysed by jazz critics, most of them found it wanting. But Henderson was not attempting to pioneer the new music, he was leading a band whose task was to record danceable versions of often trite popular songs. Jazz arranging was in its infancy, and Don Redman (Henderson's principal arranger) had no previous blueprints to study. Redman became one of the most important orchestrators of his era, but at the time that Hawkins joined Henderson, Don was only feeling his way into the jazz world.

A New York saxophonist, Adrian Rollini, was rapidly coming to grips with the innovative aspects of jazz phrasing. He was one of the few white musicians who could be classified as a jazz pioneer. Rollini, a child prodigy on piano and born in the same year as Hawkins, bought a bass saxophone on a whim during the early 1920s and was soon blowing convincing jazz on it. He was not only able to pump out solid low notes in the manner of a tuba but was also capable of soloing with a grace and elan that belied the fact that he was playing a huge unwieldy instrument, whose range was an octave below the tenor saxophone's. Rollini's successes inspired many other saxophonists to take up this musical leviathan.

Hawkins became fascinated by the bass saxophone, and intrigued by the prospects of playing on it in the rhythm section (by punching out low notes) and then swiftly moving into the role of a front-line soloist. Occasionally he tried to get a bass-sax effect on tenor, as on 'Do Doodle Oom', where he honks a long series of low pedal notes, but he soon found this to be unsatisfactory and bought himself a bass saxophone. He rapidly became proficient on the large horn and for some while doubled on the tenor and bass instruments.

Some reference books infer that Hawkins doubled on bass saxophone for most of the recordings that Henderson made during this period. This is not the case. Sometimes a bass saxophone is heard while Hawkins is soloing on tenor, which meant that one of the other reed players on the session had been drafted in to play the huge instrument. Hawkins usually made his individuality obvious when playing the bass sax (as he always did on tenor sax) by his forthright attack and his personal vibrato. He never gained a noteworthy degree of proficiency on bass saxophone, but his playing on 'Charleston Crazy' and 'Somebody Stole My Gal' shows that given time and practice he could also have been masterful on that instrument. His other brief forays into the low registers on the saxophone family were on E-flat baritone, which he sometimes played if a written part was deemed to be an essential feature of an arrangement. Later on, however, he simply transposed the music and played it on bass saxophone.

Hawkins's other doubling activities involved him playing clarinet. He was obliged to do this because so many arrangements of the period called for clarinet duos and trios. But Hawkins realized that in order to play the clarinet well he would need to devote many hours to practising it and he came to the decision that this time would be better spent increasing the boundaries of his technique on tenor saxophone. This same reasoning eventually caused him to abandon the bass saxophone; he summarized his attitude by saying, 'Don't be a dabbler on half a dozen instruments. I know there are plenty who do, but they'll never be above the average.'[4]

In later years, Hawkins virtually disowned all of his efforts from these early years and brushed aside any reference to his work on bass saxophone and clarinet. He was also far from keen to admit that he had created the tenor-saxophone solos that shine out on these early Henderson recordings. His standard reaction was to say that these sides give no indication of the real sound of Fletcher's band.

Fletcher Henderson was soon given the chance to display the merits of his band in person, as opposed to via recordings. Henderson, like Hawkins, had been making his living as a freelance musician through most of 1923. Like Hawkins he too had worked in the band led by Ralph 'Shrimp' Jones (replacing pianist LeRoy Tibbs). Jones, plagued by the temperamental reactions of his musicians, offered the leadership to Henderson, who needed to be persuaded to take over the band, which was then working at a cabaret at 65 West 192nd Street (later to be the site of the Bamville Club).

Few of the club's patrons were aware that a change had been made in the leadership of the band since Henderson, a retiring personality, continued with his duties at the keyboard and the group maintained its previous musical policy. But this experience proved to be the springboard that launched Henderson into bandleading proper. He discovered that the task of leading a band wasn't as painful as he had thought it might be and this inspired him to take the band into the Cotton Club and the Lafayette Theatre for brief residencies. By this time another trumpeter, Howard Scott (known to everyone as Kid Scottie), not quite twenty years of age, had been added to the group.

When Sammy Weiss, the owner of the Little Club, offered Henderson's band a residency, he was told by Fletcher, 'My eleven-piece band was for recording purposes only.' He was, however, persuaded to change his mind: 'I ended up by accepting his offer and this is how for the first time I became officially a bandleader. We opened at the Little Club on West 44th Street near Broadway, better known as the Club Alabam.' Coleman Hawkins accepted Henderson's offer to work regularly with the band.

Fletcher Henderson didn't direct his band from the front of the stage, choosing to remain at the piano and bringing in violinist Allie Ross to conduct the group. Fletcher was a modest leader, and a lengthy piano solo on his early band recordings is a rarity. His line-up for the Club Alabam booking was: Elmer Chambers and Howard Scott (trumpets); Teddy

Nixon or Nelson Hurd (trombone); Coleman Hawkins and Don Redman (reeds); Ralph Escudero (tuba); Charlie Dixon (banjo); Kaiser Marshall (drums) and Fletcher Henderson (piano).

Don Redman occasionally played trumpet, oboe and goofus (a novelty instrument); in addition he did most of the band's arrangements, though Howard Scott was positive that Fletcher Henderson also arranged for the band. The band's instrumental star was definitely Coleman Hawkins, a fact stressed by Scott, who said, 'That Coleman Hawkins, he was wonderful, marvellous.'[5]

Although Henderson didn't possess a strong personality, Howard Scott recalled that, in those early days, he was a firm disciplinarian: 'Fletcher was a very strict leader. Every night you had to stand up and stand inspection. He'd look at your hair, your face, see if you shaved. Your shoes, see if they're shined. You had to be perfect to suit him.'[6]

After settling in New York the affluent Hawkins gradually developed a reputation for being dressed in the latest fashions. By 1923 the 'Greasy' of yesteryear had gone for ever. An ex-colleague said, 'He would buy the most expensive garment that Ben Rocke, a favourite Broadway tailor, made'.[7] But Hawkins was still short of time when it came to having these fashionable clothes cleaned and pressed and he'd often appear in pants that had more creases than a concertina. One particular girlfriend, however, got him to change his ways.

Hawkins wasn't anti-social, but he had no close friends within the early Henderson band. He was not part of any clique, his main interest being in the ladies, many of whom responded to his laconic charm. One of them, a light-skinned dancer named Gertrude (who had worked in Mamie Smith's troupe) became a particular favourite. A romance blossomed and the two saw each other regularly. Hawkins was gradually becoming a man of the world and often took Gertrude to Glenn's, one of Harlem's most celebrated and expensive restaurants; eventually they decided to get married.

Years later Hawkins described his marriage to Gertrude (which took place on 15 December 1923) as one of 'convenience'. Gertie, as she was known to all her friends, was a little older than Hawkins and the convenience that he spoke of may well have been connected to the fact that Mamie Smith was still officially his guardian. As such, Mamie could have insisted that Hawkins rejoin the show and go out on the road again. But, if that guardianship was made void by reason of Hawkins getting married, then her powers over him were at an end.

As a well-paid freelance musician Hawkins was earning almost a hundred dollars a week, but the added security that went with Henderson's offer to play the new residency suited Hawkins for he and Gertie were just about to set up home in apartment 3J at 80 St Nicholas Place. Hawk drew a regular wage from the Club Alabam and was paid extra for any recordings. The income from these sessions was considerable; Henderson's band were recording at least three or four times a month.

Hawkins was, by this time, well aware of his remarkable musical skill, but this knowledge didn't make him egocentric. Instead it developed a presence that remained with him for the rest of his life. He was not tall, but his broad-chested frame made his five feet seven inches seem all-powerful, as though there were great strength in reserve. Rex Stewart, who later worked alongside Hawkins in Fletcher Henderson's band, said, 'Hawkins differs from the usual public conception of a musician. He is not the prototype of the affable extrovert. Coleman presents a dignified façade that often borders on the cool side, something that can be unnerving to people who do not know him.'[8]

Hawkins knew his worth and was determined that no one was ever going to take advantage of him. In May 1924, after the Henderson band had been working for several months in the Club Alabam, this side of his character was put to the test. The manager of the club asked Hawkins to leave his place on the bandstand and move on to the floor of the nightclub in order to accompany the singer, Edith Wilson. Don Redman recalled the tenor saxist's reaction:

> Hawkins was very willing, but he argued, rightly, that if he was going to work in the show he should be paid as an actor, too. So unless he got some compensation for playing in the show he didn't see why he should do any more than anyone else. So Fletcher told that to the manager of the club. The manager immediately suggested Fletcher fire Hawkins. Fletcher came back and told the band. The band decided that if he wanted to fire Hawkins we would all leave. Well, we were too big a success to let go, so Hawkins stayed and we stayed.[9]

But this dispute curdled the relationship between the club's management and the musicians, and as a result Henderson made no effort to seek a rebooking when the group's contract with the club ended in June 1924. *Variety* magazine specifically linked the dispute with the departure: 'Henderson was asked to put in an extra saxophone player for floor performance without extra compensation by the Club Alabam management, so he bowed out.'[10]

The incident shows how much the band thought of Hawkins's talent, and of the young man personally. Ironically the move from the club proved to be a lucrative one. Because Henderson's band was without a booking they were able to accept an offer to play at the Roseland Ballroom on 51st Street. They were not the first black band to be hired by that venue; Armand Piron's Orchestra (from New Orleans) had worked there briefly in May 1924. Coleman Hawkins certainly wasn't overawed by the prospect of going into the Roseland. He said later 'Fletcher didn't have much of a reputation at the time. It seemed just like another job to me.'[11]

Fletcher Henderson's Orchestra began work at the Roseland Ballroom on 16 July 1924. During its residency it played opposite various white dance bands; each unit took it in turn to play sets from bandstands situated at each end of the vast ballroom, enabling dancers to enjoy continuous music. The management insisted that bands be versatile; they were expected to play waltzes and tangos as well as fox-trots and two-steps. Abandoned improvisations were not required at the Roseland; indeed in advertising for bands to appear there the management stipulated: 'Jazz bands will not be considered.' Despite this supposed restriction on jazz the Henderson band was able to feature a good deal of spirited improvising. While at the Roseland the band was strengthened by the arrival of a fine instrumentalist, trombonist Charlie Green, whose skills as a player of the blues impressed and probably influenced Hawkins.

Throughout their bookings at the Roseland the Henderson band broadcast regularly over Station WHN, and this increased exposure brought them a whole string of private engagements, which they were able to fulfil when their initial nine-week season at the ballroom ended. The clearest indication of Hawkins's steady advancement occur on recordings that featured himself and Fletcher Henderson as the duo accompanists for blues singers Clara Smith and Bessie Brown. On 19 August 1924 the two musicians recorded two numbers with each of these admirable vocalists for the Columbia label. Hawk's twelve-bar solo on Bessie Brown's 'Pork Chop Blues' shows that his articulation was gradually becoming smoother, though his trademark of the period, a sudden thwacking descent into the low register, still makes itself obvious here and during his sixteen-bar feature on Clara Smith's 'Deep Blue Sea Blues'. On all four sides his technique and control are impressive, creating a performance exceedingly mature for a musician not yet twenty years of age.

At the instigation of Louis Brecker, the overall boss of the Roseland, booker Al Herman took up the option that the ballroom had on the services of the Henderson band and re-engaged them to play the fall season. In the short period between the first and second of their residencies the band added a young cornettist to its brass team. The newcomer created a sensation from the moment he began blowing with Fletcher Henderson's Orchestra, just as he had done two years earlier when he had joined King Oliver's Creole Jazz Band in Chicago. The young genius, whose playing was to transfigure so many aspects of jazz, was Louis Armstrong.

Back in April 1922, Fletcher Henderson had heard Louis playing in New Orleans, and he immediately realized that he was listening to an extraordinarily gifted musician. Henderson, on tour with singer Ethel Waters, asked Louis to join the troupe, but he declined, ostensibly because Henderson couldn't find a place in the show for Louis's colleague, drummer Zutty Singleton. The real reason, however, was probably that Louis didn't feel ready to leave New Orleans.

A few months later King Oliver sent for Armstrong to come to Chicago, and Louis went like a shot without making any provisos whatsoever. While with Oliver, Louis met and married pianist Lil Hardin, who understandably became ambitious for her husband. By 1924 musicians working in Chicago were well aware of the successes that Henderson's band were enjoying in New York and although it is usually taken for granted that Henderson contacted Armstrong in Chicago with an offer to join his band, there's also a strong possibility that Lil made the original overtures.

Louis Armstrong recalled his apprehension about joining Henderson: 'I could blow alright, but I hadn't counted on New York. In that big town I was just a little small-town boy and nobody much on Broadway had ever heard about me.'[12] Henderson's musicians could scarcely suppress their laughter when they caught their first sight of Louis Armstrong. Sitting at a rehearsal dressed in their expensive suits, silk shirts and hand-made shoes, the slickers observed a gauche, bashful figure who seemed to have deliberately dressed himself in the style of yesteryear. Don Redman recalled, 'He was big and fat and wore high top shoes with hooks in them and long underwear down to his socks.'[13] Drummer Kaiser Marshall also vividly recalled the scene: 'The band was up on the stand waiting when he got there, and Louis walked across the floor. He had on big thick-soled shoes, the kind that policemen wear, and he came walking across the floor, clump-clump and grinned and said hello to all the boys.' The band's wry amusement disappeared the moment Louis started playing; it was replaced by an overwhelming admiration. Don Redman summarized the reaction: 'When he got on the bandstand it was a different story.'

Although Coleman Hawkins never gave his eye-witness account of Louis's arrival, it's highly probable that he was among those who giggled at the sight of Armstrong's old-fashioned garb. Coleman was still considered as something of a boy wonder, but he was also recognized as a sophisticated young man, highly conscious of fashion. Louis's musical reputation had preceded his arrival and Hawkins's sniggering may have been partly born of anxiety, since he must have realized Louis's skills would take some of the limelight away from his own work.

Hawkins had good reason to be wary of New Orleans-bred virtuosity. He had already tangled with the great Sidney Bechet in an all-night musical joust that was talked of for years as one of the most dramatic jam sessions of all time. Eventually, at dawn, Bechet's power and invention had overwhelmed Hawkins. He did his best to make a dignified exit from the club but Bechet chased him into the street blowing a torrent of passionate phrases at the departing figure. Hawkins became a wary friend of Bechet, but something prevented him from becoming close to Louis Armstrong. And Louis, usually a model of affability, never regarded Hawkins with any great affection. All through his life Louis became riled when he detected condescension; conceivably, he sensed that Hawkins had adopted a superior attitude when he arrived to join Henderson's band. Indeed, Louis may have humbly, and unwittingly, encouraged this, because he apparently first addressed Coleman as 'Mr Hawkins'.[14]

Louis's social background may not have been as respectable as that of some of his new colleagues, but it is generally conceded that it was his playing that established Henderson's band as the foremost unit of its kind. It can be no coincidence that from the time Louis arrived in New York, Hawkins's jazz playing improved dramatically; it seems that Armstrong's phrasing and highly imaginative improvisation provided Hawk with the impetus and insight also to become a jazz giant. This wasn't a viewpoint endorsed by Hawkins. He cloaked his feelings when the subject was raised in interview or in general conversation, but one long-time colleague, Roy Eldridge, was on hand on more than one occasion when Hawkins vehemently denied any direct influence.

Trumpeter Cootie Williams, who was fond of saying that Louis Armstrong was the greatest trumpeter who ever lived, worked alongside Hawkins in the Fletcher Henderson band during the late 1920s. He said,

> No, I don't think Louis influenced Coleman Hawkins, except unconsciously, because Coleman hated Louis. It was when I was in the Fletcher Henderson band that

> I learned about this. I knew Hawk then and he just couldn't even stand the name Armstrong. I used to love Louis so much and when I'd speak about him Hawkins didn't like it at all.[15]

Whether the inspiration was direct or unconsciously assimilated must remain conjectural; what is certain is that Armstrong's arrival brought new breadth to Hawkins's musical expressiveness and, more importantly, streamlined his phrasing. The slap-tonguing that had for so long stilted Hawk's playing began to disappear during Armstrong's early months in New York. A general criticism of Hawk's early playing is based on the fact that his phrases were created almost entirely on the beat. This strategy often moulded together the disunited work of his accompanists, but in setting up a pulse within his phrases he often made the ploy too obvious and it was to be some while before he learnt to swing regardless of his surroundings. This problem did not arise for Louis Armstrong, who created phrases that were so rhythmically ingenious that even the most lumpen support could not stop him swinging.

Fletcher Henderson saw the value of having two extremely gifted young men in his band and divided the compliments as evenly as he could. Years later he said, 'Louis influenced the band greatly by making the men swing-conscious with that New Orleans style of his. The same effect that Coleman Hawkins had on the reeds, that right down-to-earth swing, with punch and bounce.'[16] Many of the recordings that Armstrong and Hawkins made with Henderson were tame, commercial efforts in which they play mundane section roles, as wasteful as having thoroughbred horses pulling milk floats. But on several of the band's 1924 and 1925 sessions Armstrong's genius is well featured and Hawk's growing talent made obvious.

Armstrong wasn't the only addition that Henderson made to his line-up that autumn. The bandleader mentioned to the new cornettist that he was looking for an outstanding clarinettist, and as a result Louis told him to send for Buster Bailey (then in Chicago). Bailey duly accepted the offer and moved to New York to join Henderson's band a week or so after Louis had arrived.

News of Bailey's move added to Hawkins's apprehension, as Don Redman recalled: 'Coleman Hawkins and I, we were not too happy because we had a lot of tricks, rhythms, licks, backgrounds that we worked out; we were afraid that the man coming in wasn't gonna be able to catch on.'[17] The incumbent reed players had no need to fret, however, because

Buster Bailey was a fine all-round musician. Bailey recalled asking his old friend Louis Armstrong about the men he was about to join. 'He told me about Big Charlie Green and about a tenor-saxophone player – Hawkins – he said, "That guy really swings". That was the first time I heard the word used that way. I caught on what he meant, because after I got to work that night I heard Hawkins'.[18]

Soon after getting on to the bandstand with his new colleagues Bailey launched into a version of 'Tiger Rag' that displayed his technical wizardry. Hawkins's reaction to this performance was quite different to the antagonistic way he acknowledged Armstrong's brilliance. Hawk realized that Bailey's skill on clarinet meant he would rarely ever have to solo again on that instrument within Henderson's band; he was further placated when he heard Bailey's journeyman efforts on the saxophone. In the same way that Hawkins funnelled most of his creative energies into playing the tenor saxophone, Bailey specialized on the clarinet: when it came to allocating the time he had for practice routines he favoured clarinet, so he never became truly proficient on saxophone. Hawkins grew to like Bailey a lot and held him in high regard for his clarinet technique; he never learnt, however, to like his jazz playing.

Measuring the solo space allocated to the newcomer, Armstrong, it is easy to see the reasons for Hawkins's apprehension and jealousy. Until Louis's arrival Hawkins was regularly, almost automatically, featured on most of the Henderson band's arrangements. This situation changed quite dramatically: Louis is accorded prominent solos on his first recordings with Henderson ('Manda' and 'Go 'Long Mule'), whereas Hawk's contribution is restricted to two brief breaks on the second title.

Those tunes were recorded on 7 October 1924; within a week the orchestra were back in the studio to record four more titles but, for some reason, Hawkins did not make this session. No one has ever given a reason for his absence. The only tenor-saxophone solo on the date ('My Rose Marie') is performed by someone who plays a competent, straight-sounding rendition of the melody. Tonally this is nothing like Hawkins's work, and such mannerisms as are discernible are very different from Hawk's style of phrasing.

Conceivably Hawkins may have been indisposed and unable to make the session, even though he was subsequently listed as having taken part. Discographers tend to forget that musicians suffer from influenza, dental problems and lumbago in just the same way as other workers do, and it is just as unlikely that the same eleven members of a band would be ever-present as it would be had they been an eleven-strong workforce in some other occupation. Nevertheless we can only conjecture at the reason for Hawkins's absence.

Hawk was certainly on the band's next recording on 30 October. He was given a solo on 'Words', as was Louis Armstrong, but the tenor saxist wasn't given a chance to shine on 'Copenhagen', whereas Louis was, and as a result created one of his most memorable early efforts. Armstrong is also heavily featured (not as successfully) on 'Shanghai Shuffle' on a November 1924 date, and subsequently makes his full thirty-two-bar chorus the outstanding feature of 'One of These Days' (a catchy melody with a strong verse and chorus). Louis again triumphs on 'The Meanest Kind of Blues', but shares honours with Hawkins on the same session's 'Naughty Man'. The saxophonist's solo is accompanied by an emphasized off-beat and this gives him an effective degree of prominence, but Louis follows up with a stop-time chorus that eclipses Hawk's efforts.

Three takes of 'How Come You Do Me Like You Do' (also from November 1924) show how Louis could maintain a consistent degree of inspiration. There is little to chose between the brilliance displayed on all three versions – each has minor differences – but they all show that Louis was intent on embellishing the melody during his solo rather than blowing abstract figures. Hawkins (and trombonist Charlie Green) prove that they too were capable of keeping up a flow of musical intensity throughout the re-makes, and all of their breaks sound inspired, with Hawkins at his most interesting on the third version of the tune.

Armstrong continued to be featured heavily on most of Henderson's recordings, but Hawkins, perhaps by request, was being allocated regular, albeit brief, solo contributions. Buster Bailey's skill on clarinet was rarely given prominence; when it was, as on '12th Street Blues', the results were effective; that particular recording showing why Bailey's reputation was so high in the 1920s. His control of the chalumeau register was excellent, as were his flights into the top register, and he also plays admirable bass clarinet on 'Why Couldn't It Be Poor Little Me'. The least-featured soloist in the Henderson band was the leader himself, though he does emerge from his shell on 'Mandy Make up Your Mind' and 'Bye and Bye'.

Charlie Green's fat-toned trombone solos were only occasionally featured, yet his two-chorus feature on 'Play Me Slow' is beautifully crafted and packed with feeling, showing that he was one of the best jazz trombonists of the early 1920s. On this same recording, Hawkins ventures a solo on C-melody saxophone (perhaps because his notoriously ancient tenor had finally been taken in for an overhaul). Hawkins continued for some while to dabble on C-melody sax, but never became a distinguished performer on it, often suffering (as on 'Me Neenyah') with intonation problems.

Hawkins still occasionally played the bass saxophone, sometimes on a recording, but his main doubling during this period was on clarinet. As Hawkins had correctly surmised that it would, Buster Bailey's arrival had relieved him of playing clarinet solos but, ironically, now that the band had a musician who could lead a clarinet trio with sureness and accuracy, the device was increasingly featured in the band's arrangements. At one point it seemed as though every Don Redman arrangement utilised three clarinets playing in harmony, so any thoughts that Hawkins may have had about putting his clarinet away at the back of a cupboard had to be abandoned.

On tenor saxophone Hawkins was beginning to experiment successfully with the use of 9th chords and augmented runs as part of his improvisations, often showing his confidence by deliberately including 'surprise notes', particularly in his breaks. The slap-tonguing effect resurfaced occasionally but was no longer part of his basic method of playing, his main weakness at this time concerning the way he projected a melody. On record he was occasionally called upon to play a tune 'as written' (on 'Swanee Butterfly', for instance). When he did so, he sounded quite ponderous and unimaginative, whereas when Louis Armstrong performs a similar take he uplifts the composer's original lines with countless subtle inflections.

Hawkins later admitted that he had a tendency to over-blow in these early days:

> When I started I played loud, using a kind of stiff reed, as I was trying to play my solos over seven or eight horns all the time. The fullness of my sound just developed as I used to work on these reeds and fool around with mouthpieces all night long. I figured it was foolish to be blowing if no one could hear you. You had to compete with guys like Armstrong, Charlie Green, Buster Bailey and Jimmy Harrison.[19]

As far as his social life was concerned, the long residency at the Roseland Ballroom allowed Hawkins to settle into a routine. He and his wife Gertie had set up home on St Nicholas Avenue, but as both of them worked during the hours of darkness and slept for most of the day there was little time for sitting and relaxing in their apartment. Gertrude's schedule as a dancer meant that she often worked later than her husband did. To while away time Hawkins usually dropped into various late-night cabarets, often sitting in at the Rhythm Club on 7th Avenue and 132nd Street. Woe betide any young saxophonists who attempted to do musical battle with Hawkins during these visits. Hawkins had a natural competitiveness and the sight of a rival musician always roused him to prove his superiority. Occasionally a promising young contender surfaced, and then Hawkins deliberately went out of his way to challenge the newcomer. Later, he said, 'When a young cat came to New York I had to take care of him quick.'[20] Pianist Don Frye, then with Cecil Scott's Bright Boys, said that Hawk's after-hours headquarters during this period was the Black Gold Grill, where 'he used to wash all the other tenor players away'.[21]

Though some leaders objected to their sidemen going out after work to blow for nothing in jam sessions, Fletcher Henderson didn't seem to mind. He was an easygoing man, and he had a genuine affection for Hawkins. In December 1924 Fletcher married Leora Smith, and these newly-weds became friends with Coleman and Gertie Hawkins. Leora, who had played trumpet professionally, took something of a motherly interest in Coleman Hawkins. A stately woman (she was five feet ten inches tall), she was able to look down on Hawkins (five feet seven) and gently chide him when she felt he needed a mild reprimand over some aspect of band discipline. Most of Leora's chiding concerned Hawkins's habitual disregard for punctuality, her husband having become increasingly annoyed at the young saxist's late arrival on the bandstand. Howard Scott recalled:

> Fletcher Henderson was strict and nice and exact in everything he did, but he threatened to fire Coleman Hawkins more than once because Coleman used to come in late. Sometimes we'd open up and start playing and here comes Coleman. But when he'd get up there, and pick that horn up, everybody was satisfied. But Fletcher didn't like it, but the band predominated and said, 'Please don't do it. Where are you going to get another saxophone player like him?' You couldn't get another tenor in New York like Coleman, Coleman was great.[22]

Coleman Hawkins's other main foible was the mischievousness he directed at his band colleagues. He was fond of starting alarming rumours and then gleefully watching how various people reacted to them. One of his regular butts was the trombonist Charlie Green (not an ideal target for pranks since he usually carried a loaded pistol). Hawkins knew that Green was constantly worried that his wife was having extra-marital affairs. Hawk was also aware that Green regularly telephoned his home, from near and far, to make sure that his wife wasn't out on the town. During band intermissions at the Roseland, several of the musicians took the air together and swopped gossip. Hawkins would position himself just within Green's hearing range and then comment on how alarming it was that so many musicians' wives, with time on their hands during the evenings, were having affairs. Hawkins would extemporize on this theme for a few sentences and then explode with laughter when Green sloped away to make yet another investigative telephone call.

3
Armstrong's Influence

The popularity that Henderson's Orchestra achieved at the Roseland Ballroom during their 1924–5 winter season laid the foundations for a long series of return bookings. During their first long stay there (from 13 October 1924 until 31 May 1925) Henderson gradually moulded his unit into an ensemble that could produce enough musical heat and power to melt away any opposition assembled on the ballroom's other bandstand.

The group's primary task was to please the dancers, but the band's performances soon became so dynamic that people came to stand as close as they could to the stage, simply to listen to the music. But all the audience, dancers and listeners, were white: the Roseland Ballroom employed many black people but maintained a strict policy of segregation towards its customers. In this respect it was like many other entertainment venues in New York, including the Cotton Club.

The Henderson musicians accepted the ballroom's racism simply because segregation was so much a part of their everyday life. At the Roseland the black musicians were not allowed to fraternize with the white customers, nor were they accorded bar or restaurant facilities. As a result, most of the musicians' intervals were spent in a spartan dressing-room downstairs, well away from the audience. The alternatives were: to find some fresh air on a balcony, or to take a short stroll out in the streets. Occasionally a friendship was established with a white musician who was working in a visiting band, but most often this sort of contact rarely got beyond a nodding acquaintanceship.

To while away intermission time some of Henderson's musicians played cards, often gambling for big stakes, and others sat gossiping and telling jokes. Hawkins was never a regular part of either school; he had already cemented his outlook on the conservation of money and at this stage of his life losing any of it at cards was a painful experience. He joined in during band-room banter sessions, but soon drifted off to size up the musical opposition or to read a newspaper, usually concentrating on the sports pages, especially during the baseball season.

Socially, Hawk was more likely to move with the pack when the Henderson Orchestra went on tour, which it did during the spring and summer months, usually playing a long series of dates through New England and the coal-mining towns of Pennyslvania. In such places, organized late-night entertainment was out of the question for visiting blacks, so out of boredom Hawkins sometimes joined in the all-night poker and 'tonk' schools that flourished when the musicians had finished work. Whenever he lost money he'd vow never to play again.

There were few personnel changes within Henderson's group during this period. This is understandable, because the musicians were earning a lot of money, playing ballroom dates, private parties and doing broadcast and record dates. One small upheaval in April 1925 saw the departure of Howard Scott, replaced by Joe Smith (who had worked with Hawkins in the Mamie Smith band). Smith was already renowned for his plaintive tone and for his skilful use of the plunger mute. Some considered him to be a rival to Louis Armstrong, but Joe, for all his mellowness and melodic phrasing, didn't possess Armstrong's rhythmic flair, technique or inventive genius. He was, however, markedly superior to Howard Scott, and his arrival made the Henderson brass team a fuller-sounding, more effective unit. Hawkins said of Smith, 'He could take a plunger and he had a very real sweet sound . . . he had a real good tone'.[1]

Smith's elegaic tone is clearly demonstrated on the May 1925 recording session that produced 'Money Blues'. The tune, a run-of-the-mill composition, has some effective Armstrong and an unsensational tenor solo from Hawkins, who displays a curious wavering on his long notes. Both these players take their solos on the song's chorus, but Buster Bailey improvises on the twelve-bar blues section and blows with a telling authenticity that is reminiscent of clarinettist Johnny Dodds.

Solos differ slightly on the two available takes of 'Money Blues', but Hawk's contributions do at least show that he had learnt the knack of imparting brief entry phrases to his solos, blowing a fleeting preliminary idea before expounding his main thesis, thus avoiding a 'square', blatantly obvious entry on the first beat of a chorus. Looking back years later, though, Hawkins could find nothing of merit in his work on 'Money Blues'.

In 1946 writer Leonard Feather subjected Hawkins to a blindfold test, playing him unannounced recordings and then asking for his comments.

One of these tests concerned Henderson's recording of 'Money Blues'. Hawk's reaction was scathing:

> That's really one of the old ones, isn't it? I hear a banjo and a bass horn. Is that Fletcher? He used to make records just like that. Sure, that's Louis Armstrong . . . that's Buster Bailey . . . say, that's me! It's an amazing thing, there are kids twenty-two, twenty-three years old who get hold of these records and they don't think anything has ever been made that's better than that sort of thing. I don't understand it! To me, it's like a man thinking back to when he couldn't walk, he had to crawl. It's hard to look back and think that you ever sounded like that. I thought I was playing all right at the time, too, but it sounds awful to me now. I hate to listen to it – I'm ashamed of it.[2]

This wasn't mock modesty; Hawkins genuinely abhorred his early work.

On all the Henderson band's recordings from this period, Smith, Armstrong, and Elmer Chambers, though tonally disparate, achieved a robust blend. There was no elbowing for prominence since each man realized that he was expected to play a different role within the band. But this combination of trumpeters didn't last long; soon after the band had completed its usual summer touring (from June until September 1925) Louis Armstrong decided to leave Henderson. Louis's ambitious wife, Lilian, persuaded him that it was time to move back to Chicago in order to benefit from the experience and prestige that he had gained during his stay in Henderson's band. Lil had organized her own band to back Louis, who responded to his wife's 'come or else' ultimatum by handing in his notice to Fletcher Henderson.

Armstrong was still with the band, however, when they returned to the Roseland during the first week of October 1925. They resumed recording on 21 October, waxing a version of 'T.N.T.' on which Louis blows a forthright, agile solo; the ubiquitous clarinet trio is heard briefly then Hawkins switches instruments and plays a four-bar tenor solo that is more legato than most of his previous work. It is not one of his best musical moments, but it is distinctly superior to his bass-saxophone contribution to another tune from the same session, 'Carolina Stomp'.

Hawkins had proved on earlier recordings (such as 'Memphis Bound') that he was competent on the bass sax, but he probably hadn't touched the instrument all summer, preferring to leave it in the boot of his car rather than haul it in and out of the many ballrooms the band played on their tour. To expect a flowing performance after such a layoff was pure optimism, and the distressing results of Hawk's reunion with the huge saxophone rank as a low spot in his career. He sounds all thumbs and out-of-tune throughout.

So the Armstrong–Hawkins recorded collaborations with the Henderson orchestra ended on a low, unsatisfactory note, but five days later, on 26 October, the two men were part of a sextet that the pianist Clarence Williams organized to accompany his wife, vocaliste Eva Taylor, on two titles, 'Squeeze Me' and 'You Can't Shush Katie'. 'Katie', charmingly sung by Eva Taylor, features Louis Armstrong, but Hawkins plays a brief (six-bar) solo on 'Squeeze Me' during which he plants a signpost indicating the direction of his future greatness. The solo is both passionate and musically ingenious, hinting at revolutionary concepts of ballad playing. He rhapsodizes around the melody but incorporates harmonic resolutions that cleverly suggest chords that are more involved than those being played by his accompanists. Stimulated by this ingenuity, Armstrong follows up with a brilliant solo, making it all the more regrettable that this was the only small-band date they did together.

Armstrong then departed for Chicago, later acknowledging that his stay with Henderson had provided him with invaluable experience: 'In that year I learned a great deal'. On another occasion Louis told writer Barry Ulanov that prior to his departure he had become disheartened by the lackadaisical approach that the sideman had gradually adopted: 'When them cats commenced getting careless with their music, fooling around all night, I was dragged, man.'

Coleman Hawkins was not one of the musicians who became careless (except about arriving on time) but he was certainly one of the instigators of the long series of locker-room practical jokes that took place at the Roseland. Most of these pranks (involving itching powder, wet fish, hiding shoes and shirts) were engendered by the routine of playing the same venue for week after week to similar audiences. Fletcher Henderson did nothing to staunch the mischief.

Louis's decision to leave Henderson was a crucial turning-point in his career. Though he had entered the band like a whirlwind, he had not benefited from the improvements that his skills had caused in others; no one, including Hawkins, could regularly offer him the sort of challenge on which he thrived. Almost all of his recorded solos with Henderson are brilliant, but there are times during the latter part of his stay where he falls into familiar patterns during his improvisations, tending to repeat himself. It is as though his musical surroundings had ceased to give him inspiration. During this same period he played masterfully on recordings with Clarence

Williams and Bessie Smith, but the Henderson orchestra's often ponderous arrangements blunted the edge of his creativity; it was immediately sharpened when he moved back to Chicago.

Henderson was extremely sorry to see Armstrong go, and as a gesture of his affection for the departing star he booked tables at Small's Paradise for a farewell party attended by the entire Henderson band. Both Louis and Buster Bailey got extremely drunk at the gathering and when Louis went over to thank Fletcher Henderson for all his help he (in his own words) 'puked all over Henderson's bosom'.[3]

Some of the assembled musicians were aghast at the incident, but the gentle bandleader accepted the dowsing with serenity. Armstrong later recalled, 'He wasn't mad, and said "Thank you, Louis".' Most of those present couldn't suppress their laughter and it is not inconceivable that Louis noticed that it was Coleman Hawkins who laughed loudest. It was part of the young Hawkins's character to find amusement in observing a minor misfortune; if the accident had happened to his dearest friend he would probably have laughed even louder. The incident highlighted Henderson's unwordly placidity and proved that his wife was not exaggerating when she said, late in life, 'In all the time I knew him he never got real mad about anything'.[4]

Armstrong's departure from New York in early November 1925 created an unpluggable gap within Henderson's brass section. Fletcher's initial strategy was to bring in a superb lead trumpeter in the shape of Joe Smith's brother, Russell (also the former husband of Henderson's wife, Leora). Russell Smith joined Joe Smith and Elmer Chambers in the trumpet section, but of this trio only Joe was capable of inspired improvisation. Chambers, deprived of the prestigious position of first trumpeter, soon departed and the band made do with the two brothers for a while.

During these latter months of 1925 Hawkins resumed his former prominence on recordings with Henderson, but perversely he spent a good deal of his time playing bass saxophone, perhaps to atone for his previous lapse on the instrument. He used it on a series of recordings that Henderson's group did for the Harmony label, using the name The Dixie Stompers for contractual reasons. On the first of these, 'Spanish Shawl', Hawkins is featured on bass sax, blowing two solos with spirit and skill. On the Fletcher Henderson Orchestra session of 18 December his bass sax is heard playing the opening melody of 'Pensacola' and, four days later, he again blew the leviathan on the first recording of his own composition 'Florida Stomp'.

Joe and Russell Smith achieve an attractive trumpet blend on all of these sides, but for all Joe's elegance (particularly on 'Then I'll Be Happy' and 'Get It Fixed') he was not the sort of player to set an ensemble alight, and at fast tempi he tended to sound flurried. Aware of these factors, Henderson decided to revert to a three-man section, persuading a young cornettist, Rex Stewart, to join the orchestra. Rex, who had originally been recommended by Louis Armstrong (before he left for Chicago) was then only eighteen years old.

Rex was, by his own reckoning, a sensitive and temperamental teenager, and the fact that he was taking the place of his musical idol, Louis Armstrong, made him particularly nervous and tense. This obvious anxiety made him the automatic target for the Henderson orchestra's funsters, especially Coleman Hawkins, who was always teasing Rex. These jibes left deep scars. Rex was eventually able to write warmly about Hawkins, but I have vivid memories of being with him on the day (in the 1960s) when he learnt that Coleman Hawkins had grown a beard. Rex appeared to smile at the information, but I was standing close enough to hear him mutter, with undisguised venom, 'Silly old fool.'

Yet Rex could not help but admire Hawkins's musical talent, and a touch of hero-worship entered his memoirs of those early days:

> Coleman amazed me by consuming more food at one sitting than I had ever seen anybody else eat. Perhaps that's where he gets his tremendous energy. A typical meal for Hawkins would start with ham and eggs and hot cakes, while his steak covered with onions was being prepared. The steak would not be a breakfast-size portion. It would be a full-size porterhouse, accompanied with hash browns or French fries. This snack would usually be topped off with a slab of pie and ice cream. Being young and impressionable I copied Hawk's eating habits with gusto, and by the time Fletcher's band had returned from our first road tour I had gained a bit of weight, jumping from 145 to 180 pounds in one summer.[5]

Trombonist Benny Morton, another eighteen-year-old, joined the brass team (at ninety dollars a week) some three weeks before Rex Stewart's arrival. Morton had an entirely different temperament, and deliberately laughed off any teasing or practical jokes:

> I had played a lot of sport before I joined Fletcher and I was used to that kind of deal. Some people do it out of spite but often it happens because they're tense or bored with being cooped up together. It didn't bother me, but I guess it got to Rex; he got worried and depressed and left for a while to get over it.[6]

At the time Rex offered Henderson a time honoured excuse for leaving: he told him his grandmother was ill. Rex eventually got his confidence back and rejoined Henderson.

Thirty years later Hawkins recalled Stewart's early days in the Henderson band:

> Rex had to do a little comedy around some of those parts he was reading, you know. Like to get to some of those passages that were kinda hard. He couldn't read them fast enough or something like that. And Rex had to stomp his foot and do something, take his horn down and twirl it up and do something at that particular spot . . . and whenever you'd look at his music you'd see there was about twenty notes right at this place, you know what I mean?'

Hawkins never seemed to experience any difficulties in reading music; outlining his method he said, 'Usually I read a line ahead of the notes I'm playing, and I've got the rest of the page photographed on my mind.' His advice was: 'When you get hold of a new piece, don't play it straight away. Read it first to see how the chords run. I always do.'[8]

The Henderson band's arrangements were a formidable test for even the ablest sightreader, since they contained a conglomeration of intricate rhythms, and were often written in keys (such as E major) rarely encountered in dance music or in jazz. Rex Stewart later became a superb all-round musician, but at this time he was young and relatively inexperienced. Hawkins, who had been something of a prodigy, couldn't appreciate the difficulties Stewart was encountering. Although Hawk later became more tolerant, quite early in his career he said, 'Six flats, five sharps. Who cares? All the notes are on the instrument. It's up to you to find them and remember them.'[9] But despite having problems in reading various arrangements, Stewart proved on 'Off to Buffalo' and 'Alabama Stomp' that he was able to improvise splendid solos.

Hawkins wasn't a sadist, but he just couldn't resist teasing his fellow musicians. Usually he desisted when he saw no reaction, but if he spotted a chink in the armour the probing would be persistent; Hawk liked to call it 'kidding'. Most of the men in the band held him in respectful affection, though none of them was close to him. So Rex Stewart said, 'He was essentially a loner.' But Hawkins could be the epitome of charm when meeting relatives of his fellow musicians, and young female fans seemed to melt when he talked to them.

During Rex Stewart's brief initial stay the Henderson Orchestra recorded on several occasions (sometimes as the Dixie Stompers). One of the orchestra sides (from 14 May 1926) was 'The Stampede', which featured a dynamic tenor sax solo by Hawkins, phrases from which soon found their way into the work of many other saxophonists eager to copy the young master's musical utterings. This particular Hawkins solo also played a part in shaping the embryo style of trumpeter Roy Eldridge, himself later to become a musical revolutionary. For his first big audition Eldridge successfully played his rendering of Hawk's solo on 'The Stampede' and got the job.

Hawkins's solo on 'The Stampede' shows how effectively he was smoothing out the jerkiness that had previously stilted his phrasing. Displaying considerable rhythmic assurance, he moves smoothly from one idea to another, skilfully linking his phrases and demonstrating that his sense of form was also developing. Despite Hawk's subsequent denials it seems apparent that Louis Armstrong's playing had affected the saxophonist's conception of soloing. The syncopations of Hawk's opening phrase and the almost trumpet-like shake that he imparts to the G that ends this stanza are patently similar to Armstrong's style, as is the pattern in the following two bars. But that said, there is also much originality within the chorus; gone are the plethora of arpeggois, in their place cleverly syncopated ideas, and the descending patterns that fill bars thirteen to sixteen are distinctly innovative. The recording of this solo marks an important landmark in Hawk's career.

Don Redman's arrangements were slowly moving away from the strict formalities that governed that era's dance-band orchestrations and he was beginning to provide Henderson's soloists with charts that were inspirational. Redman became one of the first arrangers to transfer small-band devices to a larger line-up, and as early as March 1926 (on 'Tampeeko') he incorporated call-and-answer patterns that had instrumental sections fulfilling the roles that single instruments took in small jazz bands. But despite Redman's progress he still had to churn out arrangements of poor tunes that had achieved temporary popularity, and even some of his efforts on better-class material failed to achieve any sort of climax. Like many other charts of this period they proceeded in a series of stops and starts, and contained many inconsequential novelties. The clarinet trios still provided a useful change of tone colour (as on 'Shuffling Sadie') but often the effect seemed to be included as an irrelevant diversion. Thus Hawkins was forced to keep in touch with his clarinet, but he made no effort to secure himself a solo on that instrument.

By now Hawkins was widely recognized as the leading jazz tenor saxist;

he had, almost single-handedly, made the instrument a respected jazz 'voice'. Four decades later, tenorist Johnny Griffin put the issue in perspective when he said, 'Coleman Hawkins rescued the saxophone from the oblivion of the circus.'[10] Hawkins's influence affected both black and white musicians. Bud Freeman, a pioneering white saxophonist (and an individualist in his own right) spoke of the force of Hawkins's inspiration. In early 1926, Freeman (then nineteen) was a member of Art Kassel's band, working opposite Henderson's band, who were visiting the Graystone Ballroom in Detroit: 'When I heard Hawkins I wasn't influenced by his style but rather with the idea that the tenor could be such a powerful authoritative voice in music. And so I started to play, not as a saxophone section player, but rather as a soloist on the strength of hearing Hawkins'.[11]

During the late-1926 period (following the usual summer tour) Hawkins dropped into the background temporarily on several recordings made by Henderson's Orchestra (and by the Dixie Stompers). This was perhaps due to the fact that by this time a tenor-saxophone solo had nothing like the novelty value it had (until recently) possessed; in making the instrument more popular Hawkins had made a rod for his own back. If Henderson had been a little more imaginative he would have realized that Hawk's solos were often the main talking point of a recording. Hawkins is featured only briefly on several ensuing sessions. He's heard playing an eight-bar tenor solo on 'Off to Buffalo' (on which someone else is given the chore of playing bass saxophone) and on 'Clarinet Marmalade' (from December 1926), where his brief solo sounds extremely fidgety, as though he were unprepared for it. Sometimes the variable nature of Hawkins's performance at this time was due to his tendency to experiment with reeds and mouthpieces; he said, 'I fooled a lot with reeds and mouthpieces, I wanted a strong tone'.[12]

Already Hawkins was being continually challenged for his tenor crown and he tried to use the best equipment he could in its defence. Although he gave every appearance of being abundantly sure of himself, he was still only twenty-two years of age. By experimentation he managed to develop an enormous volume of sound on his tenor, and he was able to project his considerable tone across vast ballrooms. Saxophonist Roy Butler heard Hawkins in February 1926: 'Fletcher Henderson came to Chicago and played at the Eighth Regiment Armory. The outstanding thing I remember about Hawkins was that although they had no microphones in those days Hawkins could fill that big Armory'.[13] In self-analysis, Hawkins said, 'As for my full tone, I always did play with a kind of stiff reed. When I started I also used to play very loud because I was trying to play those solos over seven or eight other horns.'[14]

Hawk's playing began to gain a whole army of imitators; almost every dance band now had a budding 'hot' tenor saxist within its ranks. On their wide-ranging tours the Henderson musicians heard plenty of these tyros. The Henderson band's main residency was still at the Roseland, but they also played regularly at other prestigious ballrooms, including the Graystone in Detroit and the Arcadia in Brooklyn. In May 1926 they were booked to play for the opening of New York's enormous new ballroom, the Savoy. Soon after the inauguration, during a return booking at the Savoy, Henderson invited the young pianist, Thomas 'Fats' Waller, to sit-in with the band. Fats did so with such success that he was subsequently often called on to guest with Fletcher's band. Though the modest leader knew that Waller was a superior pianist, he didn't resent the youngster's brilliance and even used Waller on some of the band's recordings, notably the excellent 'Henderson Stomp'.

Waller's appeal was not at all esoteric. Even at this early stage of his career his playing captivated to all sorts of listeners. The *Orchestra World* of November 1926 reported: 'Thomas "Fats" Waller, the piano wizard, relieved Fletcher Henderson once in a while and the boys and girls stopped dancing to watch his fingers.' Coleman Hawkins was positively in favour of using Waller with the Henderson band and felt the leader made a big mistake in not inviting Fats to become the band's regular pianist – a move that would have allowed Henderson to conduct out front. Thus the band would have gained a superb soloist, a master of showmanship and a supremely gifted composer; but Henderson decided against the idea. Hawkins said, 'Fats was loaded with talent. So I always thought that Fletcher made a mistake. He just should have hired Fats and kept him.'[15] Undoubtedly Henderson's drummer, Kaiser Marshall, would have greatly benefited from Waller's highly rhythmic playing. Marshall's skills as a percussionist improved steadily throughout the 1920s, and by the end of the decade he was turning in some brilliant performances, but too often it appears that his zest is hampered by the efforts of his colleagues within the rhythm section.

Henderson did make one important addition to the band in late 1926. This involved the introduction of trumpeter Tommy Ladnier, a fine soloist from the talented ranks of the Louisiana musicians. With Ladnier in the band the Henderson group cut several memorable recordings, including 'Snag It' and 'Hot Mustard', in both of which Hawkins was cast in a decidedly, subsidiary role. Ladnier and Joe Smith exhibit good teamwork on 'Snag It' and on 'Wabash Blues' (where their alternating solos have confused several annotators). Ladnier was also part of a contingent from the band who recorded two spirited numbers, 'Would Ja' and 'Sengalese Stomp', for bandleader Clarence Williams in December 1926; Hawkins plays a brief solo on the second title.

Hawk's wariness of Louisiana musicians didn't ease up during the time he worked alongside Tommy Ladnier. Ladnier wore the right clothes and was rather more sophisticated than Louis Armstrong, but he was not, as yet, expert at reading music, a fact that would not have pleased Hawkins much. Ladnier was also not averse to saying that he felt that all the best jazz musicians came from Louisiana, a point of view that caused Hawkins to smart. The new trumpeter was at his most skilful when playing the blues, but at this stage of his career Hawkins was uninterested in improvising over the traditional twelve-bar structure. He did so when called upon, but would never have dreamt of playing the blues for his own pleasure. Later in his life Hawkins re-examined his approach to the blues and by dint of his extraordinary talent became a master of the idiom.

Hawkins certainly didn't go out of his way to seek freelance recording dates accompanying blues singers. Fletcher Henderson, though, was often called upon to provide accompanists for such artists and in March 1927 took a contingent from the band (including Hawkins) to record with the immortal Bessie Smith. On this occasion Hawkins seems to have been booked as a cover for the late arrival of Buster Bailey, in that he plays clarinet for much of the session. Hawkins and Bailey play a blighted duo on the third tune of the day, 'Muddy Water', then Bailey takes over solo clarinet duties on the final number, 'A Hot Time in the Old Town Tonight', creating, with his usual aplomb, a scintillating break.

Henderson and his sidemen also occasionally accompanied Bessie Smith on theatre dates during the 1920s. On one such occasion Duke Ellington met Coleman Hawkins for the first time. The introductions took place under lively circumstances in Washington, DC. Duke recalled:

> I was playing in a joint called Jack's on Seventh Street, and Fletcher Henderson came in with Hawk. They were playing in the city with Bessie Smith and they came by to visit. I was honoured to have these celebrities with me, and everything was going fine until a fight started in the place. It began with a little throwing of things and ended up with a gun shooting and Fletcher, Hawk and me under the bandstand. I don't remember any more about our first meeting.[16]

Hawkins became close friends with yet another newcomer to the Henderson brass team, trombonist Jimmy Harrison (from Louisville, Kentucky). He was a tall, extrovert character, four years older than Hawk. Harrison, Hawkins and Buster Bailey hung out together in the band room and were soon nicknamed 'the heckling crew' by Fletcher Henderson's younger brother, Horace. According to trombonist Clyde Bernhardt, Harrison (like Tommy Ladnier) was not then a very adept reader of music, but in this instance Hawkins didn't make the shortcoming a barrier to friendship. Harrison had already developed an impressive instrumental technique and played improvisations that contained a wealth of dramatically new ideas. He was not immediately given prominence on Henderson's recordings, but even in short bursts (such as on 'Stockholm Stomp') his dexterity and warm tone are obvious. On 'Fidgety Feet' and 'Sensation' he is quite outstanding, and on 'Wang Wang Blues' holds his own alongside Hawkins.

Jimmy Harrison came in for a fair share of kidding from Hawkins but Jimmy gave as good as he got and gradually the two men became friends. Rex Stewart wrote: 'With the exception of Harrison I don't know anyone with whom Hawkins was ever really close.' Hawkins, determinedly unsentimental at most times, agreed with this assessment and said, 'Yes, Jimmy and I were real tight. He could play. He had a good beat and he could swing.' Reed player Garvin Bushell said that Harrison was 'as unusual on trombone as Hawk was on tenor', and it was probably this musical skill shared by the two men that originally formed the basis of their friendship. Hawkins also admired Harrison's taste in automobiles and began according him even more admiring respect after the trombonist purchased a new Pontiac. Trombonist Sandy Williams said of the Hawkins–Harrison friendship, 'The two of them were clowns in a way of speaking. They'd kid each other, play the dozens in other words'.[17] ('The dozens' was a teasing verbal game in which opponents tried to rile their adversaries by making the most insulting remarks they could conjure up.)

The biggest upheaval in the Henderson orchestra's history occurred in July 1927 when the group's saxophonist and principal arranger, Don Redman, left. He had been lured away to become the supremo of McKinney's Cotton Pickers, a fast-rising big band based in Detroit. As a jazz soloist Redman could never be considered outstanding; some of his improvisations were charming and occasionally ingenious, but they lacked rhythmic swing. Yet as an arranger he became the first to transfer this elusive swing to paper via his revolutionary arrangements; bands playing his orchestrations were lifted by his skilful writing. He also pioneered many effects that became standard features of later big-band arrangements. Besides the use of call-and-answer patterns between various sections, and the inclusion of climactic riffs, he also devised the mixing of clarinet and saxophone voicings (on 'Tozo', for instance, where Hawkins on tenor leads the reed section). He successfully experimented with the extension of chords so as to produce interesting new orchestral timbre and he developed the practice of writing stimulating rhythmic patterns for the entire band to play as a background to an improvising soloist. A close analysis of Redman's early writings suggest that his contribution to creating the roots of the coming swing era was far greater than that of Fletcher Henderson.

Eventually Fletcher himself took over Redman's role as the band's principal arranger – with startlingly successful results – but the bandleader's most immediate task was to find someone to take Redman's place as the lead saxophonist. He chose Jerome Don Pasquall, who had just finished his studies at the New England Conservatory in Boston, Mass. Pasquall had no trouble in reading the parts, nor in socializing with Hawkins. The two men enjoyed a courteous, almost formal relationship, with conversation circling around the merits of various reeds, the climate and other sundry matters.

The first half of 1927 had seen Hawkins becoming even more authoritative in his playing, but sometimes there were lapses when his adventurousness created swashbuckling, hit-or-miss phrases, typified by his haphazard half-chorus on 'Stockholm Stomp'. Sometimes his attack was almost aggressive, as on 'Fidgety Feet', but all the time his fingers were becoming more and more nimble as he proved on his double-time runs on 'Wabash Blues' and his fast glissandi on the various versions of 'St Louis Shuffle'.

His articulation was even cleaner than before, as he demonstrated on 'Whiteman Stomp'. Hawkins felt that this title, and its coupling 'I'm Coming Virginia', were among the best of Henderson's recordings.[18] His general technique was gradually exhibiting more facility and he was able to switch registers with the maximum of ease, as he does on 'Cornfed'. This increased control allowed him to soft-pedal comfortably on the opening of 'PDQ Blues', sounding almost tender as he warbles the main theme on tenor sax. There was, nevertheless, still a tendency for him to bustle up and down chord arpeggios on fast numbers, couching his phrases in a series of even eighth notes. It was an effect he was to revive late in his career, often when inspiration was distant, but in these early days it gives the impression that he is trying too hard.

During the latter part of Don Redman's stay with Henderson his arrangements had become increasingly bold in their use of harmonies. This suited Hawkins, who was always willing to explore the improvisational possibilities offered by an extended chord. Hawk was, at this stage of his life, willing to undergo any sort of musical test. An unusual one cropped up on tour when some of his Henderson band colleagues were injured in a road crash that occurred while they were travelling to Detroit from Kentucky. The accident put two of the band's trumpeters temporarily out of action. As a result Fletcher Henderson contacted Rex Stewart (who was working with Horace Henderson's band in Cincinnati); Stewart immediately set out for the Graystone Ballroom in Detroit to fill one of the gaps. The other place in the trumpet section was taken by Coleman Hawkins playing tenor saxophone. Hawkins sightread Russell Smith's first-trumpet parts with consummate ease, and Rex Stewart later recalled: 'he not only played the parts so well that we scarcely missed the first trumpet but he also carried the orchestra with a volume such as I had never heard coming out of a tenor sax. And the Graystone was a huge place!'[19]

Hawkins was not interested in experimentation without method; he believed that harmonic awareness and rhythmic daring were the main components of a successful jazz solo. He said that he felt Fletcher Harrison's band was at its best when it blended these two factors, as it did in the final period of Don Redman's stay; 'I think Fletcher's band should have stayed stomping . . . I think they should have stomped all the other bands out of existence until the very end. But Fletcher's band got too sophisticated . . . should have stayed just as they were, when they were used to that sound it used to have, like the "King Porter Stomp" thing.'[20]

4
Fast Cars and Silk Suits

The late 1920s marked the age of the Harlem Renaissance, an exciting awakening of black creative impulses that found a centre in the northern section of Manhattan Island, New York. Black workers from all over the United States (and from the Caribbean islands) had settled there seeking, among other things, better economic conditions. A fresh approach to life swept through Harlem, blowing new zest into music, literature and painting. A passion for entertainment developed and hundreds of clubs, cabarets and music-bars opened and flourished.

By this time Hawkins was something of a celebrity in Harlem. He enjoyed the role of man-about-town and left the Roseland Ballroom dressed in style, wearing silk or shantung suits in the summer and fine tweeds underneath a fashionable racoon coat in winter. His hand-made shoes never suffered the brunt of extensive strolling because Hawk made a point of parking his roadster – the latest, expensive model – close to his place of work, so as to give his colleagues the opportunity to envy the star saxophonist's gleaming acquisition.

Hawkins, at this stage of his life, was confident without being vain; he raised no objection to being nicknamed 'Bean' by his fellow musicians and willingly explained that he was called this because 'my head resembled a haricot bean'. Rex Stewart said that among old pals Hawk could be 'quite jovial and enthusiastic about something that interested him'.[1] He had mellowed a little and was quietly humorous with fellow jazzmen, and rarely vindictive, except at jam sessions when the sight of another tenor saxophonist in action roused a professional combativeness bordering on ruthlessness. He recalled these battles; 'Why, gangs of tenors would be coming into New York all the time from bands on the road. They used to wake me out of my bed to come down and cut people. Tenors like Prince Robinson for example.'[2]

Hawkins always emerged triumphant from these musical skirmishes.

In the 1960s, looking back over his life, he said, 'Some of my biggest moments have been in jam sessions.'[3] But through his friendship with Jimmy Harrison, Hawkins went for long periods in the late 1920s without getting involved in nightclub jam sessions. Instead Hawkins and Harrison (who lived in the same apartment block) went to each other's homes after they had finished work. Harrison, who was something of a newly-wed (he married his wife Katherine – always known as Kitty – in June 1926) had no desire to spend his nights away from home; Hawkins followed suit and temporarily dropped his habit of sampling New York nightlife. Jimmy Harrison wasn't a big drinker, and at this time Hawkins's daily intake of alcohol was only moderate.

This surfacing of domesticity had a profound effect on the development of both Hawkins's and Harrison's playing. Often the two practised together until dawn trying out new harmonies and consolidating ideas that had begun to develop on the bandstand. Hawkins was not a man to theorize about inspiration, but on one occasion he opened up a little on the subject and said, 'My playing is influenced by a lot of things I hear unconsciously and I find myself playing a lot of things I have developed out of something I've absorbed that way. But I never made any particular study of why I play as I do – it just comes out naturally.'[4]

Though Hawk gained something from studying Harrison's phrasing and jazz ideas, he fulfilled the role of teacher when it came to the use of harmony. Horace Henderson observed: 'Jimmy Harrison had a great ear. Jimmy was a great trombonist but he knew nothing about chords or anything. He just played the way he felt in his heart, but he wanted to learn how, what notes were in certain chords, and Hawk would tell him.'[5] Rex Stewart recalled the competition between Hawkins and Harrison: 'Any time Coleman Hawkins played an extra good solo, which was quite often, Jimmy would jerk up in his chair, throw a glance at Hawk and play more trombone than was natural for one man – he just hated to be beaten to the draw by Coleman.'[6]

Both Hawkins and Harrison had their fans in many places outside of New York; trombonist Sandy Williams said, 'Washington was my hometown and if the band was playing in Baltimore I'd be over there to hear the band and Jimmy Harrison, who was my real idol back in those days. I just thought that was the greatest band in the world.'[7] Other budding musicians heard the band on tour; trumpeter Bill Dillard recalled:

> I first heard Coleman Hawkins when he came to the Strand Ballroom in Philadelphia in 1928. He had a B-flat tenor, whereas most of the local guys still played C-melody saxes. When he began playing it had a tremendous effect on me; I never forgot it. I watched him get off the bandstand, he was a model of style, and he always had that style.'[8]

Drummer Jimmy Crawford's memories of the band's visit to Cleveland in the late 1920s were similar: 'I spent my last dollar to hear Fletcher Henderson. I'd heard so much about the band and Coleman Hawkins.'[9] In an interview with Stanley Dance, saxist Budd Johnson recalled his first, youthful sight of Henderson's Band visiting Tulsa, Oklahoma:

> I worked my way through right up to the bandstand, until I was standing in front of Hawk. You know, young as I was, he gave me some attention when I let him know who I was. That is one of the reasons why I always respected this guy. Hawk talked to me and from that day we were friends. He remembered me and later, when he came to Chicago with Fletcher we would hang out and drink whiskey. And he would always buy me a drink too!'[10]

Arranger Fred Norman remembers getting a kindly word from Hawkins when he took a youthful attempt at big-band orchestration along to a Washington, DC ballroom for the Fletcher Henderson band to try out: 'I passed it out and the band went through it, voom. I remember Hawkins said 'No man, we can't use this, but keep trying, keep trying.'[11]

During the spring of 1928, when the Henderson band returned to play their umpteenth season at the Roseland, Hawkins and Harrison struck up a friendship with a young white Texan trombonist, Jack Teagarden, who was then playing a residency at the Ballroom with the Scranton Sirens. After one hearing, Hawkins knew that Teagarden was a superb musician. He also realized that he could have some fun by teasing Jimmy Harrison about the newcomer's musical prowess. He went straight to the bandroom and said to Harrison, 'There's a boy upstairs playing an awful lot of trombone.'[12] He continued to heap lavish praise on Teagarden's skills to the point where Harrison swallowed the bait and became riled, but his animosity disappeared as soon as he heard Teagarden play. He knew instantly, just as Hawkins did, that here was a young man whose musical thinking was following the same route as his own. The two trombonists became easy companions. Recalling their initial meeting, Teagarden said, 'That first night at Roseland. We just didn't need any introductions.'[13]

Hawkins recalled:

Jimmy and Jack got to be the tightest of friends. After this first night you couldn't separate Jimmy and Jack Teagarden. We used to come up to my house every night and used to fool around until two or three or four in the afternoon and get no sleep. You see Jimmy and Jack were both jiving each other, each trying to figure out what he lacked that he could get from the other one, and the other one is doing the same thing . . . And I had the piano and they could play all night. We didn't disturb anybody . . . the house was all well draped and carpeted . . . so both of them got their trombones and I was playing the piano for them. This used to go on all night long. Listening to records and eating and talking, back to playing again and this every night.'[14]

Jimmy and Kitty Harrison lodged with Henderson's drummer Kaiser Marshall, who lived next door to Coleman and Gertie Hawkins. Marshall recalled: 'Many a morning we would sit up with Hawkins playing pinochle, which was his favourite game.'[15] Sometimes the nocturnal jam sessions took place in his apartment: 'Jack Teagarden used to come to our house often, sometimes staying all night. We would have a session between Hawkins, Jack would play piano, Jimmy Harrison trombone and myself on my rubber pad I kept at home. Then Hawkins would play piano, Jack and Jimmy trombones. My, what fun we had.'[16] Coleman Hawkins said of Teagarden: 'He was one of the greatest characters I ever knew – altogether different. We got into that chittlin' thing together. He always did play very pretty.'[17]

Regrettably, this was in an era before tape recorders were invented, so there are no souvenirs of these remarkable sessions featuring three of the best and most adventurous jazz improvisers of their era. Hawk made the point about neighbours being unable to hear the sessions, but for Coleman's wife, Gertie, the magnificent music, albeit muffled, must have been a mixed blessing during the small hours. Yet she seems to have accepted it all with a smile, probably happy that she knew where Hawkins was each dawn. Despite the sound-proofing the neighbours must have been reasonably sympathetic too, because whenever Hawkins was enjoying his music he stamped out the tempo with his feet.

Hawkins, Harrison and Teagarden did a lot of ballad playing at their all-night sessions, but this aspect of Hawkins's skills had to remain dormant on his recordings with Henderson's orchestra because so few of their numbers could be classified as ballads. Sometimes straightforward medium-tempo popular tunes such as 'There's a Rickety Rackety Shack' (which featured an Andy Razaf vocal) were waxed, but the only slowish melody that Hawk recorded in this period was the Dixie Stompers' 'Feelin'

Good'. Here Hawk's interpretation of the tune imparts just the sort of swagger that the lyrics suggest. Hawk immediately showed his versatility by blowing some exciting lines on 'I'm Feelin' Devilish' that reveal his subtle use of blue notes.

By now it seems that Fletcher Henderson had realized what an asset he had in Hawkins; he again started to feature him on every recording, often giving him a dominating role, as on 'Goose Pimples'. Hawk is absolutely commanding and flamboyantly rhythmic on this title, whereas the swift tempo seems to upset Tommy Ladnier's musical equilibrium. Hawkins is equally daring on Jack Purvis's arrangement of 'Baltimore' (from the same October 1927 session), creating a burst of ultra-fast fingering in the seventh and eighth bars of a spectacular solo. The saxophonist's verve also enhances the November 1927 recording of 'Hop Off', where he cocoons his fast-tempo phrases with the sound of escaping breath.

Hawkins is more relaxed, but just as inventive, on a 'Hop Off' remake (recorded in September 1928) and this same relaxation enhances Henderson's original recording of 'King Porter Stomp', where the band perform an arrangement subsequently copied by countless swing bands. Hawkins not only displays his musical imagination but also demonstrates the strength of his embouchure by suddenly plunging to the lowest notes on his instrument and blowing them with an awesome force. Jimmy Harrison's expressive muted solo precedes a call-and-answer pattern that was to echo throughout countless ballrooms during the coming decade.

From a business point of view, 1928 was not a great year for Fletcher Henderson. In February he suffered a big blow in losing a court case with booker Al Herman over commission due on past engagements, but in August he was involved in a car accident that left him with problems of a more permanent kind. His wife Leora felt that Fletcher became a changed personality after the crash, in which his shoulder and collar bones were seriously damaged. She said, 'Fletcher was never the same after he had that automobile accident down in Kentucky. He never had much business qualities anyhow, but after that accident he had even less and worst of all he would get careless.'[18]

Fletcher's passengers, Charlie Green, Joe Smith, Bobby Stark and Coleman Hawkins, all escaped unhurt when Henderson's open-topped Packard swerved off the road and fell fourteen feet into a ditch, but band dates had to be cancelled until Henderson could resume working. When he did so, his wife and his musicians noticed that he seemed uninterested in what anyone was playing, as though he were absentmindedly thinking of other matters while sitting on the bandstand. This vagueness led to Henderson starting the band off before everyone had time to pull their music out of the arrangement pad. Coleman Hawkins recalled these uncoordinated starts with wry amusement: 'We'd be starting off and half the band was looking for the music. Fletcher tapping his foot: "Alright, let's go, one, two, three, four . . ." and there was about six of them all bent over.'[19]

But the crash did nothing to curtail the mania for high-speed driving that affected several members of the Henderson band. Henderson continued to drive his Packard convertible hard, Joe Smith seemed out to break speed records in his St Claire roadster and Hawkins always tried to leave last and arrive first in his Chrysler Imperial. Trombonist Dicky Wells said, 'Smack's guys used to drive fast. Hawk got so if he wanted to go through Philadelphia he couldn't go through Princeton, he had to go down damn near to Boston. All the cops knew him, but they couldn't catch him.'[20] Another Henderson trombonist, Sandy Williams, said,

> I remember coming with Coleman Hawkins and Walter Johnson from Philadelphia and he had just got a new Imperial. He decided to open it up on a long stretch and he had it up to 103 miles an hour. That was the first time I ever did over a hundred an hour, but Hawk was a good driver. 'Hell, I don't want to kill myself', he'd tell you right quick, 'What are you worried about?'[21]

Various personnel changes occurred in the band during 1928. Saxophonist Jerome Don Pasquall observed that the dispute over previous commission payments had left the band short of work, because various bookers shied away from hiring Henderson's group, fearing that they might have to split their percentage with more than one previous agent. Pasquall left in October 1928 and moved to Chicago, to be replaced by Benny Carter. Carter, then twenty-one years old, had been in the wings for some time, having deputized for Don Redman two years earlier when Redman's father died. Carter was a promising alto-saxist and arranger, but it was really the second of these skills that most appealed to Henderson, who was eagerly looking for someone to fulfil the writing assignments that Don Redman had previously undertaken. Carter eventually became an outstanding arranger, but he was only beginning to learn his craft in 1928. Coleman Hawkins had no desire to make a name for himself as an orchestrator; he wrote occasional arrangements for Henderson's band, but in his view his piano existed to give him pleasure and not to help him work out section voicings, introduction and codas. In a conversation with Frank Driggs, Don Redman praised Hawk's skills as an arranger, saying he did 'a terrific job on "Singin' in the Rain",' but Redman was shrewd enough to add that Hawk didn't write more than two or three arrangements a year because he was basically lazy.[22]

By late 1928 trumpeter Bobby Stark was regularly with Fletcher Henderson, and was joined by the returning Rex Stewart, both the Smith brothers having departed. The new line-up was featured on 'Come On Baby', a Benny Carter score that managed to put the clock back five years in three minutes. Fortunately Carter contributed a nice alto-saxophone solo, one that seems to bear the broad outlines of Hawkins's influence. An inkling of his remarkable arranging skills is faintly discernible in the chart he wrote for 'Easy Money', recorded at the same session. Hawkins has a six-bar solo on this slow tune, which hints at the future greatness he was to display on ballads.

Despite the problems that Henderson was having in filling his engagement book, he managed to guarantee Coleman Hawkins's wages, by now keenly aware that the saxophonist was his foremost star. All of the other musicians, however, were left to scuffle. This meant that fine players such as Jimmy Harrison found other work that paid regularly. By now he was wary of Henderson's promises and became reluctant to leave New York to go on tour with the bandleader.

One of the band's trips in early 1929 took them through Ohio and gave Hawkins his first chance to hear Art Tatum, whose extraordinary piano technique caused many jazz musicians, black and white, to drive many miles out of their way to hear him perform (usually in unsalubrious clubs). Hawkins probably approached the experience with the cynicism he always showed when other musicians praised a young player, but one hearing convinced him that he was listening to a musical genius. Being a pianist himself, Hawkins was stunned by Tatum's technical mastery and swift fingering; but it was the youngster's harmonic approach and the way he implemented complex progressions and modulations that so impressed Hawkins. Tatum's skills had the same effect on many musicians; trombonist Jack Teagarden, like Hawkins, always interested in hearing harmonic ingenuity, said, 'Tatum is God.'

Tatum's example showed Hawkins that it was possible to interpret complex harmonies within rubato phrases, allowing the soloist to feel less shackled by the rigid conception of bar lines. Thus the improviser could temporarily establish a time signature that was different from the one that his accompanists were providing. Commenting on developments within Hawkins's playing, Roy Eldridge said,

> I don't think Hawk suddenly saw the light when he first heard Art Tatum, because Hawk already had a fantastic knowledge of every sort of key change, harmony, technique, you name it, but hearing Art made him realize that here was someone who had put it all together in the right way. There's no doubt that Tatum had an impact on everyone who had an ear for developments. When I first heard him in 1927 he was thirty years ahead of his time; in fact, even by 1957 they still hadn't caught on to all that he was doing. He was the 'invisible man' of jazz; guys might not realize it, but after they heard Art he was always with them, playing a part in the way they thought about improvising.[23]

Hawkins certainly found that listening to Art Tatum was inspirational and it seems to have encouraged him to further educate his sense of rhythm so that he wasn't so rigidly tied to the sturdy chugging of on-the-beat accompaniments. In order to experiment in his own time he went off to play in jam sessions at every opportunity. This often meant playing a full night's work and then jamming for another five or six hours.

This enforced routine did wonders for Hawk's music making, but it virtually destroyed his first marriage. Horace Henderson, then leading his own Wilberforce Collegians, saw the break-up coming.

> Coleman was married to a beautiful girl, but he was more interested in music and he never would come home. He would come in at seven, eight, nine in the morning, having stopped off at a place called Big John's, up in Harlem, and he'd have his band uniform on and Gertie would meet him at the door and I remember him distinctly saying to the guys one night, 'You know I got in at nine o'clock in the morning and Gertie met me at the door. She always called him 'Poopsie'. 'Hello Poopsie. How are you? Can I fix you something?' He said he'd get mad. He would want her to be mad at him for being late. She'd never get mad, and it bothered him no end, so he thought that she didn't love him and they began to become distant. Finally they divorced and she took the furniture. And of course Hawk never replaced it, except just the essential things. I think he had a four-room apartment; as you walk in the front door there's a couch in the first room past the living room and the piano. That's it. No chairs. The dining room had a small table and two chairs. In the bedroom was a bed, and he had a small dresser with a mirror. That was it. He didn't want all that stuff, no rugs, no nothing. And the man could have had a mansion. This is just Hawk, 'cause he stayed out all the time.[24]

In those years in New York, musicians who played the same instrument often organized evenings that served both as a jam session and a social supper. Trombonist Dicky Wells recalled that Hawkins was so restless in his search for places to play that he even dropped in on these semi-private functions; 'Everybody would be blowing – maybe six trombones. Hawk would always come by the session whether it was a saxophone supper or not, saying 'I just happened to stop by and had my horn.' You knew he'd come in to carve everybody.'[25] Unfortunately this intensified regime took place in a period in which Fletcher Henderson's Orchestra did few recordings, so analysing the results is impossible. The orchestra was occasionally in the studios during early 1929, but made no recordings at all from May 1929 until October 1930.

The saga of Fletcher Henderson's various bands is full of ups and downs, but it was an almighty pity that he wasn't able to retain the strong line-up he led at the beginning of 1929: Cootie Williams, Rex Stewart, Bobby Stark (trumpets); Jimmy Harrison, Charlie Green (trombones); Buster Bailey, Benny Carter, Coleman Hawkins (reeds); Clarence Holiday (guitar/banjo); Kaiser Marshall (drums) and Delbert Thomas (tuba/bass). Every horn player in that line-up was a top-flight soloist, but keeping a team of potential stars together was financially impossible for Henderson at that time.

Cootie Williams remembered with pleasure his brief stay: 'I used to listen to Hawk and Benny Carter battle each other. Sometimes they used to have jam sessions right on the bandstand.'[26] It's been said that Hawkins influenced Carter, but at least one other saxophonist felt that Hawk gained something from Carter's style. Walter 'Foots' Thomas said, 'I definitely think Benny Carter had a great influence on Coleman Hawkins. Hawkins was not playing melodically until they worked together.'[27] Carter always did his best to dissuade people from holding that view. He said, 'Coleman Hawkins had almost no one to pattern his style after, so he was really (as I consider) a great creator.' On another occasion he said, 'We all had our mentors. From whom did Hawkins copy? I don't think he followed anybody. He was a creator. He led.'[28]

The recurring bookings at the Roseland Ballroom kept income at a reasonable level for Henderson's musicians, but sometimes sporadic tours were hastily arranged when no New York engagements were forthcoming. Cootie Williams soon left and he was followed a few months later by Buster Bailey and Benny Carter (though both of the reed players later returned to the fold). After some lean spells, however, a big opportunity for the band seemed likely when Henderson was given the chance to supply the musical accompaniment for Vincent Youman's musical comedy *Great Day*. Duke Ellington had orginally been offered the job but declined it.

For much of the 1920s Ellington had been very much the junior bandleader, sincerely paying homage to Henderson's achievements, but successes at the Cotton Club and on recordings had made Duke's band a much sought after attraction.

Henderson's band began playing for the show's rehearsals prior to a Philadelphia opening. The early run-throughs seemed to be satisfactory but Henderson decided to strengthen his team in a sensational way by enlisting the services of Louis Armstrong, temporarily on the East Coast. Problems started to develop when Henderson's orchestra was augmented by a further twenty musicians (French horns and string and woodwind sections), all of them white. Henderson's conducting abilities were limited to the ballroom and he was not well versed in the technicalities of directing a pit orchestra. A white conductor was called in and he promptly took Louis Armstrong off the first-trumpet part and asked him to swop places with the second trumpeter, Russell Smith. Before that rehearsal ended, six of Henderson's musicians (including Armstrong) had been replaced; Hawkins was asked to remain.

The show opened in Philadelphia on 4 June 1929 but it failed to charm the critics. Drastic changes were made to the production and Henderson and the remnants of his original personnel were discarded. The show subsequently limped its way to Broadway, where it closed after thirty-seven performances.

After the dismissal, Henderson was forced hastily to arrange some dates in Baltimore before moving off into the Midwest. Hawkins was present throughout these engagements, having remained with the Henderson survivors. He viewed the *Great Day* fiasco with detachment, but he realized all too well that the Henderson orchestra (despite its formidable skills) had lost a lot of ground over a two-year period.

Hawkins was not drastically affected by the Wall Street Crash of October 1929. He was too wary to tie up his money in stocks and shares and had only recently learnt to trust banks with his cash. Rex Stewart dwelt on Hawk's cautiousness:

> Before he got over his mistrust of banks it was common for him to walk around with two or three thousand dollars in his pockets! One time he carried with him his salary from an entire season of summer touring, about nine thousand dollars. When we became stranded, for some reason or other, Hawk laughed while showing his roll. But he wouldn't give a quarter to see the Statue of Liberty do the twist on Brooklyn Bridge at high noon.[29]

Hawkins still spent a good deal of money on new clothes and made a point of buying extremely expensive shoes, often feeling that it was better to look good than feel comfortable. Tenorist Eddie Miller, new to New York in early 1930, went to hear Hawkins play and stood as close as he could to the Henderson bandstand. He was amazed to see that Hawkins had cut giant slits in the sides of his de-luxe footwear so as to ease the pressure on his corns.

Henderson's band returned to an even keel by playing another residency at the Roseland Ballroom, beginning late October 1929, but the wages were no higher than they had been two years earlier. Hawkins's former colleague, Don Redman, was aware that things were not looking rosy for the Henderson sideman, and as musical director of McKinney's Cotton Pickers he realized that the addition of Hawkins to his line-up would be a considerable coup. But the Cotton Pickers' purse strings were firmly in the grasp of their non-playing leader, William McKinney, and when Hawkins was informed of McKinney's top offer he simply let out a hearty, derisive chuckle. This did not prevent Redman using Hawkins as a freelance musician on sessions recorded under the name of McKinney's Cotton Pickers in New York during November 1929.

Over a period of three days this specially recruited version of McKinney's Cotton Pickers (featuring a contingent of New York's leading black musicians) recorded seven titles, several of which briefly feature Coleman Hawkins. Compared to the Henderson band of 1929 (as depicted on recordings such as 'Freeze and Melt', 'Raisin' the Roof', 'Blazin' and 'Wang Wang Blues') this edition of McKinney's Cotton Pickers was a superior unit. The tonal blends are better, as is the section phrasing and the use of dynamics; above all, the band has more rhythmic vitality than Henderson's.

Unfortunately Hawkins is never given enough space to move into top gear on the recordings of 'Plain Dirt', 'I'd Love It', 'The Way I Feel' and 'Miss Hannah', but in the first of these he manages to create an impressive sense of urgency in both of his brief solos. On the other three items Hawk has to make do with eight bars of improvisation; he doesn't lower his game drastically, but a similarity of approach is noticable as though the giant is not extending himself unduly. Hawk gets considerably more involved in 'Wherever There's a Will', where he is allocated a whole chorus. Two takes of this number were issued. They show that Hawk chose not to alter the broad outlines of his original solo to any marked degree: having conceived a dramatic opening figure for the first four bars of his solo he's content to retain it on the subsequent attempt. There are fleeting indications of a new freedom in Hawk's approach to improvisation and these are mingled with a creative restlessness, but there are no positive signs on the McKinney recordings that he was about to create his first masterpiece. Yet within the space of ten days, that is exactly what he did.

Red McKenzie, a white ex-jockey who abandoned the saddle to become a vocalist, was something of an entrepreneur in the recording world during the late 1920s and early 1930s. He organized studio sessions featuring pick-up bands and on some of these dates featured himself 'blue-blowing' (imitating wind instruments by blowing through a comb swathed in paper). McKenzie developed this novel skill to a fine art, and produced phrases that were lively and ingenious. For his 14 November 1929 session he assembled a mixed group consisting of two black musicians, Coleman Hawkins and bassist Pops Foster, and five white musicians: trombonist Glenn Miller, clarinettist Pee Wee Russell, drummer Gene Krupa, banjoist Eddie Condon, guitarist Jack Bland and himself on comb-and-paper. McKenzie's original plan was to use Joe Sullivan on piano, but Sullivan failed to show up for the session, so guitarist Jack Bland was drafted in to augment the rhythm section.[30]

In recalling the session Hawkins said, 'I'd been up all night when Red McKenzie phoned about ten in the morning and asked if I could come right down to the Victor studios. We did two tunes. We named 'Hello Lola' for the girlfriend of a rich fellow named Gordon Means who was always helping out Red and Eddie Condon who didn't even have coffee money then.'[31] It seems that Lola was a popular girl because Max Kaminsky clearly remembered her as a girlfriend of Pee Wee Russell, one who sliced up Pee Wee's clothes after they had an argument.[32]

Hawkins made no special efforts to be friendly with the only other black musician on the session, bassist Pops Foster, who had first met Hawk some years earlier in St Louis. In his autobiography Foster said, 'I never had much to do with a lot of guys around New York. Coleman Hawkins was one; he was on a different kick than we were. He was a sometimes guy; sometimes he'd look right at you and didn't know you and sometimes he did; after a while I started doing the same.'[33]

The ballad 'One Hour' is taken at a much slower pace than anything that Hawkins had previously recorded. The tempo (and the propulsive rhythm created by the combination of Foster's bass and Krupa's drums) allows Hawkins time to expound and develop ideas that had long been fermenting. In recording them he created a prototype performance that shaped the work of thousands of jazz tenor saxophonists, establishing a method by which they could improvise on ballads without sounding stiff or lachrymose. His phrasing glided smoothly over the bar lines but still retained an engaging rhythmic impetus. Hawk's poised but rhythmic style of rhapsodizing became, for many years, the universal way that jazz tenor saxists created jazz on slow-tempo tunes. Stylistically, the nearest forerunner had been Louis Armstrong's trumpet playing on 'I Can't Give You Anything But Love' (recorded earlier in 1929), but Hawk took Armstrong's rubato phrasing further into the realms of thematic development.

The recording opens with Hawkins playing a six-bar introduction; alongside him, Russell's clarinet and Miller's trombone create warm backing notes. McKenzie steps forward and sobs through the teeth of his 'instrument' a rendering of the tune that veers perilously close to the quasi-dramatic; undeterred, Hawkins shapes a lyrical preliminary phrase to announce his epic solo. There are in fact very few 'modernistic' touches, and no blue notes are included; so, with a relatively simple use of harmonies, Hawkins created a moving solo delivered in his broad, ravishing tone. Within the eighteen-bar framework of the tune Hawk had spontaneously devised a perfectly shaped melody, so expressive that it defined the direction in which the tenor saxophone was to develop.

Pee Wee Russell isn't swept aside by Hawkins's monumental creativity; he steadies himself and creates an intriguing performance. Trombonist Glenn Miller can't match the Olympian efforts of his front-line colleagues, but he doesn't disgrace himself here, or on the fast 'Hello Lola'. Russell effectively wails his tribute to the woman of the wild scissors and McKenzie stokes the proceedings with his hot, rasping intonation and energetic phrasing. Hawkins was something of an idol to these men and as a mark of their respect they allocated him two full choruses (both thirty-two-bars) for his solo. His playing on 'Hello Lola' doesn't match his efforts on the ballad, but it is still a superb performance: throaty, rumbustious and exciting. A slight feeling of tenseness still entered Hawk's work on up-tempo tunes and this often caused him to revert to the eight-note arpeggios of yesteryear. By late 1929, however, these phrases were much less even than hitherto and in consequence they swung more. On 'Hello Lola' they are projected with an impetus that inspires his accompanists, and it's interesting to note that Hawkins was deliberately inserting flatted ninths in his phrases, a positive step towards modernism.

It was to be almost a year before Hawk recorded any further solos of significant length. When he did so (in October 1930) on Fletcher Henderson's version of 'Chinatown, My Chinatown', he sounded no more advanced than he had done on 'Hello Lola'. His opening break seems bursting with promise but half-way through the solo he loses momentum. The arrangement, by a former member of McKinney's Cotton Pickers – trumpeter John Nesbitt – is one of the best that Henderson ever recorded. The writing seems to spark the band into brilliance and this feeling is strengthened by the incorporation of a string bass (instead of a tuba). John Kirby, a relative newcomer to the string bass, concentrates on two-in-the-bar patterns but still manages to infuse considerable swing into the proceedings. The issue of 'Chinatown' on record showed how speedily the recording industry worked in those days. It was recorded on 3 October and released on 24 November.[34]

The tune's session-mate 'Somebody Loves Me' has a brief, unlaboured solo from Hawkins, but its main attraction is Benny Carter's arrangement, which features the intricate saxophone scoring for which he subsequently became famous. Carter himself leads the section through the fast-flowing, difficult-to-play phrasing. Another sign of the changing times is the use of vibraphone on the coda. Jimmy Harrison recites the lyrics charmingly (in the manner of comedian Bert Williams); he also played a marvellous trombone solo on the band's next recording, 'Keep a Song in Your Soul' (waxed in December 1930). Carter again leads the saxophone section with great elan, and his arrangement includes some innovatory brass figures, eagerly answered by Hawkins on tenor, but this time John Kirby is on tuba and the previous lightness is missing. Carter was by now a superb saxophonist and clarinettist (he later became a fine trumpeter too), and he went on to achieve an unmistakable individuality, but if recordings of his alto-sax playing from this period are slowed down they sound markedly similar to Hawkins's tenor work.

An echo of former Henderson trumpeter Joe Smith's work graces 'What Good Am I Without You?' Here the slow tempo allows Hawkins to pour out a succession of passionate phrases, many of which effectively utilize bold downward glissandi, but unfortunately the elevated mood is disfigured during the last eight bars by drummer Walter Johnson, who decided to back the tenor soloist's emotive playing with some incongruous drum-skull effects.

A day after this session a contingent from Henderson's band consisting of Hawkins, Harrison, Carter, Rex Stewart and John Kirby (along with guitarist Benny Jackson and Fletcher's brother Horace on piano) did a small-band recording session billed as the Chocolate Dandies. Only one title, 'Goodbye Blues', was issued from this date. On it, Stewart's acrid-toned muted work aptly contrasts with Carter's smooth half chorus on alto sax, then Harrison's big-toned expressionful trombone playing takes over as a preliminary to Carter's inappropriate vocalizing. The vocal is not a débâcle, but it is poor enough to make any listener wish that one of the excellent soloists present had filled the space instead. Hawkins inserts some clever, dramatic pauses in his sixteen-bar solo and demonstrates his skilful use of dynamics. His improvisations, mainly couched in legato phrases, are a further example of a growing inclination to rhapsodize at slow tempos.

Another version of the Chocolate Dandies (with Bobby Stark in place of Rex Stewart) visited the recording studio on the last day of 1930. 'Cloudy Skies', the first item recorded, was a composition by Coleman Hawkins, which the octet take at a slowish pace. The composer gushingly overstates the opening melody, imparting thick layers of sentimentality on to a passably pleasant tune. The incongruity of Hawk's rococo approach is exaggerated by the relentless chugging of the tuba and banjo (no drums were used on the sessions). The rhythm section's rigidity also hampers 'Got Another Sweetie', as do the ill-sounding front-line voicings used in the first chorus of the arrangement, but by way of compensation there is some fine singing by Jimmy Harrison, and some superb tenor-sax playing by Hawkins, whose solo radiates passion but never veers towards the bathos he displayed on the previous recording; Hawk's ever-increasing interest in the use of wide harmonies manifests itself clearly in the second part of his sixteen-bar solo.

Benny Carter's fine clarinet playing graces 'Bugle Call Rag' and sets the standard for the rest of the superb solos. Harrison is magnificent, showing that his concept of swing was particularly advanced. Bobby Stark on trumpet is full of invention; he occasionally splits notes, but does so in a continual quest for spontaneous expression. Hawkins's playing epitomizes the flamboyance of the session. His entry to the first of his solos (on the twelve-bar blues section) fairly catapults him into a brilliant creation and his emphatic phrases on the sixteen-bar theme are even more impressive.

The group's finest achievements were reserved for the final number of the session, 'Dee Blues', on which every musician on the date (except tubaist John Kirby) plays a series of twelve-bar improvisations. Carter (on clarinet) goes first and sets the mood perfectly with round-toned phrases that suggest a stoic sadness rather than wringing-of-the-hands desperation.

Stark continues this mood then, by deliberately shifting the pitch of the vital notes in his solo, evokes an even more sombre feel. Hawkins takes a different tack and plays twelve impeccable bars, achieving as much expression as his colleagues had done, but without using blue notes. In contrast, Harrison's subsequent solo is based on foundations of blue notes, both minor third and minor sevenths. The guitarist picks away effectively, not revealing a substantial technique but showing that he was a competent blues player. Horace Henderson on piano doesn't produce any dramatically original thoughts, but nor does he spoil the mood in any way, allowing Benny Carter to rondo the clarinet solo that began the recording. Carter later said that he didn't like his own contribution to 'Dee Blues', but this seems to be an example of super-modesty.

Hawkins and his colleagues in the Chocolate Dandies showed on these dates that they did not have to be under Fletcher Henderson's umbrella to create memorable jazz. In fact, Hawkins's playing on the freelance sessions he did in 1929 and 1930 show that he rose to even greater heights when he was working away from the bandleader he'd served for seven years.

None of the participants in the Chocolate Dandies sessions realized that Jimmy Harrison was playing on borrowed time. During the previous August, while in Harrisburg, Pennsylvania, with Henderson's orchestra, Harrison had collapsed at a soda fountain. John Kirby and Coleman Hawkins telephoned Kitty Harrison in New York, who arranged for her husband to be admitted to Edgecomb Sanitorium, where he made a temporary recovery. But those initial pains were the harbingers of cancer, and soon after the Chocolate Dandies session Harrison's health began to fail. He died on 23 July 1931.

Hawkins had lost someone to whom he was very close, musically and socially. The sorrow that he felt had a deep, lasting effect; ever afterwards he seemed to accept the death of any colleague with a sense of inevitability.

5
The Emergence of Swing

Developments within various big bands of the 1920s and 1930s eventually produced swing music, but the transition was not a smooth, flowing process. Even Henderson's orchestra, who were in the vanguard of establishing the new style, often appeared to backtrack by producing dull recordings of the indifferent commercial songs of the day. The executives of various recording companies were partly responsible for these vacillations, being quite aware that a record packed with improvisation (no matter how brilliant) was unlikely to achieve high sales figures. As a result they encouraged big bands to continue with the tried and true policy established by commercial dance orchestras.

The trouble with Henderson's group was that by now they wanted to play as much jazz as possible within their arrangements and so when they attempted to make popular recordings they ended up producing a hybrid that satisfied neither the hot-music fans nor the general public. By 1931 it became obvious to onlookers that Fletcher Henderson had failed to consolidate the position he had gained as the foremost black bandleader of the era. His main rival, Duke Ellington, was receiving more critical acclaim, but as yet had not built up any vast following in the nation's ballrooms. Part of the reason for this had been Duke's long residency at New York's Cotton Club, but on the occasions that he took leave from that exclusive venue he fared much better in the theatres than in the ballrooms.

Harry Carney, Ellington's stalwart baritone-sax player, felt that Henderson's orchestra was more formidable in the ballrooms than Ellington's. He said, 'I can remember times when we battled with it in its prime and came away dejected. We battled with Smack several times at the Savoy, but one night in Detroit I'll never forget. They played numbers in which Coleman Hawkins was heavily featured and Hawkins cut the whole Ellington band by himself.'[1]

Most veteran musicians agree that the Henderson band in person was a formidable musical unit. Fletcher's wife recalled that the band instantly prepared itself for a battle when the leader said, 'Come on – let's take charge.'[2] Benny Carter also averred: 'The band always played better when challenged.[3] But, unlike Duke Ellington's Orchestra, it was never able to convey its full skills on gramophone recordings. Hawkins recognized this problem:

> Fletcher had a real good band, it was an extremely good swing band. The majority of that stuff was what we call 'heads'. We just made 'em up, make these things up right at a rehearsal. We'd have a rehearsal; brass would be over there doing something, saxophones over here. Finish up, we'd have ourselves another piece. We'd play this piece like mad. Come to work next night. We'd play it: *wonderful*. Maybe about two or three days later we'd go down to the studio to record it: *horrible*. Never would come out right. It wouldn't come out right at all. I don't know what it was about that band. I've never understood it. Why that band could not record. And yet in person it was the stomping, pushingest band I ever heard. Couldn't do the record the same way; I wonder why?[4]

Henderson's orchestra spent most of 1931 playing a residency at Connie's Inn, a New York nightspot that maintained a 'white customers only' policy. There Henderson's orchestra played a broad musical programme including waltzes, tangos and various novelty dances; in addition they had to accompany the elaborate floorshow. One particular benefit of working at Connie's Inn was that Columbia Broadcasting relayed radio transmissions from there. This meant that the sound of Henderson's band was brought to many new listeners. The results were generally favourable, but a *Chicago Defender* reviewer noted: 'Fletcher Henderson has changed his style of music from the "hot and dirty" to a smoothly executed style of dance rhythm.'[5]

During the first part of their stay at Connie's a feeling of unrest developed within the band (perhaps over the 'new' musical policy). As a result Henderson 'swopped' two of his musicians, the ailing Jimmy Harrison and Benny Carter, for two of Chick Webb's sidemen, reed player Russell Procope and trombonist Benny Morton (who had previously worked with Henderson). Years later, Procope modestly admitted that Henderson got the worst of the deal. This was true: the departing musicians were better instrumentalists, and Carter was already a brilliant arranger. But Carter's departure was to prove a blessing in disguise, because out of necessity Fletcher Henderson himself began to arrange regularly for his own band and in doing so created the blueprints that hastened along the advent of the Swing Era.

The recording industry had not yet recovered from the effect of the 1929 Wall Street Crash, and it was to remain in the doldrums for most of the Depression of the early 1930s, but the widespread radio exposure that Henderson's orchestra was enjoying meant that the public were once again asking for their recordings. As a result, Henderson's orchestra recorded twice as many titles in 1931 as they had done for the combined years 1928/29/30.

The first of the year's crop, 'I've Found What I Wanted in You', has the band recording a tame accompaniment for a lilting vocal by Lois Deppe (who was guesting with the band). There are four elegant bars from Hawkins but little else of great merit. Jimmy Harrison, playing on his final recording session for Henderson, buzzes effectively around the melody of 'My Gal Sal', but the main honours go to Rex Stewart, who plays a scorching solo, full of exciting moments created by his habit of deliberately reiterating notes to build up the tension. Hawkins takes an acrobatic break that establishes a new key and then resurfaces for a well-devised eight-bar solo. Jimmy Harrison's charming vocal graces 'Sweet and Hot', on which the band achieve a swinging cohesion thanks to Walter Johnson's invigorating cymbal work. Some deliberately repetitious scoring also allows Hawkins to play some terse, highly effective counterpoint.

The 'transfer' deal between Henderson and Chick Webb had taken place by the time that Fletcher's group re-entered the recording studios in March 1931. The first titled waxed was 'Clarinet Marmalade', arranged by white orchestrator Bill Challis, and deliberately based on a small recording by Bix Beiderbecke and Frankie Trumbauer. Signs of Rex Stewart's admiration for Beiderbecke's playing had figured in some of his previous work; here he mixes his respect with streaks of the musical mischief that established him as one of jazz's instrumental eccentrics. Benny Morton plays a firmly articulated solo, but Russell Procope on clarinet sounds spiky and ill at ease. Hawkins is not at his best either and, rarely for him, actually misses a note during his first phrase. In the closing chorus of this number Hawk plays a break on bass saxophone, his last recorded fling on the giant instrument.

The next tune 'Sugar Foot Stomp', was also based on a previous recording. It was a new version of the 1925 arrangement that Don Redman had modelled on King Oliver's 1923 disc 'Dippermouth Blues'. Fletcher

Henderson reset this gem and allocated himself a couple of piano choruses. This version, slightly faster than the 1925 recording, benefits from Henderson's replanning. Rex Stewart (by his own standards) gives a careful rendering of the obligatory cornet solo, then this succession of twelve-bar patterns is repeated, with considerable success, by Benny Morton on trombone, but Hawkins, soloing last, completely outshines both the brass players. The tenor saxist sounds as though he is operating at full power, and booms out a rugged low C to begin his two full-blooded choruses.

Neither this arrangement nor anything from the whole session is perfectly performed and wrong notes abound, particularly in the trumpet section, but each of the four tunes recorded was basically a jazz vehicle, with ample space left for improvised solos. On this occasion Fletcher Henderson tied his colours to the mast and adopted a bold policy, part of which was to allocate a clarinet solo to Coleman Hawkins on 'Hot and Anxious'. Hawkins had always been a reluctant clarinettist, but he was a highly competitive individual and Benny Carter's swiftly-gained excellence (so apparent on the Chocolate Dandies' sides) stirred Hawk into making a serious attempt to master the instrument. Hearing a playback of his efforts on this number seems to have changed his mind, however, since he never again took a clarinet solo on a recording, saying later, 'One instrument is all you can hope to master.'[6] In fact his twelve-bar outing is not disastrous, but it does not have the authority that was so much a part of Hawkins's saxophone playing, and his one attempt at a difficult downward run flounders slightly. The recording is notable more for the inclusion of a twelve-bar riff that gained fame as 'In the Mood' (trumpeter Wingy Manone had previously recorded the brief theme as 'Tar Paper Stomp').

The final number of the day, 'Coming and Going', showcases Benny Morton's sombre interpretation of a minor-keyed theme; Bobby Stark's solo (in the major) is also grippingly effective. Fletcher's brother Horace was temporarily at the piano. There wasn't much to choose between the two men's skills and some sidemen actually preferred Horace's playing, but here it seems to upset the cohesion of the rhythm section, which sounds disunited and poorly balanced, the guitar being too prominent at the expense of the string bass and drums.

During the spring of 1931 the Henderson orchestra recorded four titles for the small Crown label, none of them epoch-making, but the semi-sophisticated treatment of the medium-paced 'Tiger Rag' (a tune invariably played at breakneck speed) being particularly interesting.

Walter Johnson on brushes sets the mood of the performance, and the only approach to frenzy occurs when Rex Stewart (not Bobby Stark as often printed) engages in a series of four-bar chases with Coleman Hawkins. Rex sounds in fiery mood but Hawk ignores the temptation to indulge in pyrotechnics and methodically produces a succession of reasoned ideas. Procope seems more in command of his clarinet than hitherto, but unfortunately the brass section buckle slightly during the final chorus.

The other three items recorded were popular songs from various eras: 'After You've Gone' from 1918, 'Somebody Stole My Gal' from 1922 and the recently composed ballad 'Stardust'. Hawkins figures briefly in a sedate 'After You've Gone'; the banjo adopts a genteel four-in-the bar beat, Walter Johnson remains on brushes and Russell Smith gives a passable imitation of his brother Joe's trumpet work. Hawkins is distantly balanced in 'Somebody Stole My Gal', producing a solo that is top-heavy with downward glissandi, his pet phrase of this period. Trumpeter Bobby Stark could create monumental jazz on his day, but his enemy was inconsistency and on 'Somebody Stole My Gal' it stalks him down, his solo sounding full of jumbled thoughts and his cup-muted playing on 'Stardust' plagued with intonational problems. Hoagy Carmichael's lovely tune is encased in an unadventurous arrangement, the work of Bill Challis who said the leader asked him to introduce the same sort of mood and tone colours that enhanced scores played by Jean Goldkette's band. The arranger obliged, but the end result had little of the smooth warmth that Goldkette's band produced, though Rex Stewart's muted solo (a salute to Bix Beiderbecke, a former Goldkette star) lifts the rendering considerably.

In view of Hawk's ever-increasing skills as a ballad player it seems a huge pity that Henderson didn't feature him on 'Stardust', but although the bandleader was by now well aware of his tenor saxist's considerable merits he was faced with the problem of keeping his other jazz soloists happy by giving them regular exposure on recordings. It was a different story when battles had to be won on a ballroom bandstand, and then Henderson featured Hawkins a great deal, using him as his principal weapon against challenging musical opposition. Hawkins didn't mind the workload but the tactic caused some resentment among Henderson's other jazz soloists. Years later Rex Stewart still grumbled about it and said, somewhat ruefully, that on such occasions the public and most of Henderson's musicians gave their undivided attention to Hawk's playing: 'You could play a solo that was created with every ounce of your ability and no one on the bandstand even bothered to listen. Yet the minute that Coleman Hawkins started playing, all the guys would start nodding their heads in approval.'[7]

Horace Henderson was an ardent devotee of Hawkins's playing, particularly admiring the control that Coleman had over his instrument,

> He wasn't like the average guy getting ready to play a chorus, not knowing what it's going to be, searching for it. Hawk would know where his fingers lay on this thing. Whereas some of the other tenor players would luck up on a great chorus and the next time stink on the same thing. Coleman Hawkins had set patterns for certain tunes. You could play a tune three years, and if Hawk played a great chorus on that, he would keep that chorus in. This is another thing I liked about him.[8]

Hawkins himself spoke of this aspect of his performance.

> It is a strange fact that my improvisations of any one particular chorus seldom vary very much. That is to say if I have to play a chorus once and then, long afterwards, I have to repeat it, I will play more or less the same thing that I did on the first occasion. I am not conscious of imitating myself; the repetition is not so much memory as method.[9]

Fletcher Henderson's 'trump card' won him numerous musical battles, but because Hawkins was encouraged to be so expansive on live performances he began to sound desultory when called on to play a mere eight-bars on a recording. He was unsuited to the role of a miniaturist; his enormous talents were always best displayed in long solos.

One of the most charming of all Fletcher Hendersons's recordings is 'I'm Crazy 'Bout My Baby' (from April 1931). Rex Stewart and Bobby Stark are at their most engaging and trombonist Claude Jones creates a delightful muted half-chorus. In Hawkins's sixteen-bar solo he reveals early signs of his experimentations with 'broken time' phrasing, creating musical ideas that didn't fall rigidly into two- or four-bar segments. At the same session the band created another version of 'Sugar Foot Stomp' (complete with two declamatory choruses from Hawk) and a 'Just Blues' that has some elegant, gossamer-like scoring in its early stages, Hawkins unusually stressing a series of blue notes in his solo. 'Singin' the Blues' is the Henderson band's most direct tribute to Bix Beiderbecke. At the behest of the recording company's executive the band recorded an arrangement based on the Frank Trumbauer recording that had featured the great cornettist. Unfortunately it is not a worthy salute; clinkers mar the introduction and Rex Stewart, not through want of admiration, muffs some of the notes in his attempted re-creation of Bix's solo.

Later that same month the band recorded yet another 'Sugar Foot Stomp', which has Hawkins lapsing back into a series of worn ideas that suggest he had recorded this piece once too often. The saxophone section sounds cohesive and purposeful and on 'Roll On Mississippi Roll On' Russell Procope constructs a dexterous alto solo. Understandably the band decided to make another attempt on 'Singin' the Blues', managing to avoid the wrong notes but sounding prim. Stewart blows a clinker during the early stages of his tribute solo but seems more assured than on the earlier recording; nevertheless the overall results amount to nothing more than a curio.

Another freelance session with Red McKenzie (in June 1931) gives a much clearer picture of Hawkins's development than is revealed by his recordings with Henderson. On 'Georgia', following a hand-on-heart vocal chorus from McKenzie, Hawkins plays a huge-toned, majestic solo, achieving an ingenious 'turn-around' phrase during his seventh and eighth bars. Later he also provides some subtle musical repartee to Jimmy Dorsey's low register clarinet phrases. Hawkins's performance here is monumental, and his contribution to 'I Can't Believe that You're in Love with Me' is almost as remarkable: he blows some spellbinding opening cadenzas and returns to create a half-chorus of sublime rhapsodizing.

Hawkins's playing on the fast 'Darktown Strutters Ball' is no less impressive. McKenzie blows the two opening choruses, using the first to establish the melody and the second to embellish it. Though McKenzie was the leader on the session, the resultant records (like the previous ones with Hawkins) were issued as by the Mound City Blue Blowers. Condon and Bland were on both sessions, but Russell and Miller were absent and their places were filled by Jimmy Dorsey and Muggsy Spanier (on cornet); Jack Russin was added on piano, and Al Morgan on bass took the place of his New Orleans *confrère* Pops Foster. McKenzie's vocal on 'Darktown Strutters Ball' is full of exuberance, whereas the following solo by Hawkins suggests formidable strength. Swing – and a sense of urgency – mark the first of Hawk's choruses but he rises to even greater heights on the second, entering it with a complex legato phrase that combines passion with ingenuity. Fortified by Al Morgan's virile, four-in-the-bar bass playing, Hawkins never sounds hurried; it's one of the most impressive fast solos of his early career.

The last cut of the session produced a lively version of the novelty song

'You Rascal You'. Mckenzie's wrapped comb buzzes merrily as he projects the melody, then he and Al Morgan share a jovial vocal duet. Jimmy Dorsey (on clarinet) is featured on two eager choruses before Jack Russin conceives an effective piano solo. Hawkins blows sixteen forceful bars on the minor strain, then the ensemble, ably led by Muggsy Spanier, pool their energies in a sign-off chorus.

Soon after the McKenzie session Hawkins recorded 'You Rascal You' with Henderson on two different occasions, the second of these dates producing three different takes of the tune. These were occasions on which Hawkins chose to improvise freely and in doing so he creates a series of interesting variations on what is a very simple harmonic sequence. During this second part of 1931 the most important signpost in Hawkins's career occurs on Henderson's 'House of David Blues', where he is given the opportunity to rhapsodize at slow tempo. He makes most of this rare opportunity by given a sombre, sensitive performance, creating dense clusters of notes but still managing to imbue them with considerable feeling. The Canadian musicologist and bass player Alan Henderson, commenting on this solo, said, 'Hawk's playing is great here. His tone is huge and he leads into a half-note "E" – the natural 13th of the G minor 7th chord. A lot of jazz historians give the mistaken impression that no one knew much about harmony in the early 1930s. This solo proves them wrong.'[10]

Unfortunately Hawkins was not featured on 'Radio Rhythm', which bristles with effective discords and atmospheric instrumental interludes. Russell Procope on alto sax, is the main soloist. Most of the other Henderson recordings from this period are songs of the day cloaked in competent arrangements. Hawkins is never less than excellent during his artistic contributions to 'Oh It Looks Like Rain', 'Sweet Music' and 'Malinda's Weddin' Day', but (like many another jazz musician) he seems to have been defeated by the banality of 'Twelfth Street Rag'.

Fletcher Henderson's biographer, Walter C. Allen, wrote of the 'low morale' that existed within the band at this time, some of it induced by Henderson's vapid leadership. Henderson's musicians were acknowledged by their peers as the most gifted ensemble on the New York scene, yet many plum jobs were taken by lesser groups. Henderson's band confidently expected to spend the entire winter of 1931 resident at the Roseland Ballroom (following their stay at Connie's Inn), but their October return booking was a short one. During their absence from the Roseland the audience there had learnt to prefer the music of a new band led by pianist

Claude Hopkins. This band's soloists were in a lower division than Henderson's but they had won the ballroom crowd over with their cheerful presentation and earnest endeavour.

John Hammond, then a twenty-year-old jazz enthusiast who had recently quit Yale to write about music for American and European magazines, had been a fan of Henderson's band since 1926, but his admiration for the group's music didn't blind him to the leader's shortcomings;

> Fletcher Henderson was the sloppiest, the most disorganized bandleader there ever was. But he gave his soloists more freedom than any bandleader had ever done and as a result he got the best. And even though the guys in Fletcher Henderson's band made less money than the people with Duke and Cab Calloway and other bands, there was much more prestige for them playing with Fletcher than for the other bands. It was *the* band.'[11]

Trumpeter Russell Smith, who worked on and off with Henderson from 1929 until 1934, felt that the band's problems were basically caused by Henderson not being sufficiently dedicated. He said:

> Fletcher was never a natural leader, he was just a man. He didn't know how to handle the men so they just ran the band like they wanted. If a man came in late Fletcher would hang his head instead of saying something to the man; somebody else would have to jump on him. In the early 1930s Fletcher's band began to lose bookings; morale was low but the men didn't want to leave him.[12]

In 1931 Henderson was made to pay for his muddled approach to business matters. Having accepted a contract from 'Taps' Schoenfeld to play at New York's Plantation Club, Henderson then agreed (through another agent) to work at Connie's Inn. The case was settled out of court after Henderson paid Schoenfeld 750 dollars damages.[13]

Despite these backstage problems, the band completed productive recording sessions in October 1931. Over a two-day period they produced five good sides, including a version of the Jimmy McHugh–Dorothy Fields show tune 'Singin' the Blues', on which Hawkins plays a clever solo, dropping in and out of double-time phrases with consummate ease. His solo on 'It's the Darndest Thing' shows that his tone in the upper register had broadened considerably; previously he had a tendency to 'thin out' when he moved into the top octave.

Songs using the same title existed alongside each other in the record catalogues of this period, 'Sugar' was just one example. Henderson's version of the Meyer and Young song of that name doesn't contain a solo by Hawkins, but he is exquisitely (if briefly) featured on Benny Carter's tune 'Blues in My Heart'. It would have been fascinating to have heard Hawkins playing the main melody, but the appealing timbre of a muted solo from the band's new trombonist, J.C. Higginbotham, fulfils the task satisfactorily. 'Business in F' is virtually a feature for Hawkins, who pops in and out of the arrangement from start to finish without ever consolidating the strong impression he created during the opening bars. The band give a neat performance, aided by a crisp-sounding rhythm section (underpinned by John Kirby's walking double-bass line); Higginbotham follows his previous success with a blistering eight-bar solo.

In early 1932 Fletcher Henderson sensed that the normally tranquil Coleman Hawkins was becoming dissatisfied by the band's lack of progress. To counter this he began billing him in advertisements as 'Cole Hawkins, World's Greatest Tenor Saxophonist'. The billing temporarily placated Hawkins but it did nothing to improve his timekeeping. J.C. Higginbotham said, 'If Fletcher wanted you to start playing at nine o'clock he'll tell you "about seven-thirty or eight". Coleman Hawkins was always the leader on that one. He'd come in around an hour late.' Hawkins no longer allowed himself time to warm up his instrument; he simply climbed on the bandstand and unpacked his tenor sax, which led Higginbotham to remark, 'I never heard him practise in my life.'[14]

Hawkins still loved to tease people. One of his targets was George Bassman, a young white orchestrator who did some arranging for Fletcher Henderson (and who later became a successful composer in Hollywood). Hawkins recalled his kidding: 'Man, I used to give him a bit! I told him he couldn't write. I said, "Why don't you take this junk and go home".'[15] But to some people he remained steadfastly reserved. John Hammond said, 'Bean was a wonderful, quiet guy. I always liked him. I don't think he dug me particularly. He was a small, reserved, not very impressive man, but he played like a giant.'[16]

Hammond did his utmost to help Henderson's band find work. In the spring of 1932 he instigated the reopening of the Public Theatre, a 1,800-seater on Second Avenue, and arranged for the band to be the resident group there, but Henderson's slapdash leadership soon ended that arrangement. 'The first show each day was scheduled to begin at one o'clock,' said Hammond, 'and never were there more than one or two band members in the pit on time. I was very disappointed, feeling that Fletcher was letting me down and hurting himself as well.'[17]

The deluge of recording activity, stimulated by the band's radio exposure at Connie's Inn, had subsided; in the first eleven months of 1932 the band did only two studio sessions, both in March. These dates show that Hawkins was continuing to polish his skills, honing an already brilliant technique. On the puny commercial song 'Strangers' he gives another airing to his impressive double-time playing, skimming smoothly through ultra-fast fingerings, and on 'Blue Moments' he practises shading, by inflecting the same note in several different ways. But often, as on 'Take Me Away', 'I Wanna Count Sheep', 'Poor Old Joe' and 'Casa Loma Stomp' he seems content to mark time, without taxing his vast musical potential. But even though he sometimes rested on his laurels he was still acknowledged everywhere as the star of Henderson's orchestra: despite playing a subdued role on 'How am I Doing?' he is singled out for special mention by vocalist Harlan Lattimore, who asks, 'How's Hawk doing?'

For a good part of 1932 Henderson's orchestra worked in various theatres, playing week-long residencies as part of a touring show. As in years past, they also fulfilled engagements in the vast New England ballrooms, and played return dates at New York's most famous dance hall, the Savoy. The year must have seemed a very ordinary one to Henderson's musicians, and so it was, up until its final month, when the band took part in a significant recording session, organized by John Hammond.

In 1975, Hammond told radio interviewer Phil Schaap the background details:

> The recording industry was absolutely broke in the early 1930s. Columbia was in bankruptcy; it was owned by a company called Grigsby-Grunow . . . so poor old Columbia and OKeh were a bankrupt part of a bankrupt company, so there was no money for jazz at all. Finally I got hold of Ben Selvin and a man by the name of Ward who was the so-called President of the Columbia Record Division and I persuaded them that they had to record Fletcher Henderson because he hadn't been in the studio for over a year (because everybody else was broke too). I talked them into recording Fletcher at ten o'clock in the morning. That's the greatest mistake I ever made in my life. I just didn't realize you can't record anybody at ten o'clock in the morning. This was the first real professional recording date I ever had.
>
> So at ten o'clock in the morning there were three people in the studio and by 12.35 John Kirby dragged his bass in and we had exactly fifty minutes to cut four sides and balance the band. This was the days of big waxes, so there was no way of editing it. We spent too much time on a dreadful commercial tune called 'Underneath the Harlem Moon', on which Fletcher Henderson, to pay back a favour to somebody, put Katherine Handy (W.C. Handy's daughter) as vocalist. That was a commercial tune because a publisher had paid for the arrangement, I guess. 'New King Porter

Stomp' was just a run-through; there was no time to do a take. The band is very loose, and the whole thing was recorded on one microphone at a lousy studio at 55 Fifth Avenue.'

The session gives an impressive sound picture of the Henderson band at its relaxed best; they were so used to assembling in fits and starts that the late commencement didn't faze them at all. Even the denigrated 'Underneath the Harlem Moon' has some good musical moments (despite its execrable lyrics). Hawkins plays the opening melody with panache, but tends to over-embellish his lines. The middle eight is given to Rex Stewart, whose lively lip trills ornament his spirited fling at the tune; the brief solo culminates in a pedal note that more than suggests derision. Hawkins's playing on the coda is indisputably majestic.

Fletcher Henderson's arrangement of 'Honeysuckle Rose' showcases three of his important soloists: Hawkins, Higginbotham and Stark. Each man is allocated a whole thirty-two-bar chorus, the first occasion on which any Henderson recordings had continuously featured improvisations of such length. Each man justifies the exposure and Hawkins is particularly constructive, floating relaxedly over the beat, producing supple, unforced phrases. During the early 1930s Hawkins always seemed to be more inventive when playing alongside a string bass than a tuba and here John Kirby's inspiring pulse lifts the tenor saxist's performance. Walter Johnson's subtle drum rhythms blend well with Freddie White's unobtrusive guitar work, but Henderson's piano playing remains in the background.

Despite being hastily assembled, 'New King Porter Stomp' is also very successful. Stark demonstrates flair in the opening trumpet solo and Hawkins sounds lively throughout his chorus, if a little mannered. The star of the performance, though, is Higginbotham, whose muted solo is packed with stimulating ideas and whose brazen open phrases graft on extra excitement to the call-and-answer section of the arrangement.

If there was a specific point marking the beginning of the Swing Era it was the day these recordings were made. The Henderson band hit the target it had been encircling during the previous four years. The key performance was 'Honeysuckle Rose', which was used as a vehicle for improvising rather than as a commercial arrangement interspersed with hot solos. It was this tactic that set the pattern many big bands later copied.

6
The First Rival

At this stage of his life Hawkins had no desire to become a bandleader, but in March 1933 he was persuaded to co-lead a recording group with trumpeter Henry Allen (a New Orleans musician with whom Hawk always maintained an affable relationship). Three of Hawk's Henderson-band colleagues – Russell Procope, John Kirby and Walter Johnson – were on the date, and they were joined by trombonist Dicky Wells, pianist Don Kirkpatrick and guitarist Lawrence Lucie. Unfortunately the two sides that this illustrious pick-up band recorded were both rejected; happily the master recordings were not destroyed and some thirty years later 'Someday Sweetheart' and 'I Wish I Could Shimmy Like My Sister Kate' were eventually issued.

Hawkins plays an outstanding thirty-two-bar solo on 'Someday Sweetheart', featuring some highly technical improvisations but still warmly communicative. It is probably the most idea-packed solo from this part of his career, containing several superbly melodic phrases and some fascinatingly oblique harmonic flights. His musical reflexes are at their sharpest. After misfingering a phrase at the end of his first eight bars he continues confidently, without a split-second's hesitation, moving adroitly into the next series of ingeniously linked ideas. By contrast his solo on 'Sister Kate' is earthbound, taking relaxation into the realms of casualness. Henry Allen and Dicky Wells both play well in their briefish solos. Soon all three of these star soloists were to take part in a series of epoch-making recordings organized in New York by the European composer Patrick 'Spike' Hughes.

London-born Hughes, who had studied classical music in Vienna, became enamoured of jazz in the mid 1920s and was soon arranging and composing for bands in England, often playing double bass with them. He began a prolific but brief recording career writing for, and playing with, various line-ups, including big bands. In January 1933 Hughes visited

New York, principally for a vacation, but his stay soon turned into a working holiday that included organizing three recording sessions featuring famous black jazz musicians.

Hughes, a dedicated admirer of Coleman Hawkins's recordings, orginally felt certain that the tenor saxist was to be the cornerstone of what was subsequently labelled as Spike Hughes and his All American Orchestra (though the recordings were first issued as by Spike Hughes and his Negro Orchestra). Hughes wrote, 'I arrived in the States with the preconceived notion of what tenor playing should be; and I, like most Europeans, did not believe that anybody could play the tenor except Hawkins.'[1] Soon after arriving in New York, however, Hughes attended a rehearsal by Benny Carter's Orchestra and heard the tenor-saxophone playing of Leon 'Chu' Berry, a twenty-two-year-old from West Virginia, steadily gaining a considerable reputation in New York jazz circles.

Hughes, tremendously impressed by Chu's playing, was forced into a dilemma as to who should be used on the recordings: Hawkins or Berry. He recalled the problem:

> In the end I decided that I would use Chu for the very reason that he was not known. Hawkins had made many records; his name was a household word. From a purely 'commercial' standpoint it would perhaps have been more profitable to feature Hawkins; it would have attracted quite a few customers. Then came an ironic situation: Chu couldn't make the date, he was out playing in New Jersey somewhere. So being stuck for a tenor player, we had to look around for a deputy. And we chose Hawkins! I have often wondered if anybody noticed the irony of that: the world's most famous tenor player being called in as a deputy.[2]

Needless to say, the deputy performed superbly and gave a rendition of Hughes's 'Nocturne' that greatly pleased the composer. For this number (the first of the date) Kaiser Marshall sat in on drums for Sid Catlett, who arrived late at the studio.[3] Incisive writing for the brass section distinguishes 'Someone Stole Gabriel's Horn', and the saxophone section also sounds impressively united, but Hawkins's solo seems a little formal. He is at his best, however, on the appropriately named 'Pastoral', extracting a ravishing tone from his tenor saxophone in his brief solo. Hughes chose not to play string bass on these numbers, leaving that task to Ernest Hill, who reveals an amazingly modern concept in his lines. Close scoring for the trumpets pays off on the lively, unhackneyed version of 'Bugle Call Rag'. Benny Carter's alto-sax solo is a model of graceful playing and Hawkins's arpeggic chorus is full of a fascinating sense of enterprise. The orchestration of the final chorus sounds as modern as anything recorded by contemporary bands (including Ellington's) and the mordant wit of the final phrase epitomizes Hughes's deft humour. The two latter titles benefited from the arrival of the supremely talented Sid Catlett.

A month later, on 18 May 1933, a similar personnel assembled at Hughes's behest, this time strengthened by the addition of trumpeter Henry 'Red' Allen and made more dynamic by the inclusion of two tenor-saxophone soloists: Coleman Hawkins *and* Chu Berry. Hughes later wrote:

> After that first session the inevitable happened. Having heard Hawkins play my music nothing on earth would induce me to let him go. And I still wanted Chu. There was only one solution: to have one cake and eat the other. In short to have both players in the band. This we did and I believe it was a very successful experiment. I divided the solo passages between them, and the presence of the one inspired the other to play even better than usual. Messrs Hawkins and Berry were close friends and behaved towards each other as good artists should; it was a happy partnership and gave forth peculiar musical riches. The competition was good for both of them and Chu's place in the ensemble left Bean free to wander the studio and play over his choruses by the piano until he was wanted.[4]

Pianist Red Rodriguez overslept and missed the start of the second session so Luis Russell was summoned to take his place, but he too was delayed so 'Arabesque' was recorded without a pianist. This intricate slow melody (which was dedicated to the Hungarian violinist Joseph Szigeti) sounds as though it were specially written for Hawkins, who unflurriedly rhapsodizes his way through its complexities, obviously relishing the challenge. The prominence given to guitarist Lawrence Lucie pays off handsomely and the innovative flute interludes provide some elegant musical embroidery.

Hughes had this to say about his composition: ' "Arabesque" is a piece which I still find rather alarmingly complicated, inasmuch as it consisted of two themes sometimes played separately, sometimes together. Coleman Hawkins contributed more than a modest share of the final performance and I cannot conceive how the work would have sounded without him.' The recording also features another epic performance, besides Hawkins's, by trombonist Dicky Wells, who sounds startlingly daring and totally original.

'Fanfare' is a dressed-up version of a twelve-bar blues, which not only gives Henry 'Red' Allen a chance to demonstrate his musical boldness but also allows us to hear adjoining solos from Chu Berry and Hawkins. Looking back, Red Allen said, 'One of the happiest moments of my life was on "Fanfare". Coleman Hawkins and Chu Berry really fired each other. It was real happiness to hear them play that way. A wonderful date.'[5] Chu goes first, playing a thick-toned slightly less assured line than Hawkins but sounding more revolutionary in his use of chromatically altered substitute chords (a musical ploy that later came to fruition in the bebop era). If anything Hawkins sounds the more orthodox of the two in this brief exchange, but on 'Music at Midnight' the older man triumphs. Chu sets out boldly but seems to flounder a little after completing a difficult run in the ninth bar of his solo. Hawkins enters and cagily begins assembling his phrases, like a wily boxer intent on gaining a points victory. There are no wild moments but a flash of brilliance in the final bars of Hawk's solo completely settles the issue. Hawkins, Wells and Allen all play magnificently on the atmospheric minor-key 'Sweet Sorrow Blues'.

The two tenor saxists share a chorus on a jam-session version of 'Sweet Sue', Hawkins going first this time. There's a lot of bustling but neither man is at his best and the finer moments come from Benny Carter's alto playing. Red Allen's thrilling eccentricities also contrast effectively with Wayman Carver's flute solo (one of the first jazz uses of the instrument). This was strictly an impromptu performance and, as there was no arrangement to supervise, Spike Hughes decided to play the double-bass on this number. 'Throwing discretion to the winds and wrapping my fingers securely in adhesive tape to avoid blisters, I played the double bass for the first time since I landed in America.'[6]

On the following day (19 May 1933) the full band assembled again at the Brunswick recording studio, housed on the fourteenth floor at 1776 Broadway. Hawkins plays expressively on the charming 'Air in D Flat', but goes on to achieve one of the high points in his career on the recording of Hughes's composition 'Donegal Cradle Song'. Hughes modestly referred to this piece as a 'little tune'. It is in fact a perfect miniature, one that evocatively suggests the composer's Irish ancestry.

The only blemishes on 'Donegal Cradle Song' (which took three hours to record) occur in the brass section, where the muted trumpets (led by Leonard Davis) seem to have had insuperable pitching problems. To overcome the situation, a test recording was made with Wayman Carver playing the lead part on flute, but this didn't create the right timbre and Hughes reverted to using the errant brass section.[7] The wrong notes are forgotten the instant that Hawkins begins his elegy. There's a fleetingly awkward moment in the sixth bar but, unperturbed, Hawk maintains the poetic level of his improvisation. Spike Hughes recalled the performance with especial affection:

> Coleman Hawkins provided two long passages of improvisation on this pseudo-Irish theme which were masterpieces of invention, and expressed so admirably the whole mood of the tune, as I conceived it, that when the work was published some months later I insisted that Hawkins's solo should be transcribed from the record and included in the orchestration. Once having heard Hawkins's decoration of the melody no other was possible or desirable.[8]

Hughes's scoring of a part for Benny Carter to play on soprano saxophone caused a problem, since Carter's instrument was resting in the care of a New York pawnbroker. The instrument was retrieved in time, however, for the band to make an attractive recording of Hughes's bright tune 'Firebird'. Wells on trombone and Allen on trumpet are again in top form, but a chorus split by the tenor saxophonists (Berry going first) is equally potent. Hawk's well-devised solo graces an otherwise uneventful 'Music at Sunrise'; this was the penultimate number, followed by a jam session on 'Sweet Sue'. Here the informal ensemble just manages to stay on the right side of messiness; the main musical merit comes from a string of zestful solos and from Red Allen's charming, husky vocal. Hawkins goes first in the tenor-sax 'duel' and challengingly opens up with a daredevil phrase; Berry's equal share (sixteen-bars) contains nothing as startling, but it is nevertheless a highly impressive, mature display of improvising. The truly outstanding moments on this final number come from trombonist Dicky Wells, still on the threshold of fame at the time of this session but rarely playing better. Overall, his contributions to this series of recordings are no less meritorious than Hawkins's.

Thus ended Spike Hughes's New York recordings. Ironically they were to be his last anywhere. He retired from bandleading at the age of twenty-six and thereafter devoted his talents to writing (specialising in music and travel). The point at which he chose to end his career in jazz was certainly an elevated one. His New York sessions (perhaps not as well known as they should be) are full of interesting modernisms. Dicky Wells said: 'No one in the outfit had the idea that he had so much hell in that valise until we started rehearsing. It still shakes me to think of such swinging notes coming from England back in those days. Although some of them sounded Dukish he had so much Spike in the tunes that they stood up strictly on their own.'[9] Trumpeter Bill Dillard said, 'All of us were greatly impressed by the way Spike Hughes had voiced the scores; they were refreshing to play.'[10]

All the participants in Hughes's sessions were stimulated, but none more than Coleman Hawkins, who had been given the opportunity to demonstrate his sense of musical form and to show that he could be supremely expressive without overpowering the composer's intentions. In discussing his contribution to 'Donegal Cradle Song', Hawk said, 'A sweet, slightly eerie mood is set up at the onset and when it comes to my turn to take a chorus I have to study that atmosphere and develop it'. Hawkins commented on a particular phrase that he had played in the eleventh and twelfth bar on his solo: 'It is rather modern in that it goes counter to the accompanying chords.' Hawkins made this observation back in 1934, revealing that he was consciously pioneering the use of superimposed harmonies in jazz improvisation. Indeed the 'Donegal Cradle Song' recording was repulsively modern for some contemporary critics; Julian Vedey, in the January 1934 issue of *Rhythm*, called it 'This awful row'.

The Spike Hughes sessions, besides giving Hawkins the chance to experiment, also made him acutely aware that a young tenor-sax-playing rival was ready to compete with him under the exacting circumstances of a studio recording session. Hawkins had encountered Chu Berry in jam sessions and at band battles, but on these occasions he had shrugged off the young man's challenges by using marathon tactics, blowing countless superb choruses, but under the sprint conditions of the studio date, the youngster was able to offer a convincing challenge. Contrary to Hughes's judgement Hawkins and Berry never became close friends, but neither did they become enemies. They were two entirely different personalities: Chu was tubby and chuckling and Hawkins taciturn and cagey. Out of genuine respect Berry listened carefully to Hawkins whenever he could, and although Hawk feigned indifference about the prowess of other tenor players, from this period onwards he often went out of his way to hear the younger man's work.

By this time Hawkins was leading the life of a bachelor, he and Gertrude having separated. He reverted to earlier habits and spent many hours in late-night cabarets and nightclubs. By now a heavy drinker, he liked to imbibe at his own pace rather than as part of a clique, and rarely went out on the town with his Henderson band colleagues, much preferring the company of various girlfriends. He was often alone when he went to sit in.

Tenorist Al Washington felt that Hawkins's skills weren't blunted even by a big intake of spirits: 'He'd play just as well, drunk or sober, but the thing I noticed was that he became even more retiring in his personality the more he drank. He'd sit down and look half-asleep, and some young players (who didn't know better) would think, "Now's my chance," but Hawk would get up and just destroy them musically.'[11]

Hawkins was friends with, but never part of, a drinking team that formed up in the Henderson band consisting of Walter Johnson, Sandy Williams, Bobby Stark, Clarence Holiday (Billie's father) and J.C. Higginbotham. The behaviour of this coterie (known as 'the juice brothers') eventually irritated the abnormally placid bandleader. When J.C. Higginbotham fell drunk from a bandstand at a Baltimore theatre Henderson fined him twenty-five dollars, and he was even harder on Bobby Stark and Sandy Williams after they decided to celebrate 4 July by letting off firecrackers while the band were working at the Hollywood Gardens in Pelham. The two musicians' high-spirited prank caused Henderson's patience to snap and he dismissed both of them from the band.

This move brought Henry Allen and Dicky Wells into the band on a regular basis, though both had played casual dates with Henderson before this. On 21 July 1933 Henry Allen and Coleman Hawkins again assembled their recording orchestra, this time using a group drawn from the Henderson band: Dicky Wells (trombone), Hilton Jefferson (alto sax), Bernard Addison (guitar and banjo), John Kirby (string bass and tuba), Walter Johnson (drums) plus Horace Henderson on piano. Apparently the record-company executives wanted the role of the banjo to be emphasized, also requesting that a tuba be used on the date. Hawkins excels himself on 'Swinging Along on a Shoe String', imparting new dimensions to a quite ordinary tune.

The only up-tempo number on the date, 'Ain't Cha Got Music', is less successful because the first sixteen bars of Hawk's solo seem to be locked into a tediously stiff rhythmic pattern; happily, he swings out in the final eight bars. The ensemble is poorly balanced on the ballad 'River's Taking Care of Me', but Red Allen contributes a fine vocal and some passionate trumpet playing; Hawkins seems content to remain in second gear. Red's singing was featured on three of the titles recorded, but the one instrumental, 'Shadow of the Swanee', never quite defines the atmosphere it is attempting to create. Hawkins plays the melody impeccably but because the sedate arrangement is tailored in a way that allows only ultra-brief solos, one gets the impression that the recording manager had emphasized that a commercial instrumental was required. No such feeling of restriction affected the Fletcher Henderson Orchestra recordings that took place a month later.

'Yeah Man' is another early prototype of a swing arrangement (this time by Horace Henderson) replete with full-chorus solos. Procope on clarinet sounds a little like Buster Bailey here and Bobby Stark (recalled to the fold) creates some exciting phrases by suddenly jumping into his top register for one-note excursions. Coleman Hawkins plays several familiar phrases in his solo but mingled in with them are some bold new thoughts that display adventurous timing. Playing alongside Red Allen (whose work is full of ingenious rhythmic suspensions) seems to have stimulated Hawkins's sense of daring, since during this period he regularly created phrases that seem to defy musical gravity. This is particularly noticeable on the new version of 'King Porter Stomp', the arrangement of which had been revamped to include some pungently dissonant harmonies.

A partiality for new harmonic twists provided the basis for Coleman Hawkins's dramatically novel composition 'Queer Notions' (seemingly inspired by the adventurous music that Hawkins had performed on the Spike Hughes sessions). Horace Henderson's eerie arrangement allows the two soloists, Hawkins and Henry Allen, to roam freely through a series of atonal passages that resolve neatly on to straightforward, bright-sounding major chords. The middle section is based on an orthodox and agreeable melody, replaced by the fascinating discords. Hawkins then blows some swift-flowing arpeggios that spiral through the chords to form an apt conclusion to an ingenious musical endeavour.

The session ended with a conventional up-tempo tune, 'Can You Take It?', but even here there is innovation, particularly in the clever scoring that combines the brass and reed sections. Hawkins is the principal soloist, creating a bouncy thirty-two bar chorus full of pithy ideas. By now Henderson was featuring Hawkins's talent whenever he could and actually has him leading the saxophone section on 'It's the Talk of the Town' and 'Nagasaki'. The first of these has been cited as a Hawkins masterpeice; it is not, but it is a fine example of a master musician being supremely expressive on a superior ballad. The arrangement itself (by Fletcher Henderson) is uninspiring; the muted trumpets sound insipid and the burst of scored double-timed playing almost destroys the established mood. Hawkins weaves some striking patterns, glissing from one melody note to another, constructing proud phrases that bring out the best of the tune; he thoroughly deserved the label credit 'featuring Coleman Hawkins'. 'Nagasaki' has a good arrangement by Horace Henderson that showcases Red Allen's singing and trumpet playing; Hawkins's eight-bar solo proves that the saxophonist needed more space than this for his inspiration to develop. Hawkins is more emphatic on 'Night Life', moving delightfully through the rich harmonies and effectively resolving the complex modulations with ease. This session also produced a remake of 'Queer Notions'. Both the arrangement and the solos are similar to the earlier version (except for the inclusion of some double-time interludes by Hawkins) but the general effect is less stark than before and therefore less satisfactory. Both versions, however, are potent examples of adventurous jazz. Trumpeter Henry Allen, looking back, said of his work on 'Queer Notions', 'I used to drift off a bit I suppose, but I didn't have any conscious thoughts in mind of modernising anything,'[12] but for Hawkins the recording was a stepping stone towards harmonic freedom.

29 September 1933 marked the date of the first recording session on which Coleman Hawkins acted as sole leader. It was another of the dates that John Hammond organized for English Parlophone. Hammond later commented on Hawk's skills at the time of these recordings: 'He was at the very top of his creative form. He had that fat, luscious tone and complete command of his instrument. The rhapsodic edges which later blunted his cutting edge had not yet emerged.'[13] On the September session Hawk used six of his colleagues from the Henderson band and one ex-Hendersonian, trombonist J.C. Higginbotham. Except for the change of trombonists the line-up was exactly the same as on the July Allen-Hawkins session, but the musical content was markedly superior.

All three of the tunes recorded are instrumental. Hawkins is handsomely featured on each of them and there are also superb performances from Henry Allen. 'The Day You Came Along' (a song that Bing Crosby featured on film and on record) is effectively arranged. Hilton Jefferson on clarinet states the initial melody then hands over to the stately-sounding trombone. Hawkins takes the main solo (thirty-two bars), creating breathy phrases, all imbued with a rare passion. In the second bar of the bridge Hawkins soars up to a G sharp in the manner of a great opera singer then swiftly glides through an ornate phrase that takes him down to a low C sharp. From that point onwards the phrasing becomes increasingly flamboyant, often containing scalic patterns that encapsulate six notes within a single beat. But at no stage does Hawkins jettison the emotional content of his solo simply to display his technique. He delivers the coda with a towering authority, but still manages to impart a feeling of sweet adieu to his final two notes. Some reviewers criticized Hawk for being too effusive on this recording, but as this was one of Hawk's favourite tunes he was obviously determined to inject an appropriate degree of romanticism into his performance.

Hawk also used his magnificant technique to advantage on 'Jamaica Shout', offering clever paraphrases of the tune and producing cascades of notes that underline his instrumental boldness and his imagination. If there is a weakness, it is in the rhytmic construction of some of the more bravura phrases, but the good outweighs the questionable and the tenor saxist's final four-bar break is both powerful and brilliant.

Pianist Horace Henderson had nothing but praise for Hawkins's methods:

> One thing about Coleman Hawkins: even though you did something wrong he would tell you to continue playing. Even on certain record sessions I was on, he had some personnel in there that actually he could have bettered. He was a patient guy. He would never reprimand you so that you'd be embarrassed. Super genius. You could ask him things and he would always tell you. Henry 'Red' Allen was one of the few trumpet players that I know of that could run a diminished chord against a major and make it sound good. But he didn't know what he was doing. So Hawk would tell him, 'That's wrong, but it sounds good, keep it in.'[14]

On 'Heartbreak Blues' Hawkins proves that he was a sympathetic partner for Allen: the two men seem to share an identical mood in creating subdued, thought-provoking solos on this slow-paced Hawkins composition. There are no excessively technical phrases, nor even elaborate runs; both musicians stay mainly in their low registers in establishing an attractive mood that holds firm from first note to last.

Fletcher Henderson's Orchestra, recording under the nominal leadership of Horace Henderson (who did most of the arrangements used on the session), visited the recording studios on 3 October 1933. Six sides emerged, including a long, slow feature for Hawkins: 'I've Got to Sing a Torch Song' (the theme from *Gold Diggers of 1933*). An unpromising opening features an indecisive brass team and an ill-matched saxophone section, then Red Allen blows a scintillating eight-bar solo that paves the way for two choruses from an inspired Hawkins, who begins lyrically and moves majestically into the centre of a sound picture in which the band simply provide a convenient background.

In the space of eleven days Hawkins recorded three ballads: 'Its the Talk of the Town', 'The Day You Came Along' and 'I've Got to Sing a Torch Song', that show that he had perfected the ingenious style of rhapsodizing that had been developing during the previous four years. The basis of Hawk's approach consisted of him playing wave upon wave of rapid notes, sometimes producing eight within the space of one beat (all eight, thanks to his superfine technique, distinctly projected). The longest note within the three 1933 solos in question lasts for only two beats and the simplest phrase is usually the one that opens the improvisations. Hawk made no effort to suggest he was doubling up the speed of the performance; he skilfully delivers the ornate runs in a way that almost metronomically emphasizes the existing tempo. He was, in effect, pioneering the art of playing jazz ballads on the saxophone. Many of those who followed in his footsteps dispensed with the ornateness of the original, but they retained his method. In 1933, Hawkins, revelling in musical adventurousness, did over-elaborate his ballad solos, but in time he learnt to restrict the floridity within his performances.

'Happy Feet' has brief solos from Allen, Wells and Hawkins and a stirring arrangement that emphasizes the light, infectious swing of the rhythm section, which utilized the hugely underrated drummer Walter Johnson. Hawkins creates an attractive, joyful-sounding chorus on 'Rhythm Crazy', based on cleverly accented brief phrases, and he plays in a particularly relaxed manner on 'Ol' Man River' (a vocal-and-trumpet feature for Red Allen). 'Minnie the Moocher's Wedding Day' has a stirring call-and-answer arrangement and inventive solos for Allen, Wells and Hawkins; here Hawkins seems to be deliberately blowing sporadic patterns that are enhanced by effectively placed pauses. Hawk's contribution to 'Ain't Ya Glad' is brief, but whereas he usually sounds unenthusiastic in short solos, here he pours out a succession of brilliant ideas in filling the eight-bar cameo.

In November 1933 another recording session materialized for the Allen–Hawkins Orchestra, but instead of using a full contingent from Henderson's band the co-leaders recruited four musicians from Don Redman's Orchestra: Benny Morton (trombone), Edward Inge (clarinet/alto sax), Manzie Johnson (drums) and Bob Ysagguirre (string bass). Horace Henderson was on piano, but due to the execrable recording balance he is rarely heard and the main accompaniment comes from Bernard Addison's guitar (Addison does not play banjo at all on this date, contrary to published discographies).

The main purpose of the session is for the band to provide a musical framework for Henry Allen's vocal renditions of transient pop songs and nothing from the date matches up to the Hawkins session that produced 'The Day You Came Along'. Red's singing here is variable, but he plays trumpet admirably throughout the session, notably on 'Dark Clouds', where he constructs a dazzling coda. There are no inspired moments from Hawkins on this session. He's steadfastly relaxed on 'Hush My Mouth', and his solo on 'You're Gonna Lose Your Gal' is almost desultory (on this side there are moments when Addison and Hawkins do not seem to be in full harmonic agreement). Hawkins plays the melody effectively on 'Dark Clouds' but his eight-bar solo on 'My Galveston Gal' is swashbuckling to the point of being musically careless. Benny Morton's trombone playing is as reliable as ever, and Edward Inge's acrid tone adds an edge to a session top-heavy with bland, medium-tempoed material.

In December 1933 Fletcher Henderson's band played briefly in Kansas City, Missouri, a visit that allowed tenor saxist Lester Young, then twenty-four, his first opportunity to hear Coleman Hawkins in person:

> I'd always heard so much about Hawk and while I was working at the Paseo Club, Fletcher Henderson was in town. I ran over to dig him between sets; I hadn't any loot so I stayed outside listening. Herschel Evans was out there. Then one night Fletcher said his tenor man hadn't showed up and wanted to know if there was someone around that could blow. I went in, read the book – clarinet part and all – blew Hawk's horns, then ran back to my own job at the Paseo. Ran ten blocks to get back to them.[15]

Lester Young's tenor-playing cohort in the Paseo band, Herschel Evans, who was already a fervent admirer of Hawkins's work, would have loved the chance to deputize for his hero, but as Lester Young explained, 'Herschel played good, but he couldn't read.'

Lester Young's brief sojourn with Henderson impressed the bandleader, a fact that some of Hawk's colleagues pointed out to him to pay him back for his years of teasing them. Hawkins, having fallen in with good company, was his usual unpunctual self; normally Henderson shrugged off the tenor saxist's late arrivals, but for some reason (probably to teach Hawk a lesson) Henderson had asked for a temporary replacement in a city already noted for tenor saxophonists. Hawkins was surprised to learn that a deputy, with no vast reputation, had filled his chair with such consummate ease. The news stirred Hawk's alert sense of competition and he made plans to meet up with his young rival as soon as possible. Speed was of the essence, because Henderson's stay in Kansas City was coming to an end.

On the last night of the band's stay in Kansas City Hawkins finished his gig with Henderson and made his way to the Cherry Blossom Club. Many celebrated jam sessions had taken place at that 12th Street venue, but none more dramatic than the battle of music that was about to take place. Pianist Mary Lou Williams recalled the drama:

> The word went around that Hawkins was in the Cherry Blossom and within half an hour there were Lester Young, Ben Webster, Herschel Evans and one or two unknown tenor players piling into the club to blow. Bean didn't know the Kansas City tenormen were so terrific and he couldn't get himself together though he played all morning . . . when we got there Hawkins was in his vest [waistcoat] taking turns with the KC men. It seems he had run into something he didn't expect. Lester Young's style was light and it took him maybe five choruses to warm up. But then he could really blow; then you couldn't handle him in a cutting session. That was how Hawkins got hung up. The Henderson band was playing in St Louis that evening and Bean knew he ought to be on his way. But he kept trying to blow something to beat Ben and Herschel and Lester. When at last he gave up he got straight in his car and drove to St Louis. I heard he'd just bought a new Cadillac and that he burnt it out trying to make the job on time.[16]

Lester Young's challenge was confidently premeditated; years later he told Miles Davis that he had been 'waitin' on Coleman to come to Kansas City a long time.'[17] Drummer Jo Jones, who was also at the Cherry Blossom, said, 'That was the first night Hawkins was really challenged. You see, nobody in those days would walk in and set up with Hawkins, except maybe in New York where Chu Berry was just coming up.'[18] In looking back at that famous jam session it would not be fanciful to say that if Lester Young had been totally vanquished the whole history of jazz saxophone playing could have taken a different turn. He was not. He held his own against the established champion and in doing so strengthened his resolve to continue on his chosen path of individualism, forging a route that thousands of other saxophonists were to follow. Though Coleman Hawkins could never bring himself to acknowledge the fact, he must have realized after that dawn encounter in Kansas City that he had a truly formidable rival.

7
British Adulation

Not long after returning from his trip to the Midwest, Hawkins took part in an unusual recording session; he was the only black participant in a date directed by Benny Goodman. Hawkins was there at the behest of John Hammond, who had previously urged Goodman to use Hawkins on recording dates. Hammond recalled Goodman's initial reaction: 'Hawkins was out as far as Benny was concerned; "If it gets around that I recorded with colored guys I won't ever get another job in this town," said Goodman. And of course he was right.'[1] But in February 1934 Goodman changed his mind and decided to risk professional ostracism by using Hawkins (Goodman later became a pioneer in organizing mixed touring bands).

Goodman's nine-piece recording band assembled principally to back singer Mildred Bailey, but the first tune of the date was an instrumental, 'Georgia Jubilee'. Most of the arrangement was scored, but Gene Krupa makes his presence felt with some crisp drumming and Hawkins in his brief solo spot creates some sonorous improvising, making bold use of trills (an unusual tactic for him to adopt). The piece concludes with a fade-out ending, an early recorded use of this sign-off device.

Hawkins's main task on 'Junk Man' is to provide one bar fill-ins to Mildred Bailey's vocal. The idea doesn't work and most of Hawkins's interjections sound inappropriate, though he makes up for the lapse by playing very creatively on 'Ol' Pappy', first during the middle eight bars where he effectively descends to his lowest notes and subsequently in a sixteen-bar solo full of flair and rhythmic ingenuity. Benny Goodman plays particularly well on the first chorus of this tune, but throughout the date he made no effort to hog the proceedings and grants Hawkins especial prominence on the final tune of the date by featuring him playing the attractive melody of 'Emaline'.

On 6 March 1934, Coleman Hawkins took part in what proved to be his last recording session as a member of Fletcher Henderson's Orchestra. By this time Buster Bailey had returned to the reed section after a five-year absence and trombonist Keg Johnson had replaced Dicky Wells. The first tune of the date, 'Hocus Pocus', was arranged and composed by the white orchestrator Will Hudson. The basis of the tune is the simple but neat idea of having a trombonist reiterate the same single note while the saxophone section play a melody that moves in step with the accompanying chord changes. Buster Bailey soon proves that his clarinet technique is as nimble as ever, but in contrast to Bailey's eager approach Hawkins adopts a laid-back attitude, nonchalantly showing the strength of his playing by relaxedly blowing swinging, powerful phrases.

'Phantom Fantasie', arranged and composed by another white musician, Russ Morgan, is an exercise in changing tone colours. The piece contains some stolid interjections from Fletcher Henderson on piano and a solo by Coleman Hawkins that (unusually) seems to have been carefully and dispassionately manufactured. 'Harlem Madness' is a vocal feature for the straight-sounding voice of Charles Holland; Hawkins is again overtly relaxed, and Buster Bailey exactly the opposite. The date ended with 'Tidal Wave', a Will Hudson tune that sounds almost like an instrumental of ten years earlier. It is fast and dull. In fact the pace is altogether too swift for the saxophone section's fingers, but Hawk shows his class by strolling through his solo, remaining admirably coherent despite the speed and underlining his superiority by effortlessly playing complex phrases spanning two octaves. Henderson in his solo appears to be imitating Zez Confrey.

Nothing miraculous had emerged from Hawk's final session with Henderson. During his eleven-year stay with the band the saxophonist had seen the unit develop from an unremarkable nightclub group into one of the leading big bands of its era. Almost every leading black jazz instrumentalist of the period had passed through its ranks, making a number of recordings that have given subsequent generations of jazz listeners a great deal of pleasure. But Hawkins (and other participants) maintained that recordings of Fletcher Henderson's Orchestra never gave a true indication of the band's prowess.

A week after the Henderson session, Hawkins did some recordings accompanied only by pianist Buck Washington. The results contain some high peaks of creativity. On 'It Sends Me' (an indifferent composition by Hawkins) the saxophonist plays the slow ballad eloquently and uneventfully but immediately after the piano solo his imagination suddenly catches fire. He plays a dazzling re-entry phrase and moves on impressively to create a descending figure that blends ingenuity with excitement. He maintains this level of inspiration right through to the last notes, signing off with a break that was to be used later by countless saxophonists.

Highlights abound on the medium-fast version of 'I Ain't Got Nobody'. Again Hawkins opens quietly, treading daintily through the first chorus, but after Washington's chorus (full of firm left-hand phrases and right-hand Earl Hines-like tremoloes) Hawk bursts into another dimension, stressing a series of wide intervals and temporarily ignoring the pulse of the music by superimposing his own time values before majestically surging back into tempo accenting on-the-beat notes. It's a *tour de force* of ideas, all of them sounding spontaneous.

Both musicians indulge in out-of-tempo flourishes during the introduction to 'On the Sunnyside of the Street', but Hawkins's interpretation of the melody doesn't involve any substantial embellishments. Washington takes a competent solo that is neatly rounded off by a four-bar pattern introducing a new, faster tempo. Hawkins again stays close to melody for the first half of his chorus but then suddenly adopts whirlwind tactics, lifting bold harmonic ideas into his swirling phrases. The storm over, he concludes with eight bars of almost formal improvising, but adds a quirky finishing phrase that unexpectedly sails up to his top G.

During the early 1930s Hawkins had become increasingly restless with both his professional and domestic life. Since he and Gertrude had separated Hawkins had enjoyed the company of scores of girlfriends but he hadn't met anyone with whom he felt like settling down; he chose to spend as little time as possible in his sparsely furnished apartment. Outside of his flat he adopted a luxurious life style, driving an expensive car, wearing elegant and costly clothes, eating well and drinking the finest brands of spirits (even during the time of Prohibition). But something was missing and his vague dissatisfaction was fuelled by Fletcher Henderson's lack of strategy. Hawkins had worked for the bandleader for long enough to be well aware of all the opportunities that Henderson had let slip through his fingers.

During early 1934 the Henderson band were again short of work; a tour of Europe was mooted but nothing materialized. Years later Henry 'Red' Allen said that when this trans-Atlantic deal fell through it was rumoured that Henderson received some compensation, but if this was so, none of the cancellation fees reached the sidemen. Morale had been variable for some while but Hawkins's restlessness increased when Duke Ellington's musicians returned to New York full of travellers' tales about their visit to the United Kingdom.

After a gruelling winter tour through the Northern states and Canada, Henderson's band returned to New York where Hawkins met up with Henderson's former bassist June Cole, back in the USA after working for five years in Europe. During a long conversation in Big John's Bar, Cole told Hawkins of the advantages of working abroad, and advised him to contact Jack Hylton, who was then not only the most important British bandleader but also a successful booking agent.

Hawkins's playing had been the subject of regular praise in the London-published *Melody Maker*. Cuttings from this magazine had occasionally reached Hawkins, but he was doubtful of June Cole's advice, feeling that Hylton might not have followed news of the American jazz scene. Cole was positive, however, that contacting Hylton would be useful, so without further ado Hawkins took action:

> I got in my car and went down to 125th or 126th Street (between St Nicholas Avenue) and telegraphed Western Union. I sent a telegram to Jack Hylton, England. That's all I had of him. Jack Hylton, London, England. And I said, 'I am interested in coming to London', and signed my name. And next afternoon I had a cable from Jack saying he wanted me to come over and he said, 'How much money do you want?'[2]

Hawkins had correctly surmised that Jack Hylton was not fully aware of his status within the jazz world. Hylton's pianist, Billy Munn, recalls:

> Jack Hylton came to me and said he'd heard from Coleman Hawkins and asked if I knew much about him.
>
> I said, 'Heard about him? He's the greatest in the world.'
>
> 'Well', said Hylton, 'he doesn't seem to want much money so I'll take a chance.'
>
> Dave Shand (one of Hylton's saxophone players) and myself were thrilled to bits at the prospect of working with Hawkins.'[3]

Jack Hylton was able to offer Hawkins more than the 150 dollars a week he averaged with Fletcher Henderson, but it must be borne in mind that the dollar's exchange rate was then approximately four to the British pound. So Hylton only had to guarantee Hawkins £50 a week (less than he paid his star sidemen) to attract the tenor player over. Hawkins accepted Hylton's terms and then told Fletcher Henderson that he'd take leave of absence for a month or two. It was to be six years before the two men met again.

Travel plans quickly fell into place. Hawkins applied for a passport on 13 March 1934 and was granted one two days later. On the other side of the Atlantic, Jack Hylton's agency arranged with the British Ministry of Labour for a work permit to be issued. Just over a week later (on 23 March) Hawkins left New York aboard the liner *Île de France*, arriving off Plymouth, in Devon, England, on the morning of 30 March 1934.

Ben Davis, the saxophone-playing director of the Selmer Instrument Company, and Percy Mathieson Brooks, editor of the *Melody Maker*, went aboard the tender that ferried between the liner and the dock to greet Hawkins (appropriately, the name of this small vessel was the *Sir John Hawkins*). After a four-hour trainride the party arrived in London which, as it was Good Friday, was at its quietest. Hawk beamed happily at the large number of fans who had gathered at the railway station to greet him, shook hands with various well-wishers and was then driven to his London hotel. He said later, 'I didn't know until then that they knew me over there.'[4]

At his hotel Hawk was handed a telegram from Louis Armstrong (then working in England) that read 'Welcome to our country'.[5] That same evening Hawkins was taken to a party held in his honour at the London apartment of bandleader Billy Ternent. Billy Munn, like the rest of the guests at the Maida Vale gathering, was eager to hear Hawkins play:

> We soon persuaded him to get out his tenor sax, but when he first began blowing it he just couldn't get a note out of the instrument, just streams of air. We looked on aghast, but I suppose he hadn't played for a while because of travelling, but he soon got warmed up and everything was marvellous; he played like an angel.[6]

On the following evening pianist Reginald Foresythe and Hawkins played two numbers on the BBC radio programme 'In Town Tonight', then Hawk hurriedly made his way to the London Palladium where Jack Hylton's band was playing a season. Hylton decided to present Hawkins during the second part of the evening. Hawk took this bold move in his stride and went on stage to play 'It's the Talk of the Town' and 'The Day You Came Along'. A *Melody Maker* reporter, writing about the debut, said: 'Few knew who he was,' but emphasized that the audience had reacted warmly to the saxophonist's superb solos. Looking back a quarter of a century later, Hawkins recalled: 'It was my first experience of an audience in Europe. And it was a huge stage. Just to walk out there was something. And then I was very well received.'[7]

Jack Hylton was delighted both by Hawk's playing and by the public's reaction and gave instructions for his agency to organize bookings for the saxophonist covering the rest of the year, the first of which was to be a concert at the London Hippodrome scheduled to feature Coleman Hawkins *and* Louis Armstrong. The *Melody Maker* of 7 April 1934 gave details of the proposed concert (in aid of the Musicians' Benevolent Fund), planned for the afternoon of Sunday 22 April. The excited tone of that initial announcement, however, was replaced in the next issue of the magazine by a wave of fury directed towards Louis Armstrong, who had declined to play the concert. A headline: LOUIS ARMSTRONG QUITS: CONCERT WRECKED was followed by a story that began, 'Louis Armstrong, hot trumpet player from Harlem, seized with an acute attack of artistic temperament, has walked out in the best manner of "great" artists.'

The concert was cancelled, but although Louis Armstrong was questioned as to his reasons for not wishing to appear on the show, he failed to give any clear-cut answers. At the time Hawkins remained silent, but years later he said, 'I was supposed to do something with Louis. Jack Hylton had it in mind to arrange a whole lot of concerts to do with Louis, to use Louis's band. I don't think Louis had too much eyes for it. I went to the theatre to see him backstage, in the dressing room [in London].' Louis asked Coleman if he could rehearse and apparently Hawkins replied, 'What I'm going to do will be easy anyhow; nothing much to rehearse.'

In his summary Hawk said,

> So I was waiting for the time to come when I was going over to see him to rehearse. I guess there was about two days left, that's all; he cancelled the concert completely. At the time it didn't do him too much good 'cause Jack Hylton was an awful big man in England. I didn't have anything to do with it.[8]

Armstrong came in for a good deal of criticism because of his decision, but there were mitigating circumstances. Because of mismanagement, Louis had suffered a lot of problems during his stay in Europe, and as a result he became very apprehensive of entrepreneurs. His wariness increased when he read the *Melody Maker*'s original story on Hawkins's arrival, which said, 'He is to partner Louis Armstrong in a new act, which will be devised to allow the world's two greatest individual musicians to co-star.' This was news to Louis (and to Hawkins). Since the first that Louis knew of the proposed concert was from the pages of the *Melody Maker*, he felt (justifiably) that Jack Hylton should have at least consulted him before announcing the event.

Louis, so affable at most times, had a stubborn streak that rarely showed itself. During his early days in Europe he had been manipulated on many occasions; he was not a vain man but by this time he must have realized that he was more of a star than Hawkins, and so he was understandably suspicious if any publicity suggested otherwise. Louis had been featured in stage productions, on radio shows and on countless recordings under his own name, whereas Hawkins (whatever his status as a great jazz improviser) was only just beginning his solo career and was, in consequence, virtually unknown to the general public.

If Hawkins and Armstrong had been bosom pals the situation might well have been resolved – a guest appearance by one or the other might have materialized – but they had had very little contact since their days together in Henderson's band. The bizarre outcome of the contretemps, however, was that Armstrong and Hawkins moved a little closer to each other. Louis's companion, Alpha Smith (who later became his wife) persuaded Louis that it would be wise, and polite, to explain his reasons for not doing the concert to Coleman Hawkins, so the three of them met in London for an affable expatriates' reunion.

Comment about the ill-fated concert rumbled on for weeks. In the *Melody Maker* of 2 June 1934 the magazine's New York correspondent, John Hammond, wrote:

> I think it is lucky for everyone that the concert was cancelled, because 'Bean' needs really first-rate support and background in order to be 'sent' and Louis's bunch can scarcely be expected to do that. I suppose it is only fair for me to say again that I was bitterly against the Hawkins trip from the very start. As I told 'Bean' innumerable times, leaving Fletcher would do harm to himself and the band. But wanderlust had seized him. But there is good news to be told about the band. Under the Irving Mills' Agency banner the boys are at least making some money again. Lester Young, Hawkins's successor, is a sensation I was told.

Hawkins read the *Melody Maker* regularly during his stay in Britain, so there can be little doubt that he saw the item mentioning the emergence of his Kansas City adversary. Hawk was not the sort of person to get ruffled by a newspaper report; his main thoughts at this time were on making his tour of Britain a resounding success.

Hawkins's tour officially began on Monday 16 August 1934, when he was featured at the London Palladium for a week, working with an orchestra led by Ennis Hylton, Jack's wife. Billed as Mrs Jack Hylton & Her Boys, the big band fulfilled engagements on the same circuit as Jack's own outfit. Hawk's part in the show was brief: he came on stage during an interlude called 'In Town Tonight' and played two numbers, one slow and one fast. At the Palladium a reviewer mentioned that the selections were 'It's the Talk of the Town' and 'Sweet Sue'; these two turns were often used but sometimes 'The Day You Came Along' was featured instead of 'It's the Talk of the Town'.

After his week with Mrs Hylton's Orchestra, Hawkins moved off to Southport in the North West of England, where he worked with Jack Hylton's group, following the same procedure by playing a couple of numbers, often following them with a warmly requested encore. Billy Mann recalled,

> His spot in Hylton's programme was more or less a busking affair which climaxed with him playing four or five choruses on 'Sweet Sue'. It was terrific stuff. I was always so impressed with his sense of harmony. I think it was all the same to him whether he worked with Mrs Jack or with Jack himself. There was no rivalry between our band and Mrs Jack's; in fact we rarely saw them. It was always a joke in the music profession that the reason Jack got his wife, Ennis, to lead her own band was so that they need never spend any time together.[9]

During the following months Hawkins played many variety theatres in England, Scotland and Wales, mostly with Jack Hylton's Orchestra. His amazing performances left an indelible impression on those who heard them. There was something about Hawkins's playing and his stage presence that transcended the barriers that often exist between an esoteric jazz artist and lay listeners. He made no effort to adjust his style and played undiluted jazz, yet he did so with such skill and fervour that he won over almost every British audience he encountered. A typical review said: 'His performance was masterly and never have fans or musicians ever heard such power of execution, such tone, such wonderful technique, phrasing and interval playing on a saxophone.[10]

Billy Munn recalled this period:

> Hawkins had a commission to write some music for Selmer's. He started work on something that sounded a little like Dvorák's 'Humoresque' and asked me to transcribe what he played. He got stuck for a bridge passage, then suddenly played the most intricate and beautiful bars that I'd ever heard, and he said, 'Will that do?'
>
> I was flabbergasted and said, 'That's bloody marvellous,' but by then the phrase had gone clean out of his head. He'd just improvised that marvellous idea on the spur of the moment and it never returned to him.[11]

Occasionally Hawkins played in dancehalls with Jack Hylton's Orchestra. One such engagement, a late-night affair at the Astoria in Charing Cross Road, London, produced one of the few flops of the tour. The relatively high admission charge of five shillings dissuaded all but a handful of jazz fans from attending. But the gig at least gave Hawk the chance to have an extended blow (he played from 11.30 p.m. until 2 a.m.). Having been used to playing several hours a night, seven days a week, Hawkins found his working schedule with Hylton a little too easy. He welcomed any opportunity to sharpen up his technique and jumped at the chance to play at a session organized by the Number One Rhythm Club at the Gig Club (then in London's Little Denmark Street) on 6 May 1934. He was happy to play alongside local stars such as reedplayer Freddy Gardner, trumpeter Nat Gonella, saxist George Evans and bassist Tiny Winters. After playing four feature numbers Hawk ended his set by performing a request for 'If I Could Be With You One Hour'.

Bettie Edwards, a young freelance journalist, attempted to interview Hawkins at that session but didn't meet with much success. She described the tenor saxist as 'the best, or worst leg-puller let loose from Lennox Avenue.' Hawkins had already developed his own method of dealing with journalists' enquiries: he told Bettie Edwards that he was fifty years old, had sixteen children and had been in prison four times. Undeterred, the reporter fixed an interview for the following day, and during that meeting Hawkins eventually settled down and gave some fairly straightforward answers, albeit interspersing them with frivolous asides about his ambition to own a chicken farm in California.

Bettie Edwards's subsequent article showed that Hawkins had not been swept off his feet by the successes he was enjoying in Britain:

> Lots of the people who make a fuss of me don't even know what I play, and run around because it's smart and different to be crazy about hot music. Even at that, there is more real feeling here for my work than I would have believed possible. I want to come back next year with some of the boys you know – like Red Allen and Higgy (J.C. Higginbotham) – and maybe some you don't know.[12]

The tour of Britain allowed Hawkins time to follow a pursuit that he genuinely enjoyed: letter writing. Henry Allen was one of Hawk's correspondents during this time, as were various girlfriends in cities all over the USA. So too was Hawk's estranged wife Gertrude, but the person who received the bulk of Coleman's letters was a young woman he met soon after he'd arrived in England. Her name was Renée Gertler, and she and her sister Sadie had been taken by their father to hear Hawkins play during the early part of his tour. The girls, whose ancestors were Hungarian, were both deeply interested in the arts (their uncle, Mark Gertler, was a well-known painter; another relative was the violinist André Gertler). They were introduced to Hawkins, subsequently heard him play on many occasions, and he invited them to visit him at the apartment he'd taken in Jermyn Street, London W1. He gradually became closer to Renée and the two agreed to write to each other during the time that Hawkins was away on tour.

Their correspondence produced a remarkable series of letters. Interspersed with Hawkins's heartfelt and eloquent romantic thoughts there is a steady flow of background details about his tastes in jazz, in books and the cinema. The frivolous kidding interviewee is nowhere to be found, and such coyness as enters the letters is simply the gentle chiding of someone being playful with the object of his affection. In the letters Hawkins signed himself 'Coley', 'Coleman' or 'Bean'.

After playing a series of one-week bookings at theatres in London and the South of England, the Jack Hylton entourage moved up to Scotland to play for a week at the Glasgow Empire in June 1934. During this booking Hawk shared a place in lodgings with Hylton's bass player Joe Gibson. By this time he was on friendly terms with all the members of Hylton's orchestra but rarely got involved in long conversations with any of them. He kept himself to himself but was always willing to talk to fans who came backstage. A unit from Hylton's personnel backed Hawk for an extra-curricular session at Glasgow's Playhouse Ballroom, and local musicians packed themselves tight around the bandstand listening intently to every note that the star visitor played. A local reporter wrote, 'After the show he was voted a great guy on account of his unassuming and likeable demeanour.'

A Glasgow music critic's response to Hawkins was typically enthusiastic, making the point that the saxophonist's success was universal: 'It is certain that his playing will be the topic of conversation for months to come, and it is equally certain that for once public taste was found to be in complete agreement with that of musicians.'[13] In Glasgow a small party was organized in Hawk's honour. Accompanied by Billy Munn on piano, he played on a borrowed horn, then: 'Laughing, disclaiming all ability as a pianist, Hawk sat down at the piano and picked out slow, dreamy tunes, his chief favourite being a little melody he composed for Fletcher Henderson as a radio signature tune.'[14]

Jack Hylton's Orchestra remained in Glasgow for a further week but Hawkins moved south to play a week as a single act on the bill at the Sheffield Empire. On opening night in the Yorkshire city he wrote, 'rather a tough audience here but I guess I'll make it', but in another letter to Renée later that week he commented: 'The houses at the theatre have truly treated me swell. The piano player and I have honestly been doing excellently and these people are not so cold as you might expect.'

After the week at Sheffield, Hawkins was reunited with Jack Hylton's Orchestra and played a week's booking at the Palace Theatre in Manchester with them, but early in June he went off to do a series of one-night stands at Mecca ballrooms (Birmingham, Streatham, Leicester, Nottingham and York), at each of which he was accompanied by the various house bands. Hawk had no complaints about his backing groups, no matter how they played, but one report (from York) poignantly understates the problems that he encountered: 'Good as the rhythm section of the Rialto resident band is, the Hawk would have been better served had he travelled with his own rhythm men'.[15]

Following his booking at York, Hawkins travelled to Manchester to link up with the superior accompaniment of Jack Hylton's musicians for a BBC radio show, enthusiastically reviewed in the *Melody Maker*: 'Hylton did a short programme of which the high spot was undoubtedly Hawk's "Jamaica Shout" which was as brilliant as anything he has ever done.'[16] There followed a series of variety bookings, usually lasting for a week (with either Jack Hylton's band or Ennis Hylton's group), taking Hawkins to Leeds, Brighton and Newcastle.

By this time Hawkins had made it his practice to stay at the best hotels available. From the Royal Turk's Head in Newcastle-upon-Tyne he wrote to Renée: 'I don't know when I shall be returning to the States. No, I'm not homesick yet. For some unknown reason I'm not drinking as much as I was and I'm rather glad of the change.' He reported that fans often presented him with full bottles of whisky, but admitted these gifts only supplemented his considerable intake: 'I bought six bottles of Canadian Club rye whisky.' The aftermath was inevitable: 'Baby, I can hardly write this morning for my hands are so terribly unsteady. There's no reason why they should be, but they are.' But the boozing never appeared to affect Hawk's musical performances; Billy Munn said, 'He liked his tipple but he could always play supremely well.'

Because Jack Hylton undertook a long trip to the USA in 1934 the rest of Hawkins's touring in Britain that year was as part of Mrs Hylton's show. Accompanied by Ennis Hylton's Orchestra, Hawk moved into Scotland in August to play separate weeks in Glasgow and Edinburgh then travelled with the group to Wales to play Cardiff and Swansea. On tour Hawk received a steady stream of letters from the USA, some from his mother, others from Gertrude and recent girlfriends. Writing from Edinburgh, he expressed disappointment that Louis Armstrong hadn't bothered to correspond. He asked Renée Gertler, 'Have you heard from Louis yet? I presume he's doing Paris by this time. [Louis and Alpha had left England on 28 July]. He promised to write from there, but I guess he's too busy.' On several occasions, too, Hawk expressed disappointment that he had never heard from either Fletcher or Leora Henderson.

During Hawk's engagement at the Edinburgh Empire he was visited in his dressing room by a young Scottish musician, Mev Taylor, who recalls

> I had a chat with him and asked if he would like to meet some of the local musicians. When he said he would I got cracking and arranged to hire a fairly large studio with a piano. I arranged for a taxi to collect Hawkins and his saxophone. I only had time to get a pianist to accompany him. He played a few numbers and answered quite a lot of questions about his playing, his tone, embouchure, etc. Then he sat down at the piano and surprised the boys by playing some very nice numbers.[17]

Hawkins still hadn't become close friends with anyone in Mrs Hylton's troupe; he remained affable but reserved. On a quiet night at one of the provincial theatres some members of the band, who'd been drinking steadily at a nearby pub, decided to play a musical practical joke on Hawkins. Their prank was to transpose the music for his first feature 'It's the Talk of the Town' up a semitone without telling him. The band played their sign-off tune 'Hi-de-ho', then, as Hawkins was announced, the musicians played their backing notes in the new 'surprise' key of F sharp major. Hawkins walked to the centre of the stage and, without as much as a glance round proceeded to give a *tour de force* of improvising, creating the most intricate solo imaginable. The seasoned musicians behind Hawkins were absolutely staggered by the performance which, of course, was totally impromptu. Their intention hadn't been malicious; they merely wanted to test Hawkins on a point he had made in an article he wrote for the *Melody Maker* in which he had insisted that playing fluently in any key was simply a matter of practice. The Hylton musicians' 'joke' could well have caused hopeless fumbling in a less consummate improviser, but Hawkins triumphed.

If the pranksters were surprised by the breadth of Hawkins's amazing on-stage performance they were totally astounded when he showed no reaction whatsoever after the show. They thought that he would at least have said, 'You almost caught me there' or even 'Don't ever do that again', but Hawkins, in a telling example of gamesmanship, never referred to the incident. Trumpeter George Swift said later, 'It was a terrifying example of musicianship. We knew he was a marvellous player, but what he did that night was super-human. Before that incident we greatly admired him, but ever after we were totally in awe of him'.

The *Melody Maker* article that had tempted the Hylton musicians into playing their practical joke was one of a series of three that Hawkins contributed to the British publication in April 1934. The content of these pieces is worth dwelling on because they provide a good insight into Hawk's working methods and musical beliefs. In the first article (entitled 'Playing Tenor') he discussed his instrument: 'I play a highly burnished, gold-plated model with lots of engraving. My present instrument had five platings to make it sparkle like it does, but whether they improve the tone – well, that's for you to say when you hear me in action. I personally think a plated instrument is more mellow and less shrill than one in brass.' Hawkins kept faith in this belief for the rest of his life; the very last saxophone that he owned was quadruple plated.*

Also in this 1934 article Hawk said:

> The mouthpiece that I use is a metal one, specially made for me; I used to use a rubber one and found it pretty good. I prefer metal though; the lay is rigid and lasts for ever and the tone seems to be stronger and firmer too. I find that a fairly stiffish reed suits me best, a shade on the hard side if anything. Most teachers advise you to insert about one third of the reed in your mouth when you blow. Perhaps they're right, but I hold less than that – under half an inch – in my mouth and I seem to manage! The actual grip of my upper teeth and lower lip is quite light and although you might think with such a little space to get hold of that I have to bite, it isn't so. I am lucky to have an exceptionally strong underlip, but I wasn't born with it. It came as a result of continual blowing day after day for twenty years.

* After Hawkins's death this saxophone (Selmer Mark VI, model 126522) was sold to the New York musical-instrument dealer Charles Ponte. The tenor was given pride of place in Mr Ponte's business premises, then on West 46th Street. When Mr Ponte moved to Florida, he sold the instrument to New York saxophonist Mike Morgenstern, who said in a letter to me, dated 6 August 1987, 'According to Mr Ponte it was quadruple gold-plated; he had it displayed for a few years in a glass case with a $5,000 asking price. I got it for $3,000 in January 1984 because Ponte was liquidating his stock. It's too valuable to play on casual gigs. It's my "back-up" horn, partly because it's so doggone heavy from all the plating, and partly because I favor the sound of the Conn 10 M. The horn is not for sale!'

Hawk concluded his first article with the advice: 'Try to get tone in your playing, not speed.'

Hawkins began the second part of his treatise by asking, 'What are the secrets of success for a tenor player?' His answer was 'tune and tone'. He went on:

> I think Adolphe Sax himself would have agreed with me when I say that there is no such thing as a perfectly tuned horn, that is to say a sax that plays a note dead in pitch with the mechanical precision of a piano. You've got to humor your instrument, understand it and above all listen to it. That is the way to play it in tune and I regard this as one of the two main essentials of a good player. Now for tone, I'll tell you something. I'd rather hear a tenor player playing the scale of C in tune and with good tone than I would another fellow busking a lightning and intricate version of 'Tiger Rag' with a reedy tone and a just-off-the-note ear. Mere finger dexterity never made a big-timer yet. The tone of a tenor is rich and full. If you overblow it, it sounds like a bassoon, and if you want it to sound like that, why play the tenor anyway?

Hawk's final article was entitled 'Hot Playing' and contained the following advice: 'Until a player has advanced himself to such a stage that he has more or less lost consciousness of the manual side of the sax it is wrong and foolish for him to worry about playing hot.' Hawkins said that 'hot playing' required 'a perfect control of one's instrument so that musical thoughts can be automatically and unhesitatingly translated into notes; a complete knowledge of chords and harmonies; a super sense of rhythm, and the gift of inventiveness'. He went on:

> But what hot playing does not mean is a capacity for listening to hot records and using somebody else's breaks. That's the trouble with a lot of fairly advanced horn players. They spend hours listening to records, memorizing or writing down bits that sound good. I suppose this helps their technique but it also stultifies their mental powers. Listen to as many good players as you can by all means, copy their method if you like, but don't copy what they play, because that will merely make you a mimic.

Hawkins continued to work with Mrs Hylton's Orchestra, but the loneliness of the touring schedule made itself clear in letters he wrote to Renée Gertler. For over a decade he had been based in the liveliest section of one of the most vibrant places on earth: New York City. His 1934 intinerary took him to places in Britain that were decidedly less exciting. Hawkins wrote of Swansea, 'This appears to be the saddest place I've ever seen. Yet the audiences are as nice as they can be and the public house opposite the stage entrance sends ice over to me every night for my drinks.

Saw a lovely old picture yesterday; guess I shall go again this afternoon, this being the only means of amusement.'

Hanley (Staffs) soon replaced Swansea as the low spot of the tour: 'This is undoubtedly the world's most forsaken place.' Hawkins didn't drive a car on tour, relying instead on trains. He confessed that he was 'sick of travelling', an understandable reaction since one of his Sunday journeys (from Glasgow to Cardiff) took over twelve hours. During the 1930s the whole of Britain was dotted with rhythm clubs, where small conclaves of jazz enthusiasts met regularly, usually once a week, to attend record recitals and jam sessions. During Hawk's tours he attended several of these gatherings, and though his visits were brief they helped to break the monotony that he was experiencing.

When Hawkins wasn't reading, or listening to records on his portable gramophone, he played solitaire in his hotel room. Hawkins mentions reading *The Memoirs of Fanny Hill* and Aldous Huxley's *Rotunda*, but then described how he had developed what he called a 'fad' for reading detective novels: 'I believe I've read twelve in the last two weeks.' He often commented on the gramophone records that he had with him,

> I have Duke Ellington's record of 'Cocktails for Two', but I really can't see it too much. I think he had better stick to 'Stompy Jones'. The Mills Brothers' record of 'Sleepy Head' is ready: I can see it. I want to record it so badly. The Mills Brothers' record of 'Jungle Fever' is on and it's sending me so I can hardly write.

The Mills Brothers were clearly favourites of Hawkins, but he also admired another vocal group, the Boswell Sisters, even more, and wrote that he was 'crazy about' their recording of 'Coffee in the Morning'. A week later he again mentioned the same recording with real enthusiasm, following that letter with another that said, 'Connie Boswell still sends me.' In a subsequent note he said, 'Connie's record of "All I Do is Dream Babe of You" is solid.' Another favourite was Benny Goodman's recording of 'Moonglow'.

To while away the afternoons in tour towns, Hawk took every opportunity he could to visit the local cinema. His favourite movie star was Ruth Chatterton, but films he particularly enjoyed during his weeks away from London were *Villa, Villa* and *The House of Rothschild*. In many provincial towns during the 1930s, however, cinemas did not open on Sundays, a restriction that caused Hawkins to write, 'I'll go for a nice long walk. You know there's nothing else to do on a Sunday.'

Occasionally Hawkins commented on other artists on the bill with him at variety theatres. He mentioned Tessie O'Shea and said that mandolin player Dave Apollon's Orchestra was 'very good'. He also sometimes managed to listen to late-night radio programmes and wrote, 'I heard Lew Stone's broadcast Monday night. It quite pleased me; your boy Stanley Black sounded ready, as he always does.' Hawkins had been introduced to Stanley Black, then a twenty-one-year-old pianist, by Renée Gertler. The occasion was an informal party and before it was over Hawkins had played some piano duets with Black. The two men got on well, musically and socially, and this encouraged Edgar Jackson, then a prominent reviewer and producer, to suggest that the two men make a recording together. A studio session was fixed during the period in which Hawkins and the Hylton package moved south to play a series of week-long theatre bookings.

On 15 November 1934 Hawkins wrote about these plans from the Central Hotel in Portsmouth: 'I will arrive in London at four o'clock Saturday morning, sleep until nine, then off to the studio.' At the studios Hawkins met up with Stanley Black and two of Black's colleagues from Lew Stone's band, guitarist Albert Harris and bassist Frederick 'Tiny' Winters. Tiny Winters, recalling the circumstances, said,

> The session took place at the Abbey Road studios, but unfortunately we were booked into the worst studio in the building. Number 4 I think it was, upstairs near the offices. The place had an echo and the sound spread as soon as a note was played. We arrived first and got ready, then Coleman Hawkins came in and the first thing he did was put a bottle of gin on the piano. 'Help yourselves,' he said. We looked at him in amazement; we wouldn't dream of drinking at that hour of the morning. The recordings went off without a hitch. Well, he was such a marvellous player, and such a nice man.[18]

Stanley Black picked up the story:

> We soon settled into a groove, and decided on a couple of standards, 'Lady Be Good' and 'Honeysuckle Rose'. I had been asked by Edgar Jackson to provide a tune for the session so I took along a composition called 'Lullaby', which was only written out in manuscript. I showed it to Hawkins and asked if he'd mind performing it. I explained that I was always more interested in harmony than in melody and he laughed and said, 'You and me both.' So he played the tune through perfectly, full of expression as though it was part of his regular repertoire. We went through 'Lady Be Good' without any problems, and 'Lost in a Fog' was chosen by Hawkins himself. He said, 'I really like this tune. Do you mind if we do it?' Naturally we were delighted to oblige. I suggested that we change key at the end of each chorus on

> 'Honeysuckle Rose' and Coleman immediately agreed. He negotiated the modulations without the slightest problem. His sound was tremendous and the widish vibrato enhanced it. I never heard him play out of tune, even in the slightest degree.[19]

The four tunes (subsequently issued on Parlophone 78-r.p.m. records) are full of interest, even though none of them could be placed among Hawkins's finest achievements. One disappointment is that Hawk's sound is not consistently recorded; at times he seems too far from the microphone. 'Lullaby', a slow evocative piece, is given an expressive reading by Hawkins, the piano takes over and plays an interlude at a faster tempo, making clever use of an ostinato bass-hand figure, then Hawkins re-enters to create some smoothly eloquent variations on the dreamy tune. 'Lady Be Good' is taken at what used to be called a medium-bounce tempo. Hawkins lopes around the melody effectively during the first chorus, then gives way to a chorded guitar solo by Harris (backed by some slapped bass playing from Winters); Hawkins re-enters and begins pulling out the stops, moving with processional grace into a new key for the final chorus.

The remaining two tunes are duets shared by Stanley Black and Hawkins. 'Lost in a Fog' is prefaced by a crisply played four-bar piano introduction. Hawkins's opening chorus is relatively uneventful but interest mounts as the duettists begin deliberately creating some overlapping ideas. The best track from the date, though, is 'Honeysuckle Rose'; Hawk alternates between reticence and boldness during his two choruses then Black takes over and adds some vivid splashes of harmonic colouring, revealing the influences of his two particular jazz idols, Teddy Wilson and Arthur Schutt. Hawkins wraps things up with some stunning improvising, moving through a rifflike figure into a series of impressive downward flurries and culminating in a last eight bars emblazoned with rugged ideas that are impressively timed. The session doesn't possess the devil-may-care qualities of the duets with Buck Washington, but overall the recordings are almost as satisfying.

It was announced in November 1934 that Hawkins was to take part in a film to be made at the British Lion studios at Beaconsfield, near London. The film (which used the name of a currently popular radio show) was *In Town Tonight* and its format was the featuring of various music-hall acts. As no prints have survived showing Hawkins's performance it's impossible to say who backed him for the two numbers he played in the film. The

Melody Maker of 1 December 1934 cited the tunes as 'On the Sunny Side of the Street' and 'Sweet Sue' and said the accompaniment was by Howard Jacob's band, with Cecil Norman on piano. But Cecil Norman is positive that, to his great regret, he never had the opportunity of working with Coleman Hawkins.

In the last month of 1934 Hawkins worked with Mrs Jack Hylton's show, first for a week at the Birmingham Hippodrome, from where he wrote (on 5 December) to Renée:

> Have you heard the new number of Duke's: 'Solitude'? I heard from Gertrude and she said it was quite good; and pray tell me how is Fletcher's 'Shanghai Shuffle'? You may remember he made a lovely record of it years ago when Louis was in the band. I just received a letter from Red Allen and you're right, he's with the Blue Rhythm Band at the Cotton Club. I don't know about Kirby, I only heard that Duke wanted him.

The Hawkins–Gertler correspondence was as fervent as ever, and the couple were happy to see each other during the times that Hawk returned to London, but his closest female companion in late 1934 was a black dancer called Zita and he certainly spent time with her during his week's booking (with Mrs Jack Hylton's Orchestra) at the Finsbury Park Empire in London. During this period, having played his London theatre date, Hawk invited Tom Gordon-Walker and his fiancée Joyce back to his apartment. Joyce reminisced about the visit some fifty years later:

> There was a black woman there when we arrived. She was American, terribly quiet. She didn't come into the conversation. She came through from a back room and made coffee. She was in her twenties or perhaps thirties. Coleman Hawkins sat down at a small piano and played beautifully for half an hour or more. He played very well; it quite fascinated me because I did too, in my own way. Tom and I sat down and drank our coffee and listened. I was amazed. He was so charming. A quiet, unassuming man, conventionally dressed. He was completely taken up with what he was doing, enjoying himself playing the piano.[20]

For some while, Hawkins had been contemplating working on the Continent, and things suddenly fell into place when Jack Hylton (having returned from the USA) signed contracts to take his orchestra (and various guest stars) over to play shows in France and Holland. The first bookings were in Paris, where the troupe were engaged to play consecutive weeks at the Rex and at the Gaumont Palace. The entourage that crossed the English Channel included Hylton's full orchestra, the Three Gaylords, the Four Ink Spots and Coleman Hawkins.

8
Dutch Treats

Despite experiencing a hectic social life, Hawkins found time to write to Renée, 'Do I like Paris – I say I do. Seems as though when night comes I become wide-awake, my old habits of New York.' He found the five-shows-a-day routine 'frightful' but was compensated by visits to hear Freddie Taylor's band at the Villa d'Este: 'I wanted to get on the stand and play with them.' Hawkins heard Willie Lewis's Orchestra at the Chez Florence, describing the venue as 'rather an exclusive place for the elite'. He also met up with Louis Armstrong: 'I ran into your boy Louis last night, with Alfa [*sic*], sitting in a restaurant opposite Melody's Bar. I gave him your sincerest regards for which he sends many thanks.'

To keep up his energy for the five-show marathon Hawkins increased his already considerable intake of spirits. Hylton's French trumpeter Philippe Brun recalled the effects of this move: 'He used to drink a bottle of whisky, just like that. I couldn't understand it. The first show was OK, the second not so good, third so-so; fourth and fifth shows – finished.'[1] A young French jazz enthusiast, Charles Delaunay, who later became an author and impresario, first met Hawkins at the Rex:

> The Hot Club was nearby at Pierre Nourry's, 15 rue du Conservatoire, so it was easy for Pierre, Jacques Bureau and I to go and collect him in turn at the end of the afternoon show so that we could end the day with him at the club. We had dinner with him or took him back to his hotel on the Place Montholon. Our constant attendance didn't seem to bother him much and he was open to our flow of questions about bands or musicians he had played with and recordings he had made.[2]

In a letter Hawkins wrote to Renée from Paris during the first days of 1935 he mentioned hearing Louis Armstrong's recent recordings of 'Tiger Rag', 'St Louis Blues' and 'On the Sunny Side of the Street', saying that the band was 'sadder than ever'. After the marathon at the Rex had ended Hawkins felt happier with the two-shows-a-day routine at the Gaumont

Palace. His schedule there allowed him to visit the Selmer instrument company's headquarters in Paris, where he enjoyed meeting Maurice Selmer who offered to make a custom-built saxophone for him. Hawkins gratefully accepted the offer, ceased using a Conn instrument and for the rest of his life played various Selmer tenor saxophones.

On 4 January 1935 Hawkins and the Jack Hylton Orchestra left Paris for The Hague, Holland, where they were booked to play for ten days at the Scala Theatre; the travellers broke their journey by making a brief stop in Brussels. Soon after his arrival in The Hague, Hawkins went off to hear trumpeter Louis de Vries at the Tabarin: 'He seems pretty good, plays a lot of Louis's stuff.' Hawkins occasionally commented on players he heard during his travels, but rarely made vindictive assessments. He said of the British tenor saxist, Don Barrigo, 'So Don is stealing my stuff? Well, I'll have to try and get some new ideas,' and in discussing the young Frenchman, Alix Combelle, he said, 'a tenor player they call little "Hawk" and he don't do bad either'. The nearest he came to condemnation was when he described a local accompanying band as being 'petered', but added philosophically, 'that won't be anything new for me'.

Soon after Hawkins had installed himself at the Hotel Americain in The Hague he went out to buy recordings by Duke Ellington and the Boswell Sisters; 'I also have a new one by the Casa Loma Orchestra, incidentally my favorite band.' Hawkins and the Hylton orchestra completed their dates in The Hague then moved off to play engagements in Rotterdam, Groningen and Nijmegen. Jack Hylton's next bookings consisted of an eight-day tour of Germany (23–31 January), but since Nazi policies prevented Hawkins from working with the group, his place was taken by the Dutch accordionist Cavelli.

Edward Crommelin, then President of the Nederlandsch Jazz Liga, recalled the sequence of events: 'England's fine orchestra under Jack Hylton was touring Europe with Hawkins as a featured jazz soloist. He was eagerly awaited by jazz buffs everywhere, and that included Germany, but Hylton couldn't get permission to bring Hawkins into Germany, as the Master Race had no use for a black musician.'[3]

The *Melody Maker* gave a report on the situation in its issue of 26 January 1935: 'When Theo Uden Masman (leader of the Dutch big band the Ramblers) heard of the Hawk's enforced holiday he saw Jack Hylton who was then playing a concert at the Pschorr in Rotterdam, as a result of which Jack gave Masman permission to take Hawkins over for the period.' As Edward Crommelin later commented, 'Germany's loss was Holland's gain and we made the most of it.' Marcel Thielemans, trombonist with the Ramblers, explained, 'With the co-operation of the director of Dutch Decca (Henk van Zoelen) our leader Theo Uden Masman could afford Hawkins; he joined our band for five or six months.'[4]

The initial overture concerning Hawk's recordings for Dutch Decca was made by the black American pianist Freddy Johnson, then working in Rotterdam. On 17 January 1935 Johnson wrote to Eddy Crommelin at Decca's offices in Amsterdam:

> I have been talking to Coleman Hawkins this afternoon and he wants to do some recording for Dutch Decca and I should like for you to arrange this matter for him. Could you come over to Rotterdam Saturday afternoon . . . come to the Pschorr and ask for me there any time after three o'clock. You can hear 'Hawk' play if you come around four o'clock.

Edward Crommelin made the rendezvous and remembered the details many years later:

> My first encounter with Coleman Hawkins was quite revealing. Freddy Johnson had set a date for me to meet them in Rotterdam in Pschorr's dancehall. Hawkins didn't say much at first. When he decided to go to the washroom he suddenly emptied all the change out of his pockets and left it in a stack on the table. I remember thinking, 'different people, different customs.' Freddy later explained to me 'It was a sort of test. When he saw you hadn't touched anything he put the money away and decided you were alright and made friends with you.'[5]

Agreement was reached for Hawkins to record for Decca, and to work with the Ramblers. With his immediate future settled Hawkins played a brief residency at the Pschorr and began rehearsing for his forthcoming record session with the Ramblers. But Hawkins was still contracted to play one more residency with Jack Hylton's Orchestra. While awaiting Hylton's return from Germany Hawkins felt the pull of Paris and went there for a two-day holiday. In France he learnt that Louis Armstrong had returned to the USA. During the first week of February 1935 Hawk resumed working with Jack Hylton, playing at the Carré Theatre in Amsterdam; the routine there allowed him time to make his first recordings with the Ramblers (on 4 February).

Five numbers cut at this first session featured Hawkins, whose playing sounds relaxed yet full of potent drive. One of the few lapses occurs during the final stages of 'Some of These Days' when Hawk drops into a chugging pattern that contrasts starkly with the rhythmic buoyancy of his opening chorus. Just prior to the session the Ramblers had acquired a new vocalist, Annie de Reuver.

> I first met Hawkins when I was sixteen years old when he did the recording of 'Some of these Days', etc. It was ten in the morning and he came in and started to play; there were two songs he'd never heard before in his life, but for him no problem. Following my vocals he took over and my God! a cloud of alcohol came my way. When the session was over he finished a whole bottle of whisky, then he told me he wanted to take me back with him to the States, but I don't think as a 'singer', if you know what I mean.[6]

Though Annie de Reuver's delivery reveals her youthful inexperience, she sings fairly well in tune on 'Some of These Days' and on 'After You've Gone'. Hawkins creates some strong yet tender lines on the latter, aided by a discreet arrangement and the support of Marcel Thieleman's beautifully controlled high-note trombone playing. Hawk sounds supremely at ease on 'I Only Have Eyes for You', and this musical elegance contrasts with the stiff formality of the arrangement and Annie's understandably tense phrasing. Hawk's vibrant chromaticisms, however, create a satisfying finale. In a contemporary review Leonard Feather wrote, 'Hawk puts up a brave show. His chorus is really beautiful but he cannot make a silk purse out of a sow's ear.'[7]

Hawk's opening chorus on 'I Wish I Were Twins' is full of propulsion and infectious enthusiasm, but after some neat playing by the tightly muted brass he fails to build on his impressive beginning. On a second take of the same number, however, he sounds carefree and inventive throughout, and his time is noticeably freer. Second takes of all the numbers from this session were eventually issued; they show that Hawkins found the atmosphere of the Netherlands stimulating. Some of Hawk's recordings with the Ramblers were issued by Decca (on 78 rpm) in Britain, but all of the series could be specially ordered and imported from Holland; only a few of the sides were issued in the USA. Not all of the Dutch jazz fans were delighted with the records: Edward Crommelin wrote in retrospect, 'Of all the cuts we made with Hawkins and the Ramblers the only one I liked was 'I Wish I Were Twins'. I really wasn't too happy about getting the Ramblers to back Coleman Hawkins. Although they were good musicians their rhythm section was stodgy. They just didn't swing out.'[8]

The only 'ordinary' performance from Hawkins occurs on 'Hands Across the Table'. The tenor saxist was determined to record this slow ballad and declared he felt 'quite crazy about it', but despite the mellow arrangement Hawkins doesn't achieve the sensuous impact he so wanted to create. The vocal by Annie de Reuver is pleasant enough, but suffers because the singer is dealing in a language that is not her own; she's word-perfect but just too careful. The best moments on the record occur when Hawkins answers the clever instrumental scoring. The Ramblers acquitted themselves well on the date; they didn't achieve any notable swing but their phrasing blended nicely and they made no attempt to outblow their celebrated guest star. Hawk worked with the Ramblers for a week (8–15 February) at the Pschorr during which time band and guest star made their first broadcast together (from Hilversum on 12 February).

Commenting on his recordings with the Ramblers Hawk wrote, 'My session I think was quite good – I sort of pleased myself.' He went on (in his letter of 8 February):

> I've just completed a short film at the Carlton for the Dutch film company Polygoon. I was only accompanied by a piano (the pianist was the Dutch musician Leo de la Fuente). Had to speak a few words. I was thinking of you when I played the number 'I Wish I Were Twins'. Jack Hylton leaves for England, Monday, but I'm not going with him because I want to stay on the Continent for a while. Received letters from Gert and Fletcher Henderson; he wants me to help him to get his band together by promoting a contract over here, anyplace. I presume he wants me to speak to Jack.

Fletcher Henderson's Orchestra was, as ever, combining musical successes with strategic failures. Hawkins's original replacement was Lester Young (who had so impressed Henderson in Kansas City) but after a brief stay Young asked Henderson to give him a letter of release so that he could go back to Kansas City. The bandleader duly obliged, and thus ended an unhappy period for the tenor saxist. The main problems that Lester Young encountered in New York were caused by his absolute originality. Fletcher Henderson (and his sidemen) were seeking a Hawkins *doppelgänger*; they realized that it was extremely unlikely that they would find anyone with Hawkins's musical talents but they at least expected the newcomer to make an effort to duplicate Hawk's vast tone. Lester Young was, even at this early stage of his career, a highly creative improviser who was literally developing a new jazz style, but part of this originality lay in the light sound of his tone (inspired, he said, by the work of white saxophonist Frank Trumbauer) and a minimal use of vibrato.

The other members of the Henderson saxophone section made it clear to Young that they expected him to attempt to blow like Hawkins.

Henderson's wife Leora virtually commanded the newcomer to imitate Bean's approach. Young lodged with Mr and Mrs Henderson on 139th Street and each morning Leora (or 'Miss Lu' as she was known to the band) would play Hawkins's recordings to the newcomer. Young recalled, 'I wanted to play my own way but I just listened, I didn't want to hurt her feelings.' However, the experience was very unsettling for Young; 'I had a whole lot of trouble there. The whole band was buzzing on me because I had taken Hawk's place. I didn't have the same kind of sound he had. Finally I left and went to Kansas City.'[9]

The Henderson reed section heaved a sigh of relief at Young's departure, but years later Russell Procope admitted how short-sighted they had been about the newcomer's prowess. Happily, Lester Young soon found stardom within Count Basie's band. Fletcher Henderson and his musicians *were* satisfied by the efforts of the next man to fill the vacancy: Ben Webster. Ben was not, at that time, a very nimble-fingered player but he was a passionate devotee of Coleman Hawkins's style, keen to imitate every nuance of his idol's work (as he had attempted to do while a member of Benny Moten's band). Webster freely admitted that he had set out to be a Hawkins copyist: 'I had heard all of Hawkins's records and I'd studied them all. It was quite an experience taking his chair.'[10] Eventually Webster developed his own style and became one of jazz's great individualists.

Coleman Hawkins was not aware of the upheavals that had occurred in the Henderson reed section, but he was curious enough about his former colleagues' activites to make a point of listening to their new recordings. As a result he wrote to Renée:

> Fletcher's new record is nothing but 'Yeah Man' turned around slightly. I read an article in the *Melody Maker*, or some English paper, where they said I was playing on it. Funny, I must be a powerful man to be able to record over 3,000 miles of water, for I was in England when it was made and besides it doesn't sound like me.

It was, in fact, Ben Webster.

On 20 February 1935 Hawkins flew from Rotterdam to Paris in order to play at a concert organized by the Hot Club of France to take place three days later at the Salle Rameau (ex-Pleyel). Hawkins arrived expecting to find a well-rehearsed band ready to accompany him, but he was disappointed: 'I find these cats not even organized so that means I must write arrangements myself (more work). I won't, I promise you, get too commercial.'

Hugues Panassié revealed in his book *Douze Années de Jazz* that within the Hot Club was some doubt about Hawkins's drawing power. Charles Delaunay, then partnering Panassié in the running of the Hot Club, also recalled the apprehension that they, as promoters, had right up to the night of the concert: 'Before the concert started – when we looked from behind the curtains – the big hall seemed to us completely empty . . . by the time of the intermission the hall was nicely filled.'[11]

Elsewhere, he remembered:

> Despite Hawkins's great modesty and discretion he didn't hide the fact that he was hoping the concert would be very successful. He was probably fed up with having to be second best to Armstrong, a musician he thought to be, at the most, his equal. Coleman Hawkins was almost the same size as Armstrong but he didn't get noticed. He was not an extrovert but his conversation showed a fine and deep intelligence. Armstrong's playing was just like his looks and style, but Hawkins's playing seemed the opposite to his shy attitude in life. When he was playing it was as if he had freed a tremendous power held back and then exploded. The eyes closed, heavy eyelids, head low, moving his shoulders as if he were fighting his saxophone. He seemed to forget about the outside world.
>
> The concert was a great success and Hawkins's talent was acknowledged, as was that of the Hot Club's Quintette. But the financial balance sheet was a disaster. When the musicians had been paid off there remained a 6,000-franc deficit, a large amount in those days. The musicians had wanted very high fees. Django Reinhardt had first asked for an unbelievable amount. Coleman Hawkins was very pleased with the concert and offered to accept only half of his fee. I mention this because it happened only once in my life and I have organized many concerts.[12]

In the second issue of the new French magazine *Jazz Hot*, Madeleine Gautier reviewed the concert, listing the band that accompanied Hawkins: Arthur Briggs, Noel Chiboust (trumpets); Peter Duconge, Fletcher Allen and Castor McCord (saxophones); Sigismond Bech (string bass); Joseph Reinhardt (guitar); Ray Stokes (piano) and Billy Taylor (drums). She wrote, 'When Hawkins throws himself with such ardour into one of his hot improvisations his sonority penetrates you like a gust of warm air,' and after noting that Hawk relied on phrases that were 'almost exclusively legato' she commented that 'the insufficiency of the rehearsals was felt'.

Hawkins was well aware that the playing of the arrangements was extremely ragged; in a letter he wrote, 'The band was a bastard, but it didn't worry me any, I played my ass off.' It was unusual for Hawk to adopt such a self-proclaiming tone in his letters but he felt 'the concert was marvellously successful'.

On the following Saturday, the two stars of the Quintette of the Hot Club of France, Django Reinhardt and Stephane Grappelli, became part of a large band (directed by Michael Warlop) that backed Coleman Hawkins on a recording session. Only two of the musicians (trumpeters Arthur Briggs and Noel Chiboust) who backed Hawk on the Paris concert were retained for the recording session; they were joined in the brass section by trumpeter Pierre Allier and trombonist Guy Paquinet. The American sax section was dispensed with and their places taken by André Ekyan, Charles Lisee and Alix Combelle. Django Reinhardt was on guitar, Eugene d'Hellemmes on string bass and Maurice Chailloux on drums; Stephane Grappelli temporarily forsook his violin to play piano on the date.

On a slow-medium version of 'Blue Moon', trumpeter Arthur Briggs elegantly phrases the tune over a scored background. It's a charming exposition of the melody, enriched by subtle inflections in timing and delivered in a crystal-clear tone. Hawkins saunters in for the second chorus, paraphrasing the melody but adding attractive harmonies to the turn-around phrases that occur at the end of each eight-bar section. It's not a formidable example of his improvising powers but it is an admirably relaxed performance. In the closing stages the drummer's cymbal work is more enthusiastic than swinging but Hawkins seems undeterred and drifts skilfully over the cumbrous rhythm section.

Briggs and Hawkins are also featured on an early recording of the Mexican tune 'What a Difference a Day Made'. Briggs's playing is again full of class but Hawk's variations, after a chance of key, lay the foundations for a series of brilliant phrases that grace the final sixteen bars. The sound of the unrelenting rhythm section almost scuttles the opening ensemble on 'Avalon', but once Hawkins has established a strong rhythmic pulse by his determined phrasing of the melody, things settle down. Briggs again solos admirably, adding delicate lip trills to nicely conceived ideas. Django Reinhardt takes over and creates an expressive *mélange* of individualistic phrases, weaving filigree runs in with eerie blue notes, creating timeless music that exemplifies both his Gypsy origins and his deep love of jazz.

But for all Django's genius as a soloist he was often an indifferent accompanist when playing four-in-the-bar rhythm patterns, creating a chunky beat that negated swing. This is particularly noticeable on 'Stardust', where only the rhythm section accompany Hawkins. Here, unusually, Hawkins adheres strictly to Hoagy Carmichael's melody during the opening chorus; in contrast Django's sixteen-bar solo is full of shimmering invention. But Hawk re-enters and soon proves that he too can create cascades of variations and, that point made, he gently homes back to the tune during the closing bars.

Hawkins, despite having stomach trouble during the session, which he attributed to 'that rich French food', was pleased with the results of the date and wrote, 'I think they may turn out better than the ones I made in Holland.' He made no specific mention of his accompanist except to say, 'The musicians I used were the best to be found in Paris. Not the ones that were used on the concert, thank goodness.' A few days after the recording session Hawkins left Paris to visit Scandinavia for the first time. En route to Copenhagen his train made a stop at Hamburg, enabling Hawkins to spend a brief while on German soil. He used the time to visit the station buffet, where he scribbled a note to Renée proclaiming, 'This beer is solid.'

To his total surprise Hawkins found a huge crowd (estimated at 5,000) gathered at Copenhagen's Central railway station to greet his arrival (on 10 March). Welcoming music was performed by Aage Juhl Thomsen's band (who later accompanied Hawk on most of the dates he played in Copenhagen), then some enthusiastic onlookers lifted Hawkins on to an ornate chair and carried him to his taxi.

Hawk was genuinely thrilled by this reception and by the enthusiasm that greeted his performances in Copenhagen and in Arhus (where he was backed by a sextet from Erik Tuxen's band led by Kai Ewans). He finished the brief tour with a concert (backed by Ewan's sextet) at a theatre in Horsens on 25 March 1935, then left for another series of triumphs in Sweden.

Early in May he returned to Copenhagen for a brief vacation, regularly visiting the Tivoli Gardens during the warm spring weather and doing a good deal of socializing. His visit to one Danish household provided everlasting memories for jazz violinist Svend Asmussen (then a teenager). Sven's brother Ernst woke him with the news that Hawkins was down in the parlour playing piano,

> I thought it was lie, but I tiptoed down the stairs in my pyjamas. Hawkins was sitting at the piano hoarsely humming 'The Talk of the Town', which I had on record. I took out my ukulele and sang his chorus note for note – from time to time he cut in with 'Yeah boy, Yeah boy'. I showed him a sort of primitive saxophone that I had bought in Bredgade for 25 kr. It had holes instead of keys which made it impossible for the world's greatest saxophone player to produce any sound. But after I had demonstrated it Hawkins, to his great delight, succeeded in creating a sort of scream on it.[13]

Hawk was both pleased and disconcerted to discover that the girlfriend of one of the saxophonists he'd met in Stockholm had followed him into Denmark vowing her undying love, but she soon returned home and on 13 May 1935 Hawk left Denmark for the next part of his Scandinavian tour, which involved a visit to Norway.

Travelling overnight by train, he reached Oslo's central station on the morning of 14 May. A large crowd awaited his arrival, including Willy Johansen, the bandleader with whom he was to work in Oslo; a huge bunch of flowers was presented to the blushing visitor. The newspaper *Dagbladet* commented:

> Quite a few young ladies were also on hand to get a glimpse of the Negro, who of course is well known from gramophone records. Hawkins is an extraordinarily distinguished young gentleman, very well dressed, good-looking with big white shining teeth. He is considered one of the world's best saxophonists, an excellent musician who has devoted his life to jazz although he also likes classical music.

At the Hotel Bristol, where Hawk remained based during his stay in Oslo, he played for dancing, working as a featured soloist with violinist Willy Johansen's seven-piece orchestra. This ensemble (whose pianist Robert Levin later enjoyed a distinguished career as a concert artist) wasn't a jazz group, but it was a good-class restaurant orchestra. While in Norway Hawk wrote, 'I like Oslo a lot. I think I could live here for quite some time.' This was impossible, though, because he had already accepted a future booking in Denmark. He returned to Copenhagen on 27 May in good time to play a concert with Erik Tuxen's Orchestra at the Tivoli Concert Hall on 7 June. The show was completely sold out and Hawkins delighted the huge crowd by playing four encores: 'Tiger Rag', 'Dinah', 'Stardust' and 'I Wish I Were Twins'. The show was broadcast, which allowed some of Hawk's Danish friends privately to record the programme on a de-luxe American Victor machine; Hawk heard a playback at a celebration party held after the concert.

There was no chance for Hawkins to capitalize on his successes in Denmark; he was offered many engagements, but couldn't fulfil them because he was unable to obtain the necessary work permit. He wrote in a letter, 'It's terribly difficult here with permits; they don't want you to take the money out of the country.' In Britain, the *Melody Maker* commented: 'The Danish Labour Ministry has forbidden Hawk to play in that country so he spends his time playing for his fellow musicians, gratuitously after midnight, and hobnobbing with a host of admirers.'[14]

Fortunately, promoters in other European countries were clamouring for Hawk's services. Among various offers was one to join Willie Lewis's Orchestra in Paris.

Hawk declined this, saying he was particularly interested in returning to England. But by this time it was extremely difficult for American musicians to obtain work permits to fulfil engagements in Britain. Hawkins unsuccessfully put out feelers but was disappointed; he wrote to Renée, 'I think if it hadn't been for you I would have returned to the States long ago.' A twinge of homesickness occasionally surfaced; in June 1935 he wrote, 'I would love to have that old band of Fletcher's – a solid sender to me.'

But none of the offers that Hawk received was attractive enough to pull him away from Denmark, and during the summer of 1935 he remained in Copenhagen, playing only occasionally. It was not all wild revelry; sometimes he was in bed by 11 p.m. and up by 8 a.m. which was for Hawkins (a notably late riser) an amazing new routine. It was not one he kept up for long. He toyed with the idea of going to France or to Holland, being temporarily displeased that Jack Hylton seemed to have made no moves to get him back into Britain.

Having heard that Benny Carter had temporarily settled in France, Hawk considered adopting a suggestion (put forward by Renée Gertler) that he move to Paris to team up with Carter, but while he was mulling over this idea he received an offer to play a season in Scheveningen, Holland. No sooner had he opened that envelope than he received an offer to work at the Danish summer resort, Bellevue. Fearing that he might not be granted a permit for the Danish residency he accepted the Dutch offer, to discover (a day later) that the Bellevue work permit had been issued. Contracted to play in Holland, he said farewell to what he called his 'beloved Kobenhavn'.

In the last part of July 1935 Hawk began working at the Dutch seaside resort, Scheveningen, playing at the Hotel Kurhaus in the afternoon and at the Palais de Dance in the evening, guesting with local musicians. Hawkins loved the 'wonderful salt sea air' at Scheveningen, but decided to reside at his former address, the Hotel Americain in The Hague. During his spare time Hawkins composed four pieces for the tenor saxophone ('Lamentation', 'White Hat and Red Hair', 'What is the Name?' and 'Devotion'), subsequently published in 1936 by the Peter Maurice Music Company in London. He also put his portable gramophone to good use by playing various recent jazz recordings, including Duke Ellington's 'Show Boat

Shuffle' and 'In a Sentimental Mood'. This coupling impressed him: 'Very good. I think Rex Stewart is playing on them – he seems to be playing a lot cleaner and smoother, and that's what I like, for as you know, I don't like rough, loud playing.'

Hawk had regular social links with a fellow American, pianist Freddy Johnson, and the two of them sat and listened to jazz records together. One that came in for special mention was Fletcher Henderson's recording of 'Big John's Special' (dedicated to the owner of a New York bar that Hawkins had often visited). In a letter Hawk revealed that the two 'came to the conclusion that Mouse Randolph played much better than Red Allen on the record'. Hawk advised Renée Gertler to listen to the record, and particularly to 'Jeff' (Hylton Jefferson, alto saxist): 'What he plays is completely wrong with the harmony the brass is making; we had lots of fun laughing at the "corn" that Buster Bailey played.'

Hawkins also commented on 'Rhapsody Junior' and 'Rhythm in My Nursery Rhymes' by Jimmie Lunceford's Orchestra: 'I like this band very much – they are beginning to be one of my favorites.' Fletcher Henderson's 'Wrappin' It Up' and 'Happy as the Day is Long' were described as 'not bad at all. It's really too bad this band had to disperse'. Hawk also praised Red Norvo's version of 'With All My Heart and Soul', 'solid, sends me'. In his letters Hawkins occasionally offered comments on local musicians he heard. He was particularly impressed by the Belgian Fud Candrix, whose band he described as 'quite swell, play very modern. Fud himself is a very good tenor player, and also "gets off" on the fiddle awfully nice.'

On 26 August 1935 Hawkins travelled to Laren for a recording session at the Hamdorff Casino, which began promptly at ten o'clock in the morning (so unlike the staggered starts that Hawk had been used to in the States). This was another series of recordings with the Ramblers, who were benefiting from the talents of Jack Bulterman, a fine trumpet player and a gifted arranger and composer. After the date Hawkins returned to Scheveningen and pronounced the session 'very good – lots better than the other one here'. He was absolutely right: two of the sides were outstanding – 'Chicago' and 'Meditation' – and two were satisfactory: 'What Harlem is to Me' and 'Netcha's Dream'.

The opening ensemble of 'Chicago' lacks the rhythmic elan of a top American band, but the lively arrangement is crisply played. Hawkins hugs the melody affectionately during his first solo then joins the rest of the saxophones for a slightly blemished unison passage. He doesn't stray far from the tune during his subsequent solo but incorporates some marvellous shafts of exploration that seem to add zest to the band's performance. There's a brief, bright trumpet solo then the whole band regather to punch out an arrangement studded with jutting, climactic phrases.

'Meditation' is the outstanding recording from the date. It's an intriguing composition by Jack Bulterman, the arrangement full of subtle tone colours. Hawkins is at his most majestic when answering the muted brass section's whisperings; the eloquent phrases pour out of the tenor sax, then a tightly muted trumpet solo (inspired by Arthur Whetsol's work with Duke Ellington) shines out over a trombone and saxophone choir. After a piano interlude Hawkins creates a ravishing mood using the slow tempo, the interesting chord sequence and the sympathetic arrangement to remarkable effect. He realized he had created an outstanding performance, and wrote soon afterwards, 'I think it's going to be one of my best records.'

Hawkins speaks a couple of atmospheric sentences at the beginning of 'What Harlem is to Me' but his playing on this track doesn't reach the heights of his performance on the previous number. There are some impressive bursts from Hawk, particularly where he echoes the band's phrasing, but the arrangement is quite ordinary. The saxophone section fail to achieve a smooth blend, and sound almost rough at the points where the baritone sax takes the lead; the attempts to set up a shuffle-rhythm in the backings are particularly disappointing.

The final tune of the session was a Hawkins composition, 'Netcha's Dream', inspired by a Dutch girlfriend, Antoine Berger who, as Netcha Berga, sang with a group called the Rhythm Brothers. The opening block-scoring for the band gets the performance off to a good start and Hawkins's responses sound in perfect accord with the arrangement, but during his solo (played over long backing notes) Hawk starts to meander slightly, drifting casually into romanticisms; the high phrases tumble out effortlessly but there is no sense of climax. During a band interlude intonations start to stray then Hawkins tries hard to lift the performance to great heights but doesn't succeed. Even so, Spike Hughes, reviewing the recording for the *Melody Maker*, was full of praise: 'Hawkins at this tempo is to me the most genuinely moving thing in jazz. He has rarely played more beautifully than in 'Netcha's Dream'.[15] As with his previous session with the Ramblers, second takes were subsequently issued; they show that Hawkins was consistently spontaneous when working with the Dutch band.

One of the Ramblers, trombonist Marcel Thielemans, said of Hawkins:

The man was a great performer (one of the greatest!) He never played the same things and always had brilliant *nouveautés*. He always had a bottle of whisky in his pocket, which he used while he was trying out his sax in a corner of the studio. Once on a broadcast, after a whole bottle, he sang with the band 'What Harlem is to Me'. I never heard him sing again. He was always well dressed, did not talk much – a gentleman.'[16]

Soon after making the recordings with the Ramblers Hawkins returned to Laren to play a residency at the Hamdorff Hotel, fronting a seven-piece band. He found the town a little too sleepy: 'Laren is very nice, but unnecessarily quiet; it would eventually run me crazy.' He soon returned to The Hague and enjoyed entertaining Arthur Brigg's band (who were visiting Holland) at a party in his room at the Hotel Americain. Hawkins enjoyed the company of his Dutch friends, but took especial pleasure in meeting up with American expatriates, confessing in a letter, 'I'm getting tired of this broken English.'

Europe in the 1930s was not, by any means, totally free of ill feeling towards black people, but Hawkins, perhaps because of his bearing and his expensive clothes, did not get involved in any serious contretemps concerning race. He was amused, and sometimes vexed, when local jazz critics praised only black musicians, automatically excluding white performers from any listing of favourites. Having always kept an open mind when listening to jazz musicians, he had difficulty in making Europeans understand that there were some white jazz musicians whose work he genuinely enjoyed. Years later he commented on this: 'Way back, as far as the days I went to England, I had the same trouble with people believing it over there, probably from reading about it in magazines. After all, I played with Benny Goodman and all of them and I didn't know any clarinet player that played more than Benny.'[17]

During October 1935 Hawkins continued to make The Hague his base, but by then he had moved into an apartment at Spui 34. He did a series of broadcasts, some of which could be heard in Britain, others performed exclusively for transmission in the Dutch East Indies. On some of the radio programmes Hawkins worked with Freddy Johnson. One of these (broadcast from Hilversum) was reviewed in the *Melody Maker*; the preponderance of slow numbers was criticized but a five-chorus version of 'Sweet Sue' was enthusiastically praised. After one show Hawk noted, 'I had the grand compliment from a certain young lady that my creations over the radio sounded as classics.' On these shows the choice of material was left to Hawkins, who boldly (and perhaps unwisely) decided to sing 'I'm In the Mood For Love' on the 14 October transmission.

Hawkins played a concert at the Tivoli Theatre in Utrecht on 2 November with Nico van Oostrum's Hot Mixers and also worked with altoist Red Debroy's band at the Casino in Den Helder (Debroy's real name was Ben Bakema, founder of the famous Dutch jazz magazine *De Jazzwereld*). Hawk called these engagements 'intermediate jobs'; he played them while contemplating an offer he'd received to work in Switzerland. He decided to accept the invitation and left Holland in late November 1935 to journey to Zurich, where he began a December residency at the Corso Bar.

9
Family Tragedy

Hawkins's successes in Switzerland were just as great as those he had enjoyed in other parts of Europe. During the winter of 1935–36 he worked in St Moritz (where he learnt to ski), in Engelsburg, in Berne and in Lausanne. But his main base was in Zurich, where he stayed at the Pension Metzger. He formed a close friendship with a young local girl and was delighted to report that she owned a new American Buick automobile. But he also charmed numerous other women during his stay in Switzerland; so much so that when he made a private recording of himself singing and playing 'I Can't Give You Anything But Love' (in January 1936) several of these admirers fondly imagined that it was an exclusive confession of Hawk's admiration.

But Hawkins still maintained his intense correspondence with Renée Gertler, often detailing in his letters the music that was giving him pleasure. He mentioned being impressed by Ambrose's band (from England) and always tried to hear Willie Lewis's broadcast from Paris so that he could hear Benny Carter 'swinging down'; but he preferred Freddy Taylor's band: 'Now they really swing.' He was less interested in what Duke Ellington was doing and preferred listening to Fletcher Henderson's band and Benny Goodman (he was later to be impressed by the Benny Goodman Trio's version of 'China Boy'). As always, though, he listened to all sorts of music and wrote (early in 1936) how much he loved Gypsy music: 'I have a Gypsy, Hungarian friend here, simply marvellous on his violin. I'm crazy about the way they slur up and down the violin playing those beautiful Hungarian melodies.' He wrote, in March 1936, 'I only play Opera these days, no kidding.' But music wasn't the only thing he played and he ruefully mentioned losing 800 Swiss francs (almost three months' wages for the average Swiss worker) during one session of poker.

Throughout this period the Swiss writer Johnny Simmen often encountered Coleman Hawkins in Rena-Kaufmann's Record Shop in

Zurich. Hawk regularly took the opportunity to sample the latest jazz-record releases, and the youthful Simmen was delighted to note the famous visitor's reactions. When Johnny asked whether Hawkins agreed that Chu Berry was the second greatest tenor player in the world, Hawk vehemently disputed this, saying that Bob Carroll and Ben Webster were superior to Berry. Hawkins retained a soft spot for Bob Carroll's work and had praised him to Hugues Panassié during his 1935 visit to Paris. At the record store Hawkins also became ecstatic about a recording of 'Nightfall' (made in Britain), featuring Benny Carter on tenor saxophone. He said, 'That's Benny Carter, the greatest musician in the world. He was fine on alto, even on trumpet, and his arranging is tops, but now he has found the instrument that suits him best.' Hawk went on to cite his favourite musicians, naming trumpeters Bobby Stark and Roy Eldridge, and trombonists Benny Morton, Sandy Williams, Jack Teagarden and Claude Jones, adding, 'Louis Armstrong is great. That's an understatement, but that young guy Roy Eldridge is blowing up a storm.'

Hawkins did only one studio recording session duing 1936. On 2 May, after returning from a brief season in Berne, Hawk recorded in Zurich with the Berries, a Swiss band led by Bernhard 'Berry' Peritz on drums. The main object of the date seems to have been to get Hawkins's recent composition 'Love Cries' down on wax. Hawkins had high hopes for this tune, composed the previous January; at one time he even considered going to Paris to record it. Eventually he decided to record the piece in Zurich, but unfortunately he chose to sing the lyrics himself.

Two days after the session Hawkins gave Renée Gertler an uncommitted assessment of the recording: 'I don't know how it will be. I tried to express how my love cries for you.' The rendering was doubtless sincere but Hawk's vocal is lamentable. Almost every great jazz musician has been tempted to sing on record but Hawk's efforts on 'Love Cries' must be close to the bottom of any league of merit measuring such performances. The tune itself is unmemorable and its unfolding by a section consisting of Hawkins and the three reed players of the Berries is marred by ill-matching vibratos. Hawk offers saving grace in the shape of a brief concluding solo but even this is poorly recorded. Indifferent sound quality also mars 'Sorrow' (usually credited to Hawkins but actually composed by 'Roy Brooks', a pseudonym for the band's pianist Ernest R. Berner). The melody, played by Ernest Hoellerhagen, is embroidered by Hawkins's skilful obbligato, but unfortunately Hawk's succeeding tenor solo is less satisfying. A burst of passion from Hawkins during the middle eight lifts the performance and his handsome glissando into the final section provides some grandeur for the concluding bars.

The full band assemble for an agitated version of 'Tiger Rag', which is taken at a tempo that was just about as fast as anything that Hawkins had recorded at this stage of his career. Hawk, who is featured throughout, is at his most energetic, playing some dazzling breaks and creating a series of bold tonal inflections during the final chorus; less satisfactory is the surfeit of fussy, note-packed phrases. On 'It May Not Be True' Hawk gives a detached reading of an ordinary slow fox-trot melody. During the latter stages of this particular recording he rattles through a series of double-timed phrases, proving that, despite the inferior musical company, he was still in full command of an awesome technique. If anything, the final numbers were more poorly recorded than the opening pair. All four titles were issued on Swiss Parlophone (the 'Love Cries' coupling was also issued in Britain), and the subsequent rarity of these recordings was something that Hawkins came to regard as something of a blessing.

Socially and musically the Berries were delighted to have the opportunity to work with Hawkins. Over fifty years later Bernhard Peritz was full of happy memories when interviewed by Johnny Simmen:

> As a musician, colleague and human being Hawk was a gentleman in every respect and in any situation. He made no differences, musically speaking, between himself and his Swiss associates. No stuff like 'I'm the great Hawkins.' One night my tenor player Omer de Cock had taken sick and Hawk was subbing for him. When I wanted to pay him for the night he refused to take any money, insisting that it was to be given to the ailing de Cock instead.

It seems there were no signs of Hawkins's avarice during his stay in Switzerland. On one occasion when Zurich's Mascotte Bar (where Hawk and the band worked) was closed for a religious holiday, the owner offered the musicians another gig at his restaurant in the small town of Duebendorf, but he could only guarantee them food, drink and whatever admission money was taken at the door. Hawk and the band accepted the deal. The star tenorist played gorgeously and enthusiastically, stimulated by an enormous intake of free whisky, but when Berry Perritz was given the total box-office receipts he realized that each musician would get only a few francs each. Each member of the band decided to give his share to Hawkins to compensate him for his benevolent gesture in playing the gig. Hawk, however, had picked up enough of his colleagues' language to realize what they were planning to do and he flatly refused the bonus, insisting that the money be shared equally.[1]

Hawkins then moved briefly out of Switzerland to visit Paris where, on 30 May, he guested with Willie Lewis's Orchestra on a radio show. It was the first occasion on which Lewis's trumpeter, Bill Coleman, had the chance to work with one of his musical heroes. The hour-and-a-half broadcast, relayed from Poste Parisien, was picked up and reviewed in London, where the *Melody Maker* correspondent 'Detector' wrote of Hawkins: 'From the loose floridity of his style here I am almost inclined to believe the wild rumours that he now never cares to play his horn excepting when he is under an obligation to do so.'[2]

Ernest Berner (who besides being pianist with the Berries was also the editor of the Swiss Magazine *Jazz*) wrote an enthusiastic – and highly imaginative – report of Hawk's recent Swiss recordings for the July 1936 issue of *Down Beat* magazine which appeared beneath the headline SWISS FANS GO CRAZY AS HAWKINS SINGS. Someone brought this article to the attention of Coleman's mother, Mrs Cordelia Hawkins, in St Joseph, Missouri. She then contacted Ernest Berner in Zurich (via Down Beat) with the surprising news that she hadn't heard from her son since he had left England two years earlier.

Berner supplied Mrs Hawkins with Coleman's address and the family correspondence resumed. Hawkins wasn't the first loving son to neglect writing to his mother (even though he found time to send love letters to girlfriends) but the two-year silence seems inexplicable. Unfortunately his mother had the saddest tidings for her distant son. Hawk's father, William D. Hawkins, had committed suicide by drowning himself in the Missouri River. The tragedy had occurred on 4 March 1935, in front of eye-witnesses. The *Saint Joseph News Press* of that date published a front-page story detailing the incident:

> In a nonchalant manner, Bill Hawkins, colored, sixty years old, stood on the bank of the Missouri River at noon today, lighted his pipe, adjusted his glasses, buttoned his dark-blue overcoat and calmly walked into the river at the foot of Francis Street.
>
> Miss Cornelius Plato and Arthur Adams, employees of the Pioneer Sand Co, saw Hawkins in the water and said that he floated in an eddy several minutes before he disappeared. Andrew Schleicher, another witness, said that Hawkins looked at a yellow piece of paper before he walked into the water.
>
> Hawkins was employed in the shipping department of the American Electric Co and had not been to work this morning. He lived at 1713 Angelique Street. Members of the fire department began dragging the river this afternoon in an effort to locate the body.

The Saint Joseph fire department were unsuccessful in their searches for the body, and it was two months before it was recovered (in May) way down river at Atchison, Kansas. The burial eventually took place on 14 July 1935 at the Mount Mora Cemetery in Saint Joseph. William Hawkins was actually sixty-two at the time of his death, having been born on 15 June 1872.[3]

News of these sad events reached Hawkins a year after they had taken place. All his grief seems to have gone inwards; he didn't refer to the tragedy in letters to friends or to those who worked with him. His nature had always been somewhat taciturn, but from this period onwards his personality became more contemplative and he was prone to sit alone for long periods. Though his stay in Europe proved to be a long one, Hawkins never made any serious attempts to master the various languages he encountered during his travels. He learnt to order drinks and food in French, German and Dutch, and could follow part of a conversation in those languages, but he never attempted to frame a detailed answer in anything other than English.

During the summer of 1936 Hawkins again worked in Zurich, but he also played a residency at the Chikito Club in Berne. His pianist there was Martin Roman, who (while touring Switzerland with Marek Weber's Orchestra) had first sat in with Hawkins at a club date in Fribourg:

> When I left the bandstand the audience applauded and I saw Hawkins applaud too. A few days later he came over in the afternoon to the hotel where our orchestra played. I introduced Marek Weber to him and Hawkins could not get over the sound of the orchestra and the sound of Weber's violin. After our tour in Switzerland ended I went back to Amsterdam; Marek Weber went to America. After two weeks back in Holland I received a letter from drummer Morris Einhorn telling me he was starting a five-piece band with Coleman Hawkins as leader. Coleman had asked for me, and would I accept a contract at the Chikito for eight weeks with option. Excellent money and trip paid. Never in my life did I say 'yes' so fast to anything. A few days later I went to Berne. They also hired a wonderful clarinettist and alto saxist Ernst Hoellerhagen and a trumpeter from Belgium. After a few days the band sounded as if we had played together a long time. Hawkins started to play and we heard sounds, effects and phrases including modulations which were unbelievable. I rented a piano on which Hawkins liked to fool around. He was not a great pianist but he knew the chords and had very unusual chord changes. I watched him and learned a lot of his changes. Coleman and I became close friends. I had gotten him a furnished room where I lived and we spent many evenings talking.
>
> When I asked him about Benny Goodman he told me that he was invited every Friday night to Goodman's house for 'gefilte fish' which Benny's mother made. Hawk said she only spoke very poor English. One day I made a big blunder. While

> sitting and talking with Hawkins about Benny Goodman I said, 'If I could play with Benny Goodman I would play for nothing.' I realized that I had said the wrong thing. Coleman looked at me and said, 'Why would you play for nothing? If you can play with me you can also play for Goodman.' Then I realized that I was playing with the world's greatest tenor saxophonist. A little while later I decided that I wanted to go back to Holland.[4]

Hawkins and Martin Roman later worked together in Holland but, after Berne, Hawk's next long residency was at the plush MacMahon Club in Geneva (commencing 18 September 1936). There he fronted a band consisting of René Van Dyck (piano), Ernest Maznit (bass), Gustave Dupuis (trumpet), Max Oberlé (clarinet doubling piano) and Morris Einhorn (drums). After Hawkins had settled in he arranged for the twenty-three-year old Dutch singer Ann Xhofleer (Anna Johanna Mari Xhofleer) to join the band, which she did for several months commencing October 1936.

Hawkins made a genuine attempt to cut down on his drinking but found it hard to do in such sybaritic surroundings. The only thing he yearned for was the opportunity to hear some good jazz being played live, as he explained to Renée: 'I'm getting so tired of hearing tangos and waltzes. I may take a trip to the States next summer in order to hear something good in Harlem; do you want to go with me? You know I've always said I would never return without you.'

The Geneva booking stretched well into 1937; it could have gone on longer but Hawkins decided to move on so that he could take up inviting offers to work elsewhere in Europe. He quit his apartment on the rue des Paquis and terminated his stay at the MacMahon Club on 18 April. He travelled from Geneva to Paris on 20 April in order to play a concert at the Salle Chopin (Pleyel) three days later. Accompanied by Jerry Mengo on drums, Marcel Bianchi on guitar, Stephane Grappelli on piano and Louis Dupont on double bass, Hawk shared the bill with another American guest star, trumpeter Henry Mason, whose playing on the concert was highly praised in *Jazz Hot* magazine.

From Paris Hawkins went on to Amsterdam to do a broadcast, then journeyed on to Laren to another Decca recording session with the Ramblers, on 26 April. In a whirl of activity he returned to Paris and on 28 April recorded with an all-star band (featuring Benny Carter), after which he travelled back to Amsterdam to play a special gala. He then did some more recordings before settling down for what he called 'my first days at ease in eight months'.

The Ramblers' session has little of the panache that marked the previous collaborations; the band, which had experienced a couple of personnel changes, never quite recapture the liveliness of the earlier dates with Hawkins. The drumming sounds stiff and the section work stilted on Jack Bulterman's composition 'I Wanna Go Back to Harlem'; nevertheless, Hawk expresses some unhackneyed ideas and develops his solo eloquently. Here and there it seems that Hawkins was incorporating some of Benny Carter's style into his lines, particularly in his phrases in the fifteenth and sixteenth bars, but there is no blatant copying. The pity of the track is that the military precision of the band seems to curtail the mood that Hawkins was attempting to establish.

On 'Consolation', another Bulterman composition, Hawkins creates a series of sensuous phrases against a background of muted brass, this blend of tone colours effectively complemented by the clarity of the guitarist's chording. After a four-bar piano interlude Hawk begins an adventurous solo that contains some almost eerie chromatic phrases. Again the arrangement does little to enhance the soloist's brilliance and the final section of the piece is a disappointment. Hawkins's tune 'A Strange Fact' is a hotch-potch. The incongruous introduction is followed by a makeshift melody and thereafter the too-closely voiced saxophone scoring curdles the interesting, exploratory lines Hawk creates in his solo.

The British magazine *Rhythm* cited 'Original Dixieland One Step' as one of the shortest instrumentals ever recorded; it lasts only one minute and fifty-four seconds. It's an exercise in clipped phrasing by the band. Hawkins doesn't seem interested in expanding the basic chord sequence and chooses to stir up excitement by deliberately repeating a high-note pattern. As with the other titles from this date, two takes of the performances were issued; on the second version of 'One Step' Hawk takes a much lighter approach. Bulterman's arrangement of 'Smiles' begins with thirty-two bars of muted brass, then Hawkins launches an emotive solo, the opening part of which contains some effective 'crying' phrases; they may not have been apt for the tune's title but they are musically potent. Unfortunately the final bars of Hawk's solo seem to be devoted to a display of technique, as though he were trotting out virtuoso phrases simply for effect. The saxophone section seem to be influenced by their admiration for Benny Carter's style of phrasing, though their homage seems to be more painstaking than brilliant. Apart from a brief muted trumpet solo on 'Smiles', a fleeting piano interlude on 'Consolation' and the even briefer alto-sax runs on 'One Step', all the instrumental solos on the date are played by the honoured guest. Hawk ended this flurry of recordings by making 'Someone is Gonna Give Me Away' accompanied by Freddy Johnson on piano and the Ramblers' bassist, guitarist and drummer. It's a straightforward, informal work-out on an unelaborate thirty-two-bar chord sequence. The melody is an amalgam of standard licks of the time, and although Hawkins and Johnson produce effervescent solos their inspiration is sometimes curtailed by the stiff drumming.

Hawkins was pleased with the results of the session and delighted that the *Melody Maker* praised 'Consolation'. He admitted, 'I'm rather crazy about it myself.' But that an artist is not always the best judge of his own work is a fact confirmed by Hawk's assessment of the recordings he made two days later in Paris, of which he wrote, 'The records are really just "jam sessions", nothing very musical.' In fact, the French recordings from 28 April 1937 are among the finest that Hawkins ever made. Critics differ as to which is the particular masterpiece of the four titles recorded, but at least one of the tunes from this Paris date occupies a place in any listing of Coleman Hawkins's ten best recordings.

Hugues Panassié and Charles Delaunay were responsible for organizing the session; they also encouraged the idea of using a front line consisting of two alto saxophone and two tenors. For this experiment they booked two of the leading French saxophonists, altoist André Ekyan and tenorist Alix Combelle, to work alongside Benny Carter and Coleman Hawkins. Carter, who sketched out arrangements for two of the tunes to be recorded, was available for the date, having left Britain on 20 March when his work permit expired. He spent some time in Amsterdam then moved on to Paris. The rhythm section for the recording consisted of one American – drummer Tommy Benford – and three Europeans; Stephane Grappelli on piano, Eugene d'Hellemmes on bass and Django Reinhardt on guitar. A coupling from the session ('Honeysuckle Rose' and 'Crazy Rhythm') became the first issue on a new French record label Swing (one of the first specialist jazz labels in the world).

Soon after arriving in a taxi with Panassié, Hawkins took out his saxophone and by way of a warm-up blew some choruses on 'Honeysuckle Rose', accompanied by Stephane Grappelli on piano. Panassié and Delaunay were amazed and delighted by what they heard, and despite the treasures that emerged from the subsequent session Panassié always regretted that this preliminary duet wasn't recorded.[5]

On the recording of 'Honeysuckle Rose' Django Reinhardt plays a lighter rhythmic role than usual and this approach assists the flow of the opening chorus where the sax team achieve admirably smooth co-ordination. Hawkins surpasses himself in his solo, creating improvisations that form a model of passionate eloquence. During the middle section of his solo his interleaving ideas seem to have taken him to the top of a creative mountain, but the ingenuity of his final eight bars lifts him to an even higher peak. Reinhardt's brief fill-ins are a joy and Carter's eight-bar solo a perfect miniature.

'Crazy Rhythm' is taken at a fast clip, but this doesn't prevent the front line from again achieving an attractive cohesion. Ekyan emerges first and creates a lively, earnest solo, reminiscent of good, rough wine; Combelle follows on and produces a smoother blend in his chorus. Considering that these two musicians were working in close proximity to recognized masters they perform in an admirably relaxed fashion. Some years later Combelle spoke of this session:

> It was a wonderful slice of luck for us. Needless to say we were right on our toes. I can remember that after the first take of 'Crazy Rythm' Benny said to Coleman, 'Man, that ain't the way it should go,' as if to make him realize he'd have to get down to it. Obviously neither of them had anything to gain from this encounter, whilst we had nothing to lose. I dare say that's why the record came off so well.[6]

After Combelle's solo, Benny Carter enters the picture and blows some superbly balanced phrases, each cleverly linked in a way that lets the solo glide effortlessly forward. After a period during which he had been recording with inferior players Hawkins is made to realize that he again has a top-class improviser with whom to contend. He begins his defence by issuing brief, rifflike patterns that soon give way to long, loping phrases, accented in a way that generates excitement. Amazingly his second chorus is even better than his first; in it he creates a stunning mosaic by calling on his seemingly limitless knowledge of harmony and utilizing his peerless sense of rhythm. The neatly devised sign-off figure that concludes the arrangement finally staunches the flow of Hawkins's powerful ideas. So the unusual front line had triumphed, producing a succession of impressive solos without receiving any exceptional support from a rhythm section balanced in a way that left the piano practically inaudible. On the other two (unarranged) numbers from the session Carter demonstrates his remarkable versatility by moving on to trumpet; Alix Combelle swops from tenor sax to clarinet.

After an elegant guitar introduction Carter plays the opening melody of 'Out of Nowhere', using an incisive-sounding mute to give added bite to his phrasing. Hawkins then takes over and creates a masterpiece of improvisation. This 1931 melody was (according to Russell Procope) a number that Hawkins had played as a feature with Fletcher Henderson's Orchestra. Perhaps memories of earlier, happy days had suddenly surfaced within Hawk's mind, but whatever the felicitous reason, something inspired him. He moves gracefully and constructively through the intricate chord sequence, creating phrases that are rhythmically, harmonically and emotionally as satisfying as anything he had previously recorded.

Hawk's lead-in phrase, based on triplet patterns, cleverly heralds attention for the opening bars of his chorus, which are magnificently structured. He begins by playing a G for two beats, rising in the next bar to an F of similar length; he then descends to a slightly longer F sharp. This example of superior musical architecture is only one of the admirable aspects of the solo. Rhythmically there are daring runs that almost defy notation; harmonically there are shrewdly introduced deviations where Hawkins anticipates (or carries over) a chord change to make an already attractive sequence glow with modernity, and the series of glissandi in his second chorus epitomize his near-infallible technique. Above all, the outstanding feature of the solo is the wealth of feeling with which Hawkins infuses every single phrase.

'Sweet Georgia Brown' opens with a lively drum introduction, then Carter (on trumpet) announces the tune; around him his front-line colleagues chip in with the sort of phrases that exemplify a 1930s jam session. All the soloists again hit veins of rich creativity, with Hawkins managing to impart a feeling of delicacy to the second half of his improvisation. The bulk of the performance is given over to jammed ensembles in which the excitement rises and falls intermittently, making it the weakest side of the four: the spontaneity of a jam session offers one of the most exciting prospects in jazz, but all too often the necessary passion evaporates in the atmosphere of a recording studio. Nevertheless, 'Sweet Georgia Brown' retains a lot of vigour and enthusiasm. Overall this was a highly productive session, one on which Hawkins was stimulated by the skills and ardour of his fellow participants, despite being nearly exhausted by his recent helter-skelter journeys throughout Europe. The presence of Benny Carter in particular put Hawkins on his mettle, and in turn Hawk's playing stimulated Carter. This was exactly what Charles Delaunay had hoped for: 'I was sure someone like Benny Carter, who was kind of, let's say the word lazy, wouldn't do nothing special unless someone, something happened and they had to give of their best, and that's what happened.'[7]

Another factor assisted Hawk's creativity: the session in Paris didn't begin until nine at night, a time that certainly suited his body clock. Hawk loved the night atmosphere of the French capital and didn't need much persuading to sit in with various bands. The French jazz enthusiast, Maurice Cullaz, recalled: 'Once he played in a little joint on the rue Pigalle, somewhere like that, and everybody was crying, even the man at the door was crying, Hawk could play so much, with such feeling.'[8]

Hawkins returned to The Hague, enjoyed a brief, restful vacation then worked for a few days with pianist Freddy Johnson at the Negro Palace, Thorbecke-plein, Amsterdam. On 26 May the two men recorded duet versions of a couple of the tunes that formed part of the set of Hawkins's compositions that had been published by Peter Maurice in London. Hearing the sympathetic backing that Johnson provides for Hawkins, it is easy to understand why the tenorist had such a high regard for the pianist's work, but despite their empathy the duet recordings are unsatisfying. 'Lamentation' is a tender but studied etude, and 'Devotion' sounds like a painstakingly conceived aria.

In May 1937 Hawk played various casual dates in Holland, including one at Dierentuin, The Hague (on the 23rd) with his German friend, the pianist Martin Roman and two Dutch musicians, altoist Gerry Pohl and drummer Theo Koppes. By this times Roman and Hawkins had resumed their socializing. 'One day,' recalls the pianist,' I wrote a song called "Martin's Melody". He loved it so much that we started to play it. I also wrote an arrangement for him with a rhythm section and four clarinets. We recorded it but I lost the recordings, which were irreplaceable.'[9] Vocalist Ann Xhofleer (who was for a time Martin Roman's partner) played her part in this project; she recalls, 'We, Martin Roman, Coleman Hawkins and me lived in The Hague, in the same pension. We made a record with Coleman Hawkins: "Say It Isn't So". Martin made the arrangement. Whatever happened to the record I don't remember; it's too long ago.'[10]

Through a Mr Strasser of the SML factory in Paris, Hawkins heard that a Belgian promoter (F.R. Faecq) was interested in booking him for engagements in Brussels. Early in June 1937, from his apartment at Torenstraat 92, The Hague, Hawk diligently followed up this prospect by post. Letters soon flowed between the two parties, the contents of which reveal that Hawk was a shrewd operator. In his handwritten letter to Faecq (dated 12 June 1937) Hawk made his stipulation:

> Re this contract you have sent me. I shall sign it with the omission of articles 5 and 6. I can't be expected to sign such an article unless I'm guaranteed work of a more extensive calibre. I have assured you that I'm willing to pay commission on anything you might arrange for me, but if I'm in Brussels and you have nothing for me and someone else does, naturally I would take it, if it were interesting. Of course I should prefer to work under your organization and am willing to give you first choice. But I think it's rather a large request asking me not to take anything else in Brussels for four months after having only a concert guaranteed. Of course you can be assured that I won't do anything in Brussels before the concert. And you may tell Mr Packay [the promoter] that my program will consist of all the old favorites, and I'm sure he knows all of these; ask him if he has 'Blue Skies' and 'Body and Soul'.

Agreement was reached and the concert, Hawk's first ever engagement in Belgium, took place on 30 June 1937 at the Palais des Beaux-Arts in Brussels. It was here that Belgian jazz writer Albert Bettonville first met Hawkins. The youthful Bettonville introduced himself as a jazz critic, saying he'd heard all of Hawkins's recordings.

> He looked at me suspiciously. I stopped talking about jazz and said I was a professional photographer. That was also a lie; I had just bought my Rolleiflex a few weeks before. But he was more or less interested and I took some portraits of him. We met again later on and I showed him the photos. One, lit with a spot very close to his face, made us laugh for the first time together. The ice was broken. This photo to me was a flop, horrible to see. The spotlight was too near Hawk's face, and made him look like a frog and his skin was white. But he said, 'That's it, that's it!' I said, 'Are you kidding?' He said, 'I want that snap in a bigger size and I want it published.' The following year the strange photo appeared on the cover of a program. Every time we met in later years Hawk always remembered the froggy-snap and asked for more copies to offer his girlfriends.[11]

Hawk temporarily left Belgium and moved back into Holland to work at the Hotel Kurhaus in Scheveningen, where he and pianist Freddy Johnson guested with Benny Carter's Orchestra on a 22 June radio broadcast. One of the saxophonists in Carter's group was Jamaican-born Louis Stephenson, who – like the rest of the band – was delighted to be working with Hawkins:

> It was marvellous to hear that great sound at close quarters, but off-stage he was a very quiet fellow. He was certainly one for the girls, and they seemed to go for him too. The wife of someone in our band went for Hawk in a big way from the moment she first saw him. She came over to Scheveningen with her husband but she couldn't stay away from Hawk and a brief affair developed. I don't know if she ever saw Hawk after this, probably not. Years later I saw her working as a bus conductress. I didn't see a trace of musical or social rivalry between Coleman and Benny Carter;

they seemed to be jolly together, well met, both fantastically advanced musicians, but I would say that overall Benny was the more intelligent of the two.[12]

Hawk soon returned to Belgium and began working with trumpeter Roger de Kers's band at the Scala in Ostend. Albert Bettonville renewed acquaintanceship with Hawk there:

This time we were old friends. No talking much, however. After hours he was feeling lonely. The Belgian musicians were going to bed. Not Hawk and I. We had the same routine at an all-night cafe-restaurant, ordering night after night the same food: two tomatoes, two eggs with salt, gherkins, French bread, butter and whisky. Nothing else. In fact I never saw him eat differently 'after hours'.

We never talked seriously about jazz, but often about the Belgian inventor of the saxophone, Adolphe Sax. He was extremely interested to know the difficult life of Sax, and to learn about all the curious instruments that he had built. Some nights we were talking about girls and went to a few bars to find female company, but Hawk said, 'A good girl is hard to find.' Anyway, in one of these nightspots we met a girl who had heard Coleman play 'Stardust' at the Scala earlier that night; she was in love with the tune. We stayed there; she was drinking champagne and Hawk whisky, until six o'clock in the morning. Hawk didn't pay, nor did I. I was always broke, I never bought Hawk a drink and he never bought me one. So who paid that night? I think it was Pauline, the girl. And it was the same for the rest of the week.

One night, finally, we started talking about jazz. Hawk said he needed to hear another band other than the one he was working with, Roger De Kers's, good though it was. I told him that Willie Lewis was playing at the Casino in Knokke-Le-Zoute, not too far from Ostend. We immediately hired a horse-drawn cab, bought a bottle of whisky and arrived singing at Knokke at about 2.30 in the morning. The contact with Willie Lewis's musicians, Bill Coleman, Herman Chittison, Adelaide Hall, etc, was sensational. Of course, Hawk joined the band for a jam. This was now six o'clock in the morning; all the customers and all the waiters had already gone to bed, the sun was rising. About nine o'clock in the morning we all went on to the beach; all the musicians were riding bicycles.[13]

Benny Carter, like Hawkins, was enjoying a long stay in Europe. His itinerary during the summer of 1937 included a three-month booking in Holland (4 June until 5 September) at the Hotel Kurhaus in Scheveningen where he led a ten-piece 'international' band, which included the Scottish trombonist, George Chisholm. He recalled:

We played afternoon and evening sessions with Benny Carter's band at the Kursal in Scheveningen; during the afternoons we played outside in the open air. Coleman Hawkins came down some afternoons to listen. He'd sit there with a bottle and a glass, and when he'd downed that he'd sometimes go off and fetch his tenor to sit in. But the funny thing was that he'd sit in with the brass section, not the reeds. Benny

> Carter seemed not to mind this, which after all was quite a strange thing to do, but Benny was such a gentleman he wouldn't say anything and anyway there was a sort of friendly rivalry between the two. Hawkins sat next to me and kept urging me to take another chorus, sort of geeing me up.[14]

The non-American musicians within Carter's band were delighted to be working with such a distinguished leader and Carter, for his part, seemed satisfied with their efforts. Later he politely, and honestly, summarized the difference between their performances and those by musicians with whom he'd worked in the USA: 'It would be unfair to compare them to the musicians back in America. They would be found wanting. If you expected a black American musician to be proficient at playing Hungarian Gypsy music you wouldn't be quite fair either.'[15]

Benny Carter's stay in Holland led to several social reunions with Hawkins, and they soon re-established their friendship, exchanging news of mutual friends who lived in the USA and Britain. But alongside this camaraderie there was something that Hawkins once acknowledged (to Renée Gertler) as 'professional jealousy', though the feeling might have been more aptly described as 'professional competitiveness'. Leonard Feather encountered this when he began making plans for Hawkins to record with a contingent from Benny Carter's band; 'Coleman Hawkins was so reluctant to record as a sideman (even with featured billing) that I had to make a special trip to The Hague where he was working to talk him into it.'[16]

Eventually Hawkins was persuaded to take part in an August 1937 session, which also featured pianist Freddy Johnson, plus Carter and his sidemen: George Chisholm, Jimmy Williams on clarinet and alto sax, Ray Webb on guitar, Len Harrison on string bass and a black drummer from Martinique, Robert Montmarche. Benny Carter, courteous as ever, made no effort to hog the proceedings and paid deference to Hawk's skills by featuring him on each of the four titles that the octet recorded. On 'Somebody Loves Me' Carter takes the first chorus on trumpet, stressing the melody in a way that prevents the front line's jamming from disintegrating into chaos. Freddy Johnson's dexterous piano solo is followed by a chorus shared between Williams on clarinet (thin-toned and sounding anxious) and Chisholm on trombone (robust and adventurous) then Hawkins shapes an opulent solo that effectively builds up steam as he enters his second chorus. Intricate ideas flow through the agile runs, most of which are in skeins of legato phrasing. The final eight bars of the record are jammed by the enthusiastic ensemble.

In contrast, Leonard Feather's composition 'Mighty Like the Blues' is presented in a neatly scored arrangement. Carter establishes the melody nicely on trumpet, but the ensuing solo by Hawkins sounds staid, created in a way that seems to rest too heavily on the two-beat pattern the rhythm section is emphasizing. Chisholm's muted solo is impressive, but Carter's sixteen-bar outing on clarinet is the wondrously constructed highlight of the performance.

Looking back, Chisholm said:

> Playing on a recording session with Carter and Hawkins was a tremendous experience, but on that particular day I had a sore lip, which was a rarity for me; it had swollen up. I cursed and cursed. Hawkins saw that it was puffed up and said, 'I know just what will fix that.' He went away and came back with a tumbler full of clear liquid. I thought it was some kind of medicament, or a salve to put on my lip, but all he said was, 'Drink this,' which I did. It was pure vodka, and as I didn't drink at this period of my life it hit me quite dramatically. It didn't cure the swelling, but it certainly made me forget about it. In fact there's not much about that session that I can remember.'[17]

Carter demonstrates his versatility by reverting to trumpet for the jammed opening of 'Pardon Me Pretty Baby'. He then allocates Chisholm a twenty-four-bar solo showing a good deal of spirited individualism. Williams on clarinet is efficient and listenable in his brief eight-bar solo but Carter (now on alto sax) takes over and instantly moves the artistic content of the recording several degrees higher, patterning ingenious ideas into elegant cadences. Hawkins's entry seems burly in comparison, but it soon becomes clear that Hawk has chosen the right strategy because Carter, with amazing speed, switches back to trumpet for a series of four-bar exchanges with the tenor saxist. It's a close match until the final bars, where Hawkins conjures up an adventurous and highly tuneful riposte. Freddy Johnson solos well, but he is poorly balanced and ill served by an indifferent piano.

The octet finished their session with 'My Buddy', the distant piano playing of Johnson paving the way for a sixteen-bar solo from Carter, on alto sax, which is eloquence itself. Chisholm's tightly muted trombone maintains the impetus despite the ponderous sounds of the rhythm section (who have lost the lightly swinging feel they maintained for most of the session). Hawkins enters with a totally emphatic phrase, stressing the angularity with a series of masterfully placed accents. During the course of a superb solo he casually exhibits various aspects of his talent, playing with a handsome, wide tone, shifting the rhythmic emphasis by anticipating some notes and suspending others, all the while developing the contours of his improvisations in a way that grips the listener's interest. The solo is modern enough to have been dropped comfortably into his recordings from a later decade, so although the session started uneventfully for Hawkins it ended with the creation of one of the best up-tempo performances from this part of his life.

For Hawkins and Freddy Johnson the day's work wasn't over. They remained at the studio to record four duets, two of which were rejected. After a sinister-sounding piano introduction Hawk performs the melody of 'Stardust', playing it at a faster tempo than on his 1935 Paris recording. The paraphrasing is bolder than on the earlier version but some of his timing is reminiscent of his stiff playing on 'Mighty Like the Blues'. Conceivably he was indulging in explorations that appeared inviting at that particular moment, but fortunately he didn't persist with them and his final chorus is smoothly conceived, with high and low notes curling effectively into appropriate phrases.

Hawk's composition 'Well Alright Then' is studded with fragmentary riff patterns. There is nothing harmonically advanced within the construction of the thirty-two-bar tune and Hawk demonstrates how skilfully he could develop his ideas over a basic chord sequence. He also cleverly introduces a series of brief motifs and then echoes them an octave higher. His performance is energetic – and mobile: on several occasions one can hear that he has moved his saxophone away from the recording microphone. One of the rejected numbers was simply entitled 'Blues'. This was not the sort of musical fare that appealed to Hawkins at this stage of his career; the item had been included at the behest of the session's organizer, Leonard Feather. Apropos of the number, Hawkins wrote, 'Made one of the plain blues for Leonard. He seems rather crazy about the blues, I don't know why.'

At this time of his recordings with Benny Carter, Hawkins was leading his own ten-piece band at the Mephisto on Binnenweg, Rotterdam. The group consisted mainly of Dutch musicians (including the star trombonist 'Pi' Scheffer); the two exceptions were Derek Neville (from Birmingham, England) on reeds, and trumpeter Johnny Claes (whose mother was Scottish and father Belgian). Claes, who later became a champion racing driver, first met Hawkins after writing a fan letter to him back in July 1934. Hawk heard Claes and Neville working in Valaida Snow's band at the Tabaris in The Hague; subsequently he took to visiting them (and sax player Reggie Dare) at a penthouse flat that the three dwelt in near the Tabaris. Neville recalled: 'Hawkins came and drank and jammed with us and I remember a sort of blackcurrant gin called Bessen that he was crazy about.'[18]

After Claes and Neville had finished touring with Valaida they joined Hawkins's band. 'This was in Rotterdam,' said Neville, 'at a place called Mephisto which had a bar, bandstand, tables and chairs but no dancefloor. Hawkins had printed arrangements which Johnny and I struggled through because we weren't too hot reading music.'[19] Neville also recalled the nonchalant way in which Hawkins wrote arrangements for the band at the Mephisto. He leant against the piano and steadily wrote out the various parts, totally unconcerned that the band were playing a totally dissimilar piece of music alongside him.[20]

Although Hawkins was regularly receiving offers to work in various European countries, there were no prospective engagements in Britain. The omission vexed Hawk and he again contacted Jack Hylton's Agency in London expressing the hope that a way could be found to circumvent the stringent rules governing the entry of foreign musicians into Britain. During the summer of 1937 Willie Lewis offered Hawkins the chance to work as a 'permanent guest star' with his band, but as Hawk didn't fancy the prospects of being a sideman again, albeit a heavily featured one, he declined the offer.

Hawk was delighted that Freddy Johnson was able to work with him regularly on his next long booking at Amsterdam's Negro Palace during the period September–November 1937; commenting on his pleasure Hawk wrote, 'naturally that means continuous swing'. The third member of the trio was the Dutch drummer Maurice van Kleef (born Amsterdam, 1908). Django Reinhardt, touring Holland with the Quintette du Hot Club de France, called into the Negro Palace and took part in a memorable jam session with the resident trio. A Dutch reporter described the results as: 'The most interesting swing session ever to take place in Holland.'[21]

Pete Felleman, then a young jazz fan, was a regular visitor to the Palace:

> I first heard Coleman Hawkins with Jack Hylton's Orchestra. I was only about fourteen years old, and didn't speak with Hawk then, but I was tremendously impressed by him and by Jack Hylton's Orchestra, which seemed to me to be much better than the Dutch bands we had at that time; they were strictly from hunger. When Hawk played regularly in Amsterdam during late 1937 I was at the Palace nearly every night, maybe forty-five visits. it was called the Negro Palace, but then it became known simply as 'the Palace'; I don't know if Hawk suggested the change. I

got to know him and we would often talk about music. At first I only wanted to talk about Johnny Dodds and Jimmy Noone, but Hawk said, 'You're only a young man, why don't you listen to Artie Shaw and Benny Goodman?' He became my jazz teacher, mentor and guru. He totally surprised me by saying that he thought that Benny Goodman's band played Fletcher Henderson's arrangements better than Fletcher's own band had done.'

I often went to London and always came back with jazz records. Hawk would ask me what was new, and then he'd borrow them and listen to them: the Lionel Hampton sides, Roy Eldridge's 'Florida Stomp', lots of stuff on Vocalion. I think Hawk was, by this time, too tight with his money to buy records, but he loved to hear them. I used to listen to some jazz broadcasts that were relayed once a month from America (via the BBC) and I'd tell Hawk who was going to be on. Once I mentioned that the Casa Loma band were going to be on the programme, but I didn't plan to listen to them. Hawk laughed and said, 'Well they may not mean anything to you, but you should listen, particularly to their trumpeter, Sonny Durham; he's really something.'

Hawk was my first black contact. I had loved jazz ever since I was a kid, but he was the first black person I ever conversed with. He didn't stand for any racial bullshit; I am sure that he came to Europe in the first place because of the racial issue in the States. I used to sit about two metres away from Hawk when he was at the bar of the Palace. His brand of Scotch then was Black and White; he bought a full bottle from the barman at the start of the evening and by the end of the night the bottle was empty, and if one of the customers offered him a drink he'd accept a double. But he never appeared in the slightest degree drunk, he drank in a distinguished way with his pinky finger stuck out. If he did any drinking of Bessen Jenever he never did it on a gig. He kept up his macho image in public, and Bessen might be thought of by some people as a lady's drink; it was a sweet gin made from berries, and just like some men like candy, some like Bessen.

Hawk said he hated talking about music, but this wasn't strictly true because he liked discussing the records he'd borrowed from me. What he so disliked was talking about his early recordings; he'd say, 'Then was then and now is now,' and that ended the discussion. I think he hated to be thought of as being old enough to have made records with Mamie Smith. He was always a little reserved, a little superior I think, what the Americans call a 'boss man'. Even though I was a regular at the Palace Hawkins didn't pay much attention to me, but this changed dramatically when I took along my beautiful twenty-year-old sister Betty. Hawk was as friendly as could be towards me and said, 'How's the old boy today?' Girls were his hobby; he had short legs but he was very good-looking and he used to serenade the girls with his sax. They were fascinated. The tenor saxist Johnny Russell once said to me, 'Every goddamn town I ever played had a girl there chasing Hawkins.' At the Palace Hawk's regular girlfriend was called Teddi; she was Dutch, about twenty, with dark hair, fair complexion and rosy cheeks, so attractive.[22]

Occasionally at weekends Hawkins temporarily left the Negro Palace residency to play lucrative gigs elsewhere, guesting with Dutch bands. On consecutive Saturdays in November 1937 he worked with the Old Victoria Band at such places as the Casino in 's-Hertogenbosch and the plush Het Zuid Hotel in Breda. A December 1937 report of these events in *De Jazzwereld* praised Hawk's 'inspiration and fierceness' and 'his calm and modest personality'; on such occasions Hawk usually based his programme on tried-and-true standards such as 'Dinah' and 'Stardust'.

In late 1937 Hawkins left Holland to return to Switzerland where he played a season at the Sihlporte Restaurant in Zurich (en route he made a one-night 'social stop' in Paris); after Zurich he moved on to St Moritz. The Swiss writer Johnny Simmen had occasion in 1951 to discuss this period of Hawk's life with the Swiss musician Ernst Hoellerhagen who roomed with Hawk in Arosa and St Moritz. Apparently Hawk did his best to hear broadcasts by Cab Calloway's Orchestra (relayed from America via short-wave radio), his main interest being in listening, intently, to Chu Berry's tenor-sax solos. 'But,' said Simmen, 'according to Ernst, although Hawkins would praise Ben Webster and other tenor players generously, when it came to Chu he would put on an uninterested face and say, "Not bad, but nothing special." ' On one occasion Simmen himself raised the question of Chu Berry's recording and Hawk's response was similar; 'They're not bad, but they're nothing special. Alix Combelle in France is just as good.'[23]

One night Johnny Simmen had the pleasure of visiting the apartment of Ernest Berner, pianist with the Ramblers and manager of Hawkins's Swiss bookings. Berner had asked Simmen to call 'a few minutes past midnight, and bring some of your best new records along. We'll have a session with Hawk. He wants to know what's happening in the USA music-wise.' Simmen obliged. Hawkins didn't arrive until around 2 a.m. 'pretty high, very tired', but after Mrs Berner had prepared some eggs and bacon for him he perked up and after a few gins became lively company, offering a stream of comments about the various jazz recordings that were being played.

Of Louis Armstrong's 'Jubilee' he said, 'Just great. You see about ten or fifteen years ago Louis was so much ahead of everybody that he became the inspiration for all of us. Lately I heard a few records of his where I thought he was repeating himself. But of course we all have our off-days. But this one is fantastic. Play it again.'

Hawk enjoyed listening to a record by Fats Waller, but thought he should change his sideman more often to increase variety on the sessions. Ernest Berner interposed by asking: 'You like Gene Sedric?'

Hawkins replied, 'Yes, I like him.'

Berner went on, 'Robert Goffin in his book said that Sedric is one of the greatest musicians of them all.'

Hawkins simply said, 'Well everybody is entitled to their opinions.'

Hawkins was full of praise for Roy Eldridge's playing and also enjoyed hearing altoist Pete Brown on Frankie Newton's Uptown Serenaders: 'Very original style, modern and swinging. Pete Brown has been around a long time, but it's only lately that he's found himself his own style.'

Hawk was expansive about Lionel Hampton's recording of 'Buzzin' Around with the Bee', praising Hampton's ideas and harmonic sense, adding, 'Cootie Williams plays well, always does, although I don't go much for that growl stuff. I prefer him on open horn.' He also said, 'John Kirby is my favorite bass player. He's another one that I'll hire for my band when I'm home,' Hawk then went on to praise Cozy Cole's drumming.

When Hawk's recording of 'Consolation' (made with the Ramblers) was played he said modestly, 'It could be worse,' but was full of enthusiasm for Herschel Evans's playing on Count Basie's 'Sent for You Yesterday': 'He probably did listen to me, but he's got a sound of his own; that's not my sound, there are differences.' Hawk then spoke warmly about Bill Coleman's trumpet playing and Dickie Wells's trombone work on sides they had recently made in Paris with Django Reinhardt, of whom Hawkins said: 'He's the genius of the guitar.'

The nocturnal playing of records ended when a neighbour began banging on the wall of Ernest Berner's apartment, but Johnny Simmen had other occasions to observe Hawk's reactions to recordings during his continued visits to Rena-Kaufmann's record store where the tenor saxist had struck up a friendship with the platinum-blonde salesgirl. Elsewhere, Simmen had the opportunity to hear Hawkins serenading a girlfriend by singing 'I'm in the Mood for Love' (accompanying himself on the piano). This was in the back room of Zurich's der Gelbe Schnabel, and Hawk's performance of the song was so emotional that the girl finally broke down in tears.

Clearly Hawkins had lost none of the charm that so appealed to his many female admirers, but during his stay in Zurich (in December 1937) he received the news from Renée in London that she had become engaged to marry Leslie Diamond. There is no doubt that Hawkins, despite his many romances, was bitterly disappointed to learn of Renée's plans; nevertheless he sent a gallant message of congratulations: 'Every good wish for your coming marriage.' Hawkins eventually became a good friend of Leslie Diamond, but temporarily his correspondence with Renée ceased.

10
Home Again

Hawkins returned to Holland on 1 January 1938 and set up a temporary base in Utrecht, near to where the trio (Hawkins, Johnson and van Kleef) were due to play a month's residency at the Hotel Poll in De Bilt. During this booking the trio was invited (by Ed Crommelin) to play at a forthcoming Jazz Liga concert at the Dierentuin in The Hague. Hawk replied from De Bilt on 11 January 1938: 'As we will be engaged that night (12 February) until 11.30, we can arrive in Den Haag at one o'clock ready. I would have to insist upon the conditions being no less than 175 guilders for the trio.' As the average weekly wage for a police officer (or a semi-skilled workman) was then about twenty-five guilders, the quotation proves that Hawk was used to earning a lot of money in those days. Ed Crommelin accepted the price, however, and as a result the trio appeared at the concert, delighting the 4,000 people who attended.

On 1 March 1938 the trio resumed working at the Negro Palace in Amsterdam. There, Hawkins continued to impress both the public and his fellow professionals. Alto saxist Louis Stephenson, the former Benny Carter sideman back in Holland with Eddie South's group, happened to be strolling near Thorbecke plain and heard some wonderful saxophone sounds floating on the night air:

> I said to myself, 'that's got to be Coleman Hawkins,' and so it was. I went into the place, which was not much more than a little bistro. Hawk was just working with piano and drums. As you stood at the bar it seemed as though his tone, a huge growling sound, was filling the club. But as I had noticed when I played with Hawkins, the further away from him you were, the more his sound blossomed. He had a wonderful way of projecting clarity.[1]

American visitors were no less impressed, particularly the members of Edgar Hayes's Orchestra who were touring Europe. Saxist Rudy Powell was entranced by the way that Hawkins played in Amsterdam and later said, 'I knew then that Hawk was really the master of the saxophone.'[2] When Edgar Hayes's musicians returned to New York it seemed as if they couldn't stop talking about Hawkins. This sort of word-of-mouth publicity – and the regular mentions of Hawkins that appeared in the American music magazines – served to remind his rivals that the king had not abdicated; he was simply in voluntary exile.

The trio built up a huge repertoire of neat arrangements during their four-month stay at the Negro Palace; they also developed a considerable musical understanding, as they demonstrated on a recording session at Laren on 14 June. The first item, 'Blues Evermore', is listed as a Coleman Hawkins composition, but it is nothing more than a series of variations on 'One Hour'. Hawkins (as on his original 1929 recording) plays an expansive introduction then forges an intense opening chorus. Freddy Johnson moves dexterously through his solo, after which Hawk creates a dramatic effect by deliberately stressing a discordant note in his re-entry phrase; van Kleef's drumming is neat and unobtrusive.

The teamwork of the three men is exemplified on a brisk version of 'Dear Old Southland'. Johnson's left-hand patterns are fluent and van Kleef's drumming positive without being distracting. Hawkins is in an experimental mood, but all his intricate ideas are followed through to their natural conclusion. The piece ends in a swirl of arabesques and the sound of fading tom-toms. Johnson's poised, unaccompanied piano work is a feature of 'Way Down Yonder in New Orleans'; this underrated musician later highlights his exemplary rhythmic sense with a series of off-beat chords that support Hawk's solo, these two then combining to create the stop-time patterns that provide a framework for van Kleef's nifty cymbal work.

'I Know that You Know' starts out as an unpretentious up-tempo workout, but during the final chorus the muse enters Hawkins and he produces some startlingly novel ideas. He is no less impressive on 'When Buddha Smiles', creating an absorbing effect by suddenly dropping into half-tempo. The informality of the session is made obvious by the sudden reduction in volume that occurs as Hawkins turns away from the microphone to signal to his two colleagues that the end of the piece was imminent.

'Swinging in the Groove' is a fast performance of a Hawkins tune reminiscent of the sort of film music that was used to suggest the hurly-burly of an American city's traffic. The drum chorus sounds freshly conceived, with a good array of enterprising ideas, but the most dramatic moments occur in the later stages of the piece where Hawk's phrases become positively ferocious. Fury was virtually unknown in the work of jazz soloists of the 1930s, but Hawk's playing here is the exception. Like a great actor Hawkins could convey all manner of moods but in these 'angry' bursts he pioneered a trait that became commonplace in the work of tenor saxists some thirty years later. It's noticeable that during the ten months that had elapsed since he was last in the recording studios his tone had thickened and (by design) had become slightly harsher.

The trio's contract at the Negro Palace lasted from March until August 1938, but during this period they occasionally played engagements elsewhere, including a concert held at the Palais des Beaux-Arts in Brussels on 13 April. For such shows Hawkins often toned down his programme by including a few commercial items; in Brussels, for instance he and Freddy Johnson sang a duet on 'Basin Street Blues', and performed a medley from the film *Shall We Dance?* But on club appearances Hawkins invariably played long versions of material that interested him. This freedom was a factor in the continuing development of his skills as an improviser. Although Hawk wasn't often emphatically challenged in Europe, as he would have been back home in an American jam session, his self-assured explorations were uncurtailed by commercial considerations or time limitations. His actual working hours were generally less in Europe than they had been in the USA but on a club bandstand he was his own master, able to take as many choruses as he liked.

Pete Felleman heard about the trio's plans to visit Belgium:

> I learnt that Hawk and the trio were also going to play a date in Ostend during the spring of 1938 so I somehow persuaded my father to give me enough money to make the trip. They played for dancing, afternoon and evening. I saw Hawk's girlfriend, Teddi, there and danced with her. Then I led her back to her seat near the bandstand. Hawk saw this and gave me a look that burnt me up. I thought that he would like it that a seventeen-year-old boy was asking his girl for a dance, but he was as mad as hell and came up to me and said, 'Don't even do that again, young man.' Yet I always felt that Teddi was doing some hustling for Hawk.[3]

The group took a summer vacation after their residency at the Negro Palace ended in August. Freddy Johnson, now acting as unofficial manager of the group, issued a statement saying that the trio planned to get together again to play another season at the Amsterdam club, beginning on 1 September 1938. Hawk soon got restless and moved into Belgium to appear as a guest star with Arthur Brigg's band, who were playing a season at Namur. Briggs enjoyed working with Hawkins:

> We got along together nicely. He was such a wonderful person. I couldn't believe that anyone could drink so much alcohol and that it would have so little effect on him. When we were working at the Casino he would drink a bottle of brandy a day. He was featured at the tea dance. He did three numbers, so most of the time he was free in the baccarat room. He didn't gamble, he'd just be at the bar, and when I sent someone to fetch him to play he'd come straight as ever. I never knew him to practise. I think he did all his practice before he came over here. He didn't talk much but he had wonderful taste. I remember him paying twenty dollars for a pair of socks. He was crazy about beautiful shirts in silk and things like that. He would dress like a prince. I think Europe was a rest cure for him.[4]

When his brief season with Arthur Briggs ended, Hawkins accepted an offer to work with a band led by the Belgian tenor saxist Jean Omer, resident at Le Boeuf sur le Toit, on the rue du Bastion in Brussels. There Hawk shared both the billing, and a close friendship, with the Dutch vocalist Ann Xhofleer. Back in the Netherlands Freddy Johnson kept to his original plan and returned to play at the Negro Palace in Amsterdam, working there with a new tenor saxist, Jean Robert (who doubled on trumpet), and new drummer Rally Wachtel (a cousin of Maurice van Kleef, who left to tour with Ady Rosner's band).

Hawkins settled in at Le Boeuf sur le Toit and soon found that he enjoyed life in Brussels. He was by temperament a city-dweller and found much that appealed to him in the various European capitals that he visited: he liked London, adored Paris, enjoyed Copenhagen, was impressed by Oslo and The Hague and found plenty to do in Brussels. Hawk's Belgian friend, Albert Bettonville, met up with him at Le Boeuf and shared a few drinks with him at the bar; he recalls, 'He was not lonely any more, but very busy with a girl – a superb redhead.'[5]

A particularly lively event took place at the Palais des Beaux-Arts in Brussels on 5 November 1938. This was the huge Fifth International Turnoi de Jazz at which Hawkins (appearing with Jean Omer's band) met up with various musical acquaintances from all over Europe, including pianist Ernest Berner, trumpeter Johnny Claes and tenorist Alix Combelle. The densely-packed audience were treated to a jam session in which Hawkins, blowing alongside some of Europe's best jazz musicians, chose to move up a gear or two. Hawk's presence on the bandstand inspired his colleagues; in turn, their elevated performances sparked his imagination (and his competitive spirit). A reporter at the gathering observed, 'Hawkins seems to have lost his preference for over-embellishment.'[6]

Victor Ingeveldt, a prominent Belgian tenor saxist, spoke of Hawkins's inspiration:

> I had the great pleasure of playing beside him. He gave us all (besides his knowledge) a lesson in humility and humanity inasmuch as he very seldom criticized or complained. He sometimes had to play in very poor conditions; the pianist (who liked drinking) couldn't always make it to the gig, so poor Coleman had to use another musician who could play a little piano, but this musician had to rest now and then, and this left Coleman with just the guitarist. It didn't even make him bat an eyelid; he simply smiled.[7]

The question as to whether Hawk over-embellished his phrasing began to divide jazz critics; jazz listeners in Britain, hearing Hawk broadcast with Jean Omer's band from Brussels on Saturday evenings, were convinced that the giant was as omnipotent as ever. Leonard Feather regularly championed Hawk's talents; 'If the word "genius" has a place anywhere in jazz history it belongs to Coleman Hawkins, who stands for the zenith in swing improvisation.' But during the same period (1938) Feather wrote his praise, Spike Hughes was more guarded about Hawk's development: 'There is not a saxophone player in the world who does not owe something to Hawkins,' he said, but went on to suggest that the tenor saxist was over-exploiting his gift for rhapsodizing and concluded by saying, 'Hawkins's particular path led him to the Salon Piece.'

Certainly Hawkins did make a point of playing ravishing introductions when he guested with European bands; it was his way of capturing the attention of all of his listeners, and his dramatic out-of-tempo codas ensured that his features climaxed with a stirring finale. There was less need of such ploys when he worked with Freddy Johnson who, perhaps more than any other musician that Hawk played with regularly during his European sojourn, was able to provide the tenorist with inspiration and empathy at vital times. So despite having many pleasant memories of his stay in Brussels, Hawkins was happy to be reunited with Johnson in January 1939 when the two Americans began a three-month season at the Negro Palace in Amsterdam. Hawk continued to play guest-star dates with other groups. One of these, on 28 January 1939, was with a sixteen-piece band, the Collegians (led by Lou Van Rees). The climax of this engagement at the Hoky Pavilion in The Hague was a battle between four tenor saxophonists: Hawkins, Lou Van Rees, Kid Dynamite and

Johnny Fresco (a Dutchman who later moved to the USA and recorded with Harry James, among others).

Harry Lim, a young visitor from Batavia, heard Hawkins live for the first time in Amsterdam and was hugely impressed. Harry, who had organized a jazz club in his homeland, was eager to talk with Hawkins; 'He was friendly from the very start, and happy to discuss his stay in Europe, making the point that he could relax with the trio and play long numbers, whereas on stage shows a leader like Jack Hylton was continually looking at his wristwatch. When I went to see Hawk the audience seemed to be full of Dutch musicians; they idolized him.'[8]

Pete Felleman continued to be one of the club's most regular visitors:

> At the Palace, Hawk always made a point of playing 'Bei Mir Bist Du Schoen', which was strange because he never recorded it, but it was very popular at the time and he used to play long versions of it. But the most memorable aspect of this return booking was that every night I was there he worked on 'Body and Soul'; it was part of every performance at the Palace during this period so I was surprised to hear Hawk go on record years later and pretend that he only recorded the number by chance. Hawk's eventual return to the States provided me with another surprise. Hawk loved good clothes, and so did I, so when I came into the Palace one night in 1939 wearing a new suit he looked me up and down and said, 'That looks good,' This was unusual because he never gave out compliments. So I told him the story of how I got the suit. A tailoring shop called Dik had a special offer where, for seventy-five guilders, they would measure you for a suit made in London. You had the first fitting in Holland and then it was sent back to be finished in London, and even if final alterations were made they were completed in London. Well seventy-five guilders was a lot of money in those days, about nine to the pound, so I had to promise that I would do a lot of various jobs for my father in order for him to give me the money. However, my suit turned out fine and I was flattered that Hawk was impressed, but I was even more flattered a couple of years later when a photograph appeared in *Down Beat* showing the pollwinners and there was Hawkins wearing *my* suit, same pattern, same style. He'd gone to the Dik tailoring shop and ordered the London-made suit but hadn't said a word to me. I didn't mind; in fact I was so proud that my hero Hawkins had been impressed by what a seventeen-year-old was wearing.[9]

For over two years Hawkins had been writing to various people in London in his attempts to obtain return bookings in Britain, but the embargo on American musicians was still very much in force. No one at Jack Hylton's Agency in London's Shaftesbury Avenue could devise a method of obtaining engagements for Hawkins that would meet with official approval. Hawkins also contacted Elma Warren, owner of London's Nest Club, in the hope that she could secure a valid entry permit for him, but this move also proved futile. Ben Davis, Managing Director of the London branch of the instrument manufacturers Henri Selmer Ltd, however, came up with a brilliant idea that got Hawkins back into Britain. Davis and Sid Hooper of Selmer's devised a tour of the United Kingdom in which the American tenor saxist was said to be 'giving free instrumental recitals to saxophone students'.

Selmer's contacted their stockists in various parts of Britain and arranged for Hawkins (accompanied by Ronnie Wilde on accordion) to demonstrate his Selmer saxophone (and his Otto Link mouthpiece) to specially invited customers. Selmer's took a series of advertisements announcing: 'Coleman Hawkins, accompanied by Ronnie Wilde, is coming to your town in his "Free Student Concert" tour.'

Both the Ministry of Labour and the Musicians' Union gave their approval to Hawk's visit on the grounds that the tour would prove educational. Hawkins was delighted to accept Selmer's terms; he cancelled plans made with Mr Van Zoelen to record more titles for Dutch Decca and left for London, arriving on Saturday 11 March 1939. He was soon reunited with many of his former acquaintances and with Renée Diamond and her husband Leslie. On the night of his arrival he went for a Chinese meal and then visited Soho to sit in at the Nest Club. The revelry didn't stop there and after an all-night party Hawkins got to his hotel room at the Strand Palace at 9.30 a.m. on Sunday morning just in time to set out for the first date of his Selmer tour: an afternoon show at Tony's Ballroom in Birmingham, where he was greeted by a 'huge, enthusiastic crowd'.[10]

During that week Hawkins did his shows in Oxford, Liverpool, Leicester and Nottingham (from where he wrote to Renée, 'I soon get fed up in the provinces'). Sometimes, as at Leicester and Nottingham, Hawkins was accompanied by local musicians, but most often the show was performed by tenor sax and accordion. During the tour Hawkins gave an optimistic interview to the *Melody Maker* in which he outlined his future plans. Originally he had envisaged a vacation in the USA during the summer of 1939, returning to Holland by 'October or November', but the worsening international situation caused him to rethink his plans: 'I'm certainly going back to the USA and unless something unexpected turns up to delay me I shall go as soon as my trip to England is finished.'

Hawk's Selmer tour ended on Tuesday 4 April 1939 at the Angel Hotel in Northampton. There, Jeff Williams, the young son of the hotel proprietor, looked into a room and saw Hawk warming up on his saxophone. He was invited in and sat on Hawk's lap. The great man blew his tenor but allowed the child to finger the keys of the instrument. The experience proved inspirational; Jeff Williams later took up the tenor saxophone and enjoyed a long career working in music.

On the following night Hawkins took part in a jam session organized by the Number One Rhythm Club at a hotel in the Holborn district of London. Hawk's accompanists included several of Britain's top jazz musicians: George Chisholm (trombone), Tiny Winters (double bass), Tommy Wilson (drums), the brilliant blind pianist George Shearing, and on trumpet the talented Dave Wilkins from Barbados. Hawkins revelled at the chance to extend himself and said that he 'felt more inspired than at any time during my present visit'.

While Hawkins was out on his Selmer tour Jack Hylton's office had been negotiating with the Musicians' Union in the hope that the American's stay could be extended so that he could perform at various theatres with the Hylton band. Happily the union decided to regard Hawk's work in this capacity as that of a variety artist, so he was able to stay in England and guest with Jack Hylton. The *Melody Maker* passed on the news by making the story its front-page lead; Hawkins began working with Hylton at the Sheffield Empire. The opening night was successful enough and Hawk reported to Renée, 'I had those cats asking for more – not bad in Sheffield, eh?' As the week wore on, however, the enthusiasm waned and the *Melody Maker* described the subsequent audience reaction as 'cold'. Hawk admitted to a journalist that the listeners were 'very conservative'; by the end of the week he confided to Renée and Leslie: 'I'm so fed up with this place.'

Audiences' reactions didn't indicate that Hawkins was performing less well than usual; he was, according to every report, playing better than ever. The leading British trumpeter, Nat Gonella, heard Hawk on tour and said he was 'still the greatest of them all', but in 1939 jazz in Britain was going through the doldrums. Jazz records were enjoying healthy sales and rhythm clubs were flourishing, but efforts to present unadulterated jazz live on the concert platform or on stage often failed to break even. The Heralds of Swing, a band packed with the best of British jazzmen, was forced to disband in 1939, only months after it had first assembled. Veterans looking back on this period suggest that apprehension about the strong possibility of another war with Germany caused many people to look away from jazz in order to seek more transient pleasures.

Hawk's contribution to Jack Hylton's shows was similar to the part he had played in the 1934 presentations: he performed two numbers (usually 'Honeysuckle Rose' and 'Georgia') in a segment called 'Youth Takes a

Bow'. As before, he maintained a cordial but rather distant relationship with Hylton's musicians and remained affably guarded in his social contacts with the bandleader, whom he always addressed as Jack. Hylton's star tenor saxist, Joe Crossman, was delighted to work with Hawkins. He recalls:

> I found Coleman to be a quiet man, intelligent but not likely to say much. But it was obvious that he liked his drink. On the 1939 tour he'd always have a bottle of whisky up on the rack in the railway carriage and during our journeys he'd keep getting it down to take a sip. With Jack's band he didn't play in with the sax section, he was the soloist out front. Occasionally we tried something out, with him playing a part in the section, but the tones didn't match. His sound was very broad, almost harsh, extremely powerful, but very appealing. On stage he'd play chorus after chorus, wonderful stuff, pure improvising, but it didn't reap a lot of applause, the people looked on him as just another instrumentalist.[11]

After playing in London (at the Finsbury Park Empire) for a week early in May 1939, Hawkins took a brief respite while the Hylton band completed a filming assignment. He was then reunited with them for a booking at the Nottingham Exposition. While working with Hylton in Nottingham, Hawkins stayed at the County Hotel; so too did Fats Waller, who had a week's booking at the Nottingham Empire. There are no reports of the two Americans sharing a jam session that week but Hawkins wrote, 'We have been having a time together – drinking of course.' Almost thirty years later Hawkins reminisced about that week of tippling:

> We just happened to be living in the same hotel in Nottingham, only living about three doors apart. So Fats would bring me my breakfast every morning – a glass of Scotch, full glass, a water glass of whisky. You see, that was the way he drank. It would take me an hour to drink a glass of Scotch; he'd drink it in two minutes, straight down, just like he was drinking water. He was a big drinker and a big eater. Yeah, Fats was something else.[12]

When the two Americans linked up in London they created an unforgettable experience for the British jazz pianist George Shearing: 'We were in a club in London and we had heard that Fats Waller and/or Coleman Hawkins were coming by, and they both did. When everybody left they both got up and played. By the time we left that club the sun was shining brightly.'[13]

On Monday 22 May 1939 the Jack Hylton Show (with Coleman Hawkins) began a week's residency at the Holborn Empire in London. On the following day they did a broadcast together (previously they had done a short-wave radio show for American listeners); then, on Friday 26 May they recorded two titles subsequently issued on the HMV label. Hawk's former leader, Fletcher Henderson, provided the arrangement for 'At the Darktown Strutter's Ball', which is taken at a sedate tempo, one that often engenders a rocking swing. Unfortunately the Hylton rhythm section's performance precludes that possibility. The main obstacle is the drumming, which sounds as though it were being performed at a military tattoo. After a brightly played band chorus Hawk swings his way through a couple of choruses, making engaging use of dynamics. The band play a heavily syncopated chorus that has brief trumpet fill-ins and a short clarinet solo (by Joe Crossman) then Hawk zooms in again and demonstrates his prodigious musical authority. 'Melancholy Baby' has a boldly scored introduction for the trombones, then Hawk, accompanied only by the rhythm section, paraphrases the melody delightfully. The reed-section passages emphasize the theatrical nature of the arrangement, as does the eccentric trombone solo. Hawk, seemingly oblivious of these incongruities swings back into action, but even his Herculean efforts cannot lift the leaden ensemble.

Soon after the record date, Hawk attended a party held in his honour at the Palm Beach Club in London. There he jammed with a pick-up group featuring Scottish sax player Andy McDevitt and West Indian trumpeter Wally Bowen. By this time Harry Lim had left Holland to visit Britain. Lim, who later produced several American recording sessions featuring Hawkins, was at the Palm Beach Club gathering: 'It was an unforgettable experience. Hawk was marvellous, playing with unbelievable power.'

Hawkins then left London to play for a week at the Birmingham Hippodrome with Jack Hylton. The package did a Sunday concert at Rhyl in North Wales, then moved east to appear for a week at the Palace Theatre in Manchester. During that residency (on 8 June 1939) Hawk wrote a letter to Renée, mentioning a tune that was to play an all-important part in his life: 'Thanks so much for liking the way I played "Body and Soul", you know that's always been one of my favorite tunes.' Hawk had also mentioned 'Body and Soul' in a letter written to Renée four years earlier; as Pete Felleman has pointed out, it had been part of his regular repertoire for some time.

The Hylton show played in Glasgow in June, moved south to Bridlington in Yorkshire, then made the long journey to Brighton, Sussex, for a week's booking at the Hippodrome, which concluded Hawkins's stint with Hylton's band. He returned to London where he had taken an apartment in Phoenix House, and spent the early part of July 1939 socializing (including making a non-playing appearance on 8 July at another party held in his honour at the Palm Beach Club). During early July Hawkins imparted his latest plans to the *Melody Maker*, who published them in their next issue: 'He has already been approached by Willard Alexander (of the William Morris Agency) who is considering building a big band around him. Though sorry to leave his many friends on this side of the Atlantic he is looking forward to settling permanently in the States and declares it unlikely that he will return to Europe.'[14]

Coleman Hawkins left England on 9 July, crossed to Holland to collect the various goods and chattels that he had accumulated during his five-year stay in Europe, and then sailed direct to New York. Hawkins's long-time musical partner, Freddy Johnson, decided to bide his time in Europe – with disastrous results: he was trapped by the tide of war and spent two years in a Bavarian prison camp.

During his voyage across the Atlantic Hawkins had ample time to think about his future plans. He had not dismissed the offer from agent Willard Alexander but he delayed his answer until he had had the opportunity to make his own assessement of prospects for a big band. The competitive side of Hawk's nature was eager to hear his tenor-playing rivals in person. He had kept abreast of developments via recordings and short-wave radio transmissions, but he was well aware that there might be many fine young players whom he had never heard. Hawk was too wise to have been made complacent by European adulation, typified by the results of a *Melody Maker* poll in which Hawkins received 1,520 votes, his nearest rival (Bud Freeman) polling 217.

However, in an American poll organized by the Associated Negro Press, he was not listed (being ineligible, having not worked in the USA during 1938). Hawk was told about this poll just before he left England. The results of it did not unduly surprise him; in fact the information made him all the keener to joust with the musicians who occupied the first two places in the tenor-saxophone section: Chu Berry and Lester Young.

In the late stages of his voyage Hawk's plans were given positive direction by the arrival of a cable from Ralph Watkins, owner of the New York club Kelly's Stable. Watkins, a former sax player, had known Hawkins since the early 1930s, and he offered the tenor saxist the chance to take his own band into the club, situated at 141 West 51st Street.

Subject to a suitable starting date being agreed upon, Hawkins took an option on the offer.

When Hawkins disembarked on 31 July 1939 he was met by a small welcome-home contingent organized by Ed Harris, then President of the National Swing Club of America, who described Hawk as being 'handsomely dressed' with 'an air of charming sophistication', and 'somewhat slimmer than the "Bean" of five years ago. His hair had thinned, his mustache was neatly trimmed.' Hawkins's first plans were to visit Harlem. Harris reported: 'The tremendous popularity that Hawkins enjoys is a tribute to his artistry, character and good fellowship. He was greeted with gladness, respect and affection – and a thousand well-intended offers of employment by many of his contemporary artists.'

Harris continued:

> Benny Carter, one of Hawk's best friends, played host to us during the celebrations that followed Hawkins's docking. First it was the Savoy Ballroom where we listened to music by Lee Norman's nine-piece jump outfit and to the late Chick Webb's band, which now features Ella Fitzgerald and drummer Willie Beason. After jumping at the Savoy we drove to the Famous Door to hear Count Basie. Here we formed a party which included Fitzgerald, Jimmie Lunceford, Billie Holiday, Charlie Shavers, Russell Procope, Satch Crawford, Jean Walker, Norman McCoy, Buster Bailey, Taps Miller, Hawkins, myself and several whose names I can't recall. At 4.30 a.m. we went up to Harlem's Jimmie's Chicken Shack and, motoring through Central Park, we viewed the daybreak of 1 August, a new era for Coleman Hawkins. Hawk was back and we were as high as a kite.[15]

Hawkins took a temporary lease on an apartment at 15 Central Park West, New York, and pondered on a course of action. He was delighted by the warm reception that fellow musicians had given to him and pleased that he was still fondly remembered. During his long absence *Down Beat* and *Metronome* had given his odyssey mentions and this kept people aware of his name, but listeners in America had had little chance of keeping up with Hawk's playing. Of nearly fifty sides he made in Europe during the period 1934–39 only six had been issued in the USA (four – from Holland – on American Decca and two – from France – on RCA Victor).

Hawk's most immediate task was probably shaped by what he had heard coming out of Lester Young's saxophone during his visit to the Famous Door. Hawkins must have realized that Young was his foremost rival for the tenor-sax crown because he decided to take part in a jam session with him as soon as possible. Lester had experienced Hawk at close quarters in Kansas City six years earlier, and just how closely he kept tabs on Hawk's playing in the intervening years is conjectural, but he mentioned having heard the 1937 Paris recording of 'Crazy Rhythm', which he described as 'great'.[16]

The results of the musical combat between Hawkins and Young made front-page news in the September 1939 issue of *Down Beat* magazine. Under the heading 'Hawk and Les Young in Carving Contest' the magazine described what had happened at Puss Johnson's Tavern in Harlem. There Hawkins and Young had locked horns in an epic jam session; *Down Beat* inferred that Hawkins had triumphed: 'The two aces tangled for an hour in a carving contest, and according to members of Fats Waller's band it stopped when Lester said he'd had enough.'

However, singer Billie Holiday, who was at the club, had other ideas about which of the tenor saxists had emerged as the victor. She went out of her way to put her point of view to the staff at *Down Beat*, and as a result they published an item in their 15 October issue headed 'Les Young wasn't carved – Holiday'; it contained Billie's statement: 'Young really cut the Hawk, and most everyone there who saw them tangle agreed on that.' The great controversy as to which of the two musicians, Hawkins or Young, was the greater jazz tenor saxophonist had started in earnest.

Hawkins decided to accept Ralph Watkins's offer and began assembling a band to play at Kelly's Stable, but he soon discovered that star sidemen wanted to be highly paid for their work; Hawk was still thinking in terms of 1934 wages. Several of the musicians he wanted were bandleaders themselves, or about to become so. His original shortlist optimistically contained the names of Benny Carter, Benny Morton and Henry Allen; he also went to hear trumpeter Roy Eldridge and said, 'That boy's wonderful. I want him in my band.' Roy was delighted to jam alongside Hawk in after-hours sessions, but by this time he was leading his own successful group and had no desire at that juncture to become a sideman again. Years later Roy said:

> When Hawk came back from Europe he heard me play and said 'Yeah, I like that legato approach.' That was the first time I ever played with him. I had previously met him years before in Pittsburgh when he and some of the other guys from Fletcher's band got me to play against Rex Stewart, to get Rex mad, because I was only a kid. They didn't call it carving in those days, they called it 'signifying'.[17]

The band that Hawkins eventually assembled for the debut at Kelly's Stable contained promising young musicians, but no stars. Jackie Fields was the lead alto saxist, Eustis Moore played alto sax and clarinet,

Tommy Lindsey and Joe Guy were the trumpeters, and Earl Hardy the trombonist. Gene Rodgers was on piano, William Oscar Smith on double bass and Arthur Herbert on drums; the band's eighteen-year-old vocalist was Thelma Carpenter. All of the band except Arthur Herbert and Hawkins were in their twenties.

Thelma Carpenter recalled those days:

> I had been singing with Teddy Wilson's band and that stay came to an abrupt end. I found out that Coleman Hawkins was looking for a vocalist so I went round to see him at Kelly's Stable. As I walked in he looked at me and said, 'Ah, ah, they're making them like this in America now I see.' I got the job and learned a lot from Coleman about music and about life. First he taught me to put expression into singing ballads, and he did it by saying, 'Carp, if you're putting a song across, you've got to regard it as if you're making love. You greet the song, then you slowly get closer to it, caressing it, kissing it, and finally making love to it, and when you bring your performance to a climax you don't just end it there and then, you have to be just as tender as you were when you began, so that your audience feels the flow of your expression and they end up peaceful and satisfied.' Well I sat there full of interest; here was I a teenage girl and virginal, listening to this great sophisticated musician talking like that to me. He'd tell me all about the various European countries he'd lived in; it was all fascinating.
>
> Musically he was pure genius; his playing was magnificent and so were his arrangements. He didn't often write but when he did, it was done in the most casual way in the kitchen at Kelly's where he could spread out several sheets of music at the same time. He didn't write vocal arrangements for me. My feature on 'He's Funny that Way' was done by Hazel Scott, at least she started doing the arrangement but she never got around to completing it and in the end her mother, Alma (who was also a fine musician) finished the arrangement and we recorded it.[18]

Trumpeter Tommy Lindsey recalled how all of the young musicians in the band were thrilled to be working with Hawkins. Lindsey arrived in New York city from Buffalo as a member of the Seven Dukes of Rhythm, led by Buster Harding. When work for this group became scarce Lindsey joined Hawkins; so too did his leader, as Hawk's principal arranger. Lindsey is proud to have been in that band: 'Coleman Hawkins's tenor playing has left its mark on me as a trumpet player. His ability to tell a story with his horn moved me no end.'[19]

While Hawk was organizing the new band's rehearsals he was offered the chance to play on an all-star recording session set up by Lionel Hampton. He accepted with alacrity, knowing that he was going to work alongside two of his tenor-playing rivals, Chu Berry and Ben Webster (soon to join Duke Ellington). Beside these three musical heavyweights the front line also benefited from the talents of Benny Carter on alto saxophone and John 'Dizzy' Gillespie on trumpet (soon to be acknowledged, along with Charlie Parker, as one of the innovators of modern jazz).

On 11 September 1939 the Hampton group recorded four sides, two featuring Hawkins's tenor sax. At the last moment, though, it looked likely that Hawk would be barred from the session, because the recording company discovered that he hadn't yet renewed his Musicians' Union card since returning from Europe. After some urgent negotiations Local 802 gave permission for the date to go ahead with Hawkins. Lionel Hampton didn't play piano or drums on the date; instead he concentrated on his best instrument, the vibraphone.

The first number was Benny Carter's ingenious composition 'When Lights Are Low', the first sixteen-bars of which are stated by Dizzy Gillespie's cup-muted trumpet. From the first moment it's apparent that the rhythm section of Cozy Cole (drums), Charlie Christian (guitar), Milt Hinton (bass) and Clyde Hart (piano) have achieved a remarkable blend. Each man's contribution is clearly discernible yet the overall impression is of one emphatic pulse. Carter contributes a brief, elegant solo then Hampton creates a series of breaks that link with the beginning of Hawk's improvisations. Hawk adopts an aggressive approach to the gentle contours of Carter's tune, sounding unshaven and slightly out of practice. Although the rhythm section was better than anything he'd encountered for years (or perhaps *ever*) he doesn't seem to be lifted by their swing. A second take shows that an improvisatory spirit filled the session, for the second attempt at the arrangement was slightly revamped and the idea of including breaks abandoned. Hawk's ideas are interesting but they are delivered in a rough tone, and the end of the solo is blemished by an awkward 'baton change' between him and the pianist. Wrongly-performed notes in the written trumpet part further mar the second attempt, making the first version the natural choice for the original issue.

But even a Hawkins who was not at his supple best delighted the French critic André Hodeir, who found ample merit in the tenor saxist's playing on 'When Lights Are Low'. In 1948 Hodeir wrote: 'He's aggressive, and tense to the point of exasperation, showing off in the treble of the instrument with an amazingly powerful sound, utilizing an unusual "growl". He takes a solo with ferocious roughness, shaking everything around him, neglecting the melody for a sensual excitement which is not without beauty.'[20]

Clyde Hart's poised piano introduction launches Hawkins's rendering of the 'One Sweet Letter from You' melody. The tenorist's exposition consists of clever paraphrases that keep the tune in focus but the performance is less impressive than many of his Europe recordings, despite the multi-talented backing. Hawk moves closer to top form in his concluding eight bars, but the ideas seem to be held in check. The stand-out feature of the track is Hampton's idiosyncratic vocal, which is inspiringly backed by Christian's crisply chorded guitar fill-ins. Hawkins didn't solo on 'Hot Mallets', which features Gillespie (again using a cup mute) and Chu Berry, who was increasingly intent on incorporating new harmonic twists into his bustling, skilful solos. The other tenorist on the date, Ben Webster, is given his chance to shine on 'Early Session Hop', a truly innocuous theme. Webster's allegiance to Hawkins's style is obvious, but at this stage of his career Ben hadn't developed his musical poise and here he lets his solo trail away in the closing stages.

Coleman Hawkins's nine-piece band opened at Kelly's Stable on Thursday 5 October 1939. Press advertisements were headed DIRECT FROM EUROPEAN TRIUMPHS and throughout the run old friends and fans called into the club to offer welcome-home greetings, but a good proportion of each night's audience was hearing Hawkins for the first time. After the first few nights of the booking, business slackened off, but the band's morale soared when they learnt that a recording contract was in the offing; Leonard Joy, an executive at RCA Victor, had contacted Hawkins and offered to record the band. As a result, the unit went into the studios and recorded four titles for issue on the company's subsidiary label Bluebird.

11
Body and Soul

The first two titles that Coleman Hawkins's Orchestra recorded on 11 October 1939 make it abundantly clear why the group was having difficulty in setting New York alight. All of the musicians perform competently but the arrangements fail to achieve any sort of climax, and the material is poor. 'Meet Doctor Foo' and 'Fine Dinner' (both riff-type compositions by Hawkins) are untuneful and therefore unmemorable.

After the indifferent theme of 'Meet Doctor Foo' (arranged by Hawkins) has been offered, Hawkins re-presents the basic phrases of the release before constructing his solo on the main melody. He obviously thought it would be commercial to hammer home the tune but, as the theme was threadbare to begin with, any repetition tends to stress its tedious qualities. Trumpeter Joe Guy blows a capricious eight-bar solo that is effective and drummer Arthur Herbert does his considerable best to lift the group but the overall impression is of a nine-piece band trying too hard to sound like a sixteen-piece unit.

'Fine Dinner' (arranged by Gene Rodgers) also tries to maintain the same illusion. The three-piece sax section sound ill-matched (Hawkins is too prominent) and the widely scored brass writing has the trumpets straining for their high notes. Gene Rodgers plays eight bars of nicely controlled flamboyance and Earl Hardy (despite an opening fluff) sounds to be a promising trombonist, but the paucity of the material failed to gain the radio plays that would have helped to establish the new band.

On the original 78 rpm issue 'Doctor Foo' was coupled with Thelma Carpenter's vocal feature 'He's Funny that Way'. Apart from a slight pitching lapse in the middle eight Carpenter sings the number expressively. Hawk takes a full chorus that begins with some magnificently poetic flourishes, but after an enterprisingly conceived descending phrase he seems to get bogged down by repetitive patterns and the last part of his chorus is little more than a high-class example of a great musician simply marking time. Gene Rodgers again proves, in a brief, flowing solo, that he was an underrated pianist.

It is Rodgers who provides the four-bar introduction to the final number of the session, 'Body and Soul', a 1930 composition by Johnny Green that had previously been recorded by a number of jazz musicians, including Louis Armstrong, Henry Allen, Benny Goodman, Roy Eldridge and Chu Berry. Hawk decided to treat the song informally, making it a two-chorus ballad feature for himself. His first thirty-two bars are accompanied by a simple two-in-the-bar pattern on the double bass, light chording from the piano and unobtrusive brush work by the drummer; even when the full band enters for the second chorus their role is merely to blow long notes. Backed by what was the simplest of arrangements, Coleman Hawkins achieved the apotheosis of his entire career, creating a solo that remains the most perfectly conceived and executed example of jazz tenor-sax playing ever recorded.

In a supreme burst of inspiration this great musician created a masterwork that showed him at his best, harmonically, rhythmically and technically. It was a performance that captured Hawkins at the pinnacle of his expressiveness, and it was this quality that somehow touched countless listeners who were not jazz fans. Hawkins's performance was adored not only by the general public but also by all of the musicians reaching out for new jazz frontiers. It became one of the music's most important and influential recordings, giving a positive musical direction to thousands of saxophonists and leading countless instrumentalists to realize that the use of sophisticated harmonies could enhance the beauty of a jazz solo. Even those who staunchly resisted the onset of modernisms in jazz were hugely impressed by Hawkins's performance on 'Body and Soul'.

Looking back, Hawkins said:

> I had no idea of recording 'Body and Soul' when we went into that session. That tune was the least of my ideas. There were other tunes I preferred. I used to play 'Body and Soul' as a solo or extra tune on stage in Europe. And when I got nine pieces together in Kelly's Stable when I got back to America, maybe once in a while in the middle of the night I would play 'Body and Soul'. Every time I played it different and the people seemed to like it enough. Then I got a call from Victor to do this date and started fixing up tunes. We didn't have 'Body and Soul' in the thing at all.
>
> I had done three numbers at the record date when Leonard Joy called me over and said, 'Do us a favor. One of the guys called up from Trenton. He heard you do 'Body and Soul' at the club and would like to hear it on record.'
>
> I said, 'I have another song I'd rather do,' but he said, 'You could do that one some other time. Let's just make one take of "Body and Soul".'

I didn't even have an arrangement on it. I didn't want to play it at all, so I just played it through once and made up the ending when I got to it. The ending, as it turned out, was one of the funniest things I ever played in my life. Like the way the horns came in on the last chord.[1]

Pianist Gene Rodgers confirmed how informal the planning was:

I remember Coleman, just as if it happened yesterday, he reached over some place and got a bottle of Cognac and he took a good healthy sip, laid it down and then he got right under the middle of the microphone and he said, 'Make an introduction on "Body and Soul"' . . . so I made the introduction that became the legend with the record. I don't know where it came from, I just put my hands down and it came out. I think that the reason for the success of 'Body and Soul' was that Coleman played from his heart. The musicianship that this man possessed. There was no shackles of an arrangement; he just played with no interruption, flat-footed, and he probably didn't even hear the accompaniment. His eyes were closed and he just played as if he was in heaven.[2]

Hawk realized later that the lack of a formal arrangement had been a blessing in disguise, 'I hadn't written any notes or nothing down. I'm glad I didn't now. One take, no rehearsal.' Hawk was prone to suggest that 'Body and Soul' was just another tune to him at the time of the recording but, as noted, he'd specifically cited it as one of his favourite pieces (in his letter of June 1939) and he'd mentioned it in a letter four years before. This, of course, doesn't in any way diminish the merits of his amazing performance. He said later:

It's funny how it became such a classic. Even the ordinary public is crazy about it. It's the first and only record I ever heard of that all the squares dig as well as the jazz people, and I don't understand how and why, because I was making notes all the way. I wasn't making a melody for the squares. I played it like I play everything else and yet they went for it. I thought nothing of it. I didn't even bother to listen to it afterwards.[3]

Hawkins first heard his recording of 'Body and Soul' on a radio programme:

I was sitting up in Fat Man's [Fat Man Charlie Turner's Rib Place in Harlem]. A bunch of us was at the bar; this was shortly after the recording session. It was on Martin Block's program, the one that used to come on about 6.30 at night. This thing came on; a girl sitting there said to me, 'Did you record "Body and Soul"?'

I said, 'Yes.'

She said, 'Is that your record?'

I listened and said, 'Gee, that's my tone . . . that's funny.' It actually sounded good and I was surprised.[4]

Hawk was not the only one who was surprised by the widespread popularity that the recording gained. He recalled:

Thelonious Monk said to me, 'You know you never did explain to me how these people, these old folks and everybody, goes for your record of "Body and Soul". Because I've listened to the record and I could understand if you played melody because that's what they like; they sure won't listen to anything else that's jazz. There's no melody in there, what are they listening to?'

Hawkins said,

You know when the record first came out, everybody including Chu Berry said I was playing wrong notes on it. They just weren't making these changes. But the changes I made on 'Body and Soul' are the only changes to make. They thought I was wrong. But at that time you make some type of a D change going into D flat and that was wrong. At that time you had to make an A flat 7th (they didn't know that was relative chord to D anyway) to go into D flat. They heard that D and it had to be: 'Oh, that's terrible.' It became common after that, but it certainly wasn't common before I made 'Body and Soul', I can tell you that.[5]

Pianist Teddy Wilson always appreciated the merits of Hawk's performance and described it as 'the best solo record I ever heard in jazz'.[6] Another pianist, Randy Weston, said, 'For me it's one of the greatest works of music of any kind from any era. When I first heard it I played it note for note on the piano . . . it was something that blew my mind.' Every sort of jazz instrumentalist was given new insights into improvising by the harmonic vocabulary that Hawk employed on his recording of 'Body and Soul', but its presentation was to inspire tenor saxophonists for generations. Illinois Jacquet recalled the recording's effect:

The first time I actually heard Hawkins was when Nat 'King' Cole took me into a little bar on Central Avenue in Los Angeles so I could hear Hawkins's record of 'Body and Soul' on a jukebox. That was the first time I really heard the saxophone played from the bottom to the top. I realized I was listening to the master of the horn.[7]

A later jazz master, John Coltrane, said, 'The first time I heard Hawk I was fascinated by his arpeggios and the way he played. I got a copy of his "Body and Soul" and listened real hard to what he was doing.[8] Howard McGhee, a pioneer of modern trumpet playing, said, 'After I heard "Body and Soul'', Hawk made such a masterpiece of that, I had never heard anyone play music like that. I had never heard a horn play two choruses in a row.'[9]

Some critics failed to appreciate 'Body and Soul' when it was first issued. An unnamed reviewer in the 22 December 1939 issue of *Jazz Information* went as far as to write: 'Hawkins plays almost entirely without inspiration. His variations are mechanically constructed of clichés and are without much logic.' However, 'Barrelhouse Dan' in *Down Beat* redressed the balance by describing Hawk's performance as having 'a full biting tone and fantastic ideas'; he went on to express disappointment that the record had been issued too late to be listed under the 'best of 1939'.

One notable critic, John Hammond, saw 'Body and Soul' as marking a crucial point in Hawk's career. In 1975 he summarized Hawkins's achievements:

> 'Body and Soul' was an extraordinary virtuoso performance. I thought Hawk was wonderful but a little in danger of becoming too much of a rhapsodist, too florid. The same thing happened to Louis Armstrong after he went to England. He was never the same after he got back from England and I have the feeling that the same thing happened to a lesser degree to Coleman Hawkins. He became more the exhibitionist, less the interweaving jazz-ensemble artist he grew up being.[10]

Hammond's comments seem strange, coming from such an astute listener, particularly as Hawkins had never in his early days distinguished himself as an ensemble player. However, the long stay in Europe (rather than the bookings in England) may have played a part in creating the way in which Hawkins conceived his original recording of 'Body and Soul'. A strange sidelight on Hawk's recording came from Albert Bettonville, who recalled a night out with Hawkins in Ostend in 1937; 'We went to an Hungarian nightclub to hear a *tzigane* violinist playing and also improvising with *maestria*. Hawk was extremely interested and talked a lot with him about harmony. When I met Hawk again after the war I congratulated him for his superb ''Body and Soul''. He only said, ''Do you remember that Hungarian violinist?'' '[11]

It was to be a while before the revolutionary implications of Hawk's 'Body and Soul' (and other tributaries of modernism) affected the general course of jazz. Meanwhile a growing enthusiasm for the revival of Dixieland and 'vintage' jazz caused several record companies to assemble small pick-up groups whose tasks were to revive the jazz favourites of the 1920s. Hawkins, who had let it be known that he was available for any sort of record date, became part of one of these groups, the Varsity Seven, in which he teamed up with two musicians who had also worked a lot in Europe during the 1930s; Benny Carter (playing trumpet and alto sax here) and the white clarinettist Danny Polo. This front line was supported by Joe Sullivan, piano; Ulysses Livingstone, guitar; Arthur Shapiro, bass and George Wettling, drums. The vocalist was Jeanne Burns.

The solos on the session are more attractive than the ensemble sound, which often sounds like a pastiche of Dixieland, which wasn't surprising as no one in the front line was a specialist in that style. Polo's thinnish, slightly nasal clarinet playing sounds at its best on 'Easy Rider', which has some good robust melody playing by Hawkins. Livingstone's guitar solo is outstanding on 'Tight Like That', but George Wettling's use of woodblocks behind Sullivan's piano solo seems an inappropriate anachronism; the drummer's work on the snares, however, rocks the band to a swinging finale. On this track Hawkins hints at his growing partiality for creating rifflike patterns in his solos. The tenorist's best moments occur on 'Save It Pretty Mama', where he builds climactically throughout the final two choruses, blowing barrel-chested variations that tie in effectively with the ensemble's four-bar sign-off phrase.

'Scratch My Back' is the only recently composed tune on the session. It's a pert little theme written by Leonard Feather, who was co-organizer of the date together with Warren Scholl, the *Melody Maker*'s former North American correspondent. The best moments on this track come from Benny Carter's alto-sax playing (elsewhere on the date he plays superbly on trumpet); the other lively attributes of the performance are the effective tenor-sax-and-clarinet unisons and Joe Sullivan's flamboyant, rolling piano solo.

Hawkins's next recording session also featured Benny Carter and Joe Sullivan. It took place a week after the Varsity Seven date and produced some vastly superior music. These recordings, made on 21 December, under Lionel Hampton's name, show Hawkins in a more favourable light than on his previous session with the vibraphonist. Hampton gives a potent demonstration of his knack of getting newly-assembled groups immediately to establish a swinging unity.

Benny Carter on trumpet is featured at the beginning of 'Dinah'; he makes a fleeting reference to the melody then blows a series of warm-toned variations that include a striking step-by-step descending pattern that exemplifies his extraordinary compositional sense. Hawk's entry phrase is rifflike and deceptively simple, like the laying of the lowest card in a royal flush, but this ingenuity is soon eclipsed by the linked phrases that fill the middle section of his solo, which seem to hint at a superimposed time signature, yet each of these intricacies swings effortlessly. The chorus can be counted among Hawkins's greatest achievements. It seems to inspire Hampton, who surges into his solo, determined to maintain the same remarkable level of rhythmic intensity. The tension is given one more twist as the vibist-leader continues to play over the front line's incisive riffs, concluding this superb example of informal jazz.

The performers immediately tried another take and, amazingly, almost equalled their recent achievements. Each of the main soloists (Carter, Hawkins and Hampton) explores creative alternatives based on ideas he had formulated on the first attempt, but both the phrasing and the note content of these new endeavours are different from the originals (giving a fine insight into the mental agility of these three superb jazz musicians).

Nothing else from this session quite measures up to 'Dinah', but both 'My Buddy' and 'Singin' the Blues' have excellent contributions from Hawkins. On 'My Buddy' he shares an engaging duet with clarinettist Edmond Hall (whose role elsewhere on the date is a subdued one), and the vigorous tones of the two men add a lively bite to the musical sparring. Hawk had first recorded 'Singin' the Blues' almost a decade earlier (with Fletcher Henderson); here his playing is ultra-relaxed. His near-tender solo is couched in a breathy subtone that many young tenorists began to copy. Echoes of Hawk's pioneering of this approach can be heard in the work of today's tenor saxists; Hawk's leading disciple, Ben Webster, chose to develop a heavier, more cavernous version of the effect.

So Hawk's final session of 1939 was a momentous one, symbolising his continuous progress. During the early months of that year his career had seemed almost directionless, but his homecoming from Europe had re-established his eminence. Hawk's rivals, and some critics, had formed the mistaken idea that the returning musician would be less of a jazz player than the man who had sailed to Europe in 1934. They reasoned that because Hawk had been playing mostly with indifferent rhythm sections and unchallenging front-line partners he would have lost his dominating jazz skills. They did not take into account that Hawkins listened carefully and regularly to gramophone records imported from the States, and to short-wave broadcasts, and therefore had a clear idea of the main course of jazz developments back home. In his frequent periods of solitude Hawk listened adoringly to modern classical music, pondering on the fact that the harmonic riches in that music had hardly been tapped by any jazz saxophonist and becoming increasingly determined to rectify that situation. So despite being thousands of miles away from the fountains of jazz, Hawk continued to nurture and develop his remarkable talent, as he proved with his epoch-making version of 'Body and Soul'. That recording would eventually be seen as one of the first positive signposts towards modernism, but a more immediate accolade shows that Hawkins had swiftly regained his position as the most acclaimed tenor saxist in jazz. The annual *Down Beat* poll (published on 1 January 1940), showed that Hawk had easily won the top placing, polling over 500 more votes than his nearest rivals: Charlie Barnet, Eddie Miller and Chu Berry. Lester Young, who was to prove such a challenge in the coming decade, took an outsider's role, gaining seventh place.

By the second week of November 1939 Hawkins's band had complete its brief season at Kelly's Stable. The run (during most of which the band worked opposite the Spirits of Rhythm) was never really successful; 'a good and well-drilled outfit' was about the most flattering line in any review, and one report commented that 'business was disappointing'.[12] During the latter stages of the booking the band was augmented by the arrival of Kermit Scott on tenor saxophone and Bill Dillard on trumpet, making the unit eleven strong (four saxes, four brass and three rhythm).

Bill Dillard spoke of his inauguration:

> I joined Coleman Hawkins in late 1939 – after they'd recorded 'Body and Soul'. As a bandleader he was easy to get along with. He knew exactly what he wanted, but he also knew if a thing was not possible, which is important, otherwise you have musicians ill at ease. He adjusted his requirements when he saw that such-and-such was impossible for a musician, and he didn't react badly if things went wrong. The most he'd do on the bandstand was to glance back at a musician or at a section if something did go wrong, just to let you know he knew. He was very nice to his musicians.[13]

The outlook for the new band brightened considerably when Hawkins gave them the news of a two-week booking at the Arcadia Ballroom, and the promise of a season at the newly-opened Golden Gate Ballroom. This new dancehall, at 142nd Street and Lenox in Harlem (two blocks away from the Savoy Ballroom), had been functioning only since October 1939; it could hold 6,500 people. The proprietor was Jay Faggen, who had previously controlled the Roseland (where he first met Hawkins); he had also been involved in the administration of the Savoy Ballroom in the 1930s.

But it was not Faggen's previous acquaintanceship with Hawkins that secured the Golden Gate booking for the new band. The engagements at the Arcadia and at the Golden Gate had been negotiated by Hawk's new agent, Joe Glaser, who at that time also represented Louis Armstrong and Billie Holiday. Glaser, then operating from a suite at 30 Rockefeller Plaza, decided to use exactly the same tactics to present Hawkins to the public as he had done a dozen years earlier when he had billed Louis Armstrong in Chicago as 'The World's Greatest Trumpeter': for the Arcadia opening Hawkins was advertised as 'The World's Greatest Saxophonist'.

Hawkins added a guitarist at the Arcadia. The newcomer was Lawrence Lucie, who had recorded with Hawk on the 1933 Spike Hughes sessions:

> I heard Hawk was looking for a guitarist for his big band so I went along to the Arcadia and saw that three or four other guys were after the same job, one of them, Eddie Gibbs, a fine player. I don't think Hawk remembered me. The audition consisted of playing a set with the band, in front of the dancers. Some of the arrangements were difficult to read, but I must have done OK because Hawk said, 'I'll take that boy,' pointing at me. He had been listening closely to me and I had deliberately played as much as I could like Clarence Holiday (Billie's father). Lib-lab, as we used to call him, had a way of accenting the backbeat a little and this set up a terrific swing, so I tried to do that and it clicked with Coleman; he had been used to that sort of guitar playing with Fletcher Henderson.
>
> I found Hawk a relaxed man to work for. I never saw him get upset. He had a respect for musicianship and if you were doing your job OK then everything was fine. When the band started hitting it he'd smile in a certain way. Hawk's band was very good, and Arthur Herbert on drums was wonderful. He was dynamic, but so modest. He was perfect at shuffle tempo, playing four-in-a-bar but with accents, sometimes four beats against two. It created a different feeling from Fletcher's old drummer Walter Johnson, who you might say had a gospel beat. My rhythm buddy, Johnny Williams, was on bass. There was a very brotherly feeling in the band.[14]

The band's pianist, Gene Rodgers, also held Arthur Herbert in high esteem, describing him as 'a phenomenal drummer' and recalling him 'battling successfully' against Buddy Rich (then with Dorsey's Orchestra).

The Arcadia Ballroom booking (from which broadcasts were relayed twice a week) served to get Hawk's band into shape for its residency at the Golden Gate. At the Golden Gate the support band, led by Buddy Wagner, featured the electric organ. Besides these two units there was also a steady flow of visiting bands. Jay Faggen encouraged competition and gave Golden Gate audiences (the majority of whom were black) evenings packed with variety. One of his presentations at the ballroom in late 1939 was 'a piano jam' featuring Count Basie, Teddy Wilson, Mary Lou Williams and Jelly Roll Morton.

Lawrence Lucie recalled:

We moved into the Golden Gate as the house band, we'd play a set routine, half an hour on the bandstand, then we'd hand over to whoever else was sharing the booking. The bandstand was big enough for two bands and at the other end of the ballroom there would be an organist. We were pretty formidable at the Golden Gate, but a house band should always be able to outdo the visiting bands because the house band knows the tempos the local dancers want. When Count Basie brought his band in I heard him say to Hawk, 'I know I'm going to get cut tonight.' I joined Fletcher Henderson after Hawk had gone to Europe, but his name was always being mentioned; it was a band joke that if anyone was always late then they were copying Coleman Hawkins. His biggest problem was getting to work on time. When he had his own big band he was always late for the rehearsals – and he'd called them. Everyone would be waiting and Hawk would come in and say, 'Sorry, I've been jamming all night and I just couldn't get up in time.'[15]

Bassist Johnny Williams recalled the Golden Gate was a huge place:

You could put the whole of the Savoy Ballroom in there with no trouble. For a time Teddy Wilson's band played there with us, but on Sundays various guest bands came in, like Tommy Dorsey, Glenn Miller, all of them. The place had good acoustics and the band had a good repertoire, all interesting arrangements. Hawk was a beautiful guy to work with, usually very jolly; I never saw him get angry.

Most of the arrangements that Williams mentioned were written either by James 'Buster' Toliver, Lavere 'Buster' Harding or Andy Gibson, but some were penned by Gene Rodgers and a few by Hawkins himself.

Bill Dillard remembers the fierce but friendly competition that went on between rival bands at the Golden Gate:

When we battled Basie's band Lester Young was playing at the top of his form, but in my opinion Hawkins simply took over. Basie's band was being talked of as *the* up-and-coming band but this didn't faze Hawk at all. He had such great confidence in himself. The moment he came on stage everyone was aware of this. He had his own style of walking on stage. You knew and the audience knew before he'd blown a single note that he was a master.

Buddy Tate, however, playing tenor sax with Basie (alongside Lester Young) when the two bands battled, looked back on the occasion forty-five years later and said:

> Frankly I think we came out on top. It was one of Basie's very best bands, doing what Basie always wanted: 'playing like five pieces'. It swung at any tempo. Coleman Hawkins's band was well-rehearsed but it hadn't got that loose swing. The musicians hadn't had time to get it together properly. All the notes were right but it was a bit stiff, and they kept playing up-tempo numbers. Basie's band could play fast but they could also drop into a very effective slow groove.[16]

This was a happy time for Hawkins: 'When I opened with my own big band at the Golden Gate in 1940, they wouldn't let us off the stand. I enjoyed the period very much and being leader didn't worry me. The band was very good – too good in some ways.' After Hawk's band had finished its initial residency at the Golden Gate it was sent out on the road by Joe Glaser, in January 1940, to play a week each in three theatres: the Royal, Baltimore; the Howard, Washington and the Earle, Philadelphia. Experienced musicians had played this trio of linked dates so often they nicknamed it 'The Circuit'.

Whereas Hawkins had usually triumphed on his theatrical tours in Europe he found playing 'The Circuit' hard and uninviting. Coming on stage for several shows each day to entertain audiences who hadn't come primarily to hear jazz – no matter how skilfully performed – proved a daunting experience. *Metronome* said of the tour, 'Coleman Hawkins disillusioned many of his admirers,' and *Down Beat*, commenting on the show at the Howard Theatre, said, 'His attitude was listless.' Basically the problem was that Hawkins was not an extrovert leader; although his announcements were clear they were rather formal and the band's presentation lacked the sort of gimmicks that made the general public sit up and take notice.

But despite the lack of frenzied applause Hawk kept his sense of humour, soon to be tested by Slim Gaillard, also touring 'The Circuit' on the strength of his success with the recording of 'Flat Foot Floogie'. Slim decided to play a trick on those fans in the audience who had come especially to hear Hawkins play 'Body and Soul'. Gaillard, a talented multi-instrumentalist (who could play guitar, piano, vibes, trombone and tenor sax) pushed the bell of his tenor through a gap in the stage curtain and blew the first notes of 'Body and Soul', and when the applause began simply stepped out and played a few more notes before introducing Coleman Hawkins, who seemed to enjoy the joke as much as anyone. Gaillard remembers, however, that Hawk was often downcast when he visited him in his dressing room, and recalls that he had heard a rumour that Hawkins was depressed at the time because a girlfriend in

France, whom he had invited to join him in America, had declined the offer.[17]

The theatre bookings had not achieved the success for which Joe Glaser had hoped, so Hawkins and his band returned to New York and on 2 February 1940 began another residency at the Golden Gate Ballroom. By this time the group had been augmented by the addition of three more musicians: trombonists Claude Jones and Billy Cato and tenor saxist Ernie Powell. Trumpeter Bill Coleman, who had just returned from a long stay in Europe, heard this band and was greatly impressed: 'The orchestra was superb. I sensed a shiver go through me.'[18]

But business at the Golden Gate was severely affected when the ballroom had its beer licence revoked because of a contravention of the liquor laws. Faggen decided to minimize his wage bill and dispensed with Hawk's band (soon after they had begun their new residency) with the assurance that they could resume the booking when the situation improved. As none of Hawkins's musicians was paid a retainer by the bandleader it was a case of every man for himself during this period. Trombonist Claude Jones began working in Zutty Singleton's small band at Nick's Club in Greenwich Village, but the magazine *Jazz Information* noted, 'Jones is expected to rejoin Hawkins who is laying off at present.'

Count Basie, aware that bookings were becoming scarce for Hawk's band, toyed with the idea of adding Coleman Hawkins to his unit to vie with Lester Young in what would have been one of the greatest jazz coups ever (Basie's previous foil to Lester, Herschel Evans, had died in February 1939, his place taken by Buddy Tate). But Hawkins, despite enjoying a warm friendship with Basie, was not interested in becoming a sideman again, no matter how big the billing.[19] But soon after the offer was mooted Hawk guested with Basie's band for their Apollo Theatre opening on 24 May 1940. Leonard Feather gave an eye-witness report: 'Coleman Hawkins got so worked up by about the tenth chorus of "One O'clock Jump", Lester Young, who was standing by, nervously went back to his seat. But they called him out again and he had the ordeal of following the greatest of them all.[20]

On the following day Feather organized a small all-star group of ex-Fletcher Henderson musicians for a series of recordings on the Commodore label. They were issued as by the Chocolate Dandies and remain some of the most vibrant and inventive small-band recordings of the era.

'Smack', the first tune recorded, was Feather's compositional tribute to

Fletcher Henderson's nickname, but neither Fletcher nor his brother Horace was available for the session, so it went ahead pianoless. Benny Carter, on alto sax, loosely establishes the melody then, with a growing sense of urgency, weaves a bold but involved chorus. Roy Eldridge on trumpet, intense and febrile, plays thirty-two bars of hard-hitting phrases without moving far from his middle register, then Hawkins, sounding more rugged than usual, powerhouses his way through some intensely rhythmic ideas. Sid Catlett's drumming is superfine, establishing an inspirational swing behind Carter's solo, maintaining it on the cymbal patterns he uses to back Eldridge and bringing it to full fruition in the shuffle-beat rhythms that galvanize Hawk's improvisations.

Each fresh take of 'Smack' brought forth a whole new series of spontaneous ideas from the soloists. The three front-line players were such gifted improvisers that they could afford to discard the epic phrases that they'd effortlessly created, simply replacing them with others equally ingenious. There are two takes of 'I Surrender, Dear', a ballad feature for Hawkins in which he ignores the harmonic approach he had taken on 'Body and Soul' and reverts to the sort of performance he had recorded in Europe in the 1930s. To fill out the rhythm section Carter played piano on this number, simply as an accompanist. Roy Eldridge creates a smouldering solo on each take, demonstrating the big part he played in pioneering the use of alternative-harmony 'turn-around phrases' in the seventh and eighth bars of each stanza.

Hawkins plays the opening melody of 'I Can't Believe that You're in Love with Me' with an infectious zest, then develops some energetic variations that rocket from his saxophone but, for all the energy and skills that he displays, his work is soon eclipsed by one of the finest solos that Roy Eldridge ever recorded, an outstanding amalgam of heat, technique and harmonic awareness. Yet in turn Eldridge's work is overshadowed by a brilliantly conceived solo from Carter on alto. Few jazz solos have been more perfectly formed. While maintaining a formidable swing, Carter shows his advanced musicianship by stamping certain phrases with subtle rhythmic accents. He augments these effects with ideas that move smoothly to logical conclusions; in some cases, as in the second chorus step-by-step descent, the logic assumes breathtaking proportions.

The group followed up with a much slower take, but this is, by comparison, ordinary. Thus far through the date Hawkins was not quite in top form, having been forced to take a back seat while Carter and Eldridge displayed their brilliance, but on the final tune of the day, another Leonard

Feather composition called 'Dedication', Hawk returns to his full powers. His lines are superbly shaped, and each chord change is garlanded with a fresh, appealing idea. Unfortunately the support he gets from the rhythm section doesn't sound substantial enough for such a weighty solo. Feather himself described the situation by saying that the tune's 'complex changes were not too clearly spelled out by Bernard Addison's guitar and John Kirby's always understated bass'.[21]

Despite Hawkins's ability to play great jazz under varying circumstances and his undisputed status with fellow professionals there were few openings for his big band; he had to take what he could get. A week's work at the Apollo Theatre (from 5 April 1940) had allowed Hawk to regather his scattered musicians, however, and he was able to maintain a sense of continuity by telling them that he had signed a contract to take the band into the recently opened Fiesta Danceteria on 42nd and Broadway, near Times Square, New York.

12
The Rise and Fall of a Big Band

Unfortunately, soon after Coleman Hawkins's Orchestra began their May 1940 residency at the Danceteria, Hawk and the management had a clash of interests over musical policy. The owners, who were embarking on a novel scheme whereby customers bought a minimum of sixty cents' worth of cafeteria food and then listened or danced to live music free of charge, felt that the band's music wasn't commercial enough for the casual visitor that the Danceteria attracted; they also said that the band was 'too loud'.[1]

Despite needing a long residency for his band, Hawkins decided to quit the job after the first week. He said, 'Mine isn't a Mickey Mouse band, and if I can't play the music I want I'd rather not have the job.'[2] The last straw for Hawkins came when the management asked him to play stock arrangements of currently popular tunes such as 'The Woodpecker Song' and 'Playmates'. Hawk's reaction was scathing: 'If they want that kind of music let them hire Blue Barron or Reggie Childs. That place was ruining the morale of my men. You can't expect to develop a swing band by having your men held under wraps.'[3] Hawk went on to explain that he was asked to play stock arrangements until 11 p.m. and thereafter it was requested that the brass section played muted for the late-night session; 'I have to play the music that I feel and I can't feel the kind that the Fiesta asked me to play.' Hawk said that he was considering offers from two other ballrooms, but added, 'I still won't play Mouse stuff.'[4]

The only engagement that Hawkins had in the offing was a rebooking at the Apollo for the week of 14 June 1940. By then Charlie Buchanan and Moe Gale, the two principal owners of the Savoy Ballroom, had taken over the rival Golden Gate Ballroom. They decided not to put Hawkins back in the Golden Gate but instead offered him a residency at the Savoy (which paid slightly less); Hawk accepted immediately.

Due to the lay-offs and the stop-start bookings of earlier months some of Hawk's original personnel had drifted into other jobs. There were thus several new faces in the band when it began its Savoy residency on 4 July 1940. The biggest headache for Hawkins had been caused by the departure of three key sidemen – Bill Dillard (trumpet), Johnny Williams (bass) and Lawrence Lucie (guitar) – who had been aked by Joe Glaser to join Louis Armstrong's Big Band. Their immediate replacements were Eugene Fields (guitar and vocals), Nick Fenton (bass) and Lincoln Mills (trumpet). Other newcomers were Martin McKaye, who replaced drummer Arthur Herbert, and trombonist Jimmy Archey, who briefly took Earl Hardy's place before being superseded by one of Hawk's old friends, trombonist Sandy Williams. Soon after the Savoy residency began Hawkins added a fourth trumpeter, the high-note specialist Tommy Stevenson, who was a former star of Jimmie Lunceford's band.

Lawrence Lucie recalled this period:

> Somehow Hawk's band didn't catch on and it could only get low-paid dates. Playing at the Roseland was alright; I think that was fifty-five dollars a week, but the usual rate for the Savoy Ballroom was about thirty-six dollars a week. Some of us got the offer to join Louis Armstrong and we took it. Hawk wasn't in the least bit upset; he was happy for us. You see in those days it was like baseball today: you left a band for more money and nobody got bitter.[5]

Bassist Johnny Williams endorsed those remarks: 'When I left Hawk there was no loss of friendship; whenever we met later he was always fine.'[6]

Jazz fans were delighted by the band's performances at the Savoy. Russell Sanjek described his visit to the ballroom for the *Hot Record Society Rag*: 'The trombone section was playing heads on some standards the night I heard them, amazing Hawk with one sample of fine section and solo work after another. I firmly believe that the Hawk's trombone trio of Claude Jones, Sandy Williams and Billy Cato is one of the finest to be heard in any man's band.'

Hawk's new young drummer, J.C. Heard, outlined his early days with the band,

> I went straight from Benny Carter at the Savoy into Hawk's band, also at the Savoy. It was a fine big band, very jazzy. Basie and Ellington were, of course, very popular at this time, but Hawkins never really made any scheme to get that popular. He was carefree and easy-going, but a giant of a player. He was very interested in his music, and in the girls too, but beyond that he wasn't a disciplinarian. He was beautiful people, always nice. He wasn't quite the same with guys who couldn't play their instruments, but if you could play he was always fine. We had good arrangements, some by Buster Harding, Andy Gibson and Buster Tolliver, but we also had some by

Jimmy Mundy and Edgar Sampson, and Eugene Fields, the sax and clarinet players in the band, did a couple.

Hawk's unit wasn't intimidated by any other bands that visited the Savoy Ballroom, and the leader seemed to welcome any challenge issued by a fellow tenor saxist. In an interview with Peter Vacher, pianist Gene Rodgers recalled:

One night we were playing at the Savoy and a guy walked in, got up on the bandstand, pulled his horn out, didn't even say good evening but turned around to me and said, 'Hey man, play some blues.' Coleman Hawkins is standing there and this guy didn't even speak to him, just started blowing up a storm. It was Chu Berry. The people sensed that this was something special. Nobody but the rhythm section played. He caused such excitement. When he got through Chu never said a word, just put his horn in a little bag and walked off.

Coleman looked at me and said, 'It's a damn shame he walked in on my bandstand; he didn't even speak to me.' After this everybody's standing there waiting to see what Hawk is going to do. So Hawk said, 'Alright, play some more blues.' Then he started a riff that became one of the greatest riffs ever. The band started shouting behind him, just off the top of their heads, and Hawk turned that riff around so many different ways and kept that theme going. Pretty soon the whole Savoy Ballroom started dancing to this thing and the place started shaking. We played to three or four thousand people dancing at once. It was a very memorable occasion.[7]

Vocalist Thelma Carpenter also saw Hawkins stung into action by the work of a competitor at the Savoy:

I vividly recall one incident there. We were taking an intermission and Erskine Hawkins's band was playing. All of a sudden their tenor player, a dark guy, Paul Bascomb I believe, began playing a feature on 'Body and Soul'. This was unthinkable, this was absolutely Hawk's tune. Much as I liked Ethel Waters I wouldn't dream of singing any of her material if she was within a hundred miles. It was one of the few times I ever saw Hawk vexed. I said, 'That's not fair,' and he nodded, solemn but fuming. Then we got back on the bandstand and *he* played 'Body and Soul', and in all the times I heard him play it, this was the greatest version. It was as though he was determined to put everything in that performance, and he did. The crowd went wild and the Erskine Hawkins band kept well away from that tune for the rest of the run. One of the pleasures of the job was that I had a chance to hear how well Hawkins played night after night. I used to sit on the bandstand, which is what the singers did at that time; some nights Hawk was kinda loaded with drink, he'd walk about while he was playing, but he kept his eyes closed. Sometimes I'd have to shout, 'Look out, you're right at the edge of the stage.'[8]

On 9 August 1940 Hawkins and his fifteen-piece band made their only studio recordings. The personnel was the normal Savoy Ballroom line-up with the exception of Billy Taylor, subbing on string bass for Nick Fenton, who had been injured in a fight. The first title recorded, 'Passin' It Around', emerges as a half-hearted attempt at commercialism. Hawkins leads the reed section in a slow, bumps-and-grinds-type melody that sounds like the great-aunt of 'The Stripper'. An emphatic off-beat keeps things rocking, but over-repetition of the theme soon wears thin in an arrangement that loses its way; Hawk has one brief interlude in which to improvise. Its coupling, 'Rocky Comfort', has no striking theme but its ordinary thirty-two-bar sequence launches Hawk into a solo that is a mixture of jump phrasing from the 1930s and the frenetic sounds that many future tenorists were to use in order to get concert audiences screaming. Hawk's climactic build-up sounds a little contrived but the effect is impressively spirited. Trumpeter Joe Guy's solo contains some bold harmonic flourishes but no appealing shapes.

Hawk's skill breathes life into the ballad 'Serenade to a Sleeping Beauty', but apart from eight bars of plush improvisation from him, and his ornately embroidered ending, the piece is about as undistinguished as vocalist Gladys Madden's rendering of 'Forgive a Fool', which is enhanced by Hawk's restrained eight-bar solo. This tune was composed by twenty-one-year-old twins Kay and Sue Werner, who had several songs recorded by big bands during this era. Kay Werner (now Mrs Catherine Kent) spoke of the girls' friendship with Hawkins:

> I first met Coleman through my sister's husband, Jim McCarthy, who was doing publicity for Count Basie at that time. This would have been just prior to the making of 'Body and Soul', because my sister and I went to the studio for that recording session. I think Leonard Feather was there and also a Dutch girl-friend of Coleman. It may seem unreal to say this now, but at the time we were certain it would become an all-time great recording, though of course there were so many other wonderful recordings by Coleman.
>
> As a person he was shy and reticent, and so wrapped up in his music that he didn't really give any time to planning anything, so Sue and I did our best to organize things for him, getting publicity and acting as managers, though in those days it was just about impossible for women to be thought of as managers. We didn't do this to make money, just to enable Coleman to concentrate on the musical side of things, for which he was so gifted. He was well aware of the racial issues that existed in the United States at that time; I think he felt things keenly having just come back from Europe. He had a chance to take his band into all-white ballrooms and he turned them down. He was careful with his money. When he came back from Europe he

brought back *a lot* of money with him, but he kept it all in a closet at his home on Edgecombe Avenue. It was one of the signs that he was an eccentric person. As far as the band, and his personal life went, he just wanted to do what *he* wanted to.[9]

Pianist Gene Rodgers gave his views on the band's lack of success:

Coleman's big band never recorded to its full potential. It should have been a tremendous band. Coleman was a marvellous musician, but as far as being a bandleader was concerned he was always up in the clouds. Sometimes pay-nights you couldn't find Coleman. He'd gone off somewhere. He wouldn't even say goodnight to anybody. He's in a cab surrounded by a bunch of floosies. The women that Coleman handled were numerous. I have never met an individual that lived that fast. He lived for the moment. His performance on the bandstand was just superb; the power and the exuberance that he portrayed was breathtaking. The people would stand agog. But he was no businessman, definitely not! Often the guy had the place would say, 'Well, who am I gonna pay? Coleman isn't here to get the salary.'

'So why don't you give me the power of attorney to collect the money? I know how much everyone gets.' We were all getting the same anyway.

So he said, 'OK,' just to get it off his back. So everybody was calling me the straw boss after that.[10]

Hawkins's band played at the Savoy throughout the summer of 1940, during which time NBC relayed three broadcasts per week from the ballroom. Some of these radio shows were privately recorded off the air by diligent fans (on wire recorders) and years later were issued on microgroove. Despite the fact that some of these broadcasts suffer badly from fading, indifferent sound balancing and poor recordings, they give a reasonably clear idea of the band's considerable spirit and the leader's continuing brilliance.

A long work-out by Hawkins, full of hoarse dexterity, is the main feature of a fast 'California Here I Come'. J.C. Heard on drums plays some rocking rimshots in the background before creating a supple, exciting drum solo. The trombone section is a trifle rough but this seems to add to the fervour; Joe Guy's brief trumpet solo is full of flair. The trombone section again display an indifferent blend on the opening chorus of 'The Sheik of Araby', but Claude Jones's trombone solo is a model of smooth brilliance. Hawkins constructs two ingenious choruses, pouncing on his ideas, shaking the substance out of them and then moving on. Gene Rodgers's piano solo reveals his admiration for Teddy Wilson's talents, but also shows that he had much to say for himself. A fastish 'Blue Moon' is again introduced by the trombones; Hawk twists neatly around the melody but the unsympathetic backing figures are distracting. A well-articulated, block-scored chorus by the entire ensemble launches Hawkins into a solo that veers perilously close to incoherent wildness, but this dynamic show of energy comes to a sudden end as the arrangement abruptly concludes.

Joe Guy's trumpet playing was closely patterned on Roy Eldridge's, but despite his range and speed Guy never possessed Eldridge's gift for creating instant excitement, a failing that becomes apparent on 'Chant of the Groove'. Guy plays well enough, but there's a lack of conviction, and the searing notes that give his mentor's solos their zing are missing. Hawkins again parades some spellbinding ideas, building his solo to dramatic peaks during his second chorus. One of the supreme moments from the whole set is Hawk's rendering of 'I Can't Believe that You're in Love with Me', on which he's accompanied only by the rhythm section. It's an unusually slow version of the tune, with thoughtful accompaniment from Gene Rodgers (who inserts a highly effective triplet pattern in his backing for Hawkins). Hawk effortlessly produces wave upon wave of phrases that suggest the inexorable power and beauty of ocean breakers.

The arrangement of 'Chicago' gets off to a brilliant start, impressively maintained during Joe Guy's trumpet solo and throughout Eustis Moore's clarinet improvisations. Though the stage is perfectly set for Hawkins, a series of distracting riffs take the edge off his interesting solo; happily a bold modulation relaunches the excitement but then the arrangement pulls up with another unsatisfactorily sudden ending. 'I Can't Love You Anymore' is one of the few commercial charts that Hawkins chose to broadcast. Claude Jones's trombone establishes the melody of this fleetingly popular song, then Hawk takes over for a chorus of rhapsodizing; the band play eight bars of orchestration before Hawk re-enters to introduce a contrasting mood, one that he creates by shouting out gruff phrases on his tenor sax, as though he'd lost patience with the banal material.

There are some commercial trimmings around 'The Breeze and I', including clarinet-and-tenor-sax unison passages that give a Glenn Millerish flavour, and a competent male vocal, but more interesting are the effective tom-tom patterns played by J.C. Heard and Hawk's smooth low-register work. Unfortunately there's yet another anti-climactic ending. Hawkins used one of his premier soloists, trombonist Sandy Williams, sparingly, but he is given the chance to shine on 'Sweet Emaline', which has a spectacular high-note ending from trumpeter Tommy Stevenson. Williams's lusty, highly emotive style is particularly effective on 'When a Congressman Meets a Senator', which has a vocal by J.C. Heard. None of the sections of Hawkins's band is consistently good, but the saxophones are close to their best throughout 'It's a Wonderful World'. The piano solo by Gene Rodgers achieves a pleasant, lilting swing and there is another punchy high-note finish from Stevenson. The oddity of this track concerns Hawk's solo, which for some reason he imbues with an emphatic vibrato that sounds ungainly.

These samples, taken from the many broadcasts that the band did from the Savoy, offer clues as to why Hawkins's career as a bandleader didn't flourish. Although he used 'Body and Soul' as an occasional theme song he made little effort to highlight his ballad playing within each programme. He also ignored short, snappy numbers that might have stimulated the interest of casual listeners, instead playing long instrumentals, but he was often forced by time restrictions to cut the number off before it had reached any sort of climax. Often the backing riffs cut right across the soloist's lines, and while in person this sometimes added to the excitement, on an indifferently balanced radio show it meant the listener at home heard only the riffs. Jazz listeners were thrilled to hear the master play long, involved tenor-sax solos but undiluted jazz in such quantities is too strong a brew for the general public.

Hawkins only half-heartedly went along with suggestions that the band feature more vocal numbers; a good percentage of radio listeners of that era particularly wanted to hear – and learn – the lyrics of various current songs, so they were not attracted by Hawk's avoidance of what he considered trite material. Though the jazz fans found such an approach commendable, it was not a strategy that delighted booking agents and ballroom managers. Overall the jazz content of Hawkins's big band was admirably high, but the commercial value of Hawk's programming was suicidally low.

In an attempt to drown out the perceivable sounds of the band's death rattle, Moe Gale's press agent put out some highly imaginative press stories about Hawkins. One said that his $15,000 home in Paris had been destroyed in a German air raid and another announced that his 'English estate, in the suburbs of London, was being used as a British Army hospital'.[11] Needless to say, Hawkins didn't own any property in France or England.

In person the group's lack of gimmicks and the leader's subdued presentation failed to win over the general public; the dancers at the Savoy Ballroom liked the band's music but found nothing it its make-up that made them want to be fans. Several of Hawk's musicians, sensing that the future of the band was in doubt, went off to audition for other jobs and, during the late stages of the Savoy residency, a number of subs worked briefly in the group, including trombonist Billy Butler and reed players Jimmy Hamilton and George James.

To keep the band working Moe Gale offered to fix up a wide-ranging tour, using another of the agency's bands, Al Cooper's Savoy Sultans, as the support group. Realizing that this was the only way of keeping the band intact, Hawkins accepted the offer. So, in September 1940 the Hawkins band bus (chartered from the Greyhound company) rolled its way through a string of one-night stands that stretched right through the South and also included bookings in Kansas City, St Louis and Chicago.

A new bassist, John 'Jack' Jarvis, joined the band for this trip. Hawkins made contact with Jarvis after arranger Andy Gibson had recommended the youngster. The audition for the job took place in Hawkins's apartment, with Hawk accompanying the bassist on piano. Jarvis enjoyed his stay with the band, which was only for the duration of the tour; he said, 'Hawkins was a genius. He was a quiet, brilliant man. If the mood was right he could sit back and talk about many things. There was nothing boisterous about him, easy come, easy go, but when he got on that horn it was a different story.'[12]

Throughout that tour trombonist Sandy Williams travelled in Hawk's car:

> We'd ride mile after mile. I just enjoyed his conversation; it was so interesting. The man was always jolly. We had always been good buddies, right from the Fletcher Henderson days on. While the other band members travelled by bus, Hawk wanted me to be with him in his car. He drove fast and always left much later than the bus. We often arrived late at certain gigs and all of the band were already on the stand. 'Here comes the two bosses,' they said, and you could see that some of them were jealous of the way Hawk seemed to prefer me. I didn't like that at all but Hawk just laughed it off.[13]

On another occasion, Williams reminisced further:

> It was rough travelling in those days, particularly down South. One would travel all day and all night and then you had to find some place to sleep and get something to eat. It was rough. We got as far as Coleman's home town, St Joe. I remember having the honour of meeting his mother. She was a beautiful lady, snow-white hair, the type you'd see on a Mother's Day card.[14]

Drummer J.C. Heard said, 'We covered a lot of miles on that tour, mostly ballroom dates, I seem to recall. We went to Detroit, Chicago, Cleveland, Minneapolis and so on down to New Orleans, then we come back and played some dates in West Virginia before making our way back to New York.'[15]

Attendances at the various ballrooms were disappointing and those that did hear the band were favourable rather than feverish. Hawk himself made no effort to smoothtalk the various ballroom managers; he played his sets then cut out for the next date. Agent Moe Gale checked on the ballroom operators' reactions and was dismayed by their lack of enthusiasm. With openings scarce in New York and no prospects of further tours Hawkins had no option but to disband.

Under a headline ARE NEGRO BANDS DOOMED AS MONEY MAKERS? the 1 December 1940 issue of *Down Beat* reported the band's demise: 'Coleman Hawkins's recent tour with a large band was not successful. The day it returned to New York in November the band dissolved.' The magazine mentioned that Count Basie's band was not working steadily and even Duke Ellington's Orchestra was experiencing a lean time. The music that these bands played delighted the jazz fans but in this part of the Swing Era it was the more commercial bands, almost all of them white, that drew the biggest crowds.

In his last days as leader of a big band Hawkins virtually lost interest and this attitude resulted in a critical magazine feature headed COLEMAN HAWKINS IS DECLINING, written by 'Duane Woodruff' and published in *Music and Rhythm*. Commenting on the failure of Hawk's big band, the writer said,

> Hawkins's physical condition has been a contributing factor. He has been leading his own band for a year, and poor bookings, which necessitated long jumps, coupled with inevitable business worries, have taken part of his attention from music-making. He seems to have developed an indifference towards his public. Not long ago I went to hear him and his band play for a one-nighter. I paid the better part of a dollar to gain admission but I heard him play for only an hour and a half. He disappeared entirely for almost two hours, letting his badly-rehearsed band take over. Maybe some of the trouble lies in excesses in his personal mode of living. That's strictly his business, but when it interferes with his playing it isn't.

In Britain the *Melody Maker*, reporting on the demise of Hawk's big band, said, 'Lack of organization and discipline is blamed for the downfall of this once promising crowd.' Hawk's musicians were disappointed that the band couldn't survive: 'That was a terrific big band,' said Sandy Williams. 'I was sorry to see the band break up, but there was no place to play.[16] Hawkins was not the only jazz giant to suffer the ignominy of being forced to disband during this era. Benny Carter's superb unit broke up, and so too did Teddy Wilson's big band. Hawkins and Carter were eventually able to shrug off the disappointment (Carter went on to lead other big bands) but Teddy Wilson's dismayed rancour about this particular setback stayed with him for much of his life. Failure to win over the public didn't affect only black bandleaders; white jazz musicians such as Bunny Berigan and Jack Teagarden bankrupted themselves trying to launch their own big bands. Being a superb improviser didn't guarantee success on the ballroom circuit.

During this period *Down Beat* magazine gave its readers a fascinating insight into Coleman Hawkins's style by publishing (in two parts) a transcription of the tenor saxist's recording of 'Body and Soul'. The publication of this solo (in the issues of 15 September and 1 October 1940) played an important part in making many jazz musicians broaden the harmonic scope of their work. Jazz publications had previously published brief excerpts from famous recordings but nothing as substantial as Hawk's celebrated solo had been made so readily available. Its publication gave a fillip to young musicians eager to explore new harmonic avenues. Countless tenor saxists did their best to learn the solo note for note; most of them found it a daunting task. Arnett Cobb was one; 'I never could get Coleman Hawkins's "Body and Soul" verbatim; a little bit too tough for me at that time.'

Early in November 1940, Hawkins, using a nucleus of musicians from the disbanded unit (including Sandy Williams, trumpeter Peanuts Holland and drummer J.C. Heard), returned to Kelly's Stable (now located at a new address: 137 West 52nd Street) to lead a seven-piece band. The pianist in the group was Clyde Hart, the guitarist Eugene Fields and the bassist, a youthful newcomer to the profession, was twenty-year-old George Duvivier. Duvivier, who was completing his studies at New York University, decided to write to Coleman Hawkins when he heard that he was contemplating forming a new small band. He later described his action as 'sheer nerve' and was both surprised and delighted when Hawk telephoned him about five days before the opening date at Kelly's. He recalled Hawkins saying, 'I got your letter; are you doing anything this afternoon? If not, bring your bass up and play for me.' The route from the Duviviers' family apartment to Hawk's flat was all uphill, but the young bassist willingly trudged over with his instrument and played duets with Hawkins at the keyboard. When the audition was over Hawkins asked, 'Do you have a tuxedo? Alright, Monday night. Nine o'clock. Kelly's Stable.'

Duvivier looked back on his stay at Kelly's with affection: 'The hours were long. We went on at nine until three or later. In the three or four months I was there it was like two years in University'. The young bassist had the utmost respect for his leader. 'I couldn't ask for a more helpful human being. He'd say, 'If you mess it up don't worry about it, just keep doing it.' Coleman was very loose as a leader. He figured this way: "I've got good sidemen so I don't have to tell them what to do. If they make a mistake they're the first ones to know it." ' Hawkins drove the young bassist home each night in his 1939 Cadillac. Duvivier recalled these trips as 'hair-raising'. 'Coleman observed no traffic lights whatsoever, from the time he went in Central Park South to Central Park North. He never got caught.'

Speaking of the clientele of Kelly's, Duvivier said, 'They came in principally to hear Coleman; he was the great attraction then.' The band played at least two warm-up numbers before Hawkins came on stage: 'He was in the back having a little Calvert's, that was his favourite drink at the time. We'd have a phalanx of tenor-sax players there for the last set – those who were playing elsewhere and got off earlier would head for our last set.' One night some of the tenor players joined in a warm-up number and jammed the blues in B flat. 'Hawk walked across the stand, turned and said, "Blues in G flat." People left the stand. Then, when he said, " 'East of the Sun' in B," we lost everyone.' Duvivier felt that Hawk's gifts extended far beyond dexterity in every key and cerebral ingenuity:

> He could destroy other tenor players by sheer power. You couldn't believe what came out of that tenor. He also had an unorthodox way of playing, in that barlines meant nothing. He'd play a phrase that was five bars and three beats then carry the next phrase right through the eighth bar, maybe two and a half bars into the next eight. It would kind of throw people. Kind of unsettle his adversaries.[17]

The ballroom dancers and general public had failed to devote much admiration to Hawkins's skills on the bandstand, but American jazz fans let the tenor saxist know via the *Metronome* popularity poll that he was still highly regarded by them. They voted him the top tenor saxist, and as a result he was featured with other musicians who had enjoyed success in the poll on a recording session for RCA Victor, the proceeds of which went to charities operated by Local 802 of the Musicians' Union. Ralph Watkins, the owner of Kelly's Stable, co-operated by allowing Hawkins time off from the club so that he could take part in the session scheduled for the early hours of 16 January 1941. All of the musicians involved waived their performance royalties and simply took a basic session fee; the nominal leader was Benny Goodman.

As was often the case on recording dates, Hawk chose not to arrive early. He entered with his good friend, Count Basie, with whom he had shared a drink or two on the way to the studio. Even so, they were not the last to arrive. Tenor saxist Tex Beneke, who had to dash to the Studio after finishing his gig with Glenn Miller, arrived after Basie and Hawkins, but the final entrant was Tommy Dorsey. The session eventually got under way at 1.20 a.m.

While waiting for the late arrivals, alto saxist Toots Mondello tried to get Hawkins and Benny Carter to run through the two arrangements selected for the date, Deane Kincaide's chart of 'Bugle Call Rag' and Count Basie's 'One O'clock Jump' sketch. Neither Carter nor Hawkins showed any enthusiasm for Mondello's suggestion; in fact, Hawk delayed opening his tenor-sax case and sat down to doodle random phrases on the piano. Leonard Joy, the session supervisor, was used to Hawkins's habits and let him stay at the keyboard, and after a few minutes Hawk decided to unpack his instrument and joined in the hubbub of tuning up.

Because there was only just over three minutes' playing time available on a ten-inch 78 rpm disc, this assembled plethora of fine improvisers could be allocated only brief solos. Tommy Dorsey and Tex Beneke voluntarily relinquished their chance to be featured; as a consolation Beneke was allocated some breaks on 'Bugle Call Rag'. No one managed to reach top gear in the limited time available and Hawk's abrasive approach to 'Bugle Call Rag' suggests he wasn't yet in the mood for the date; his simply constructed riffs on 'One O'clock Jump' are much more effective. Overall the high standard of the performances says a good deal for the participants' stamina. Harry James, for instance, had played five shows at the Paramount Theatre before arriving at the studio.

Hawkins continued to lead his septet at Kelly's Stable, but it was obvious both to him and to the management that he would eventually wear out his welcome if he stayed at the club too long. Knowing that the end of the residency was in sight, Peanuts Holland and Sandy Williams accepted offers to join Fletcher Henderson, who was re-forming a big band.

The brilliant young trumpeter, Dizzy Gillespie, joined Hawk's band at Kelly's Stable but left after a week. Gillespie recalled the brief encounter:

> I told Coleman Hawkins, 'I'm not gonna work for sixty-six dollars, I want seventy-five a week.'
>
> 'Yeah, yeah' said Hawk, 'you deserve it.'
>
> But Hawk wasn't the one who was paying the money, and things kept going back and forth between him and the owner. So at the end of the week they gave me sixty-six dollars. I didn't show anymore and that was the end of my engagement with Coleman Hawkins. They paid Coleman the money he asked for; he was getting his money by saying, 'I want so-and-so for myself; those other musicians will work for scale.'[18]

Gillespie's brief stay at Kelly's played a part in changing the song 'How High the Moon' from a transient 'pop' into a jazz standard. Dizzy recalled: 'Nat "King" Cole was working there with his trio. He showed "How High the Moon" to me and I thought it was beautiful. I took it down to Minton's and I showed it to Thelonious Monk, then we started playing it.'[19]

Minton's Playhouse, at 208–210 West 118th Street in Harlem, was an informal nightspot that stayed open until 4 a.m. During the early 1940s it rapidly became the central point in the development of modern jazz. The owner, Henry Minton (a former saxophonist), left the musical policy to ex-bandleader Teddy Hill, who became the club's manager in 1941. Drummer Kenny Clarke recalled that, previous to this, the club 'was a rather drab place frequented by old men'. Clarke saw it change dramatically: 'Monday night was always a free-for-all at Minton's. Dizzy Gillespie had gotten on a new kick working out his ideas with Charlie Parker, Thelonious Monk, Nick Fenton and myself.' Pianist Duke Jordan said, 'Minton's Playhouse was a nightclub. They had a bar in front, and in the back they had this room where you could buy drinks and sit down and listen to the music.'[20] A report from the Christmas 1941 issue of *Swing* magazine mentioned: 'Every Monday night Teddy Hill has Celebrity Nights at which negro and white musicians sit in together for all-night jam sessions. Always the host, Teddy serves these exponents of swing dinner on the house. Among these who have been sitting in at recent sessions are some former members of Hill's old band, Roy Eldridge, Coleman Hawkins and Joe Guy.'

Hawk's long booking at Kelly's Stable ended on 27 February 1941. Pianist Clyde Hart stayed on at the club to work with Lester Young's incoming group, J.C. Heard went to work with Teddy Wilson's band and George Duvivier joined Eddie Barefield's Orchestra. All of these men went with Hawk's blessings; he had no regular work to offer them. A little over a year after he had returned from Europe in a blaze of glory, Hawk thus found himself without any prospects of leading a regular band in New York City. He played a few casual dates in and around Manhattan and was featured on a couple of engagements in Providence, RI. On the first of these Sunday dates in Providence Hawk's performance was lambasted by the outspoken critic George Frazier, but his return booking soon afterwards was highly praised by the same man.

Beginning in late December 1940 Hawkins often played at the Sunday-afternoon jam sessions organized by Ralph Berton at the Village Vanguard (178 Seventh Avenue), sharing the bandstand with various star musicians such as Lester Young, J.C. Higginbotham, Pee Wee Russell, Sammy Price, Teddy Bunn, Rod Cless and Max Kaminsky, but these sort of casual dates would hardly keep Hawkins in socks. After the stint at Kelly's ended, Hawkins admitted that he had no definite plans. he told *Down Beat*, 'I've had a couple of offers in Chicago and may cut out there for a time.' The magazine commented, 'He doesn't seem concerned about his status and says Joe Glaser, the booker, will "fix me up with something when I'm ready".'

As neither Moe Gale nor his brother (and co-director) Tim had any work to offer Hawkins, he decided to approach his former agent, Joe Glaser, to enquire about prospects. Glaser, who still had strong connections with the club scene in Chicago, soon found an opening for Hawk at a venue owned by Sam Hunt and Benny Skoller at 343 East Garfield Boulevard, Chicago. This nightclub operated for some while as Dave's Cafe, but it had recently been renamed Dave's Swingland (it later became the Rhumboogie); Dave was the manager, Dave Heighley.

13
Chicago Siesta

Hawk's task at Dave's Swingland was to front a big band. It was billed as Coleman Hawkins's Orchestra and consisted entirely of musicians based in Chicago: Darnell Howard, Ernest 'Pinky' Williams, Robert 'Bob' Crowder (reeds); Ed Sims and Milton Fletcher (trumpets); Ed Burke (trombone); Prentice McCarey (piano); Jesse Simpkins (bass) and Oliver Coleman (drums).

The band had been organized by tenor saxist Bob Crowder. Hawkins brought some of the band's arrangements with him from New York, but Crowder wrote a lot of material and also scored several features for Hawkins to play. Hawk's performances on these new numbers greatly impressed his sidemen who, by word of mouth, spread the news that Hawkins was playing better than ever. *Down Beat* reported, 'The Hawk is drawing local musicians in droves to Dave's Cafe, South Side black-and-tan nitery.'[1]

Prentice McCarey was delighted to be accompanying Hawkins, saying: 'He was just about the nicest, easiest guy that I ever worked for. Some genius-types are difficult to work with, but Hawkins certainly wasn't.' Trumpeter Ed Sims echoed this viewpoint: 'Hawk was one of the finest of all bandleaders. He didn't like any kind of responsibility. He delegated people to take care of what had to be done. I was musical director for shows; somebody else took care of business, that was it. He just played his horn.'[2]

The band opened at Dave's on 12 April 1941. After finishing work, Hawkins left his saxophone at the club and went back to his hotel room at the Ritz on Oakwood Boulevard and South Parkway. When he got to work the next evening he found that several keys on his saxophone had been bent out of line. A rumour began that a rival clubowner, angry that Skoller and Hunt had secured such a powerful attraction for their venue, had damaged the saxophone. This story is refuted by someone who knew the Chicago club scene well: 'Nobody would be dumb enough to cross those guys over something like that.' The mystery was never solved. It's possible that a fan, or an admiring musician, simply took Hawk's tenor out of its case to look at it and accidentally dropped it, without ever owning up. Hawkins himself seemed unconcerned about the incident; he put the tenor in for repair and simply borrowed a horn from a sideman and blew just as magnificently as he had on the previous night.

Tenorist George 'Big Nick' Nicholas first heard Hawkins live at Dave's, having been hugely impressed by two recordings that Hawk had made in Europe: 'Stardust' and 'Meditation': 'Until then my two favorites were Ben Webster and Chu Berry. I was always a "sound" man, and I went for Coleman's sound. Near to Dave's there was a Cadillac showroom and that was where I had my first real conversation with Hawk. He was always in there discussing new models.'[3] Record producer and writer Dave Dexter never forgot the power of Hawk's playing at Dave's: 'You could hear his tenor outdoors and across the street from the ballroom.'[4]

During the band's six-month residency at Dave's there were various personnel changes: Leon Gray came in on sax in place of Pinky Williams and Claude Roberts was added on guitar (Omer Simeon occasionally subbed in the reed section). Hawkins was also persuaded to add a male vocalist. He chose a tall young man who had previously sung with Jimmie Noone's band; this was Joe Williams, later to gain international fame with Count Basie's band. Williams recalled: 'Coleman Hawkins had a *good* band out of Chicago. I was singing at the club; he paid me double what I was making: eighty dollars a week to join his orchestra and sing ballads.'[5] Eddie Jefferson, who later became a well-known vocalist, also worked at Dave's as part of a dance team billed as 'Billy and Eddie'.

While living in Chicago, Hawkins met a local white girl named Dolores Sheridan, who was then just twenty-one. Dolores made it her business to hear in person the musician who had made the sensational recording of 'Body and Soul'. She not only heard Hawkins but entered into conversation with him; a romance blossomed over the next few months and the couple were married on 16 October 1941.

During his honeymoon Hawkins learnt of the accidental death of Leon 'Chu' Berry, the man generally considered to be his closest rival on tenor saxophone. Berry, who died in an automobile crash while touring in Cab Calloway's band, said in the last interview he ever gave: 'A tenor man who was a combination of Coleman Hawkins's originality and Freddy Martin's tone couldn't be beat.'[6]

Hawkins himself had a high opinion of Berry's talents, even though he sometimes chose to disguise that admiration. Two months before Chu's death Hawkins selected a listing of his twelve favourite tenor saxists for *Music and Rhythm*. As that magazine was published in Chicago, Hawkins was able to deal with the matter direct rather than through an agency publicist. His choice was (in order of preference):

1. Ben Webster	5. Charlie Barnet	9. Vido Musso
2. Chu Berry	6. Bud Freeman	10. Sam Donahue
3. Lester Young	7. Don Byas	11. Babe Russin
4. George Auld	8. Dexter Gordon	12. Eddie Miller

Hawk explained the reasoning behind his selections:

I like Ben Webster's nice big tone the best of all. Ben is excellent at phrasing too. Chu Berry is one of the fastest men in the business on his horn. Add to this his original ideas on phrasing and his firm sense of harmonic changes and you have a tenorman who ranks among the best. Lester Young is great on phrasing, for originality of ideas I would rank him first. Les plays with lots of feeling and most important he constantly strives for originality. George Auld's tone is second only to Ben Webster's. Charlie Barnet's instrumental attack is hard and powerful – he has plenty of what we musicians call 'guts'. Bud Freeman has a lot in common with Les Young; he phrases well and puts a lot of thought into his phrasing.

Don Byas's strongest point is execution. Don is young and has plenty on the ball. Vido Musso has a good tone and plays with the right feeling and expressiveness; he gets directly to the heart of the jazz spirit. Sam Donahue gets the 'jump' into his horn without seeming so brutal about it as Barnet. Babe Russin, his sense of harmonic change is excellent. Eddie Miller's solo tenor work is marked by a firm, clean attack and although he doesn't attain the drive of most of the tenormen I have selected he compensates for it by the conciseness of his execution.[7]

Eleven of the players Hawkins listed were well-established musicians but as if to confirm that he always kept his ears alert for the work of promising newcomers, Hawk included Dexter Gordon, then a teenaged member of Lionel Hampton's band. It was an early acknowledgement of the skills that created a long and illustrious career for Dexter.

Fletcher Henderson, who had employed the first three in Hawkins's list at one time or another, had recently become leader of a big band again (having spent two years working for Benny Goodman). Henderson brought his new band to Chicago in May 1941 and Hawkins went along to hear it. It was the first time that the two men had met since Hawk had left for Europe in 1934. Hawkins spoke of the encounter: 'Fletcher was playing and knew I was in the audience. He sent the waiter over with a note saying, "Hope you have your saxophone with you. I think it's about time your leave of absence was over." '[8] But the reunion was a fleeting one and neither man made any particular effort to re-establish their earlier close friendship.

Count Basie was one bandleader with whom Hawkins always remained on friendly terms. By coincidence the Count's band were in Chicago when Hawk arrived there in April 1941, and as a result Basie invited the tenorist to join them for a recording session. By this time Lester Young had left the band. On '9.20 Special', Basie and trumpeter Harry Edison create solo phrases that swing unerringly the split second they are created. After a modulating bridge Hawkins enters and blows a series of forceful ideas that interject with the band's crisply played figures. In the background drummer Jo Jones's wristy playing marks yet another superb performance by the nonpareil rhythm section.

'Feedin' the Bean' is a simple twelve-bar blues riff that is topped and tailed by Buck Clayton's softly blown plunger-muted trumpet. Hawkins's playing is the meat in the sandwich. He starts in a restrained mood but gradually begins to increase the drama by emphatically reiterating single-note patterns before surging his way through the fifth and sixth choruses. On both tracks it's noticeable that Hawkins appears to be paying a tribute to the Basie band's deceased tenor saxist Herschel Evans. It's more than a question of association; Hawk seems deliberately to include some of Evans's phrases. Hawkins was known to like Herschel's playing; Evans himself had worshipped Hawk's tenor style, so much so that Lester Young once said, 'Most of the time Herschel sounded just like Hawk to me.'[9] Jo Jones felt that the admiration might have been a sore point between Basie's two tenor stars: 'You couldn't say anything bad about Hawkins to Herschel. Some of the friction between Herschel and Pres may have had something to do with that.'[10]

When the record came out, Basie again jocularly asked Hawkins to join the band but Hawkins humorously declined the offer, saying he had no plans to become a sideman again. After playing briefly at White's Emporium (formerly the Golden Lily) at 309 East Garfield Boulevard (close to Dave's), Hawkins decided to take his Chicago band out on tour. A few of the group didn't want to leave Chicago, but most of the musicians who had worked with Hawk throughout 1941 went out on the road with him. Prentice McCarey said, 'We set out on a series of one-night stands, and it was half-suggested that we might even take the band on to New York if things worked out alright; it was a good band. But when we got to Indianapolis, Indiana we heard about Pearl Harbor being bombed. So that ended the tour and all of Hawk's plans; he told us all to go back home.' Joe Williams recalled that the band played one further date in Memphis, Tennessee, before heading back to Chicago.

During the first weeks after the USA entered World War II the entertainments business was plunged into total confusion about its future. No one knew what sort of regulations would be introduced, so club and ballroom owners temporarily stopped booking bands in advance. However, just as had happened in Europe in late 1939, things gradually returned to something approaching normality, though almost every band was affected by draft notices conscripting musicians into the armed services, and by the rationing of gasolene, which made touring very difficult.

In January 1942, while guesting with Jimmy Williams's seven-piece combo at White's Emporium, Hawkins was offered the chance (by the club's black owner, Ed White) of leading his own small band there. Accordingly Hawk formed a group featuring Alvin Burroughs on drums, Gail Brockman on trumpet, Eddie Johnson on tenor sax and 'Goon' Gardner on alto sax. By this time several of Hawk's former Chicago sidemen were already in the services. Prentice McCarey recalled the period; 'By the time Hawk got his next band jobs fixed in Chicago those that hadn't already been drafted were fixed in other bands.' Singer Joe Williams returned to work with Hawkins at White's because a collapsed lung made him ineligible for the services.[11]

The new residency suited Hawkins. He said at the time: 'I'm tired of a big band, of one-nighters and long hops, and I want to settle in one spot with my own small combo and relax. I believe I can play better that way. I think the majority of rising colored bandleaders would be smart to concentrate on small outfits. The number of places where big Negro bands can go on location is becoming limited.'[12]

Draft calls continued to decimate established personnels. Being over the age fixed for the first recruitment draft was a mixed blessing for Hawkins because he did not want to admit being considerably older than his sidemen. To please his own vanity he pretended that he might be called any day. He even kept up this ploy with friends such as Roy Eldridge and John Kirby. Kirby, increasingly exasperated by Hawk's tactics, said to him one day, 'Damn it Bean, if you get any younger you'll have to go back into diapers.'[13]

Tenor saxist Eddie Johnson spoke of working with Hawkins's band at White's:

> I remember some nights Hawk would get so bored he would drink a little more of his Seagram's Seven than he could comfortably handle, and when he got up to solo he wouldn't stand in front of the band. He would get in the arch of the grand piano in order to brace himself so that he wouldn't fall off on his face. He would open up on his horn some nights and blow for an hour and a half, non-stop. The rest of the band just sat gap-mouthed and listened. He seldom, if ever, had to tune his horn. Hawk always managed to stay in tune. Regardless of where the piano was [in pitch] he was in tune. I don't understand it to this day. I remember that we always tried to get next to Hawk but he was a very shy and private person and stayed to himself. To get him to talk was an effort.[14]

Hawk's band stayed at White's for four months, until the club closed temporarily. *Down Beat* gave the reasons for the closure as 'so-so business and politics'. Two other venues on Chicago's South Side, the Plantation and the Grand Terrace also closed that same week. In order to keep the band together Hawkins was forced to take it out on the road. After playing a series of one-night stands the group took up residency at a nightspot known as Benny Mason's Farm, situated near Cleveland, Ohio. They returned to Chicago several weeks later, played briefly at a newly-opened White's Emporium then disbanded through lack of work.

Hawkins faced a repeat of the situation he had encountered the previous year in New York but, as before, he faced the future with cheerful optimism. *Down Beat* of 15 September 1942 reported: 'Coleman Hawkins is still around town [Chicago] and is now reportedly rebuilding his band. Nothing is lined up but Hawk doesn't seem too worried about things in general.'

As Hawkins's links with Joe Glaser had terminated, he contacted a local Chicago agent, who secured him a two-week residency at the Fox Head Tavern in Cedar Rapids, Iowa. For this October 1942 club stint Hawk led a band consisting mainly of musicians he had gathered up in Chicago. The line-up was Johnny Board on alto sax, Ellis 'Stumpy' Whitlock (an ex-Louis Armstrong sideman) on trumpet, James Woode on piano, Chuck Barksdale on double bass and Joe Marshall on drums.

Altoist Johnny Board spoke of this residency with Dempsey J. Travis, author of *An Autobiography of Black Jazz*:

> We worked the Cedar Rapids nightclub six nights a week and when we finished playing the last set on Sunday morning Hawk would head back to Chicago because

he said he didn't want to spend a weekend in a hick town. He and I would travel back alone; the other fellows wanted to stay over. Hawk always drove a brand-new Cadillac and we would glide along, sipping his Seagram's Seven and talking. The roads were narrow in those days and Hawk drove between eighty and a hundred miles an hour. But for some reason, with Hawk behind the wheel, I didn't worry about anything happening.

Les Zacheis wrote a graphic description of Hawkins's visit to the Iowa club for the spring issue of *Jazz Quarterly*:

A shrewd and far-sighted management has bearded the lion. In the heart of the corn country where Little German Bands thrive and the Mickey Mouse bands are a dime a dozen we find an oasis of Righteous Jazz. What's more, people will listen to it. And there's no dancing either. The bands need make no concessions to dancers here. So it doesn't pay off? The STANDING ROOM ONLY sign is up nightly. Just try and get a booth or table for a party after nine. Indeed, a great tribute to the drawing power of Le Jazz Hot when we consider that in the state of Iowa hard liquor over the bar is taboo. It's beer or pop, brother. The Hawk is on the stand in the flesh, adjusting that golden horn to a comfortable angle. Can this be Cedar Rapids, Iowa?

At the Cedar Rapids club Johnny Board had the opportunity to observe Hawk's bizarre method of arranging a new number:

Hawkins did not write out a musical score for the band. He brought in an alto part one night, a piano part the next and so on, until everyone had a part. I couldn't figure out how he could remember the part he had written the day before, or the day before that. Ordinarily an arranger will write a score and then he can see at a glance exactly who is playing what note at any given time, but to write it in segments as Hawk did is remarkable. It was an education to watch Hawk work out nightly. He made tenor-sax playing seem effortless – that is, if you weren't aware of his tremendous musical training and discipline.[15]

When the Cedar Rapids residency ended Hawkins continued to make Chicago his base, but after playing a few guest appearances with local bands he decided it was time to move back to New York and set up home there for his new wife, Dolores. They moved east and settled into Hawk's apartment at 555 Edgecombe Avenue.

Hawkins took up an offer to return to work at Kelly's Stable. He opened there on Christmas Eve 1942 guesting with Kenny Clarke's band (Clarke, drums; Ike Quebec, tenor sax; Willie Nelson, trumpet; Earl Hardy, trombone; Ray Walker, piano and Al Lucas, double bass). *Metronome* devoted a whole page to Hawkins's auspicious return to New

York. Under a headline COLEMAN HAWKINS BETTER THAN EVER Barry Ulanov wrote:

> Coleman Hawkins is still the top man on tenor saxophone. Hawk today is more relaxed than at any time in recent years. The changes of key and chord, the plethora of notes that Hawk blows have confused or annoyed or bewildered many of his listeners in the past. And casual listeners can't help occasionally being swamped into boredom or uncertainty by his playing. There will be somewhat less of that reaction in the future however, because this is a more lucid music that Hawk plays today.

Each night at Kelly's Hawkins did two numbers in each of the band's three sets; he also played one feature in the shows that WMCA broadcast from the club several times a week. Ulanov, after commenting on some of the breakneck tempos chosen by Hawkins, made a plea (in his feature) to the management at Kelly's, asking them to feature the tenor-sax star more frequently.

Business boomed at Kelly's and Hawk's contract was extended several times. He continued to work as a guest star, appearing with a variety of accompanying groups. In February the club featured Hawkins (billed as the King of the Saxophone), Billie Holiday, Red Allen's band and a jam session organised by tenor saxist Jerry Jerome, who recalls:

> I had the relief band at Kelly's Stable on Monday nights. It was a kick to hear Hawk. What a player! He used a Selmer balanced-action tenor and an open-lay Otto Link mouthpiece (metal). He used a very stiff (four or five) Rico reed and he'd tighten the ligature with a pair of pliers. I could hardly get any air through his mouthpiece. He had a very strong jaw and clamped down very hard on the mouthpiece. He was a very gentle man and was always co-operative.[16]

On his days off from Kelly's Hawk showed no inclination to rest and instead played guest appearances, sometimes moving far afield as he did on 21 February 1943 when he (and Red Allen's band) went all the way up to Boston, Mass for a one-nighter. Frank Stacy, reviewing Hawk at Kelly's, noted that he was 'well received', but suggested that the star 'was coasting' by playing too many ballads. But the strategy of playing ballads followed by very fast riff numbers suited the clientele at the club and Hawk's residency at Kelly's went on and on. A band led by pianist Nat Jaffe accompanied Hawkins for several weeks then Jaffe moved on to play at the Onyx Club, leaving his group behind to continue working with Hawk. This arrangement continued briefly, then Hawkins decided to organize his own small band again.

Hawkins broke the band in at Kelly's, and also played a date with them (on Sunday 3 May 1943) at the Hurricane Club (on Broadway at 50th Street), where they worked opposite Duke Ellington's Orchestra. Hawk then temporarily took leave of New York and took his new group to play at the Top Hat Club in Toronto, Canada for a week in late May. The band returned to work briefly at Kelly's then, while that club was closed for structural alterations, they travelled up to Boston to fulfil an engagement at the Tic-Toc Club from 6–20 June 1943.

The new band consisted of Lem Davis (alto sax), Roy Stevens (trumpet), Al Lucas (double bass), Helm Mitchell (guitar), Wally Bishop (drums) and Danny Negis (piano). It was a racially-mixed group, Stevens and Negis being white. The group's original guitarist was Remo Palmieri, a particular favourite of Hawk's, who had worked with him often at Kelly's Stable. In May 1943, while working with Hawkins in Canada, Palmieri caught scarlet fever and had to remain there for a month in a service isolation hospital. Forty years later, Palmieri recalled his disappointment at having to leave the group through illness; 'Playing in Coleman's group was a dream come true; I had idolized him all through my youth.'[17]

Drummer Wally Bishop recalled that on the return trip from Toronto Hawkins got the members of his band to carry various items through customs so that he could avoid paying any import duties. Bishop retained a great admiration for Hawkins but didn't let this blind him to the tenorist's parsimonious ways: he said, 'Hawk was a great man. You were supposed to buy him a drink – not that he'd buy you a drink.' Bishop was flabbergasted one day when Hawkins offered to buy him a drink during a visit they made to Greenwich Village. Bishop declined, fearing he might drop dead if he accepted it. It was, Bishop suspected, Hawk's way of letting him know that he was being eased out of his job. Soon afterwards, Hawk replaced him with Kenny Clarke; Bishop remained philosophical about the change and said, 'He'd got somebody better on drums than me.'[18]

The group's trumpet player and vocalist, Roy Stevens (later to become a high-note trumpet specialist), had many happy memories of working with Hawkins. Stevens was leading his own band at the Famous Door on 52nd Street when he heard that Hawkins was looking for a new trumpeter:

> I went over to Kelly's Stable, walked into the room and there were quite a few guys waiting to audition. Finally it's my turn to come up. I figured I'd pick a ballad, a good tune, and by the time I got into my second chorus I'd start taking some real

liberties. Anyway, I started to play but just as I was getting to the middle of my second chorus Hawkins comes up to the stand and stops me. I thought, 'Was I that bad?' My heart dropped. He raised my hand and said, 'Thanks, fellows' to the others who'd auditioned, 'Roy's got it.' I opened up with him at Kelly's Stable. I ran the band for Hawk. We had a jazz following we had to play for; there we weren't just blowing a club-date job. We used to talk a lot, 'cause I ran the band for Bean. As a guy he was just superb.

I said to him, 'I didn't know how to get going when I auditioned for you.'

He says, 'Don't forget man, I've got ears.'[19]

Stevens's work with Hawkins included a USO tour in which the band played at services bases:

He used to say to me on those dates, 'You keep this band jumping with the singing you do.' And whenever he felt we were lagging on the date he'd say, 'Let's get 'em with a tom number. Lay one of your tom numbers down on them.' The 'tom' numbers were for the white audience, squares. He was not a complicated man; musically he was the most complicated man. He was way ahead of Charlie Parker and all those guys.[20]

Hawkins continued to work with this band at Kelly's Stable until the autumn of 1943. He then reverted to his role as the club's guest star, blowing with whichever group had been booked into the club as the house band. Thelma Carpenter had returned to sing at the club on a regular basis; the rest of the bill changed regularly: Babe Lawrence, the tapdancer, was sometimes featured, as were a jubilee-type song group called the Four Chocolate Bars; trumpeter John 'Harlem' Harley also worked there briefly as a speciality act. In addition the club maintained a resident trio which, during the late months of 1943, was led by pianist Clarence Profit. Hawkins still used up some of his spare time by blowing in jam sessions. During one 1943 Sunday bash at Jimmy Ryan's, Hawk crossed swords with a young up-and-coming tenor player, Joseph 'Flip' Phillips. Phillips's brilliance in the duel became a talking point in jazz circles for weeks afterwards.

Despite the excellence of the music performed during this era, no commercial recordings were offered to the public, due to a ban on recordings enforced by the American Federation of Musicians. The union strike began in August 1942 and lasted for over a year. It was instigated by the union's president, James Petrillo, in an effort to gain remuneration for musicians from the performance of recordings on radio and on jukeboxes. In late 1943 some of the smaller record companies decided to resolve their differences with the union and thus reached a productive agreement before the major companies did so. These companies ended the drought by flooding the jazz market with hastily-organized recording sessions, speedily issued on independent labels.

Hawkins, by reason of not having an exclusive contract with any of the major recording companies, benefited greatly from this burst of studio activity. During the first twelve-month period after the strike ended he took part in over twenty recording dates, all for various independent labels. The first of this huge batch was for Commodore, in a date organized by Leonard Feather and billed as his All Stars. The group that convened on 4 December 1943 consisted of Hawkins, Cootie Williams on trumpet, Edmond Hall on clarinet, Al Casey on guitar, Sid Catlett on drums, Art Tatum on piano and Oscar Pettiford (making his first recording) on doublebass.

The most outstanding feature of an excellent session is the swing and cohesiveness achieved by the rhythm section; anyone who believes that the individual brilliance of Tatum disqualifies him from being considered as a fine accompanist cannot have heard these sides. Tatum is superlative, both in his backing role and as the creator of flowing solos that swing ceaselessly.

'Esquire Bounce', a deft thirty-two-bar theme written by Leonard Feather, first features a relaxed, loosely phrased guitar solo by Al Casey. Ed Hall then plays an ebullient middle eight before Hawkins blows some full-blooded riffs to open his chorus. But instead of discarding the riff idea and moving on, Hawk repeats the phrase several times, extracting every bit of swing out of it and in doing so provides an invigorating indication of future trends whereby rhythms-and-blues tenor saxists employed similar tactics (without, alas, any of Hawkins's ingenuity). The middle section of Hawk's chorus utilizes the same sort of thematic development that graced his 1939 recording of 'Dinah'; he blows a striking idea then revamps it through a series of linked phrases that move up through an octave.

By the time the second and third takes of 'Esquire Bounce' had been created Hawk's thoughts had moved on in a different direction, one in which his ideas are more challenging but not so effective as the rocking, apparently simple phrases of the first attempt. There were two versions of the other numbers (all of them issued years later on microgroove), but there is little to choose between them because the standard of excellence is so consistently high.

'Mop Mop' utilizes an idea (subsequently kicked to death by various bands) of heavily emphasizing the first two beats of each four-bar pattern. Hawk's solo on take one is determindedly harsh, but his fingers do not seem quite in synch with his mouthpiece articulations. He is gentler on take two, but no more effective. 'My Ideal' is a showcase for Hawkins, the sort of ravishing ballad that had become (as Leonard Feather pointed out) 'a *sine qua non* of every Hawkins session'. Hawkins's lush ideas and warm sound-textures enhance the fine melody, and he is well supported by Art Tatum, whose brilliance is exhilarating. Hawk, sounding inspired, blows his voluptuous ideas over long soft backing notes, ending the passionate offering with a series of gentle cadenzas.

The date ended with a medium-tempo blues that allowed everyone in the group, except drummer Sid Catlett, the chance for a brief solo spot. Hawkins chose to superimpose riff patterns on the twelve-bar sequence, and they bristle with unexpected intriguing notes and gain from being propelled by Catlett's powerfully struck drum beats.

Within that same month (December 1943) Hawkins completed three sessions for another small company, Signature, managed by Bob Thiele, then serving in the US Coastguard (stationed at the Military Morale Department, Manhattan Beach, New York). One of Thiele's service colleagues, drummer Shelly Manne, played on two of these dates with notable success.

The first Signature session opens with a simple tune, 'Voodte', devised by Hawkins. After two run-of-the-mill themes the blanket of ordinariness lifts as trumpeter Bill Coleman plays a mercurial eight bars, and is fully rolled back as Hawkins's energetic solo develops. Hawk is featured throughout 'How Deep is the Ocean', a ballad he'd been playing regularly at Kelly's Stable. It's a magnificent rendering, built on a web of cleverly linked ideas. This was one of Hawk's own favourite recorded performances, and years later he said that he was surprised that it hadn't achieved the sort of success that his version of 'Body and Soul' enjoyed.[21]

'Hawkins' Barrel House' is a solos-for-everyone jam on a twelve-bar blues. All the improvisations are adept with Hawk again choosing to structure his phrases on riff patterns. The date ended with 'Stumpy', a theme Hawkins had devised on the harmonies of the old evergreen 'Whispering'. Ellis Larkins's piano playing and Bill Coleman's cup-muted trumpet work are models of grace, but Hawk himself seems in a parrying rather than thrustful mood.

A quintet session, with Hawkins and a four-piece rhythm section, stoked by the brilliant young drummer Max Roach (who had been introduced to Hawkins by Dizzy Gillespie), produced a buoyant 'Lover Come Back to Me' and a lively, boogie-ish 'Blues Changes', which spirals through a series of key changes, but the finest items from the Signature sessions were created a few days later when Hawk waxed four titles with Eddie Heywood, piano; Oscar Pettiford, double bass and Shelly Manne, drums (mainly utilizing brushes).

Up-tempo versions of 'Get Happy' and 'Crazy Rhythm' follow a similar pattern: theme/piano solo/tenor solo/theme, with Hawkins becoming increasingly adventurous as he moves further into his solos, but these fine performances pale against the achievements on 'Sweet Lorraine' and 'The Man I Love' (issued together on a twelve-inch 78 rpm record). 'Sweet Lorraine' is filled with the passion that graced Hawk's finest ballad playing; there is no over-decoration but the exploration of new avenues of harmonic thought is obvious. Shelly Manne's positive brush work gets 'The Man I Love' (played at medium tempo) off to a swinging start, and his efforts are soon consolidated by one of the finest solos that pianist Eddie Heywood ever recorded, packed with ideas and delivered with an infectious *joie de vivre*. The drive of Pettiford's double-bass solo is emphasized by his audible gasps of effort, his skill made obvious by his exquisite choice of notes and his resonant tone.

Hawk's solo opens boldly with a phrase that places an E natural against an E-flat chord, but he skilfully resolves this pungent discord and begins rocking his way through a series of strongly played middle-register phrases. The streamlined eighth notes that form the basis of the solo are delivered with a swinging impetus, so different from the eighth-note patterns prevalent in his early work. The ingenuity flows ever faster as the sixty-four-bar chorus (played in long measure) develops, and reaches a point of breathtaking grandeur as Hawk vaults into a powerful second chorus; in this section Hawk utilizes a two-octave span of notes. One of his greatest skills was his gift for increasing the rhythmic excitement in a solo without sacrificing one iota of his harmonic acumen. His best solos utilize equal quantities of cerebral and physical effort; 'The Man I Love' is a perfect example of this blending, remaining one of his supreme achievements.

Bob Thiele hadn't planned for this number to be issued on a twelve-inch disc but, realizing that Hawkins was in full flight, he wisely decided not to interrupt the continually soaring ideas. He recalled, 'We almost lost 'The Man I Love'. The engineer almost stopped recording because of length. Bean just wouldn't quit. I shouted, "Hell, it'll be a twelve-inch record . . . so what!" '[22]

Hawkins was not a boaster. Fellow tenor saxist Budd Johnson summed this up when he said, 'He never was too much to brag on himself.'[23] But the achievement of recording 'The Man I Love' temporarily stripped away the veneer of modesty; Hawk turned to Thiele and said, 'Bob, there isn't a musician alive who can match me when it comes to working with chords.'[24] The imperishable quality of Hawk's performance of Gershwin's tune was emphasized forty years after it was made when Branford Marsalis, hearing the record for the first time simply said, 'God, I loved it.'[25]

14
A Deluge of Discs

For several years running, Coleman Hawkins had been voted the top tenor-sax player in polls organized by *Esquire* magazine, so he was an obvious choice for the Esquire All-American Jazz Band, which gave a war-bond concert at the Metropolitan Opera House in New York on 18 January 1944. The full line-up consisted of one of the most illustrious collections of jazz musicians ever assembled: Louis Armstrong, Roy Eldridge (trumpets); Jack Teagarden (trombone); Barney Bigard (clarinet); Coleman Hawkins (tenor sax); Red Norvo (xylophone); Lionel Hampton (vibes); Art Tatum, Teddy Wilson (piano); Al Casey (guitar); Oscar Pettiford (double bass) and Sidney Catlett (drums); vocalists Mildred Bailey and Billie Holiday also appeared on the show.

Hawkins did not play a dominating part in the concert – often his role is restricted to filling in what gaps there are in the busy ensembles, – but he was given the centre of the stage for his feature on 'My Ideal' (one of several sides from the concert that were issued for the armed forces on V-discs). Hawk's phrasing is not quite as masterful as on the recent studio recording of the tune, but he seems undaunted by the concert atmosphere and makes no attempt to play to the gallery; Art Tatum again shares the solo glories on this number.

Poor recording balance mars the tenor-sax work on the opening 'Esquire Blues', but Hawk finds better placement for his brief solos on 'Muskrat Ramble', 'Stompin' At The Savoy' and 'Basin Street Blues'. On this last title he follows Louis Armstrong's vocal confidently enough but, in a rare lapse of concentration, allows his solo to disintegrate. Hawk is appropriately robust on the jammed versions of 'I Got Rhythm' and 'Flying Home' (where he is stimulated by Lionel Hampton's fervent vocal exhortations) but his most interesting playing is on Oscar Pettiford's feature 'For Bass Faces Only', where he and Roy Eldridge phrase the nifty arrangement impeccably and then venture a whole series of forward-looking ideas.

During 1944 Hawk took part in eight recording sessions for a newly-established recording company, Keynote. Harry Lim, the label's diminutive owner, had known Hawkins since pre-war days in Europe. The two men enjoyed an easygoing relationship:

> Hawk never drove a bargain with me over the price for his record dates. He was always nice and co-operative. it was always interesting to hear him talk about other jazz musicians; he evaluated all the new players. I can remember him making a point of praising Illinois Jacquet's work long before anyone had ever realized what Illinois was capable of, and Hawk was certainly the first to mention Thelonious Monk to me. He was truly a sharp cat.[1]

In fact, Hawkins's recording schedule during this period was overloaded, which meant that he wasn't automatically full of zest and inspiration on all the record dates he played in 1944. Even so, few of his solos have a laboured quality, and his tone, technique and chordal knowledge always produce something of merit even when he is temporarily coasting or when his imagination is taking a nap.

Each and every take that was recorded by Keynote was eventually issued in the 1980s, and they reveal just how fertile Hawkins's mind was during this period of his life. In the 1930s, pianist Horace Henderson had praised the tenor saxist for his ability to repeat the same solo over and over again without ever making it sound listless. By the 1940s Hawkins had abandoned that method of working – indeed various second takes from the 1930s show that Hawkins was improvising – but Horace Henderson was speaking principally about Hawk's work with Fletcher Henderson's band. The Keynote takes (sometimes as many as four on one tune) are positive proof of Hawk's musical adventurousness.

On the first of his Keynote dates Hawk worked alongside Roy Eldridge, supported by a neat rhythm section consisting of Teddy Wilson (piano), Billy Taylor (double bass) and Cozy Cole (drums). Hawk and Roy jam their way through three evergreens and one original: 'Bean at the Met' (written on the chords of 'How High the Moon'). On the session Eldridge chose to introduce the opening chorus of each piece by playing with a cup-mute in his trumpet, and Hawkins zooms ingeniously around this burring lead, providing an object lesson in jazz counterpoint. The variations within Hawk's solos on this date are not simply the reshuffling of his previous ideas, they are examples of pristine musical thoughts. One take might have at its core a motif of fast chromatic runs; the next attempt is based on wide-intervalled phrases embracing top and bottom registers.

Hawk's moods also change: on one version of ' 'S Wonderful' he sounds gentle and subdued but on the next attempt he seems full of swagger and enterprise. Take two of 'I Only Have Eyes for You' has a series of breathtaking glissandi and 'I'm In the Mood for Love' is a model of controlled fervour.

On a February 1944 session for the same company, Hawkins again worked with Wilson and Cole, this time with Israel Crosby on bass. The resultant music fails to reach any high point of inspiration. Wilson, one of the most graceful and inventive of all jazz pianists, seems on this session too urbane for the Hawkins of this period, who was by then used to working with the chunky intricacies of Thelonious Monk's keyboard work. Even so, there is much to admire in Wilson's playing on these sides, particularly the admirable elan displayed on 'Flamethrower' and 'Night and Day', and his ingenious use of left-hand tenths on 'Imagination'.

This assembly of master musicians went through four numbers without deeming it necessary to essay another take, and if their intention was to create four smooth sides then they succeeded admirably. Even the rush of blood in 'Cattin' at the Keynote' (seemingly inspired by the chordal framework of 'My Gal Sal') sounds to be inspired by the eagerness of men who had other engagements to attend. The most surprising aspect of the date is the manner in which Hawkins approaches 'Imagination', performing it in a way that could (allowing for the superior American rhythm section) have been created during his pre-war stay in Europe.

Hawk's next Keynote date was as part of Cozy Cole's All Stars. The young guitarist on the session, Teddy Walters, was the only member of the pick-up group without a distinguished reputation, but his contributions are no less admirable than the work of his colleagues on this fertile occasion. Joe Thomas's ultra-relaxed style of trumpet playing seems to epitomize the mood of the date.

Pianist Earl Hines demonstrates his unique sense of timing during a dramatic solo on 'Blue Moon' which even the ingenuity of Hawkins's subsequent solo cannot eclipse, but Hawk's shouting vibrancy takes the honours on 'Father Co-operates' which is further enlivened by a brief, dynamic drum solo from Cozy Cole. The four versions of this tune all contain strikingly inventive playing by the entire group. The richness of Hawk's subdued tone, elegant as brocaded silk, is the stand-out feature of 'Just One More Chance'. Trombonist Trummy Young, sounding as keen as mustard throughout the date, reaches a high point in his illustrious career on his own catchy composition 'Thru' for the Night' (based on

'Honeysuckle Rose'). Young's technique and spirited blowing seem to stimulate Hawkins into producing some resounding ideas. It's easy to understand why Cozy Cole cited this track as his own all-time favourite recording.

A collaboration between Hawkins and Teddy Wilson in May 1944 produced happier results than had their February date. The inclusion of Sid Catlett on drums brings a glow of excitement to the up-tempo numbers and his rhythmic liaison with bassist John Kirby guarantees a rock-steady beat. Hawkins shows his admiration of Wilson's work by allocating him the lion's share of 'Make Believe'. The outstanding track is the ballad 'Don't Blame Me'; here the playing has a polite exterior but lurking just beneath the surface is a layer of sophisticated intensity. Wilson's piano playing here is elegiac, full of perfectly resolved ideas. He modulates back to the original key and then it is Hawk's turn to expound his rich statements. The effect is of two eminent raconteurs sharing their best tales.

Piano and tenor sax combine to create a bold introduction to the swift-running 'Just One of those Things'. Sid Catlett (who remains on brushes throughout the date) maintains an enlivening rhythm by playing some perfectly struck off-beat patterns. Hawkins unexpectedly loses the thread of his thoughts during his opening solo on 'Hallelujah', then Catlett and Kirby are featured briefly in what turns out to be prelude to the fascinating moment when Hawkins and Wilson surprisingly shy a set of magnificent four-bar phrases at each other. Regrettably there is only one such exchange; it would have been engrossing to have heard more.

Harry Lim's adventurous policy at Keynote brought together a front line consisting of four eminent saxophonists: Hawkins and Don Byas on tenors, Tab Smith on alto and (from Duke Ellington's Orchestra) Harry Carney on baritone. Carney, an avowed Hawkins disciple, is his customary robust self, the bonus being that he is given the rare opportunity to stretch out, to which he responds by blowing superbly, notably on 'Three Little Words'. This was a golden period for Don Byas and he offers a serious challenge to Hawkins on every track.

Tab Smith is amply featured, and his concluding cadenzas (lasting for almost a minute) impart a notably dramatic ending to 'On the Sunny Side of the Street'. He was a master technician whose style owed something to the influence of Johnny Hodges, but Smith possessed his own creamy sound and his articulation was a model of precision. Hawkins plays a succession of double-time runs on 'Sunny Side', but doesn't inject them with any notable ideas, reserving his ingenuity for 'Louise' and 'Three

Little Words'. The backing throughout the date is lively, with Sid Catlett again providing a fount of inspiration. Pianist Johnny Guarneri's playing on 'Battle of the Saxes' (a work-out on 'China Boy') is particularly deft and witty.

The strong line-up (Teddy Wilson, Buck Clayton, Slam Stewart and Denzil Best) that Hawkins assembled for an October 1944 Keynote session produced some variable results. Most of the problems seem to exist within the rhythm section, where Wilson plays a heavy, *um-chung um-chung* pattern while backing the soloists. The group made an indifferent start with a bitty version of an undistinguished contemporary song called 'I'm Yours'; only Wilson constructs a meaningful solo. Hawkins seems content to issue double-time phrases without any grand design, but immediately raises his game several notches on an arresting version of 'Under a Blanket of Blue'.

Bassist Slam Stewart bows an ingenious, but totally incongruous, introduction of a fast version of 'Beyond the Blue Horizon', then Buck Clayton contributes an elegant cup-muted solo before Hawk blows a series of solo phrases that seem to have been stamped out of a matrix, being all similar in shape and length, the symmetry of Wilson's backing chords seeming to underline the impression. The group achieve a light swing on 'A Shanty in Old Shanty Town', with Slam Stewart bowing (and simultaneously singing) some clever paraphrases of the melody. Buck Clayton's burnished open tone expressively delivers a solo chorus before Hawkins takes over the limelight. He is certainly musically cogent here, but the overall impression is that he was tired out.

By the next day he had bounced back to form as a member of Charlie Shavers's All American Five (also on Keynote). Shavers managed to combine tenderness and daring on the group's version of 'My Man', and Hawk's huge tone sounds totally appropriate for the Gallic melody. The two men then romp into a twelve-bar riff, 'El Salon de Gutbucket', on which the trumpeter's braggadocio approach stimulates some lively thoughts from Hawkins, who seems to be nonchalantly amusing himself by playing a few phrases in the manner of Tab Smith. Inspiration dips on 'Embraceable You', and the fourth title of the date, 'Undecided', remained unissued for years. Rejection was based on the blemishes that disfigure the riffs and the concluding phrases; Shavers is particularly brilliant on take three of this, his most famous composition.

Hawk's final session for the glorious, but shortlived, Keynote label was a somewhat indecisive affair that has solo space divided evenly throughout a talented front line consisting of Hawkins, Jack Teagarden, trumpeter Joe Thomas and clarinettist Hank D'Amico. A positive musical director might have eliminated some of the diffidence that mars the ensembles, and he might also have ensured that the head arrangements were better devised. As it is, the sequence of events alters from take to take as the band strive to find the most effective way of presenting four standard tunes.

Happily Jack Teagarden's laconic, mellow singing is heard on 'Home' and on 'You Brought a New Kind of Love to Me'. On this latter title he is adroitly backed by Herman Chittison's piano, but overall the rhythm section of Chittison, George Wettling (drums) and Billy Taylor (bass) never settle into a cohesive groove. Joe Thomas's huge-toned melodicisms are effective throughout, but D'Amico's clarinet playing is unenthralling, though his lines begin to bite on the second take of 'Too Marvellous for Words'. As for Hawkins, it was an unexceptional date; on 'Somebody Loves Me' he seems to allow torpor to blunt his skills and contentedly trots out a looped succession of busy-sounding phrases.

The 1944 recording sessions that attracted most attention to Hawkins were two dates he did in February for Apollo, a newly-established independent label launched by Teddy Gottlieb and Hi Siegel from their Rainbow Music Store in Harlem. These Hawkins sides were subsequently hailed as the first recordings of bebop: the new jazz style pioneered by Charlie Parker, Dizzy Gillespie and Thelonious Monk. The recordings were of particular interest to the growing number of people who were following every nuance of the modern-jazz movement because Hawkins made a point of featuring Dizzy Gillespie, also commissioning arrangements reflecting the new spirit.

Budd Johnson, who played saxophone in (and arranged for) the twelve-piece band, recalled the background to the date:

> I had known Coleman since about 1926. We lived around the corner from each other. He lived in a place called King Haven on 151st Street and I lived on 152nd Street between Convent and Amsterdam. He said, 'I've got a record date coming up and I want to know about all of these cats who are playing the new music, because I'm going to pick up on what they're doing.'[2]

Elsewhere, he remembered:

> It wasn't a studio band, it was jazz musicians who were playing on the Street, because he wanted his coat to be pulled with this kind of music, and he wanted to be in first. Hawk, Dizzy and I did the writing for the date. The thing that I wrote, Clyde

Hart and me, was a tune called 'Bu-dee-daht'. Well, this was a beginning for this stuff being put down on paper, because the cats used to just play it and teach each other. But see, we started writing it.[3]

The first tune recorded on the February 1944 sessions was a Dizzy Gillespie composition, 'Woody'n You', of which Gillespie said: ' "Woody'n You" came from a minor-sixth chord to the dominant seventh. That's the influence of Thelonious Monk.'[4] The tune was dedicated to Woody Herman, but Woody himself chose to play the tune under the title of 'Yenta'; later Gillespie recorded it but changed the name to 'Algo Bueno'. In hindsight this piece, like everything else from the session, does not sound particularly revolutionary, but there is no doubt that at the time of issue these recordings created a minor sensation in the jazz world and (in some cases) instantly converted listeners to the new style. The catalyst and leading exponent of the modernisms displayed on the recordings is Dizzy Gillespie, whose trumpet playing, having shed the direct influence of Roy Eldridge, now possessed a strikingly individualistic approach to harmony and rhythm.

It's an indication of Hawkins's already highly developed harmonic sense that he copes easily with the various chord substitutions and unusual resolutions that crop up on the session. As far back as 1934 Hawkins had said that he was positively interested in modernism in music, but he never, throughout his career, became part of any musical cult. So although the young modernists were delighted that their efforts were being recognized and sponsored by a master jazz musician, most of them realized that he was not totally devoted to bebop.

Hawkins made it clear that he was not interested in becoming a bopper, regarding the 'new' jazz as a logical extension of the old. He explained his attitude: 'When I came back [from Europe] I was disappointed with what had happened in the music. Charlie Parker and Dizzy were getting started, but they needed help. What they were doing was "far out" to a lot of people, but it was just music to me.'[5] Trumpeter Benny Harris, often cited as a key figure in the development of bop, said, 'When Hawk came on the scene everything was pretty well set, and 52nd Street was opening up. He had the foresight to see what was happening, whether he liked it or not, because he had come back from Europe looking for and expecting new developments.'[6] Bassist Leonard Gaskin, who worked with Hawkins at Kelly's Stable in 1943, summarized Hawk's attitude during this period: 'He was looking for a new identity. He had to come up with something other than 'Body and Soul'.[7]

On the Apollo session Hawkins interprets the exotic melody of 'Woody'n You' with feeling and insight, but he leaves the drama of high exploration to Gillespie's trumpet. This particular track became a favourite with dozens of young trumpeters, including Miles Davis. Dizzy's playing is no less startling on 'Bu-dee-daht' even though the sequence, with its more or less conventional use of diminished chords, is not as challenging. Hawk's solo, replete with powerfully blown high notes, gives the impression that he is attempting to force the pace.

'Yesterdays' is a feature for Hawkins, who plays over some adventurously scored background figures. The tempo, veering towards medium pace, seems to take much of the wistfulness out of Jerome Kern's usually evocative ballad. Hawkins is inventive throughout, but none of his phrases possesses the beautiful contours that he was eminently capable of creating. After a modulation he takes the unusual step for him (on a ballad) of making a deliberate foray into the extreme part of his high register, almost whistling out a top B flat.

The original plan was to record six numbers on 16 February 1944, but time ran out because some of the band were having problems in playing the complex new arrangements.[8] The same personnel reconvened six days later and tackled 'Disorder at the Border', the beginning of which suggests an Ellington small group (with bassist Oscar Pettiford particularly reminiscent of Jimmy Blanton). Gillespie and Hawkins are the main soloists on the twelve-bar sequence, with the trumpeter again providing the more daring improvisations. Hawkins in his four choruses builds up a considerable head of steam without branching off into new territory. Not everyone was enamoured by the new material and *Down Beat* emphatically panned this particular track, calling it, 'The worst thing Coleman has ever put on paper. Whether muted or open Dizzy Gillespie's trumpet makes little sense.'[9]

'Feeling Zero' was, according to Teddy Gottlieb, 'named for Hawk's girlfriend Zero, who was there.'[10] The reed section play a novel, medium-tempo theme which is answered by brass countermelody. Hawk sounds subdued but alert as he blows some well-shaped ideas over soft accompaniment. His vocabulary is obviously harmonically advanced but, as before, he doesn't display any bop emblems. The final tune of the session was a remake of 'Body and Soul', using a similar format to the October 1939 'hit' version. Hawkins decided to call this rendering 'Rainbow Mist' so that he could claim composer royalties, feeling that by making only a fragmentary allusion to the melody of 'Body and Soul' he

Mamie Smith and her Jazz Hounds c 1922
Cutie Perkins (drums), Bubber Miley (trumpet), Cecil Carpenter (trombone), George Bell (violin), Mamie Smith, Coleman Hawkins (saxophone), Bob Fuller (clarinet), Harvey Brooks (piano)

The Jazz Hounds, Long Beach, California, early 1923
Unknown violinist, Bob Fuller (clarinettist) holding drum sticks, Cutie Perkins (drummer) holding clarinet, Cecil Carpenter (trombone), Coleman Hawkins (saxophone), Harvey Brooks (piano-conductor) and Joe Smith (trumpet)

Fletcher Henderson's Orchestra, 1932
(l to r) Russell Procope, Coleman Hawkins, Edgar Sampson, Clarence Holiday, Walter Johnson, John Kirby, Fletcher Henderson, Russell Smith, Bobby Stark, Rex Stewart, J.C. Higginbotham, Sandy Williams

1713 Angelique Street

St. Joseph, Missouri

Passport Agent
Subtreasury Bldg.
Wall Street
New York City, N. Y.

Gentlemen,

THIS IS TO CERTIFY THAT We, Cordelia Coleman Hawkins and William D. Hawkins, Negroes, 1713 Angelique Street St. Joseph, Missouri are the Mother and Father of Coleman Randolph Hawkins, Apartment 3J, 80 Saint Nicholas Place, New York City, New York, born November 21, 1904 at 1713 Angelique Street, St. Joseph, Missouri. Doctor Preston M. Edwards, attending Physician.

Signed: Cordelia Coleman Hawkins

Cordelia Coleman Hawkins

MAR 21 1934

State of Missouri
County of Buchanan

I, Edna O. Wilson, a Notary Public for and within this County, in the State of Missouri, do hereby certify that Cordelia Coleman Hawkins, personally known to me as the real person whose name is subscribed to the above affidavit as having executed the same, appeared before me in person and signed and properly swore that the above is absolutely true and full.

Given under my hand and seal, this 14th day of March 1934.

My Commission Expires June 30, 1934

Edna O. Wilson

Edna O. Wilson
Notary Public

Affidavit signed by Coleman Hawkins's mother, 1934

Jimmy Harrison

Jack Hylton

Leon 'Chu' Berry

Fletcher Henderson

From Coleman Hawkins to Renée and Sadie Gertler

Coleman Hawkins arrives in England, March 1934
(l to r) Frank Barnard, Coleman Hawkins, Ben Davis and Percy Mathieson Brooks
(From the files of Max Jones)

Sadie and Renée Gertler, c 1935
(Photograph courtesy of Mrs Wendy Formisano)

Coleman Hawkins with members of The Berries in Engelburg, Switzerland, winter 1936–7
(l to r) André Berner (ten-year-old son of Ernest Berner), pianist Ernest Berner, saxist Omer de Cock, Coleman Hawkins, Laddy Sterry (*maitre de plaisir* at the Dancing Matter), Clairette Berner (wife of Ernest Berner), drummer Bernhard Peritz
(Theo Zwicky collection, Zurich, Switzerland)

Coleman Hawkins in Ostend, Belgium, summer 1937
(Photo by Albert Bettonville)

Coleman Hawkins with Willie Lewis's Band in Knokke-Le-Zoute, Belgium, summer 1937
(l to r) (standing) Willie Lewis, Bill Coleman, Billy Burns, Coleman Hawkins, Billy Butler, Ted Fields, (kneeling) Frank 'Big Boy' Goudie
(Photo by Albert Bettonville)

Coleman Hawkins, Theo Uden Masman and Jack Bulterman in Laren, Holland, 1935
(Photograph courtesy of Herman Openneer)

Coleman Hawkins at Le Boeuf Sur Le Toit, Brussels, 1938
(l to r) Jean Delahau (bass), Coleman Hawkins, Christian Serluppens (drums), Victor Ingeveldt (clarinet), Ann Xhofleer (vocaliste), Rudy Bruder (piano), George Clais (trumpet), Louis Sims (dancer), Mike Engelen (guitar)
(Photo by Albert Bettonville)

Lionel Hampton recording session, September 1939
Dizzy Gillespie (trumpet), Cozy Cole (drums), Ben Webster, Benny Carter, Chu Berry, Coleman Hawkins (saxophones), Clyde Hart (piano)
(From the collection of Frank Driggs)

Metronome All Star Band, January 1940
Ziggy Elman, Cootie Williams (trumpets), J.C. Higginbotham, Tommy Dorsey (trombones), Benny Goodman (clarinet), Buddy Rich (drums), Tex Beneke (tenor sax), Benny Carter, Toots Mondello (alto saxes), Coleman Hawkins (tenor sax)

Thelma Carpenter and Coleman Hawkins
(From the files of Max Jones)

Metronome All-Stars recording session, 1946
Coleman Hawkins, Johnny Hodges and Harry Carney
(From the collection of Frank Driggs)

Louis Armstrong, Roy Eldridge and Coleman Hawkins at the Esquire Metropolitan Opera House concert, January 1944

Coleman Hawkins and Don Byas, 1944
(From the collection of Frank Driggs)

Keynote recordings session, New York City, February 1944
Harry Lim (producer), Coleman Hawkins at the piano
(From the collection of Frank Driggs)

Coleman Hawkins, Norman Granz and Ella Fitzgerald,
c 1950

Coleman Hawkins arrives at London Airport (December 1949), with bassist Pierre Michelot, drummer Kenny Clarke and pianist Jean-Paul Mengeon
(From the files of Max Jones)

Sarah Vaughan (vocals), Joe Benjamin (bass), Coleman Hawkins and Illinois Jacquet. England, October 1954
(From the files of Max Jones)

Recording session, New York City, 1958
(l to r) Doc Cheatham, Buster Bailey, Coleman Hawkins, Juanita Hall, Claude Hopkins, George Duvivier, Jimmy Crawford
(From the collection of Frank Driggs)

Coleman Hawkins and Sonny Rollins, 1963
(Photograph by Joe Alter)

Barry Harris (piano), Coleman Hawkins and Roy Eldridge. Chicago, April 1969 (Photograph by Stephen Hale)

The end of the road. Coleman Hawkins in Chicago, April 1969 (Photograph by Stephen Hale)

could cite the performance as his own composition. Hawkins told Budd Johnson at the time, 'I own the solo, so I'm going to call it something else and record it over.'[11] But Hawk's attempt to increase his composer royalties was only partly successful because several reissue records listed 'Rainbow Mist' as 'Body and Soul'.

Hawk's efforts on the challenging sequence are certainly as dexterous as on the 1939 version and he produces a succession of admirable new ideas, but the creative magic of the original is missing. By 1944 Hawk's technique was even better than it had been five years earlier, particularly his playing of fast legatoed runs. His earlier recording contained a sprinkling of orthodox grace notes but by 1944 he had changed his manner of adding appoggiatura, creating a similar effect by using immensely rapid triplets.

The 1939 disc is obviously the blueprint for 'Rainbow Mist' (the four-bar piano introduction and the concluding cadenzas make this obvious) but there are an enormous number of fascinating differences. Even so, Hawk keeps the original in mind, basing the opening of the first bridge on the same note pattern as previously, and repeating his ploy (in the closing stages) of ascending to a high E flat, followed by an E then an F but, on the 1944 recording, the climb is even more ingenious (and more dramatic). The concluding cadenzas are longer (and more abstruse) than before, which is perhaps why they are not as effective. Hawk's re-examination of 'Body and Soul' is almost a classic in its own right, and some listeners, including the talented saxist Pat LaBarbera, prefer it to the 1939 recording. The crucial difference, however, is that the earlier performance broke entirely new ground and established broad paths for countless musicians to follow.

Although Hawkins spent a good deal of time in the recording studios during this period, he still managed to appear regularly at Kelly's Stable throughout the first months of 1944. It wasn't exactly a sinecure, but Leonard Feather wrote that Hawk spent a lot more time in the club's kitchen than he did on the bandstand, 'emerging every two hours to play two numbers'.[12] Hawk usually sauntered into the club at the last moment, picked up his saxophone, which had been unpacked and assembled by the club's handyman 'Red', and then blew a couple of numbers before leaving the bandstand for an hour or two. Various house bands were hired and fired but Hawkins remained the unchanging factor in a shifting scene. One of the club's most durable units was organized by non-musician Clark Monroe (a former husband of Billie Holiday); this group featured talented youngsters such as pianist Duke Jordan, tenor saxist Ray Abrams and bassist Leonard Gaskin, and they too played their part in stimulating Hawk's interest in trying out new tunes and fresh sequences. The Billy Moore Trio worked for a while at Kelly's, as did the Vivienne Gray and Arv Garrison duo, as well as trumpeter and dancer Joseph 'Taps' Miller. Eventually the repetitive routine at the club caused Hawkins (in the spring of 1944) to repeat the tactics he'd employed a year earlier; he formed his own band to play bookings in Boston and Toronto.

The co-star of this new outfit was Don Byas, emerging as a leading contender for Hawk's 'king of the tenor saxists' crown. Recalling the situation, Leonard Gaskin said, 'Don Byas was a great threat and quite frankly in many instances Don Byas was the preference.'[13] Choosing such an adept rival was a bold move by Hawkins, even though Byas readily admitted that Hawk, Benny Carter and Art Tatum were his musical idols. Byas was by this time a supremely accomplished technician full of bold ideas that utilized his vast harmonic knowledge. He also possessed a naturally competitive personality containing a streak of aggressive awkwardness that could surface without warning when he had too much to drink.

All of Hawkins's new signings had worked in name bands. Byas had recently been in Dizzy Gillespie's group and before that he was with Count Basie's band; Don's manner of giving Basie notice typified his character: he said, 'Basie, in four weeks I will have been gone two.'[14] But Byas's stay with Hawk's sextet was harmonious on and off the bandstand. The group's trumpeter, Benny Harris, who had recently been with Herbie Field's band, was in the forefront of that era's adventurers, as was the sextet's pianist, Thelonious Monk. Drummer Stan Levey played some of the group's early dates, but he didn't tour with them and his place was taken by Denzil Best.

Denzil Best had been a promising trumpeter, but when a lung disease forced him to give up that instrument he began playing the drums and became one of the finest percussionists of his era, particularly adept with the brushes (he was also an outstanding composer and arranger). Best recalled his inception into the group:

> I worked at the Two Deuces for two months (with Ben Webster) and then the job closed. I stopped in there one night not long after that and Coleman Hawkins was standing there. He said, 'I've been looking for you. I'm going to Canada next week and if you come I think you'll like it.' I was standing there with a 'Who Me?' feeling.[15]

Eddie Robinson was the original bassist in the group, but he opted out of the trip to Canada. Selwyn Warner (originally from the Caribbean), who had recently been working with Hazel Scott and Hot Lips Page, took Robinson's place. The band travelled up to Toronto where they played at the Top Hat Club (on Lakeshore Road and Parkside Drive). Warner recalls the trip:

> Denzil Best recommended me for the job. We went up to the Top Hat in Toronto then came down to play an engagement in Boston. Hawkins was a very nice man, beautiful to work with. Everyone in the band got along with each other. Thelonious Monk was coming along in those days, getting his chips together. He was very bright, quiet and cool, but not eccentric. Monk did arrangements for the band; so too did Benny Harris and Denzil Best. Hawkins and Don Byas made a huge sound together. The group played all sorts of interesting new things, but I never heard anyone in the group use the words bop or bebop; they were just thought of as new arrangements. Of course at the matinees in Toronto they got a young crowd and they would keep shouting for 'Body and Soul', so in the end Hawk said, 'We'll just do a couple of choruses like the record and that'll quieten them down,' and it did. When we got back to New York I handed the job back to Eddie Robinson.[16]

Hawkins was delighted with the way the band had shaped up and later spoke of this particular group with real warmth: 'We had a good little band, well rehearsed. We used to rehearse every day. Benny Harris kind of lost his lip a bit; once upon a time he had a very good lip.'[17] On 25 May Hawkins took the new group into the Downbeat Club (managed by Monte Kay and Pete Kameran) which was functioning on the same site (66 West 52nd Street) as the recently closed Yacht Club. An abundance of fine tenor-sax playing could be heard there, since besides Hawkins and Byas, Herbie Fields was also in attendance, leading his own trio. Soon after the club's opening, altoist Pete Brown took over as the relief band's leader. The mistress of ceremonies there was Becky Harding, whose job was sometimes made difficult as boisterous servicemen, on furlough, tumbled in and out of the club, paying little attention to what the jazzmen were playing. It was a bad summer for violence and there were many incidents of white servicemen getting into fights with black musicians on 52nd Street.

A note of aggression also crept into some of the record reviews of the period as discs that featured Hawkins with the young modernists were released. The war between those who liked old jazz and those who followed the new style was about to begin. The work of the innovators was originally described by the supposedly onomatopoeic word 'rebop'; this was soon renamed 'bebop' and later shortened to 'bop'. Those who felt these descriptions were frivolous simply called it modern jazz. The lines of reference between old and new were sometimes blurred. 'Rainbow Mist' from the so-called 'bop' session was an obvious reworking of the 1939 version of 'Body and Soul'; the RCA Victor recording company were soon aware of the marked similarity between these two performances and 'found a solution short of the law courts' (as *Down Beat* magazine put it) by reissuing the 1939 version on its thirty-five-cent Bluebird label in an attempt to win sales over the $1 10c Apollo issue.

Hawkins had developed an ambivalent attitude towards performing 'Body and Soul'; he naturally realized the important part that the tune had played in furthering his career, but disliked a situation in which he felt forced to play any tune, whatever its merits. Eddie Johnson, who had worked with Hawkins in 1942, said, 'I remember he detested playing 'Body and Soul', but he had to play it. So in order to avoid boredom he would actually change key every eight bars. He might start off in F, go to D, and then to A. You could hear the piano player modulating from one key to another and Hawkins was gone. The man was a genius.'[18]

Yet the tune could still stimulate Hawkins into giving some amazing performances. Trumpeter Roy Stevens recalled one such occasion at Kelly's Stable on the night that Hawkins's first child, daughter Colette, was born:

> Hawk was at the hospital; his wife was having a baby. I was getting up to the mike and saying, 'We expect Coleman Hawkins to be in soon.' Finally he walks in.
>
> I said, 'Well, what do you want to play?'
>
> He said, 'I'm gonna play some "Body and Soul".'
>
> I don't know how many incredible choruses he took, maybe seven or eight. He usually played two, like on the record, so we laid out, but he just kept going. When he finished the audience broke up, they all stood up and cheered.[19]

Hawk's band continued its residency at the Down Beat until 17 August 1944. Personnel changes occurred during the latter days of the run as various members of the group, such as Don Byas and Oscar Pettiford, accepted offers to lead their own bands at other clubs then thriving on 52nd Street. Several young musicians worked briefly with Hawkins during this period, including the Washington pianist John Malachi.

This was the golden era of 52nd Street and live jazz could be heard pouring out of dozens of clubs along 'The Strip'. For a time the sound on the wind was an amalgam of old and new styles – one club might feature a Dixieland group, the next an innovative jump combo – but gradually exploration became the order of the day. It was not unknown for customers (and visiting musicians) to drift haphazardly from one spot to another, sampling a few tunes in each. Even the musicians who worked on 52nd Street regularly called into rival clubs to hear part of a set. If a promising newcomer surfaced, the news of his arrival spread like wildfire among those who played the same instrument.

If it wasn't possible to sit in and challenge the tyro, the old hands made sure that they tested the youngster's nerve by making him acutely aware of their presence. Tenorist Lucky Thompson recalled his baptism by fire:

> I found myself replacing Ben Webster in Sid Catlett's quartet at the Three Deuces on 52nd Street. The first night I was to play, who was in the house but Coleman Hawkins, Don Byas, Lester Young and Ben Webster, all of them there at the same time! I don't know how I survived, believe me, it's one of the mysteries of my life, because for the first time I found my fingers in between the keys.[20]

Many young musicians were unnerved by having Coleman Hawkins standing close by them, arms folded, unsmilingly listening with great care to what they were playing. Julian 'Cannonball' Adderley recalled: 'A young tenor player was complaining to me that Coleman Hawkins made him nervous; I told him Hawkins was supposed to make him nervous for forty years.'[21]

15
Bean and Bop

Hawkins's long residency on 52nd Street gave him a vantage point from which to assess talented newcomers. He was also able to observe at close quarters the growing acrimony between those who liked old jazz and those who listened only to bop. The rivals might have co-existed more easily if magazines and disc-jockeys hadn't fanned the sparks of controversy. Hawkins found the animosity and prejudice absurd, summarizing his attitude: 'Wherever there's good musicians you'll always find me. I don't think about music in the way other people do. I don't think about music being new or modern. Music doesn't go seasonable to me.'[1] As a result of this stance Hawkins determindedly maintained his role as an encourager of emerging jazz talents. Pianist Billy Taylor said, 'Coleman Hawkins was sympathetic to the newer musicians as the Street became more modern.'[2]

Drummer Stan Levey, who worked with Hawkins in 1944, said:

> He always kept the younger musicians in awe of him, not on purpose, but his demeanour demanded it. He was like a prince; his clothing was perfect, in the latest style, etc. In a word he had *class*. Also he didn't get stuck in time. His ears were always open to new music. Hawk was a great help and always urged you on to play better.[3]

Another percussionist, Max Roach, echoed this praise: 'When the new movement was in its infancy Coleman was the guy who encouraged many of us. Some of my first gigs were with him. He always made me feel I was something.' These words from two magnificent drummers – one white, one black – underline the fact that Hawk's encouragement was not restricted to any particular ethnic group.

Trumpeter and pianist Buddy Anderson, then at the centre of new developments, said, 'The musicians involved included some of the older jazz stalwarts as well as some of the younger, experienced musicians. It was a healthy tonic for popular music. The idea was mainly influenced by

Dizzy Gillespie, and it was fostered principally by Coleman Hawkins.'[4] Gillespie himself said, 'Benny Carter and Coleman Hawkins had the great taste in music to understand my generation and to come with us. There wasn't much we could show them in harmony, for instance, only to let them see where we put accents in going from one note to another.'[5] Benny Carter, like Hawkins, always kept abreast of new approaches to improvising jazz. When asked how he had reacted to the advent of bop, he simply said, 'I welcomed it.'[6]

Hawkins had always been fascinated by new developments in jazz, going back to the 1920s and 1930s. His training and enormous natural talents enabled him to analyse any music he heard; in this way he became aware of the harmonically adventurous individualists such as Dizzy Gillespie, Charlie Parker, Benny Harris, Fats Navarro and Thelonious Monk, he liked what he heard and continued to encourage the new music's development. This was the music of the young and, by temperament, Hawkins always wanted to be thought of as a young man.

Hawkins acknowledged that many people were openly critical of him when he hired Thelonious Monk; he was asked, 'Why don't you get yourself a piano player? What is that guy trying to do?' Monk for his part always revered Hawkins's musicianship and said years later, 'Nobody can pick up a tenor sax without playing some of him.'[7]

Hawkins made no secret of the fact that he was in favour of new developments in jazz, but this didn't mean that he abandoned his previously held values, nor did he condemn veteran musicians whose work didn't incorporate modernisms. Art was timeless for Hawkins; unlike for some of the young musicians, who made spiteful remarks about veterans whose only failing was that their improvisations were not influenced by recent innovations. Mere modernisms were not enough for Hawkins: he also wanted to hear rhythmic and harmonic ingenuity, individualism, tone, inspiration and ideas. He was too mature artistically simply to praise the clichés and repetitions that soon pockmarked the work of the copyists who abounded in bop.

Hawkins worked at the Club Bali in Washington DC from 25 August until 8 September 1944, then returned to the Downbeat Club, which, because of stiff competition from rival clubs, had increased its complement of musical attractions. In late 1944 the club featured Hawk's band, Billie Holiday, Red Norvo and the compere-musician Harry 'The Hipster' Gibson – Gibson's presentation epitomizing the growing popularity of the boppers' approach to new words, a flamboyant style of dress and fresh attitudes. Besides these resident attractions, the Downbeat employed a support band that varied from month to month, various bandleaders included Pete Brown, Trummy Young and Tiny Grimes.

Occasionally Hawkins took time of from the Downbeat to fulfil a one-night stand out of town and in the autumn of 1944 he took a quintet to the Footguard Hall in Hartford, Connecticut and played to over a thousand dancers, picking up a very hefty fee in the process. In this same period Hawkins and his quintet played a date at the Apollo Theatre in Harlem, reviewed by Leonard Feather:

> Everything Hawk did was great; Vic Coulsen's Gillespie-ish trumpet showed improvement; Thelonious Monk's piano always covers fertile ground and the bass and drums rounded out a solid rhythm team. But Hawk needed a build-up announcement and a little stagecraft. The show ended with the Hawkins and Tommy Reynolds bands joining forces for a little One O'Clock Jump.[8]

Coleman Hawkins had certainly achieved financial security by the mid 1940s, since besides his well-paid club work, concert dates and radio shows he also earned money via his composer royalties and all this was supplemented by the fees he got for his many recording sessions. Saxophonist and arranger Walter 'Foots' Thomas, a longtime fan of Hawk's, booked him to play on several recordings in the 1940s. He said, 'I got him for a hundred dollars a day, twice union scale, but it was cheap; he was worth two guys. He simply asked, "Where's the piano part?" and he went to the piano and played it through; that was all he needed.'[9]

Soon after one such session for Joe Davis's label (in October 1944) Walter Thomas wrote a summary of events for the *Music Dial* magazine:

> The record date had to start at midnight as Cab Calloway's band was playing at the Adams Theatre in Newark [three of Calloways' musicians – trumpeter Jonah Jones, bassist Milt Hinton and alto saxist Hilton Jefferson – were on the date]. Hawkins was playing at the Downbeat and Cozy Cole was appearing in the *Carmen Jones* musical show. Everyone was on time except Hawk who, due to the switching of his night off, had to play until one o'clock at the club. However we utilized the time while waiting for him by rehearsing and timing the numbers. When Hawkins arrived we lost no time in getting down to business and making the records. We did four tunes in two and a half hours. Great is not the word for Hawkins. It is super-colossal. We have yet to find anything comparable to this genius musician, who has a combination of humbleness and respect for his fellow musicians. This outstanding quality creates a great sense of admiration and esteem for Hawkins from all his fellow musicians all over the world. One incident occurred on a test recording: Coleman played an out-of-this-world melodic passage that accidentally ran into

Hilton Jefferson's alto solo. This upset Hawk very much and he began to openly apologize.

On 19 October 1944, eight days after the session that Foots Thomas described, Hawk recorded four tunes with his own quartet. It was an auspicious occasion because it marked the recording debut of pianist Thelonious Monk. In his brief solos on 'Flyin' Hawk' and 'On the Bean' Monk serves notice that he was well on the way to becoming a highly influential jazz musician. His original manner of voicing inversions and resolving chords, both in his solos and his accompaniments, was already quite out of the ordinary.

Mingled in with Hawk's vast 1944 output of recordings were some commendable sessions for the Savoy label in a group called the Cozy Cole-Coleman Hawkins All Stars (which featured trumpeter Emmett Berry and pianist Johnny Guarneri). Both sessions (on 1 May and 14 June) are well planned and utilize skilful arrangements. Hawkins, stimulated by the group's clean playing, sounds purposeful on the up-tempo numbers and emotive on the slow tunes, but he shares honours with trumpeter Emmett Berry, an underrated jazzman, whose huge, expressive tone and smouldering mute work adds considerably to these fine sessions.

Cozy Cole is featured on 'Ol' Man River', but for most of the time contents himself with stoking the group along; only on 'Stompin' at the Savoy' does he sound leaderishly obtrusive, backing Hawk's chorus with ineffective paradiddles and shuffle strokes. The concluding riffs on this track later formed the basis of Hawk's celebrated composition 'Stuffy'. Hawk plays a pedigree sixteen-bar solo on 'Wrap Your Troubles in Dreams' (a top-class arrangement) and sounds admirably spirited on 'Riding the Riff' and 'Jump Awhile', but his feature, 'On the Sunny Side of the Street', is the outstanding part of the session. After an arranged introduction Hawkins caresses the melody for sixteen bars, then gradually becomes more expansive, climaxing an empyrean performance with a spirited cadenza tinged with modernisms.

During this part of the 1940s several of Hawkins's contemporaries on tenor saxophone were capable of sharing a bandstand with him without disgracing themselves. Through Hawk's all-pervading influence, men like Don Byas, Ben Webster, Flip Phillips, Dave Matthews and Corky Corcoran could create big-toned solos that were harmonically interesting, but when it came to the playing and shaping of a ballad feature Hawkins remained a long way ahead of his rivals. His performance on 'On the Sunny Side of the Street' makes this point very potently.

Less successful were the sides Hawkins recorded under Cozy Cole's name for the Continental label. Anyone who believes that the microgroove era was solely responsible for spawning hackneyed middle-of-the-road sessions should listen to what Cole's octet produced on 14 and 21 November 1944. The basic problems are created by the bittiness of the arrangements and the poor quality of the original compositions (in reality nothing more than a reblending of well-worn riffs). The planning of the session is unimaginative; no sooner has a soloist begun to settle in than he is shunted away and, distressingly, no one took stock of the fact that on six of the numbers recorded the final solo is allocated to Slam Stewart's bowing-and-singing routine. The leader's drumming is volatile and flexible on 'The Beat' and 'Look Here' but Hank D'Amico's clarinet fails to convey any flair throughout the date. The admirable pianist Clyde Hart (who did some of the arrangements) is on the first session, but doesn't solo; his replacement is the talented Johnny Guarneri, who remains equally unlit.

Don Byas is given more solo space than Hawkins on the second date, but both men are featured, in tantalizing miniature, on 'Memories of You'. If there was a star performance on this undistinguished session it came from trumpeter Charlie Shavers, who does his best to inject some spirit into the proceedings and also demonstrates the near-impossible by playing cup-muted solos perfectly in tune, in every register.

Also for Continental, Hawkins formed part of Leonard Feather's All Stars in a session that sensibly granted a feature number to each of four soloists. Trumpeter Buck Clayton has an effective two-chorus workout on 'Scram' and guitarist Remo Palmieri (despite being under-recorded) creates succinct ideas on 'Esquire Stomp'. Edmond Hall's slightly rasping tone propels his two lively choruses on 'Esquire Jump' and, as if to show that he too could rough things up a little, Hawk blows thirty-two guttural bars. The tenor-sax feature is 'Thanks a Million', which is given the 'Body and Soul' treatment: the opening chorus is a series of paraphrases of the melody that develop against some muted long-note backings and not surprisingly, the piece ends with a series of cadenzas, but in this instance they sound mandatory rather than inspired.

Hawk's follow-up session for the Apollo label was rather more conventional than the two February dates that had featured Dizzy Gillespie, but it had an unorthodox twist in that it featured a front line consisting of three tenor saxists; Hawkins, Ben Webster and George Auld (who also doubled alto sax on the date). The trumpeter was Charlie Shavers and the accompanists consisted of Billy Rowland (piano), Hy White (guitar), Israel Crosby (bass) and Specs Powell (drums), at that time the rhythm section of Raymond Scott's group. The session started after midnight so as to allow George Auld time to get from the Apollo Theatre (where he was leading his own band) to the Apollo recording studio.

Ben Webster sounds in fighting mood on 'Pick up Boys', but his solo is overloaded with vigour and his tone hoarse with effort, whereas Hawkins's subsequent improvisations are nimble, powerful and interesting. In the middle of these two heavy-weight offerings Auld plays a driving, well-constructed solo. Considering the plethora of big tones present the sound of the saxophone voicing on 'Porgy' is disappointing; Hawk's phrasing of this Field–McHugh melody is luscious and Auld, sounding distinctly relaxed, creates a warm-toned solo. The main talking point about 'Uptown Lullaby' is that it is one of those rare occasions on which Ben Webster played clarinet, but *Metronome* magazine put the issue in context by saying, 'Webster tremulously supplies clarinet work in the background.' The tune itself is a close reworking of Leonard Feather's 1940 composition 'Reunion in Harlem'; this version has a fine alto-sax solo by George Auld, which benefits from Hawk's absorbing obbligato. Charlie Shavers is at his mercurial best on 'Salt Peanuts', but Webster resumes his earlier musical onslaught again, making Auld's work sound more enjoyable. The peaks of exploration and swing, however, are achieved by Hawkins's solo.

Towards the end of 1944 the charms of his long booking at the Downbeat Club began to fade for Hawkins; wearying of the routine, he even contemplated forming another big band. He pondered for a while then decided not to, but he needed no second thoughts when invited to take a small band out to California, an area he hadn't visited since his 1923 trip there with Mamie Smith. The offer related to a November 1944 opening in Los Angeles, and Hawk prepared for the booking by asking Don Byas, Thelonious Monk, Denzil Best and Selwyn Warner to travel with him. Unfortunately, though, the Californian entrepreneur Billy Berg encountered a snag in leasing the site of the new club and was forced to postpone the opening.

When the contract for a February 1945 opening was finalized it became obvious to Hawkins that he would have to organize a new line-up: Thelonious Monk was adamant that he wouldn't leave New York, and both Don Byas and Selwyn Warner had other plans. Drummer Denzil Best agreed to make the trip westwards and Hawk managed to persuade Oscar Pettiford to join the group on bass. Pettiford then introduced Hawkins to a trumpeter, who became part of the new quintet.

The newcomer was twenty-six-year-old Howard McGhee, who had already worked with Lionel Hampton, Andy Kirk and Charlie Barnet. He recalled the circumstances of his joining Hawkins: 'In December 1944 in New York I ran into Oscar Pettiford. Hawk's going to California, was I interested? Damn right I was. I wanted to get to California. December in New York was too cool.' But McGhee had to endure a colder place than New York City before the group reached California: 'We went from New York to Buffalo for two weeks. Was it cold up there? It was so cold even the cabs wouldn't run.'[10]

During the group's two-week stay at McVann's Club in Buffalo they took every opportunity to introduce and perfect new arrangements. McGhee said of Hawkins:

> He was modernizing his own self, he didn't want any of the old guys in the band at that time. Pettiford, myself and Sir Charles Thompson were quite young; we were learning from him and he was learning from us. It made a close-knit thing. Hawk had a young mind; he wasn't the kind of guy that says, 'Just because I can play "12th Street Rag" I'm gonna stay on it.' He kept right on going. It was a pleasure to go to a rehearsal with him because he had something like changing key every two bars. You had to listen. He didn't say, 'You've got to play the way I play,' or anything like that. He just did things on his horn that you heard. The man was a genius at lyrical chord changes.[11]

Eventually, after playing dates in Detroit and Chicago, the group reached the West Coast and opened at Billy Berg's club on Vine Street (just south of Sunset Boulevard) Los Angeles on 1 February 1945. There Howard McGhee became totally familiar with the group's arrangements: 'Coleman hipped me to a lot of music. I had to get hip to Monk's tunes. I had the chops and the range but I didn't know the melodies. Hawk and I were pretty tight together; only differences were over money.'

Although Thelonious Monk was no longer on piano the band continued to play some of his tunes; they also played a number of arrangements written by the man who had replaced Monk, Charles Thompson (recently nicknamed 'Sir Charles' by Lester Young). Thompson said:

> I was more or less a utility piano player on 52nd Street. In fact this is when I met Coleman Hawkins, during that period. I refer to Coleman Hawkins as a 'College of

> Music'. I've met people like Art Tatum and I put Coleman Hawkins in the same category. Hawkins was more of a teacher because he'd sit down at the piano and show you chord progression; he was a great listener to classical music. You know, the man could play a ballad like Art Tatum played on the piano, and he could invert those chords and he could get so much expression in them. We played in New York and we travelled, a brief tour of the Mid-western states and on to California where we played in Billy Berg's famous club. We were considered to be one of the first organized groups to play the type of music which was considered to be modern.[12]

Coleman Hawkins's quintet did good business at Billy Berg's newly-opened club, sharing the bill with a trio led by Slim Gaillard (which featured drummer Zutty Singleton) for part of the run. A fillip for the Hawkins group occurred when they were chosen to appear in a Universal movie *The Crimson Canary* featuring Noah Berry Jr. Henry Blankfort, scriptwriter for the film (originally called *Hear that Trumpet Talk*), was a jazz fan, so he included interludes for improvised music. Ted Cain, then head of Universal's music department, saw that Hawkins's group was at Berg's club, and agreed with the company musical director, Nat Young, that it would be a fine idea to feature them in the film.

The quintet went to the studios to record two numbers and subsequently mimed to their own music when they were filmed playing a nightclub sequence. Hawkins wasn't carried away with the prospect of becoming a movie star; his preparation for the filming was to stay up all night revelling. He later said that he hadn't slept for two days before shooting began.[13]

Hawk's group (with Eddie Robinson on bass instead of Oscar Pettiford) had recorded six titles for the Asch label in January 1945, just before they left New York. The sides are not well recorded but they show that the quintet's arrangements were full of contemporary ideas; the group kept one foot in the swing groove but stuck the other limb out in determined exploration. Sir Charles Thompson's economical, lightly played interjections suggest a modernized Count Basie, and his style of accompaniment allowed freedom and space for the soloists to insert their own passing chords. Howard McGhee, though nothing like the revolutionary that Dizzy Gillespie was, plays technically daring solos that contain broad shafts of experiment.

It was a growing practice during this era, for those with modern inclinations, to construct tunes on the chord sequences of popular standards. Hawkins followed this trend by writing 'Bean Stalking' on the harmonies of Jesse Stone's tune 'Idaho', and in doing so composed a clever, tuneful and lasting orginal. But not all of the items from the Asch session were as durable and 'Night Ramble' sounds like a montage of early bop clichés. The same sort of riffs and 'new' melodies cropped up and over and over again on recordings made by modernists during the 1940s. Often the composer was the musician who had the foresight to copyright the theme first. Sordid opportunism gained composer royalties for some people who had played no part in the origination of a particular melody, but sometimes the stealing was innocently created by osmosis when musicians wrote down a theme that had seeped into their ears as they strolled along 52nd Street. A typical example of this borrowing process concerned a riff tune based on the chords of 'Oh, Lady be Good'. Hawk first recorded the catchy theme on a December 1944 date with Mary Lou Williams's Orchestra; it turned up later under Hawk's name as 'Rifftide' and later still (purportedly written by Thelonious Monk) as 'Hackensack'. Who is to say which musician put the original idea in the melting pot? In late 1944 the Downbeat Club in New York was almost next door to the Spotlite Club (which then housed a band featuring Benny Harris and Budd Johnson), and a *Metronome* reporter commented on the similarity of material used in the two venues: 'Hawk's bunch and the one at the Spotlite play many of the same head arrangements and riffs, and it's amusing to jump from one door to another to compare the performances.'

The real pity concerning many early bop recordings is that so much of the precious three minutes available was given to unison renderings of fairly trite little themes, at the expense of the soloists. The Hawkins quintet fell into this trap, but there is enough improvising space for Howard McGhee to demonstrate his technical facility (particularly strong in the upper register) and his confident lines. He was never glib but (like Joe Guy) sounded similar to Roy Eldridge but without the intensity. McGhee's cup-muted playing on 'Ready for Love', a slowish ballad, shows a pleasing degree of subtlety and warmth, and Sir Charles Thompson gives an early indication of his inimitable touch in the way he block-chords 'Ladies Lullaby' (a tune he composed as a tribute to Billie Holiday). Hawk's ballad feature 'Leave My Heart Alone' shows the master giving his standard (admittedly extremely high) treatment to yet another ballad – complete with swirling cadenzas. Throughout the Asch date Hawk veers to and fro between the past and the future, but within some of his phrases are traces of Don Byas's playing, as though some of Don's ideas had rubbed off during the months the two tenor stars had worked side by side.

Neither Hawkins nor anyone in his group was modern enough to be offensive to the ears of patrons at Billy Berg's club – whereas out and out revolutionaries such as Gillespie and Parker were given the cold shoulder by the clientele when they played at the club later that same year – but a lot of this type of reaction was simply a question of the crowd accepting an established jazz giant's explorations while decrying similar efforts by people then less well-known. Howard McGhee spoke of the quintet's stay at Berg's:

> When we got to California the group was very tight; we had been working together for eight weeks, working every night. That tightens up a group. We had quite a few arrangements. At a lot of places we could rehearse during the day and play at night. California people knew about Coleman Hawkins but they didn't have the slightest idea what the band was like and so when they came they said 'Oh man, what a band! We haven't heard music like that, ever!' So I guess Coleman was the one who opened the West Coast up as far as modern sounds in jazz.[14]

But some visitors *were* surprised by the new group's musical policy; one of these was the veteran trombonist Kid Ory, who ruefully asked Howard McGhee, 'Why doesn't he play the way he used to play?'[15]

Soon after arriving in California Hawkins found himself working on the same bill as Kid Ory's band. The post-war jazz-concert boom was just starting and big all-star packages were regularly assembled for one-off shows. The leading promoter in this field was twenty-five-year-old Norman Granz. Granz organized one of his concerts at the Los Angeles Philharmonic Hall on Sunday 18 February 1945; it featured Kid Ory's band, a Gene Krupa unit (with guests Illinois Jacquet, Peanuts Holland, Vic Dickenson and Eddie Heywood) and Coleman Hawkins's trio (Hawkins, General Morgan on piano and Harold Hahn on drums). A reporter for *Jazz Record* said the highlight of the entire event occurred in the finale when Hawkins blew six choruses of the blues, backed by Joe Sullivan's piano.

Norman Granz made use of Hawk's services whenever he could during the tenorist's stay in California. Granz's package shows became known as Jazz at the Philharmonic (or JATP); they were to play a regular part in Hawkins's subsequent career. The use of the Philharmonic's name soon became ironic because the hall's management (in a move that emphasized the *infra dig* qualities that jazz had at that time) made it impossible for Granz to book their venue for his presentations.

Record producer Dave Dexter, who had formerly worked for *Down Beat* magazine in New York, was by 1945 settled in California and producing recording sessions for the recently-organized Capitol company.

He seized the opportunity of recording Hawkins and his group and gave Hawk what was described at the time as 'the biggest advance of his career'. These Capitol sides, issued as by Coleman Hawkins and his Orchestra, were recorded in three batches during late-night sessions held in February and March 1945 at the Radio Recorders' Studio on Santa Monica Boulevard, Los Angeles. The white guitarist, Allan Reuss, was added to the quintet for the recordings.

The strategy of using two standard tunes and two boppish originals on the first session (23 February 1945) set the pattern for subsequent dates. On 'April in Paris' Hawk regulates a steady flow of warm-toned ideas as he rhapsodizes around the melody; McGhee shows the Eldridge influence in his sixteen-bar solo by quoting snippets from Roy's famous recording of 'Old Rockin' Chair'. The trumpeter subsequently phrases the beautiful verse of 'Stardust' elegantly but in so doing exposes the ribs of his thin tone. This tune was one of Hawk's major successes of the 1930s and he lives up to the challenge by using a larger palette of harmonic colourings in this new version. 'Rifftide' allows McGhee to demonstrate his technical flexibility and Hawkins effortlessly to superimpose a series of complex grace notes into his fast-moving solo.

Dave Dexter described the background to the naming of the final tune of the date:

> Hawk had an original, a bit boppish, but no title. I suggested we call it 'Stuffy' in tribute to the best disc-jockey in California, Gene Norman, whom I had nicknamed Stuffy on our two-hour broadcast every Wednesday on KFWB. Bean said, 'Fine,' and it was the hit side of the album. Gene Norman used it as his program's theme for many years after.[16]

The group sound super-confident on 'Stuffy' with Hawkins displaying an effect that was to figure heavily in his later work, namely his way of opening a solo by playing a loud, aggressive cluster of notes. The theme itself, and the quilted lining of arranged passages, were contemporary examples of what might be called riff-bop.

Sir Charles Thompson later inferred that he had been partly responsible for composing the melody of 'Stuffy', just as Howard McGhee felt that he and Oscar Pettiford had written part of one of the tunes assigned to Sir Charles. There was a tangle of claims and counter-claims over who wrote what, but in general the group worked well together, though a faint whiff of acrimony occurred when Pettiford began chiding Sir Charles for playing backings that were too sparse.[17]

The only real trouble connected with the Hawkins group's stay in California occurred at the Capitol recording session on 2 March 1945, when a contretemps developed between Howard McGhee and Dave Dexter that left a good deal of ill feeling. A British visitor to the studio, Bob Higham (then serving in the Royal Air Force), described the scene for readers of the *Melody Maker*. For this recording session the band had been further augmented by the addition of trombonist Vic Dickenson; he was in the studio when Higham arrived but there was no sign of Howard McGhee. The visitor described the scene: 'Upon entering the control room the mystery of the missing trumpet player was speedily explained. Loud snores emanated from a chesterfield in the corner and closer inspection revealed the recumbent figure of Howard McGhee. Dave Dexter sadly explained that the trumpet man had arrived "carrying a load".'[18]

Years later, Dave Dexter filled in the details;

> McGhee I believe was not drunk. He was on some kind of narcotics. He was belligerent and unco-operative from the start of the session. He fluffed every bar and Bean was embarrassed. In sheer desperation I telephoned Red Nichols, a dear friend of mine, who lived not far away and he drove to the studio with his cornet. But while McGhee sat on a chair giggling poor Red couldn't cut that near-boppish music and after a couple of hopeless takes he went home. He and I were humiliated but somehow we concluded the session sans trumpet.[19]

Hawk's own account of the incident appeared in *Metronome*. 'This trumpet player [Nichols] was so completely lost he couldn't do a thing and Howard McGhee forgot he was mad and almost killed himself laughing.' In turn McGhee gave his side of the story, complaining that Dave Dexter 'rode in Red Nichols to play in my place. He didn't have the slightest idea what he was supposed to be playing. Pettiford would look at me and laugh and finally they decided he wouldn't make the date.[20] Elsewhere, he recalled: 'Hawk ran down a tune he wanted to play, 'Too Much of a Good Thing', based on the chords of 'Fine and Dandy', but when Red Nichols started to play he couldn't read that. He was in the wrong setting.'[21]

Bob Higham, who remained throughout the all-night session, reported, 'Hawkins was as steady as a rock, bouncing through arrangements and solos with never the slightest suspicion of a falter. I was amused to note that at no time during the seven hours of the session did the Hawk remove the hat which was jammed precariously on the back of his head, neither did his imperturbable drummer.' Higham went on to say that the president of Capitol records, composer Johnny Mercer, came in to the studio at about three o'clock in the morning carrying a large bottle of whisky; 'Vic Dickenson had, by this time, decided to call it a day and had departed.'[22]

It was not one of Dickenson's most successful sessions. He sounds ill at ease on 'Hollywood Stampede', and, as that was only a revamping of 'Sweet Georgia Brown', it cannot have been the harmonic sequence that fazed him. Most probably he was feeling the warning vibrations of the impending dispute. Howard McGhee employs one of his standard soloing ploys here, first playing a subdued eight-bar pattern and then following it with a dramatically impressive flight into the top register. Hawkins adopts a bold line, blowing phrases that confirm that he had dozens of ways of adding notes that extended common chords. The fascinating aspect of the arrangement is that the band include part of the melody of 'Ornithology' (which later became one of the anthems of the early bop movement), but Hawk's Hollywood session took place months before the tune was first recorded. Benny Harris, co-composer of 'Ornithology', had been Hawk's previous trumpeter and it's conceivable that he first grafted the theme into Hawk's arrangement of 'Hollywood Stampede'.

By the time the group recorded 'I'm Through with Love' McGhee was out of action. A relieved Dickenson displays some of his inimitable musical guile and humour, and Hawkins booms out some highly satisfying low notes. Hawk's huge tone is also a feature of 'What is There to Say?' but despite the impeccable support of Pettiford's driving bass playing a feeling grows that the clipped strokes of the rhythm guitar are acting as a corral for Hawk's ideas. Hawk concluded the date by using only the rhythm section on 'Wrap Your Troubles in Dreams', but again the *chunk-chunk* of the guitar beat seems to restrict him.

A problem of a different kind affected the third and final Capitol session (held on 9 March 1945). During the week that had elapsed since the previous recordings, Oscar Pettiford had suffered one of the hazards of a bassist's life by splitting the skin on one of his plucking fingers. Normally the soreness soon disappears and the skin hardens, but on this occasion Pettiford developed an infection – blood poisoning set in – and at one time it seemed as if he might have to have a finger amputated. Mercifully things began to improve without surgery but, for a two-week period, bassist John Simmons was called in to deputize for Pettiford, both at Billy Berg's club and at the 9 March recording session.

The group's first task was to record 'Too Much of a Good Thing', the tune on which Red Nichols had floundered. But even McGhee had trouble in playing the trumpet part. Dave Dexter recalls: 'McGhee spoilt so many masters we wound up with a poor track. I think we tried twenty-seven takes and we never did get it right.'[23] These minor blemishes riddle the arrangement of what is, after all, an innocuous theme (penned by Hawkins). The piano solo sounds relaxed and inventive but a desultory quality, probably caused by repetition fatigue, disfigures both McGhee and Hawkins's solos.

'Bean Soup', a wittily disguised 'Tea for Two', also has some elegant piano playing from Thompson, but McGhee's thirty-two-bar solo underlines the fact that the modernisms he used were being superimposed on an existing swing-based style. McGhee could be innovative, and proved this by the spectacularly exploratory playing that he contributed to the band's brief sequence in *The Crimson Canary* movie. Hawkins skilfully bustles his way through 'Bean Soup', giving the impression that he was warming up for a spectacular second chorus that was never played through lack of disc time. Hawk moves much closer to his earlier style of playing by rhapsodizing his way through 'Someone to Watch Over Me' and 'It's the Talk of the Town', this last title (backed by 'Stuffy') becoming a big-selling 78 rpm record for Capitol.

In summing up the three recording sessions Dexter said, 'I found Hawkins easy to work with, aside from that one bad night. He had no objection to my bringing in Allan Reuss on guitar. He was in good humor, and accepted my tune suggestions eagerly. All the other tracks came off well, I think. I didn't like Howard McGhee after that incident and avoided him.'[24]

Hawk's other 1945 session for Capitol was as a member of an all-star group, assembled by Dave Dexter, which consisted of three of Hawk's former colleagues from the Fletcher Henderson band; Benny Carter, John Kirby and Buster Bailey. The rest of the illustrious group were trumpeter Bill Coleman, pianist Nat 'King' Cole, guitarist Oscar Moore and drummer Max Roach. Vocalist Kay Starr sang on two of the four tracks.

As might be expected, the calibre of the musicians meant that no serious mishaps occurred. Inspiration is rarely at its highest points on 'All Star' sessions, but fluency is ever-present, as it is in Nat Cole's sensitive half-chorus on 'You Can Depend on Me' and the elegant solos blown by Carter and Coleman. On this tune Hawk is given a prestigious full chorus and uses it to prove that he wasn't reserving his use of substitute harmonies for exclusive use at Billy Berg's. On the Kay Starr vocal vehicle 'If I Could Be With You One Hour' he implements his growing tendency to include broken-time phrases in his ballad solos. 'Stormy Weather' is a vocal feature and the final title, 'Riffmarole', produced a series of high-class but urbane blues choruses from the celebrated musical cast.

Hawk's quintet finished their residency at Billy Berg's club in mid-April 1945. They played some local dates and also appeared on Sunday 17 April at a concert Norman Granz organized at the Russ Auditorium in San Diego (Nat 'King' Cole, Willie Smith, Slim Gaillard and Bam Brown were also on the bill). A day later, Hawk's group began working at Shepp's Playhouse, Los Angeles, taking over there from Eddie Heywood's band, who moved into Billy Berg's club.

Howard McGhee felt that the time was right for him to ask for an increase in salary, but his plea fell on deaf ears. He said later:

> The band busted up on account of the money problem. Coleman didn't see fit to keep it together. They didn't ask for outrageous money; he just wouldn't get up off what he had promised to pay. The guys figured they were worth more than that, the group had gone over so well. We had a tour set all the way back to New York. The promoters wanted the band that everyone had been hearing about. Hawk was a tight son of a gun. He didn't believe in giving up a quarter. I told him, 'I think I deserve a raise. I know all the tunes.' He had different ideas and said, 'I'll get Joe Guy.'[25]

But Joe Guy, who was then Billie Holiday's consort, had other plans, so Hawkins enlisted the services of Bill Coleman, in California as a member of John Kirby's sextet (then temporarily without work). Bill recalled the situation: 'At the end of two weeks at Shepp's Playhouse Hawkins asked if I could stay longer, but Kirby had finally found an engagement at a white club in Baltimore.'[26]

Hawkins had no intention of asking Howard McGhee back, and decided that it was time to move back east. Thirty years later, McGhee viewed the contretemps philosophically:

> Hawk was, to me, a very strange man, in a sense that him being in Europe made him stand out from the rest of the fellows. I guess he knew more about the world than we did. It meant he acted differently and he lived different. We weren't out to set a new thing. We were just doing what we felt like doing. All the guys in the band had their own creative ideas and we just put them together and it turned out to be a group ahead of its time.[27]

16
Jazz at the Philharmonic

McGhee, Thompson and Pettiford remained in California to follow their own devices. Hawkins mulled over the idea of working his way back to New York by using a trio consisting of himself, Denzil Best on drums and Roger 'Ram' Ramirez on piano, but he changed his mind and journeyed straight back east. He arrived in New York in May 1945, played a date at the Detroit Institute of Arts on the 25th (guesting there with a band led by drummer Art Mardigan), then on the 30th he returned to work at the Downbeat Club as the resident guest star.

Hawkins played at the Downbeat for most of the summer and autumn of 1945, often co-starring with Billie Holiday. Guitarist Tiny Grimes was regularly on the bill, as was trombonist Trummy Young; Art Tatum appeared there occasionally, earning (it was rumoured) a thousand dollars a week. Hawk soon fell into the same sort of routine he had adopted during his other long New York club runs, occasionally taking leave from the Downbeat to play brief residencies elsewhere on the East Coast. The main difference in his schedule in 1945, as compared to 1944, related to his recording activities. His contract with Capitol precluded him from recording with his own band for rival companies, or from receiving label credit on recordings with other groups. As a result of these restrictions he made only one session (with Sidney Catlett's All Stars) during the remainder of 1945.

Despite featuring a strong line-up, the Catlett All Stars' recordings from October 1945 failed to produce any memorable music. Hawkins and pianist Billy Taylor flirt with bebop while the other soloists, Dick Vance (trumpet), Hilton Jefferson (alto sax) and Tyree Glenn (trombone) remain firmly in the swing mould. The fussy arrangements are tinged with bop ideas but lack the excitement of the fast-running unison figures that so appealed to that era's modern-jazz fans. On 'What's Happening?' Hawk sprinkles a few bop licks into his first chorus but it's noticeable that he sheds this type of pattern as he romps through his second thirty-two bars. On the one slow number of the session, 'Before Long', Hawk is restricted to playing arranged passages with Glenn, Vance and Taylor taking the solos that support the straight, powerful vocal by Matthew Meredith.

For part of his run at the Downbeat Club Hawkins resumed his role as bandleader, but (as before) he often left it until the last moment before booking his sidemen. Bassist Al McKibbon, one such late addition, spoke of his inauguration:

> I went to visit 52nd Street with a friend and Coleman Hawkins didn't have a bass player that night; he was opening at the Downbeat. Big Sid Cartlett said, 'Hey, why don't you go and play with Hawk? He needs a bass player.'
>
> I said, 'I don't know Hawk and I don't have a bass.'
>
> He said, 'That's all right, I'll introduce you to him.'
>
> I borrowed a bass and played. So he gave me the job. Miles Davis used to come in; he was in Juilliard [Juilliard College of Music] at that time. He used to come in with his horn and he'd sit up on the bandstand and he'd listen to us play, watch what Monk was doing. And sometimes Monk would hit something strange and Miles would figure it out on his horn, but he'd never play. He would just sit and listen and laugh to himself.[1]

One of Hawk's most devoted disciples, tenorist George 'Big Nick' Nicholas, had settled in New York by this time:

> I got to know Hawk well during the time he played on 52nd Street. By then I dressed like Hawk and had grown a mustache like him. I used to go to hear him so often the guys in the band got to know me and they'd say 'Hallo'. One night Hawk was very late getting back after intermission; I don't know where he went to but the guys saw I had my tenor with me and they invited me up to play. Hawk came in and he wasn't put out at all. He always called me 'son' and answered any questions that I asked. He was a quiet man, but with me he was serious and truthful. He invited me to his home and played the piano for me, and he showed me his various tenor saxophones, all of them Selmer's. He had an automatic record changer, the very first one I ever saw. I was terrifically impressed by his ways.[2]

By the summer of 1945 Charlie Parker had firmly established a place for himself on 52nd Street. The talents of this wayward genius of the alto saxophone had long been recognized by his fellow musicians, but his impact on the jazz public, and on New York's clubowners, was not fully felt until 1945. Hawkins took a close interest in Parker's playing and was able to listen to him regularly when the altoist played a residency at the Three Deuces, right next door to the Downbeat. Parker's front-line partner for that booking was Don Byas, who used to play his sets with Parker and then, during intermissions, move into the adjoining club to play duets with Hawkins. The ensuing tenor-sax 'battles' were the foreunners (by some years) of quintets that featured tenor-sax duelling between Sonny Stitt–Gene Ammons, Al Cohn–Zoot Sims, Dexter Gordon–Wardell Gray and various other pairings.

Late in 1945 Charlie Parker played a residency at another 52nd Street club, the Spotlite. When his stint there ended he was replaced by Coleman Hawkins and his group. This move didn't involve Hawk in any dramatic change of routine since the new club was situated at 56 West 52nd Street, just a few steps away from the Downbeat. The Spotlite was then managed by Billie Holiday's first husband, Clark Monroe, who had some support from outside interests. Monroe had played a part in nurturing bop at one of his former clubs, the Uptown House, and he continued regularly to book young modernists into his new venture at the Spotlite, giving them the opportunity to share billing with established stars like Hawkins.

On 20 November 1945 Hawkins took time off from the New York club and went with his rhythm section (Thelonious Monk, Denzil Best and Al McKibbon) to play in an all-star concert held in Philadelphia; others on the bill were Art Tatum, Dizzy Gillespie and guitarist Mary Osborne. A *Metronome* reviewer was impressed by Hawkins but commented, 'The trio was hampered not a little by pianist Thelonious Monk.'[3] It was to be some years before Monk's talent was generally acclaimed, but Hawkins always championed the pianist's work: 'Monk,' he'd say with emphasis, 'That's originality.'[4] Occasionally Hawk became quite vehement in crusading for modern jazz. In 1946 he said, 'It's amazing to me that so many people in music won't accept progress. It's the only field where advancement meets so much opposition. You take doctors – look what medicine and science have accomplished in the last twenty or thirty years. That's the way it should be in music – that's the way it has to be.'[5]

Clarinettist Tony Scott first got to know Hawk at the Spotlite Club:

> He wasn't an open talker, but he was one of my idols. I first heard him at Kelly's Stable, not long after he had recorded 'Body and Soul'. That record hit us young musicians, it really opened our noses, just three notes of melody and it still became a hit. The Spotlite Club was very quiet on Tuesday, Wednesday and Thursday; if I was sitting there listening on one of those nights he'd beckon me to sit in. One night he suddenly called from the stand, 'Take over Tony,' so I got on the bandstand with my clarinet and he left me, saying, 'I'm going around the corner to the White Rose,' which was a bar on 6th Avenue near the club.[6]

Hawkins's first stay at the Spotlite lasted only a few weeks then, by prior arrangement, he left to join impresario Norman Granz's newly-organized JATP touring unit. The package was considerably larger and more star-studded than the Granz shows that Hawkins had worked in during his stay in California. In the interim, Granz had decided to organize a three-week national tour, which would also visit Canada. Some of the participants, such as Arnold Ross (piano), Barney Kessel (guitar), Corky Corcoran (tenor sax), Willie Smith (alto sax) and Vido Musso (tenor sax) were based permanently on the West Coast; others, including Howard McGhee (trumpet), Lucky Thompson (tenor sax) and Meade Lux Lewis (piano), were temporarily dwelling in California. The five who flew in from the east to link up with the main contingent were Hawkins and his rhythm section (Best, McKibbon and Monk) and trumpeter Roy Eldridge. Helen Humes was the featured vocalist with the touring show.

The tour began with a concert at the Los Angeles Philharmonic Hall (on 26 November 1945) that delighted the 2,600 audience. The itinerary had originally been scheduled to cover a four-week period, but Granz (who was always a passionate enemy of racism) insisted that the management at each venue agreed to his booking clause which said, 'There shall be no discrimination or segregation concerning admittance of the audience'; some managers in the South refused to sign such a contract so Granz cancelled that part of the tour, reducing the duration of the trip to three weeks. Business, and audiences reactions, convinced Granz that there was a willing market for regular jazz-concert tours.

Hawkins returned to New York, took a brief rest then, in December, resumed his residency at the Spotlite Club, which had temporarily returned to more traditional music fare by booking Henry 'Red' Allen's band to work alongside Hawk's group. In February 1946, while Hawkins was still at the Spotlite, Leonard Feather organized a recording session for Victor that featured Hawk on two titles. To tie in with the release of these discs, Feather wrote a pen-portrait of Hawkins: 'Coleman has a warm, friendly personality. He takes life easy and rarely gets excited over anything.' He also alluded to the problem that faced those who reviewed Hawk's recorded ballad performances: 'Like every record he has made since "Body and Soul" you may be tempted to describe it as his "greatest since . . ." '[7]

The version of "Say It Isn't So' recorded at the Victor session wasn't as distinguished as the epic that Feather mentioned, but it is still a superb ballad performance, one in which Hawkins evinces romanticism without resorting to sentimentality. 'Spotlite' (based on the chords of 'Just You Just Me') was a tribute to Hawk's place of work. Mary Osborne on guitar and Jimmy Jones on piano create some subtle improvisations on the medium-paced tune, then Hawk enters and begins a fidgety exposition of some of his bop licks. He doesn't seem totally convincing, however, whereas Charlie Shavers, who follows him, sounds (as ever) flamboyantly assured.

Leonard Feather had also booked the young white tenor saxist Allen Eager to play on the session. Feather reasoned that Eager's lightish tone and gently wrought phrases would make an interesting contrast with Hawkins's huge-toned dramatic lines, and he suggested that the two musicians swop four-bar phrases during the recording of Denzil Best's tune 'Wee', here called 'Allen's Alley'. Feather recalled in his book *The Jazz Years* that Hawkins did not take to the idea at all: 'We tried one take but Bean was clearly uncomfortable and the concept did not appeal to him; on the take used we let Allen Eager and altoist Pete Brown divide the honours.' Hawkins had played four-bar chases on record with other musicians, notably on a previous session organized by Feather in 1937, but in 1946 he declined to joust with Eager. This was perhaps because it was obvious that Eager's playing style was inspired by Lester Young's work, but this hadn't always been so. He had taken lessons from Ben Webster and recalled saying to him, 'Ben, you're the greatest,' to which Webster replied, 'No, Coleman Hawkins is.'[8]

At the Spotlite Club, Red Allen's band gave way to Dizzy Gillespie's group. Dizzy, who had not long returned from a near-disastrous booking at Billy Berg's club in Hollywood (with Charlie Parker) had formed up a new small band, featuring Leo Parker on baritone saxophone, to work opposite Hawkins's group. A felicitous combination of enormous musical talent and an instinct for gaining publicity led to Gillespie being hailed as the most important figure in the bop movement. As a result of this acclaim the Spotlite Club began to enjoy what *Downbeat* magazine called 'sensational business'. Gillespie was given the go-ahead by the Spotlite's management to increase his band to a seventeen-piece unit, and he was invited to remain at the club indefinitely.

Hawkins never went out of his way to criticise fellow musicians, but he was not averse to making candid assessments in interviews, even about men he worked alongside. In 1946 he said, 'I like modern – very modern – but the bands that are playing modern stuff don't have enough cleanness and finesse. The bands that do play clean generally play old-style arrangements, so I find it hard to listen to either kind. Dizzy sounded great with just six men; now he has a big band that plays the right kind of music but sloppily.'[9]

Hawk was on hand to see the initial surge of business at the Spotlite but in April 1946 he returned to California to take part in concerts that heralded the start of another national tour by the Jazz at the Philharmonic unit. The itinerary again commenced in Los Angeles, but this time the inaugural show was at the 1,800-seater Embassy Auditorium, Granz having found it impossible to deal with all the various restrictions upon which the Philharmonic Hall management insisted. After appearing in Los Angeles the package moved on to San Diego, San Francisco, Oakland, Portland and other West Coast venues before commencing a vast cross-country itinerary that included Kansas City and Detroit. The tour ended at New York's Carnegie Hall in late May 1946.

There were fewer musicians in the troupe than previously, but the quality of talent more than compensated. The group's only trumpeter was the former Count Basie star, Buck Clayton, just released from the US Army. The two tenor saxists were Coleman Hawkins and Lester Young; Charlie Parker and Willie Smith were the altoists; Irving Ashby was on guitar; Billy Hadnott and Al McKibbon shared the double-bass duties; Kenny Kersey was the pianist and Buddy Rich and J.C. Heard alternated on drums. Pianist Meade Lux Lewis and vocalist Helen Humes guested with the show on many of the tour dates and various other jazz stars were added to the bill at specific concerts.

Recordings made at the Los Angeles concerts give a clear indication of the skills of the formidable improvisers in the troupe. From the 22 April concert a medium-tempo 'JATP Blues' has a series of vibrant solos, with Lester Young deliberately reiterating a low note to produce a spate of genteel honking that pleased the crowd. Hawkins's tone gives off more aggressive vibrations and his strong fingers seem to be punching out his busy phrases; he climbs dramatically into the high register, but these excursions are not created to please the audience; instead, they are the effective climax of his spectacular upward runs. Hawk is also more ornate than Young on 'Slow Drag', where again the intricacies are thoughtfully developed, Lester settling into the low register and establishing a bitter-sweet mood, using relatively few notes. Buck Clayton's high-note playing has never been shown to better advantage than on this session. On 'Slow Drag' his solo is peppered with strong, high blowing and he ends the final ensemble by playing a C that is an octave above top C. The composer credit for both of these impromptu blues was given as N.G. Shrdlu, which was both the standard sign-off word for linotype operators and the *nom-de-plume* of Norman Granz.

Buck Clayton effectively continues his high-note excursions on 'I Got Rhythm'. Willie Smith's alto playing is lively and graceful and Hawkins maintains his vigorously combative approach, so much so that his tone develops a rasp. Charlie Parker, who sounded restrained on 'JATP Blues', plays an even sparser solo here. Though Parker's awesome technique made it easy for him to produce cascades of notes, his output here is much more economical than Hawkins's, yet it is Lester Young, whose solo is full of understated, lithe phrases, who creates the most effective work on this track.

Young introduces the melody of 'I Surrender, Dear', lightly embellishing it. Clayton is again a mixture of grace and strength but Hawk's solo is intriguing: in the seventh and eighth bars he plays some typical half-bar bop changes, but in the next eight bars he adopts a totally orthodox harmonic route. Kenny Kersey's filigree figures and subtle voicings are well in evidence throughout the date, but unfortunately the piano became more out of tune as the concert progressed, which spoils the overall sound. Willie Smith's concluding solo epitomizes the admirable control that he consistently maintained over his intonation, high and low.

On a recording of 'I Found a New Baby', made on the following night, Lester Young triumphs. His joyful choruses make a mockery of those who said that his skills were crushed by experiences suffered while he was serving in the US Army. His playing here has all the spirit and swing of his pre-war discs, and as if to underline his buoyancy he humorously includes quotes from solos he'd recorded with Count Basie in the previous decade. Clayton again produces some ultra-high notes in his ingenious weavings then Hawkins bustles his way through two choruses without engendering a vast amount of swing. Willie Smith is also less impressive than usual, and quickly decides on the strategy of playing stock licks. A pyrotechnic drum solo from Buddy Rich propels the front line into an every-man-for-himself final chorus.

Charlie Parker and Willie Smith were absent from the Carnegie Hall concerts on 27 May and 3 June 1946, but several more big names were added to the show, including Illinois Jacquet, Gene Krupa, George Auld and Charlie Ventura. The added vocalists were Sarah Vaughan (on 27 May) and Billie Holiday (on 3 June). The concerts were reviewed in *Metronome* by Leonard Feather, who wrote:

> Norman Granz, who has been touring the country with presentations of this kind, is doing a good thing for jazz. He is presenting, for the most part, modern music and progressive musicians; he is using almost all Negro talent and he is featuring saxophones very extensively. Musically there was much on the plus side. Coleman Hawkins, George Auld, Illinois Jacquet and Lester Young all blew some great choruses.

Leonard Feather continued:

> Only two major musical criticisms: for the sake of form, contrast and climax, the men should work out riffs and routines for some numbers instead of doing nothing but solos and unco-ordinated ensembles. And Norman should be censured for his very shoddy treatment of Coleman Hawkins. At both concerts Hawk had one solo speciality. The audiences screamed to get him back but Norman hurried on to the next number. Lester Young, his solo spot saved for the end, was allowed three or four numbers and remained on-stage fifteen minutes. Lester is great, but Hawk is still the greatest tenorman of all time, as his contributions here make very clear.[10]

Norman Granz may not have been delighted by the points raised in Feather's critique but he made no attempt to answer the complaints in print; during the coming months there was to be a deluge of criticism, often from writers with only a fraction of Feather's musical insight. Later in 1946, D. Leon Wolf, in a full-page *Down Beat* review, headlined his onslaught on a JATP Chicago show 'Granz Bash a Caricature on Jazz – Everything Bad in Jazz Found Here'. Wolf lambasted almost every aspect of the presentation and made a swingeing attack on Rex Stewart's cornet playing. Few of the participants were given even a hint of praise; typical was his comment on Coleman Hawkins; 'The Bean sounded like a little sewing machine, playing everything at top speed and buzzing along with scarcely a trace of his old feeling for logically developed ideas and relaxed phrasing. More than a trace of bop has crept into his playing.'

This time Granz did not remain silent and wrote, in the following issue of *Down Beat*, 'My show is predicated to pleasing as many people as possible. Hawk wasn't playing with a trace of his old ideas, but is, instead, playing with completely new feeling for modern logically developed ideas.' It seems that Granz took heed of Feather's suggestion, though: on a follow-up tour (beginning in San Francisco on 6 October and ending in Brooklyn a month later), Granz made a point of announcing Hawkins as 'The World's Greatest Tenor Saxist.'

A great deal of flak was fired at the JATP presentations but they flew on undaunted, drawing huge crowds to most of their concerts. Granz's wage bill was colossal – even with seats priced around the three-dollar mark he only just managed to clear, even on sell-out nights – yet the more he was criticized the more determined he became to carry on with the touring show. His encouragement came from the musicians, who simply shrugged off the diatribes, and from the delighted audiences whose enthusiasm often reached fever-pitch.

It was partly these displays of excitement that irked critics, because they felt that the JATP musicians were tempted (perhaps unconsciously at first) to play honks on the saxophone or stratospheric trumpet notes so as to gain a loud response from the crowd. On one occasion Granz said wryly of his various saxophonists' ploys, 'Even if it's honking it's the best honking.'[11] Certainly none of his musicians was commanded to 'grandstand'; most of Granz's instructions concerned the timing available on stage and how it could best be used. He said, 'I've made suggestions but they're usually confined to advice on what frills to cut out.'[12]

Grandstanding has played a part in many jazz concerts and, in the highly competitive JATP shows, no virile musician wanted it said that he couldn't 'move' an audience with his work, so at times effects were wantonly repeated that had previously brought shrieks of pleasure from listeners. But the live recordings made at JATP concerts prove that an enormous amount of worthwhile jazz co-existed with occasional forays into exhibitionism: 'I Can't Get Started' (from the 27 May New York concert) is a model of lyrical understatement, containing poignant solos from Hawkins, Young and Clayton.

Thinking back to the 1946 JATP tour, Buck Clayton felt it was one of the most enjoyable musical experiences of his life. He remembers feeling that he could hardly wait to get on stage to work in a front line with Lester Young and Hawkins. Buck was so moved and fascinated by these two musicians' improvisations he almost forgot to come in to play the next solo. He feels that both men were absolutely at the peak of their powers at this time, stressing that whatever musical rivalry existed it never interfered with the affable relationship the two men enjoyed off-stage. Clayton said of Lester Young: 'He'd just come out of the army and was feeling refreshed. I knew how he felt because the same thing had just happened to me. On the shows he was in competition with Coleman Hawkins, which was very good for him. Neither he nor Hawk wanted to let anything go while the other was around.'[13] Norman Granz was adamant that those who suggested that Young's army experiences diminished his powers as an improviser were totally wrong:

I think I heard Lester play his last gig before going into the army and I heard him play his first dates after leaving the service. I actually arranged his journey from Monterey immediately after he was released so no one could have had a clearer picture of events. I can say emphatically that Pres was playing as well when he came out of the army as when he went in.[14]

Since 1939 the music magazines had regularly brought up the subject of rivalry between Hawkins and Young. Gradually readers began to take sides. During the early 1940s Hawkins was the overall favourite with most jazz fans, but slowly, in the middle of the decade, an ardent following for Lester Young developed. It was quite easy to get a huge amount of satisfaction from the work of both of these magnificent jazz improvisers but, in keeping with a long-established jazz 'game', fans began to drift into one camp or another. You were either for Hawkins or for Lester. Many jazzmen, particularly young white saxophonists, began to incorporate Young's phrases into their solos. Bud Shank said, 'Lester Young became my idol. I sensed that Coleman Hawkins was very creative and sophisticated, but he didn't have what I needed.'[15]

At first the two rivals observed the situation with detached humour, but there came a time when they were both irked to find that almost every interviewer (and many bold fans) automatically questioned them about each other's work. Some of this mounting irritation seeped into an interview that Lester Young gave to *Jazz Record* during the summer of 1946. The scene was Young's hotel room; Allan Morrison conducted the interview, but several jazz fans tagged along.

'What about Hawkins?' someone asked him.

Lester looked up without changing expression: 'What about Hawkins?'

'Didn't he give you ideas?'

'There you go again,' Lester said, showing some slight irritation, 'must a musician always get his ideas from another musician? I don't think so. I never did have a favorite tenor. I never heard much of Hawk except on an occasional record. Everybody was copying him. The whole jazz world was on a Hawkins kick.'

He lay back on the bed and closed his eyes. He continued talking about Coleman Hawkins, of his importance to jazz and the tremendous influence he has exerted on tenor players the world over. One got the impression that Lester is no devotee of the Hawk's, that the two greatest tenormen in jazz are worlds apart temperamentally and musically. Noticeable too in his voice was a slight trace of contempt for tenor players who slavishly followed the Coleman Hawkins pattern. 'I couldn't see copying the Hawk or any of the others. You got to have a style that's all your own. A man can only be a stylist if he makes up his mind not to copy anybody.'[16]

Howard McGhee, who worked with both Young and Hawkins, offered an interesting comparison: 'Hawkins knew more about the horn and he knew more changes and the harmonic structure than Pres did. Although Pres could float through it like a butterfly and you'd still enjoy it, Hawk really made you get into where it really was, because he insisted upon playing the right changes.'[17]

During the summer of 1946 the management of the Spotlite Club reintroduced Coleman Hawkins to their bill, making Hawk's group an additional attraction alongside the highly successful Dizzy Gillespie Big Band. They also decided to cash in on the Hawk v. Pres controversy by adding Lester Young to the package. Perhaps the two men had recently seen enough of each other on the Jazz at the Philharmonic tours; whatever the reason, they did little socializing during this shared residency. Pianist Argonne Thornton (aka Sadik Hakim) recalled the lack of liaison: 'I once watched Pres and Coleman Hawkins drink next to each other at a bar of the Spotlite Club for two weeks without speaking.'[18]

Lester Young soon moved on, and so too did Dizzy Gillespie's band. Beginning in August 1946, the Spotlite's new presentation consisted of Hawk's group and a big band led by Roy Eldridge. During this period Hawkins employed various pianists, including Al Haig and John Malachi, but then settled the issue by regularly using a brilliant youngster, Hank Jones, who had been working at the Spotlite as an accompanist for singer-compere Billy Daniels, and in a trio led by Buster Bailey. Jones became a regular member of Hawk's band for some while: 'I worked with his little group on 52nd Street, and I did some one-nighters and little jobs in and around New York and Massachusetts and whatnot.'[19]

Hank Jones was one of several gifted young musicians Hawkins used on a December 1946 recording session for the small Sonora label. The front line consisted of Hawkins, Fats Navarro (trumpet), J.J. Johnson (trombone) and Porter Kilbert (alto sax), with a rhythm section of Jones, Curley Russell (bass) and Max Roach (drums). 'I Mean You' showed that Hawkins was eminently capable of writing a convincing bop theme, as opposed to the bop-tinged swing tunes some other veterans were featuring in an attempt to brush hair over their bald patches. The sharing of solos is extremely democratic, with each member of the front line (and Hank Jones) taking eight bars apiece. Navarro and Johnson are fluently innovative and it's fascinating to hear them improvising phrases that became the clichés of their copyists.

Vibraharpist Milt Jackson was added on 'Bean and the Boys' (based on

'Lover Come Back to Me') and is granted the longest solo; Hawk joins wholeheartedly in the boppish spirit that prevails and doesn't sound out of place. The front line were not required on the two ballad features, but Milt Jackson stayed on to strike some apt backing phrases for Hawk's supple variations of 'Cocktails for Two'. This was Hawk's first recording of the Coslow–Johnston tune, and it became one of his favourite ballads: during the next decade he recorded it on several occasions. 'You Go to My Head' is given a mellow rendering, but one in which Hawk makes it clear that he was now intent on expanding the harmonies he used in his ballad playing. Although he had made his intentions admirably clear on 'Body and Soul', he had not consistently developed the methods he had used on the 1939 recording, and sometimes reverted to his less adventurous pre-war style of rhapsodizing. From this point on he usually underlines the chromaticisms and extensions that he used on ballads, particularly when he was supported by a rhythm section fully conversant with sophisticated harmonies.

In 1946, studio recordings that gathered together magazine poll-winners were still being made. In December of that year Hawk took part in the *Esquire* winners' studio session and played an eloquently decorative version of 'Indian Summer', complete with his own spontaneously devised introduction. 'Indian Winter' (based on 'How High the Moon') has J.J. Johnson devising more new phrases for other trombonists to use. Charlie Shavers again shows himself to be the daredevil of all trumpeters, while Hawkins creates a solo in the musical 'no man's land' that existed between bop and swing. Hawk doesn't solo on 'Blow Me Down', 'Buckin' the Blues', or 'Dixieland Stomp' (also issued as 'Mouldy Fig Stomp'). This last curio was waxed in high spirits at the end of the session and issued as by Chubby Jackson and his Jacksonville Seven. It's a dixieland pastiche, and although Hawk joins in the 'cod' mood during the opening and closing ensembles he refrains from soloing, leaving the individual corn-making to Teddy Wilson, John Collins and Harry Carney.

Later that same month, Hawkins was part of the Metronome All Stars, backing a Frank Sinatra vocal on 'Sweet Lorraine'. The thirty-two-bar instrumental chorus is shared four ways, between Lawrence Brown (trombone), Johnny Hodges (alto sax), Charlie Shavers (trumpet) and Hawkins. Each man shows his class during the two available takes, with Hawkins seemingly content to create a similar solo on both attempts. The Nat 'King' Cole–June Christy vocal duet 'Nat Meets June' begins with a booming blues chorus from Harry Carney on baritone sax. After the vocal, Buddy Rich's lively drum break takes the band into an up-tempo allocation of one-chorus solos for the front line and bassist Eddie Safranski. The whole performance is filled with an attractive exuberance, and this time Hawk sounds very much in the mood to improvise.

Financially, 1947 was not a successful year for the 52nd Street clubs. After the immediate post-war boom created by returning servicemen catching up with developments on the jazz scene, and stimulated by all the publicity about bop, business was much quieter than in previous years. This mini-recession didn't make too much of dent in Hawk's earnings, which were by now heavily supplemented by his regular appearances in Norman Granz's travelling concerts. Following the success of the wide-ranging tour in the autumn of 1946, Granz soon organized another package which, this time, began its trek on the East Coast, playing its initial concert at Brooklyn's Academy of Music on 6 February 1947.

This JATP unit featured Hawkins, Buck Clayton, Willie Smith, Trummy Young, Kenny Kersey, Buddy Rich, young bassist Benny Fonesville and vocalist Helen Humes. As in the past, various guest stars were added and subtracted as the tour proceeded, among them Illinois Jacquet, Roy Eldridge and Flip Phillips. A 'How High the Moon', recorded in Pittsburgh during the tour, features a triumphant performance by Hawkins and some inspired piano playing by Kenny Kersey.

Hawkins continued his practice of always listening carefully to the musicians with whom he worked, and though he admired Illinois Jacquet's playing he sometimes put on a rueful smile if the crowd went wild when Jacquet (or some other tenorist on a JATP show) honked on one note for minutes on end. Roy Eldridge recalled:

> Hawk used to pull a face and say that there were certain ways that any tenor player could break up the house. So one night in Washington, DC I had an idea, and Hawk went along with it. I could play the tenor sax a bit in B flat so Hawk loaned me his instrument and when it came to my turn to go on stage I went out with his sax and started blowing this low-note phrase over and over again. It broke the place up; people were screaming and hollering. I handed the sax back to Hawk and that was that. But when we went back to Washington all sorts of people came around and asked, 'Are you going to play the tenor sax again?' One of the police chiefs down there came and said, 'Everyone wants to hear you play the sax.' So I thought, I'll do it again. But this time Illinois Jacquet was smart; instead of coming on after me, which was usual, he went on before me and played exactly what I was planning to do. So that ended my tenor-sax feature. Coleman and I laughed about it for years afterwards. People did funny things on those tours. I remember Lester Young and Flip Phillips working out a little dance routine that broke us all up.[20]

Joe 'Flip' Phillips, who had started out on 52nd Street as a clarinettist in Pete Brown's band, gradually developed into one of the world's foremost white tenor saxists. His big, warm-toned playing was full of swing and he possessed a good deal of individualism. Soon after his 1947 tour with JATP he was asked by *Down Beat*, 'Who is your favourite tenor-sax player?' He replied, 'Give me Coleman Hawkins. Hawk is the Daddy. Knows the horn inside out and blows it full. When he steps into a chorus it's the final word.' That year Phillips had finished second in the *Down Beat* poll, one place behind Vido Musso and one ahead of Coleman Hawkins. A few years earlier various writers had forecast that it would be Don Byas who eventually overtook Hawkins in the popularity polls, but by 1947 Byas had quit the USA. Finding that the work situation had worsened, Byas toured Europe with Don Redman's band in September 1946, and the atmosphere was so conducive for him he decided to make his home there.

Like Flip Phillips, Charlie Ventura, who was enjoying enormous success at this time, was also a confirmed Hawkins disciple. He echoed Flip's comments: 'Coleman Hawkins is the Daddy of the tenor sax. He always knew his horn. He was one of the reasons I took up tenor – he and Chu Berry. He was so far ahead of everybody when he cut "Body and Soul" '.[21] Charlie Barnet, another leading white tenor saxist, later offered his homage: 'My style was greatly influenced by Coleman Hawkins. He had an amazing facility for working the chord progressions while swinging all the time. He would play the most beautiful ballads and then turn around and swing everybody out of the joint.'[22] Corky Corcoran, Harry James's long-time tenor star said, 'We're all out of that stable – influenced basically by Coleman Hawkins.'[23]

17
Return to Paris

Box-office business was excellent for most of the long 1947 JATP tour. The climax of the long trek took place when the package, plus additional guests (such as Harry Carney, Billy Strayhorn, Oscar Pettiford, Charlie Parker, Kai Winding and Lennie Tristano) played a series of concerts at New York's Carnegie Hall in May 1947.

After his long odyssey Hawkins played dates at New York's Three Deuces Club then briefly took time off to relax with his family. By this time he had two young daughters: Colette who was four and Mimi, two. The family apartment in the King Haven block on 153rd Street needed all its spaciousness to house both the growing children and Hawk's ever-increasing collection of classical records (in those pre-microgroove days one symphony could stretch across eight twelve-inch 78 rpm discs).

Hawkins always believed in quality buying. His gramophone was a vastly expensive Capehart, costing over a thousand dollars. The advantage of this particular model was that it could play a stack of 78s by turning each record over, allowing Hawkins to listen to an opera all through at one sitting. He'd recline in a comfortable chair, sipping a drink, the tears streaming down his face as he listened to the epic music. Hawk gradually acquired a formidable library of scores and books on classical music, but he also needed space for various transient hobbies such as collecting model trains and model autombiles. His chief relaxation when at home, however, was playing the piano, which he did most days. In season his early evenings were spent listening to baseball games on the radio; for a while he also became interested in fishing.

Hawk rarely bought jazz records. He kept in touch with musical developments by calling in to various Manhattan clubs and listening carefully to any promising players new to New York. He had begun praising Miles Davis before most people in the jazz world had ever heard the name, and he took pleasure in employing the young trumpeter, soon to establish himself as one of the most individual of the modernists. Davis, the proficient Danish-born trombonist Kai Winding and veteran alto player Howard 'Swan' Johnson joined Hawkins in the front line of a recording group, backed by a contemporary rhythm section consisting of Hank Jones, Curley Russell and Max Roach. Two of the four sides from the session were standards, 'Isn't It Romantic' (given a slightly acerbic treatment by Hawk) and 'The Way You Look Tonight', on which the tenorist-leader cruises lightly around the sumptuous melody and then creates some pithy answers to the arranged bop-tinged phrases. The other titles were 'Phantomesque', a harmonically interesting ballad, and 'Bean a Rebop', a quirky little theme that spawns some bright forward-looking solos.

Hawkins made a point of verbally encouraging young musicians. Big Nick Nicholas cites an example:

> When I recorded 'Manteca' with Dizzy Gillespie, Hawk went out of his way to find me and compliment me. He always kept up with everything that was happening, not necessarily to use for himself but just to be aware. I know all of his records; he sounded happy on the European sides but he never stopped creating, whereas Don Byas and Lester Young often resorted to clichés and set phrases. Hawk was always improvising.[1]

Forty years later Max Roach recalled the supportive role that Hawkins played during this period;

> Miles Davis and myself, we toured with Hawk with a small band, up and down the East Coast (Baltimore, Boston and places like that). He always gave us the impression that what we did was OK; but he had checked us all out, me, for example. No one played a ballad like Hawk and he knew that you would treat a ballad as a ballad and you wouldn't just try to smoke a person out. The taste was there, that's why he hired people. Like Charlie Parker, Hawk never told you exactly what he wanted. Hawk left you to do it and figure it out for yourself, and if you didn't, then the next week he wouldn't call you.[2]

Hawkins continued to feature young modernists on his record dates, and they too paid tribute to Hawk for his trailblazing. Trumpeter Fats Navarro's views were typical; he described Hawkins as 'one of the peaks of jazz, because whatever happens he knows.'[3] Navarro was on a Hawkins session for Victor that Leonard Feather organized in December 1947; trombonist J.J. Johnson was also in the group. The arrangements for the nine-piece unit were by Tadd Dameron, who had established himself as one of the first to transfer convincingly the nuances of bop into written orchestrations.

Dameron displays his skills on 'Half Step Down Please', an arrangement that includes a thirty-two-bar solo by Navarro and twenty-four-bars from Johnson. The links with the swing era are maintained by the four-in-a-bar rhythms guitarist Chuck Wayne strums behind Hawk's raffish solo. Wayne creates a flowing solo on the fast 'Jumpin' Jane'; Budd Johnson (on alto sax), Hank Jones, Johnson and Navarro take sixteen-bars apiece. Navarro's spectacular entry phrase is an exciting example of how completely he'd grasped the concepts of the new style, but the eight-bar drum solo by Max Roach (with its broken time patterns and novel accents) is even more revolutionary. Hawkins sounds at ease in these settings but his work here hasn't the exploratory qualities his colleagues display.

Hawk sounds monumentally assured on the ballad feature 'Angel Face' (a Hank Jones–Coleman Hawkins composition). The tenor saxist takes full command after an apposite piano introduction and performs with guile and expression on an interesting melody. His work on the other ballads recorded on the date is less successful, being somewhat hampered by the background figures. Tadd Dameron was undoubtedly a pioneer of modern arranging, but here he is too intent on spreading the chords by writing wide harmonies for a small line-up. The resultant voicings do not always flow smoothly and some jagged accompanying figures mar 'April in Paris' and the sombre 'How Strange'.

On the day before this session Hawkins had taken part in a more orthodox date, accompanying the smooth but bland singing of Leslie Scott. Hawk, aided by strings and a rhythm section, blows some deft obbligati and also contributes excellent, if brief, solos. His commencing lines on 'You Were Meant for Me' are truly magnificent and even on indifferent material like 'Never in a Million Years' he sounds flawless. Another vocal backing task, this time accompanying Delores Martin, was less productive. On 'The Old Song' and 'You Said Goodbye' (the total output of the date) Hawk's task is simply to introduce the melody; he does so with aplomb, but the vocals lack warmth and the studio-assembled 'Orchestra' gives an indifferent performance.

The slump that had affected the New York club scene in 1947 worsened in 1948 and 52nd Street was pronounced dead in several music magazines. The obituaries were premature but several old-established venues underwent a metamorphosis that dismayed jazzmen. Kelly's Stable became a Chinese restaurant, the Spotlite introduced a 'girlie' show and the Onyx began using a resident disc-jockey. For the first time in years Hawk found work scarce on the New York club scene, and as a result he began taking regular bookings in Philadelphia and Cleveland. As in the 1930s, his thoughts turned towards Europe, and his enthusiasm for a trip across the Atlantic was stimulated by news brought to him by various members of Don Redman's band, recently returned from an exciting (if slightly haphazard) tour of the Continent.

Hardship was still rife in post-war Europe and currency controls made it difficult for visiting American musicians to take their earnings back to the USA, but there were ways of side-stepping that problem. Hawkins liked Paris a little more than any other European city, so he was distinctly amenable to an offer that French promoter (and writer) Charles Delaunay sent via the New York agent Billy Shaw. As a result, it was agreed that Hawkins was to be the principal guest star on the first big jazz festival to be held in the French capital since before World War II.

A big party of American jazz musicians disembarked from an Air France plane at Orly Airport, to be welcomed by French musicians, journalists and fans. Hawkins was the star (and senior member) of the contingent, which included Erroll Garner, Slam Stewart, Howard McGhee, Kenny Clarke, John Lewis, Percy Heath, Specs Wright, Jessie Powell, Vernon Biddle and John Collins. The female star of the festival was the veteran blues singer Bertha 'Chippie' Hill.

Though jam sessions took place all over Paris, the main site of the festival was the Marigny Theatre, where the first concert took place on Monday 10 May 1948. On the opening show, Howard McGhee's sextet, Erroll Garner and Chippie Hill were all received enthusiastically, but when the Belgian critic Robert Goffin announced Coleman Hawkins the applause was thunderous. The festival was an emotional event for local jazz fans and the presence of Hawkins, who had thrilled Parisians in pre-war days, ignited an enormous flare of emotion. Hawkins himself seemed to be affected by the atmosphere and blew his heart out during a forty-five-minute set. He had intended to keep 'Body and Soul' for an encore, but the requests for it became so frantic he changed his mind and performed it as the second number in his programme. The delight of the occasion seemed to transport Hawkins into an almost boyish mood, and he charmed the audience by roaming all over the stage blowing at each section of the crowd, using dance steps that he had learnt back in the 1920s with Mamie Smith.

Hawk used a variety of accompanists throughout the week. Many

French musicians took part in the festival and on Hawk's second night he was backed by Jack Dieval on piano and Emmanual Soudieux on bass, with Kenny Clarke on drums. The highlight of the following night was the jam session featuring Hawk, Hubert Rostaing on alto sax and Aime Barelli on trumpet. On Thursday's matinee Hawk worked with Howard McGhee's rhythm section but surpassed himself in one of the four separate jam sessions that made up that evening's presentation. During a long version of 'Stuffy', which Hawk chose to play each night at the Marigny, he totally eclipsed everyone on stage.

Hawkins was given a day off on Friday 14 May, and though he hadn't neglected any of his old friends during the week, the free time gave him the opportunity to concentrate on reunions. Among the British contingent at the festival was Hawk's old buddy, saxophonist Derek Neville (Graeme Bell's band from Australia added to the international flavour of the event, as did the presence of groups from Belgium, Denmark and Switzerland). One of Hawk's pre-war girlfriends from Holland, vocalist Ann Xhofleer was also part of the festival; several other ladies, not singers, went out of their way to renew Hawk's acqaintance.

On the Saturday show Hawkins played several numbers with Aime Barelli's big band but was then overtaken by the exhausting way he had spent his 'rest' day. For one of the few times in his career, Hawk had to rest awhile so that he could finish the concert. He swiftly regathered his strength, though, and played in a quartet of saxophonists consisting of himself, Hubert Rostaing (alto), Robert Mavounzy (alto) and Harry Perret (tenor). It was originally hoped that Alix Combelle and André Ekyan could take part in this section of the show, in order to re-establish three quarters of the team who had made the sensational recordings of 1937, but neither man could make the concert (Combelle was in Lyon and Ekyan in Deauville). Hawk's final featured appearance at the festival was backed by a sparkling rhythm section consisting of John Lewis, John Collins, Slam Stewart and Kenny Clarke. On his way back to the dressing room Hawk was heard to say, 'I've seldom had such a good backing as I had tonight.' The festival had not been a huge financial success but it would be difficult to say who was the more disappointed that it had ended: the listening fans or the participating musicians.

Hawkins flew back to New York and was naturally delighted to be reunited with his family, but his return to the American club scene must have seemed something of an anti-climax. He played a succession of East Coast dates that summer then moved to his old stamping grounds to fulfil a residency in Chicago. This September booking at the Blue Note club was such a success that Hawk and his locally-recruited musicians (Paul King, trumpet; Percy Walker, drums; Frank Smith, piano and Eugene Wright, bass) were retained until 10 October. During this period Hawkins made the acquaintance of the pianist Herman Blount (later to gain jazz fame as the Arkestra leader Sun Ra); Hawk was apparently fascinated by Sun Ra's voicings. Val Wilmer, in her book *As Serious as Your Life*, described how Hawkins asked the pianist to write out his arrangement of 'I'll Remember April'. Years later, in New York, Hawkins had to be reminded that he had met Sun Ra in Chicago, but the saxist swiftly gathered up his memories and said to the pianist, 'Yes, you wrote a number out for me that I couldn't play. It was the only music I've ever seen that I couldn't play.'[4]

After returning home, Hawk prepared himself for a new, wider-ranging JATP tour. This seventh national show was scheduled to play in thirty-five cities from coast to coast, beginning with a Carnegie Hall concert on 6 November 1948. Several previous JATP tourists were in the troupe, including Hawkins, Flip Phillips, Charlie Parker and Howard McGhee; the rhythm section consisted of Al Haig, piano; Tommy Potter, bass and J.C. Heard, drums. Two young up-and-coming musicians, trombonist Tommy Turk (one of Pittsburgh's new jazz stars) and the brilliant altoist Sonny Criss (from Los Angeles) made their JATP debuts with this troupe. Criss recalled the tour:

> Tommy Turk and I were the youngest guys on the tour. We were twenty years old but Hawk would always hang out with us and not the older guys. He'd listen in the wings and sometimes I'd hear him phrase things the way I had. Not that he'd copy me, he was too original for that, but there is no doubt about it: he'd listened to what I was doing, though it would still come out like Hawkins, and that for me was the greatest thing.[5]

Hawkins was absolutely on top of his game throughout the tour, inspired and rejuvenated by his experiences in France earlier in the year. Conversely the brilliance of Charlie Parker was temporarily dimmed on some of the tour dates. A *Down Beat* reviewer dwelt on the contrast betwen the two great saxophonists' performances at the JATP Shrine Auditorium concert in Los Angeles, which took place near the end of the great trek: 'Charlie Parker blew virtually nothing. In contrast Coleman Hawkins was brilliant. His taste in presentation and timing were that of a master. Hawk wrung everything from both his horn and his audience. He had to beg off after two encores.' A sign of times to come occurred at that

Shrine concert – a local television station asked permission (not granted) to relay the show to its viewers.

JATP was becoming increasingly successful, and almost every jazz fan in America was by now aware of the show's itinerary. Granz, who also acted as compère, had set up an efficient organization to handle the administrative problems connected with transporting a large crew of backstage workers and musicians across huge distances. Often Hawk did not travel with the main entourage, particularly if they were going by air – he went through a period of avoiding flying – but this meant he sometimes had to drive vast distances. After one evening concert in Lancing, Michigan he left to drive full speed to Buffalo for a show beginning at 1 a.m. Various other musicians also chose to go by road; Lester Young and Flip Phillips often travelled together by car, with Phillips doing most of the driving. Sometimes Lester rode as a passenger with Hawkins, but most times Hawk left later than the rest and drove alone. When there was time to kill at a new venue Hawkins, Phillips and Young talked over various aspects of the city they were in, but always ended up discussing the sports news of the day. Phillips, who was the handyman of the party, often repaired or overhauled the other players' saxophones.

A sort of camaraderie developed on the long JATP tours, even between those the public thought of as rivals. Illinois Jacquet spoke of the friendliness that Hawkins and Young showed towards him:

> They were wonderful to me, though they were years and years older than I was, they accepted me. We got along fine. The papers used to write about bitter rivalry and all that, but it was completely professional and we worked well together. Sometimes for a laugh each of us would play the others' licks, then we'd chuckle quietly on stage. Hawk was a very subdued person for a lot of the time; you really had to get him in the spirit of talking but I gradually got to know him on the JATP circuit.[6]

It seemed as though the 1948 winter JATP tour had only just ended when the spring package took to the road in March 1949. Shelly Manne, Ray Brown and Ella Fitzgerald were added to a line-up that visited many regular ports of call, including the Chicago Civic Opera House, which had audiences as vociferous as any that the show encountered during their travels. One reviewer described the March 1949 JATP show's audience as 'probably the most ill-mannered to have hit the Civic in years; they clapped, shouted and booed loudly'. Without ever ostensibly playing to the gallery, Hawkins managed to please almost everyone who attended the JATP shows. His presence on stage, developed through years of experience, commanded an audience's attention and the strength and skill of his music ensured a favourable response.

On 20 April 1949, soon after the JATP tour ended, Hawkins's third child (his only son) Rene Etienne Hawkins was born. Coleman was not often on hand during his children's early years, usually being away on tour, but during that summer of 1949 he spent a good deal of time in New York playing a residency at the newly-renovated Cafe Society club. His quintet there consisted of Al Haig, piano; John Collins, guitar; Nelson Boyd, bass and Shadow Wilson, drums; he used this line-up to accompany him on a record date in August, augmenting the group on various tracks by using either J.J. Johnson or Bennie Green on trombone and Cecil Payne on baritone sax.

The stand-out performance on the session is 'There's a Small Hotel', taken at a slow, wistful pace. Hawkins seems to revel in the tempo and builds an intriguing solo that begins and ends in understatement. There's also the original version of 'Skippy', the coyest tune Hawkins ever wrote, which is in marked contrast to the sophisticated contours of 'Platinum Love', on which Hawk and Bennie Green achieve a velvety blend of tone colours. Hawk seems in a mellow, restrained mood throughout, particularly noticeable on the twelve-bar blues 'The Big Head', where he follows a long quote from 'How Long Blues' with a chorus of genteel honking on a pedal B flat.

September 1949 marked the start of another JATP tour, one that rolled through a twenty-eight city schedule. Roy Eldridge had been added to the cast, and Ella Fitzgerald was there to consolidate the enormous success she'd achieved on her debut tour earlier in the year. The superb rhythm section featured on this edition of Granz's travelling show was Hank Jones, Ray Brown and Buddy Rich. Three numbers from the Carnegie Hall concert of 18 September featured Hawk with this rhythm team, and he sounds in excellent form. After being introduced by Granz as 'The Master himself' Hawk plays a fertile 'Body and Soul', and a lively 'Rifftide', on which he takes four choruses rich in ideas and swathed in enthusiasm. His gentle 'Sophisticated Lady', replete with delicate glissandos, quietens a restive audience.

All of the participants in the tour were experienced travellers; displays of back-stage antagonism were rare, but there was always an air of competitiveness during performances. Roy Eldridge recalled a dance date that the package played in Chicago: 'Someone suggested that we play "Stuffy". Well, we used to play this on our set in the show so Coleman had no eyes for it. They kept on insisting, so he started 'Stuffy' in A natural. You never heard so much scuffling in your life.'[7]

As soon as that tour ended, plans were finalized for Hawkins to make a return trip to Europe, this time involving an itinerary that was to take him to several of the capital cities that he had worked in during the 1930s. On 29 November he flew from New York to Paris, slept for two hours then briefly rehearsed the group with which he was to tour: Nat Peck (trombone), James Moody (tenor sax) and Kenny Clarke (drums), plus French musicians Hubert Fol (alto sax), Jean-Paul Mengeon (piano) and Pierre Michelot (bass).

Hawk's concert at the Edouard VII Theatre in Paris was every bit as successful as his previous year's triumph at the Marigny Theatre. Playing a programme consisting mainly of standard tunes such as 'Sweet Georgia Brown', 'Body and Soul' and 'Lady Be Good', Hawk and his group had the audience demanding more. Those lucky enough to follow Hawkins's path through the St Germain district after the show heard him play several numbers with a band led by the French tenor saxist Jean Claude Fohrenbach. But Hawk still had energy left and an observer noted, 'Coleman was last seen in the twilight, setting out to have a good time somewhere.'[8] His stamina was remarkable, because he was due to play in Berne, Switzerland on the following day, after which he was booked to appear in his pre-war 'home' city of Zurich. Zurich retained a lot of its attraction for Hawk and during the early 1950s he seriously contemplated moving there with his family.[9]

Looking back on that European tour, tenorist James Moody recalls that it was a happy one:

> I had first heard Coleman Hawkins in person on 52nd Street, but then the conversation was only a sort of 'Nice to meet you' affair. At that time I was closer to Lester Young's playing, but as the years went by I realized what a master of changes that Hawkins was. He was always a pleasant man, not flashy, but he had discernible class. His clothes were perfectly made, he drove a big car, he had a magnificent Rolleiflex camera. I thought of him as a polished diamond, whereas so many other guys were just paste. When we were in Paris he stayed at the best hotel, Claridge's I think it was. Hardly anything ruffled him, the only bother I saw him in was when we were about to enter Germany. Hawk discovered he'd lost his passport, but even this didn't make him mad. He was allowed to enter Germany. The passport was soon found and given back to him, but the official who handed it over read out Hawk's name and date of birth – he didn't like this – but it was soon forgotten.
>
> He listened to all of the musicians he worked with but never said anything harsh. I've always remembered the advice he gave me; he looked at me and said, 'Slow

> down, take it easy, learn how to relax.' That was all. He always listened intently and I remember some years after the tour he came to hear me work with Dizzy Gillespie in New York and he stood immediately in front of the band. He didn't say anything but smiled gently and nodded his head, I guess in approval.[10]

Hawk's European tour proceeded smoothly and successfully until Sunday 11 December, the date of his arrival in England. This trip was described at the time as a social visit, ostensibly to allow Hawk to act as godfather at the christening of a child belonging to an old friend, Anthony Hughes. But Hughes and his friend James 'Bix' Curtis thought that it would be a fine idea also to have Hawkins play at a jazz concert they were promoting in London on 11 December. The big snag about this idea concerned the stringent rules that governed the employment of foreign musicians in Britain. The British Musicians' Union had been involved in a long-standing dispute with the American Federation of Musicians which had resulted in a ban on the hiring of American musicians. Coupled with this was a law implemented by the Ministry of Labour that forbade foreign musicians gaining employment in Britain without the possession of a valid work permit.

A few weeks prior to Hawk's arrival, Sidney Bechet (also in Europe on tour) had been brought into London to guest at a jazz concert with Humphrey Lyttelton's band, and his performance had resulted in the promoter of the show being prosecuted. Anthony Hughes, having been told of Hawk's availability by the French promoter Charles Delaunay, decided to apply to the Ministry of Labour for permission to feature Hawkins at a London concert; the Ministry refused the request on 15 November. Undaunted, Hughes and Bix Curtis decided to invite Hawkins over (ostensibly for the christening) and they took the precaution of advising Hawkins not to bring his saxophone, but in the meantime they scouted around to find someone in London who might lend them a Selmer model similar to the one that Hawkins played.

Bob Burns, a Canadian-born saxophonist who had made his home in Britain, recalled the search: 'Bix Curtis asked me if I could loan my balanced-action Selmer to Coleman Hawkins. I was only too pleased to help. I had bought the sax in Toronto when I was about fifteen; they were made in France but assembled in the States. Hawk borrowed the sax but used his own mouthpiece, a metal Otto Link. Sadly, many years later, someone stole that sax (No. 28639) from me.'[11]

So a suitable saxophone awaited Hawk's arrival; the next big hurdle was in getting him through the British immigration control point. Ronald Geoffrey Smith, the immigration officer on duty, interviewed Hawkins for over an hour on his arrival at London Airport on the morning of Sunday 11 December. Smith also asked Hughes, Curtis and Bert Wilcox (representing *Jazz Illustrated*) some probing questions and they volunteered the information that Hawkins might well attend a jazz concert that night and might well have a spotlight turned on him. Smith then asked Hawkins if he was going to play the saxophone, to which Hawk replied, 'How can I? My saxophone is on its way to Brussels.'[12] Despite remaining suspicious, Smith stamped Hawkins's passport and informed him of the conditions of entry: 'That he did not enter into employment, paid or unpaid, and did not remain in the United Kingdom longer than three days.'

Once he was through the airport barriers Hawkins linked up with some people who had also flown over from France, namely the rhythm section with whom he had been working on the Continent: Kenny Clarke, Jean-Paul Mengeon and Pierre Michelot (with them was Jean Finsterwald, the representative of French *Vogue*). The party joined up with Curtis and Hughes who, knowing of Hawk's love of big automobiles, had laid on a special vehicle. Curtis recalled the details: 'We laid on a big Lincoln Zephyr for Hawkins. I was driving a little old battered Austin 7 and Hawkins for some reason took a liking to this and walked past the big car and got in with me.'[13] The travellers paid a brief visit to Bix Curtis's home then made their way to a large pub in Willesden, north-west London, called the White Horse, where Curtis's Music Makers' Club held Sunday-lunchtime sessions. After listening to a local band featuring tenorist Jimmy Skidmore and trumpeter Hank Shaw, Hawkins was 'persuaded' to borrow Bob Burns's tenor sax and sit in. The session was not quite as impromptu as was later stated in court, because everyone in the 300-strong audience had arrived expecting to hear Hawkins play.

When the session ended Hawkins left the pub surrounded by well-wishers and journalists. The question that the writers were itching to ask the great man was: 'What do you think of bebop?' Hawk's answer was mischievious and playful;

> Bop? Man, I ain't ever heard of bop! What is this bop? I understand it as a name, the name of a street. Bop Villa and next to it you have Pop Villa. Do I like the sound of the word? Yes, it sounds all right. I don't know any bop music. I only know one music – the music that's played. There's no such thing as bop music, but there is such a thing as progress. What you are talking about is probably a commercial phrase, huh? A phrase that has been used to make something sell.[14]

Hawkins recorded an interview for the BBC, had a fish-and-chip lunch, listened to some young modernists playing at London's Club Eleven and then took a quick look at the Princes Theatre, where Hughes and Curtis were staging their concert that night. When evening arrived Curtis and Hawkins visited a pub near to the theatre and while there Hawk received an invitation to visit the theatre to say a few words to an audience of 1,400 people. Hawkins went backstage and found Bob Burns's saxophone again at his disposal and, as if by telepathy, his accompanists (from France) were already in place so Hawkins walked on and blew a magnificent set that evoked a response as wild as any that ever greeted the finale of a JATP show.

There were no experimental selections in Hawk's set; he played 'Stuffy' and 'The Big Head' and two ballads, 'It's the Talk of the Town' and 'Body and Soul'. In reviewing the concert for *Jazz Journal*, Stanley Dance wrote:

> Hawk's stage presence is admirable. There is dignity in his strong figure, something like sternness in his manner. Instead of ingratiating smiles on all sides he is more often frowning in apparent concentration as he listens to the other musicians. His left shoulder is extremely expressive, hunching in emphasis at vehement notes and phrases, shrugging down as the music rolls smoothly away again. To him, music is obviously a serious thing, he isn't kidding, and on stage he is himself, a man, acting in a way more musicians might copy.[15]

In a *Melody Maker* review, Max Jones and Sinclair Traill commented:

> Last time, in the thirties, when we first heard 'Bean' in person, we were struck by his excessive power and attack and also by his inventive faculty. This time, the force of his playing seemed as great as ever, although the tone was harsher and the phrasing more angular. One of the things that nobody could help observing was Hawkins's adherence to swing playing. He moved on the beat and swung like no tenor known to bop. Many of the progressives present were disappointed in 'Bean' because, as they argue, his stuff was dated. We can only repeat the obvious: dates have nothing to do with musical quality and little to do with criticism.[16]

When the concert was over Hawkins linked up with various people who had known him in pre-war days. Curtis and Hughes felt that the wonderful music that had been created more than compensated them for all the tensions and hazards connected with the visit. But their troubles were not over and their actions eventually landed them in court to answer charges that they (and Herbert Wilcox) 'allegedly falsely represented to an immigration officer that Coleman Hawkins would not take employment paid or unpaid in the United Kingdom'; they were also accused of aiding and abetting Hawkins in contravening the Aliens' Order. When the case was heard at Bow Street Court in London during the following June all three were found guilty and fined heavily. This case, and one involving Sidney Bechet's entry, were heard together. The court's decision dissuaded anyone else from trying to beat the embargo and it was some years later, in 1956, that the British and American Musicians' Unions worked out a system of exchange that ended the ban.

Hawkins flew out of London on 12 December (without being charged with any offence). He arrived in Belgium and was reunited with the rest of his touring group. The group played a concert on 13 December at a venue familiar to Hawkins, the Palais des Beaux-Arts in Brussels. After the concert Hawk went out with his old friend Albert Bettonville to a musicians' club called Carlton's. It happened to be a fancy-dress night there, so in order to gain admittance Hawkins and Bettonville borrowed outfits from the club's manager. For his 'disguise' Hawk chose to wear a melon hat (similar to a derby or bowler) and a large white beard.

The group soon returned to Paris where (minus James Moody) they recorded seven numbers for Vogue on 21 December. These sides underline the fact that this was a fertile and at times exploratory period of Hawk's career, but his performances show why some European fans (expecting him to present the latest bop licks) were disappointed by his work on this tour. There is no parading of bop clichés; instead Hawkins proves that he had absorbed those aspects of bop that he had found appealing and had incorporated them into his method of improvising. 'Shi Sha' is a twelve-bar blues (with a boppish tinge) on which Hawk blows four variegated choruses. He is more experimental on 'Bah-u-bah' (based on 'Sweet Georgia Brown'), where his performance, stimulated by an Afro-Cuban-styled backing, strongly suggests the hard-bop approach that was to emerge some ten years later, so in the midst of a seemingly conventional date Hawk's playing acts as a signpost to the future.

Hawk's front-line partners play the various themes with smoothness and assurance, but their only solos (eight bars apiece) appear on 'It's Only a Paper Moon', a number on which Hawkins (in both takes) flies through a series of double-time phrases as though on automatic pilot. His blues playing, unusually, takes on an almost down-home quality on the slow 'Bean's Talking Again'. The date ended with quartet versions of 'I Surrender, Dear', on which Hawk shakes off the melody to begin building his own musical superstructures, and 'Sophisticated Lady', where he pays full homage to Ellington's melody by wrapping it in thick, fur-lined phrases.

Hawkins spent Christmas in Paris. He had several close friends in that city, some of whom he had known since the 1930s. In looking back to his pre-war days in Europe he said that the most receptive countries to jazz in those days were Denmark and Holland; 'France didn't have quite the interest.' In post-war years, however, he said of the French jazz fans: 'They've been studying. They come to the concerts with books and research.'[17] But regardless of location, Hawkins never became the ideal subject for a researching interviewer, as the French musician-writer Jean Ledru discovered when he visited him in his 2,600-francs-a-day apartment at Claridge's Hotel in Paris during this period.

Ledru arrived at 3 p.m. to find Hawkins (as was usual at that hour) having his breakfast, wearing an extremely expensive dressing gown. Ledru observed that Hawkins was in a good mood and said to himself, 'At long last I'm going to be able to get something out of him,' but his hopes were only partially realized. Hawk did say, however, that he didn't like French beer much, and preferred Dutch lager. He loved to drink champagne but found he got drunk on only three glasses of it. The subject of reeds was then discussed and Hawk said he was now very wary about telling people he had found a good reed since he had one taken off him by Vido Musso when the two men worked together. He expressed a liking for Montmartre, loved French perfume but found it too expensive. Ledru redirected the conversation so that he could ask for details of Hawkins's favourite musicians. The Frenchman later observed that obtaining the answers was as difficult as trying to extract butter from croissants, but his persistence was eventually rewarded. Hawk praised the playing of Fats Navarro, J.J. Johnson, John Collins, Gene Ammons and James Moody ('when he ripens some more'). After expressing a great fondness for Charlie Parker's work, Hawk added that he was sorry that Parker's popularity was decreasing owing to too many people copying him. Hawk made special mention of Oscar Peterson's talents, adding the names of other favourite pianists, Hank Jones and Art Tatum. Baritone saxist Cecil Payne was 'fantastic and incomparable' and Milt Jackson was 'fine, even though his set of vibes are dreadful'. As far as swinging drumming was concerned he preferred to work with Shadow Wilson. Hawk liked Flip Phillips, adding – with humour – 'especially after he introduced me to a sensational French girl in Mexico'. But Hawk expressed general disillusionment with audiences, saying that their understanding rarely went above his belt, and seldom beyond his shoulders, which was why he usually played easy-listening numbers like 'Stuffy' which he 'loathed'.[18]

In January 1950 Hawkins moved into Germany to continue his tour. His accompanists on this leg of the trip were as before: Peck, Moody, Fol etc, but for the dates that he played in Sweden and Denmark (later that month) he was backed by local musicians. Two titles recorded with Leo Mathisen's band during a concert at Copenhagen's KB Hall show Hawk in fine form. Both tunes ('The Man I Love' and 'It's the Talk of the Town') always seemed to stimulate Hawk's imagination, enabling him (as he does here) to create some fascinating new ideas. At the concert he took them as solo features; the front line's task is simply to provide soft, sporadic long notes in the background.

Soon afterwards, when Hawk had returned to the USA, he was able to reflect on the minimal interest his homecoming had caused compared with the furore that had greeted his 1939 return. Then every jazz writer in New York had contacted him for a quote, every recording manager had called in to see him to congratulate him on his achievements. In 1950 his arrival home after a triumphant European tour went almost unnoticed. No recording dates were offered, no lucrative residencies were mentioned, even the poll results were not in his favour: Stan Getz had won the *Metronome* award; Hawk was placed seventh.

18
A Dynamic Partner

By 1950 modern jazz had blossomed and the efforts of the young 'progressive' musicians were widely acknowledged. They continued to respect Coleman Hawkins's paramount skills, but did not invite him to play on their recording sessions, well aware that his style and his phrasing did not fit perfectly in with the nuances and mannerisms of their music. Hawk spoke the language of modern jazz with great fluency but always with his own discernible accent.

Hawkins had been happy to co-exist with the bebop fraternity and to share their excursions into expanded harmonies, but he remained his own man musically. During this period the noted French critic, André Hodeir, wrote, 'In 50 to 100 years from now, some knowledgeable and patient researchers will make an inventory of jazz; let us hope that they will give Hawkins his due share. His own evolution sums up jazz evolution.'[1] But whereas Hawkins continued to listen to, and praise, the modern-jazz movement, some of his contemporaries had come to regard bop as a form of musical cancer. One of these was Hawk's former bandleader, Fletcher Henderson, who said, 'Of all the cruelties in the world, bebop is the most phenomenal. Coleman Hawkins can play bop when he wants to, but he always goes back to playing Hawkins again.'[2]

The length and breadth of Hawkins's recording career tended to work against him during the late 1940s and early 1950s when most record companies and jazz magazines seemed desperate to unearth new sensations, but some bold critics were not afraid to stress the unfashionable fact that Hawkins was as modern and forward-looking as anyone on the 1950 jazz scene. Michael Levin of *Down Beat* made that point when reviewing Hawk's recording of 'Picasso', an unaccompanied tenor-sax solo that formed part of a 78 rpm *Jazz Scene* album devised by Norman Granz for his new Clef label. Levin wrote, 'Hawk's changes have always been as complex as the boppers' best,' adding that the tenor saxist's performance on 'Picasso' indicated that he was 'the most consistently fertile and progressive musician in the last two decades of jazz.'

Hawk's idea of recording an unaccompanied, improvised jazz solo on saxophone was revolutionary, one that required a combination of talent, boldness and patience. The project involved innumerable run-throughs in the recording studio. A prototype performance, also unaccompanied, had previously been recorded for issue on 78 rpm by the Selmer instrument company. This earlier solo was a *tour de force* of instrumental technique more than an exploration of the frontiers of jazz, but it was still brilliantly innovative and a challenging display of Hawk's musical powers. 'Picasso', however, is positively avant-garde. It involves the presentation of thirty-seven phrases that are unconnected by harmonic progression or tempo (many of the stanzas are deliberately played at differing speeds). Despite the mood of atonality the note clusters are usually built around a centrifugal point. At one stage (a third of the way through the piece) the patterns seesaw between swinging twelve-tone studies and quirky runs played with 'straight' time values. One reviewer naïvely suggested that the piece was 'Body and Soul', but this is incorrect; the improvisations are not based on any standard harmonic progression.

'Picasso' was the result of intensive planning, and although the lines have the air of being the stream-of-consciousness utterings of a master musician they are the ingenious sifting and shaping of intricate ideas whose creation can be likened to the process that gave birth to James Joyce's *Finnegan's Wake*. Hawkins never took as much trouble with any of his subsequent (or previous) recordings. The idea of recording unaccompanied had intrigued him for a long time; he had first mentioned the idea to Keynote record producer, Harry Lim, during the early months of 1944, citing as his inspiration the solo work of cellist Pablo Casals (one of Hawk's heroes), but although Lim was enthusiastic about the project it didn't materialize at that time.[3]

In the same way that Hawkins liked to pretend that the original recording of 'Body and Soul' was totally unpremeditated, so he also chose to give the impression that 'Picasso' was an unplanned achievement, saying, 'It came out spontaneously, that morning.'[4] In his review of 'Picasso' Michael Levin called Hawkins 'the cat that walks alone'; this description was doubly apt, both for Hawk's personality and for his method of working in an era when he was being increasingly employed as a 'single', guesting with resident rhythm sections at various clubs. Previously he had usually formed a band (sometimes hurriedly) for his out-of-town residencies, but now, to avoid the headaches of bandleading, he was content to do what he had done so often in Europe: journey alone to an engagement and take pot luck on the skills of the musicians booked to accompany him. He followed this strategy during the summer of 1950 by playing a season in Chicago (where he was almost guaranteed to be backed by excellent players); from there he moved on to a six-week booking at the Tropical Lounge in Des Moines, Iowa.

Hawk's only studio date in 1950 was a quintet recording for the Roost label. It was an unspectacular session embracing four goodish tunes, all of which feature a melody-conscious Hawkins who, perhaps with commercial intent, plays with a faster, more dramatic vibrato than usual. The cast is good, but the play is poor. Billy Taylor (piano) and John Collins (guitar) are allocated brief solos, and there is plenty of Hawkins, but inspiration is in short supply.

One of Hawk's club stints in New York consisted of a residency at Birdland in the late summer of 1950. This club was enjoying considerable success, so much so that the Levy brothers, who owned it, could afford to hire three major attractions at the same time. Hawk (using a front line consisting of Miles Davis and J.J. Johnson) shared the bill with Dizzy Gillespie's combo and Charlie Parker with strings.

Charlie Parker and Coleman Hawkins were always respectful to each other, but they never became close friends. Hawk often praised Parker, calling him 'one of the most original of all jazzmen'[5] and describing him as 'one of the best blues players you ever heard',[6] but their dissimilar personalities kept them apart socially. Hawk listened especially closely to Parker and as early as 1946 had been well enough aware of his style to recognize immediately (in a blindfold test) Sonny Stitt's credible imitation. Hawkins admired Parker's harmonic approach, and pointed out that the alto saxist used substitute chords only when they enhanced a composition and not as a matter of course. Commenting on Dave Pell's recording of 'Can't We be Friends?' he said, 'The harmony of this piece is very pretty the way it was written; they didn't have to change it. You lose more than you gain. The record Bird made on this was very nice, because they stayed right with the piece.'[7] Hawk also said of Parker, 'He sounded loud. I used to notice something about a lot of the boys that were trying to copy Charlie; a majority of them had a little tiny sound, and they had to use a microphone.'[8]

Unfortunately Hawkins and Parker did only one studio recording together. This was in October 1950 when they made 'Ballade', originally intended to be part of a film soundtrack. The performance is an extremely informal one. After a relaxed four-bar piano introduction (by Hank Jones) Hawkins blows eloquent phrases for the first half of a standard thirty-two-bar chord progression, then Parker enters and sprays some filigree patterns during his sixteen-bar solo but keeps his true brilliance under wraps. Hawk comes forward again for another burst of relaxed musings but his half-chorus ends abruptly, suggesting that someone in the control booth had signalled that enough had been recorded for a particular interlude.

In 1950, when the New York police clamped down (temporarily as it transpired) on the ever-increasing number of clubs that had abandoned jazz in favour of strip-shows, optimists hoped that these venues would revert to live music, but very few did. Birdland, however, thrived on its music policy; it was in a good location and its topical name (linked to Charlie Parker's achievements) appealed to young jazz listeners. But not all of Hawk's dates were at such prestigious spots and during the early 1950s he often worked at small clubs in Philadelphia, Providence, Rhode Island and other places close to New York City.

The JATP autumn tour set out from New York on 15 October 1950. It featured the tenor triumvirate of Hawkins, Young and Phillips, working alongside trombonist Bill Harris and altoist Willie Smith. Three of Hawk's feature numbers from a pre-tour Carnegie Hall concert on 16 September were issued on record. They demonstrate how his artistry triumphed over the sometimes rowdy audience. A powerfully emotive version of 'Yesterdays' is rapturously received, and the muscular delivery of the intricate ideas on 'Hawk's Tune' (Disorder at the Border) also pacified the crowd. But the most positive indication of Hawk's formidable musical presence occurs on 'Stuffy'. Ignoring the infantile cries of 'Go Man, Go!' he commands attention by dropping his volume to pianissimo, then in the manner of a great lecturer he barks out a series of tough phrases that bring him a huge ovation.

The rhythm section on this tour consisted of JATP regulars, Hank Jones, Ray Brown and Buddy Rich. The young Canadian pianist, Oscar Peterson (who had made a highly successful guest appearance with the show at Carnegie Hall during the previous year), was added to the tour as a special attraction; Ella Fitzgerald was again the featured vocalist. Hawkins had been championing Peterson's skills for some while and had made special mention of him during the 1949 visit to Europe. He had first heard the young Montreal pianist while unwinding at the Cafe St Michel after a JATP concert. Hawkins was greatly impressed by the pianist's work and remained quietly seated in a corner of the club until the last customer had gone; he then approached Peterson, who always remembered Hawk's initial request. The great tenorist leant forward and said, 'I'd like to hear "It's the Talk of the Town", but I'd like to hear it in B major.' When Peterson passed this difficult test and went on to perform a couple of other awkward pieces that Hawk asked for, the veteran left the club satisfied with what he had heard and determined to bring the young pianist's talents to wider attention.

Hawkins was always pleased to acknowledge musical promise but, unlike most of his contemporaries, he was more than willing to employ a promising youngster. Max Roach recommended that Hawk listen to drummer Art Taylor (then just twenty-one years old). Hawk took Roach's advice and was much impressed. When the JATP autumn tour ended, Hawk temporarily reverted to leading his own group and he made sure that Taylor was in that line-up, alongside pianist Kenny Drew and bassist Tommy Potter.

These young musicians felt it was an honour to be working with such a star as Hawkins. Kenny Drew recalled:

> I first heard Coleman Hawkins on 52nd Street when I was about seventeen years old, and naturally I was very impressed. A whole team of us youngsters, Sonny Rollins, Arthur Taylor, Jackie McLean, used to hang around a diner in Harlem on 148th Street and St Nicholas Avenue and occasionally Hawk called in there. There was no live music, just a jukebox, food and coffee. Though I would say that Charlie Parker was our foremost musical hero we were always in awe of Coleman Hawkins; we used to hang on every word he said when he talked about his life in Europe. A few years later I did a few loose jobs with him but around 1950 I worked with him regularly; the line-up was myself, Arthur Taylor, Tommy Potter and Sweets Edison on trumpet, and we played in Chicago, Montreal, Toronto etc. Hawk was an amazingly relaxed leader, but he listened intently to what everyone in the group played. One night I played the solo that Sir Charles Thompson had recorded on Hawk's version of 'Stuffy', and he was aware of this in a flash. He was a beautiful guy to work for; the only problems I had at that time were those of my own making, and Hawk was tremendously tolerant.[9]

A poorly-recorded concert (from February 1951) with trombonist Bennie Green in place of Harry 'Sweets' Edison underlines the rhythm section's unity and enthusiasm, but most of the offers that Hawk received at this time were for him to work as a soloist, so the group never had a chance to flourish. In 1951 he played many guest dates with local rhythm sections and he worked briefly with Marian McPartland's trio at the Embers in New York. In December 1951 Hawk and trumpeter Hot Lips Page played a very lively date at the University of Syracuse; regrettably these two dynamic musicians never made commercial recordings together.

Hawk's recording career was again at a virtual standstill; he went for over a year without fulfilling a studio date. The drought ended when Decca invited him to their new Pythian Temple studios in New York to record what would now be termed a single. In October 1951 he cut two slow themes, 'Sin' and 'And So To Sleep', using an octet packed with top-class jazzmen, including trumpeters Benny Harris and Idrees Sulieman, trombonist Matthew Gee and baritone saxist Cecil Payne. Their presence was hardly vital, considering that the material was nothing more than unelaborate pop songs of the moment (another version of 'Sin' briefly topped the Hit Parade in 1951); Hawkins simply did the musicians a favour by using them on the recording date.

None of the record critics could find a good word to say about Hawk's excursion into such obvious commercialized pastures. *Metronome* lambasted the venture, calling the release 'Feeble explorations of two pops by a legendary figure who will fast destroy the legend with such uninspired, grating indulgences as these.'[10] Undaunted, both Hawkins and Decca continued with a similar policy for several subsequent releases; on each of these Hawk was backed by a studio-assembled group, sometimes containing a string section. If the tune was good Hawk paid it respect, and in doing so created commendable versions of 'Lost in a Fog', 'If I Could be with You' and 'I Can't Get Started', but just as often he parodied popular saxophone playing by using a wide, even vibrato, and on a sour brew entitled 'Lonely Wine' he plays some uncharacteristic, schmaltzy glissandi. One of the offerings, 'Wishin' ' (musically the worst of the lot) was actually accorded grudging acceptance by *Down Beat*: 'You'll be flabbergasted to hear the tenor-sax veteran bogged down by a thudding rhythm section, but "Wishin" ' has sales potential for the old master.'

The series soon ended. It was a strange interlude in Hawkins's career. Everyone who makes records does so in order to sell them, but sometimes great artists can be tempted into endeavours unworthy of their enormous talents. The temptation is usually created by news of a rival's huge royalties, or by the prospects of gaining a new army of idolizing listeners; whatever Hawk's reasons, he had no qualms about making the recordings and later said he regretted not being featured with a choir.[11] Ironically his final date for Decca produced an attractive, swinging version of the blues,

'Lucky Duck'. On this occasion the orchestra was directed by Neal Hefti; he and Hawkins literally stayed up all night finalizing plans for the session. The series must have sold reasonably well because Decca sent a renewal contract, but Hawkins decided not to sign it. It was to be a year before he made any more recordings.

During this period a development occurred that was to play a regular part in Hawkins's musical life throughout the next fifteen years. It concerned trumpeter Roy Eldridge, with whom Hawk had begun recording in 1940. Thereafter their paths often crossed; they had toured with JATP together and had also taken part in numerous jam sessions. During the late 1940s they played occasional club bookings together, but from the summer of 1952 they began to work as co-leaders of the Coleman Hawkins–Roy Eldridge Quintet.

One of this partnership's first dates together (under the new regime) was at the Capitol Lounge in Chicago, where they began a residency on 20 July 1952. For this booking they used pianist Norman Simmons, whom they had recruited locally. Simmons recalled the circumstances:

> I was recommended for the gig by Erroll Garner. Erroll was playing the Chicago Theatre, which was next door to the Capitol Lounge where Roy and Hawk were opening. Hawk set new standards for me. He was fluid on any changes, in any key, at any tempo. Playing fast was popular then and Hawk loved it. He would ask if I knew a particular song that may have had tricky changes and I would proudly say 'yes'. Then he would call the key and I'd choke. Then I'd ask how fast he wanted the tempo and he'd reply, 'As fast as you can.'[12]

After Hawk returned to New York he began a residency at Birdland, using another fine young pianist, Horace Silver:

> I played at Birdland twice with Hawk and bassist Curly Russell – once with Roy Eldridge and Art Blakey, once with Howard McGhee and Art Taylor. It was a privilege and an honor. Like most great artists, Hawk showed not only genius but consistency. Not hot tonight, cold tomorrow – these cats could produce every night. They kept you on your toes because they always came up with something unique. Hawk was always on the ball, firing some great sounds at you, calling interesting tunes and tempos.[13]

Recordings taken off the air from the midnight broadcasts emanating from Birdland in September 1952 were issued on albums some twenty years later. The sound (and the balance) of the quintet leave a lot to be desired but the duration of each number (averaging six minutes) allows Hawkins and company the chance to stretch out – with happy results.

Blakey on drums concocts a feast of stimulating rhythmic patterns and Silver's positive (but sparse) accompanying style and melodic solos underline his musical maturity. On the series of shows, the personnel varied, with Howard McGhee and Connie Kay playing on the earlier sessions in place of Eldridge and Blakey.

Although they worked together regularly Hawkins and Eldridge were free to follow their own recording activities and to play dates independently, but the prospect of performing organized arrangements and new originals alongside a highly competitive (and supremely gifted) partner appealed to both men. During the years 1952 and 1953 the Hawkins–Eldridge Quintet played in many locales, including New York, New Haven, Rochester, Washington DC, Baltimore and Montreal, Canada. At first, work was plentiful enough for both men to decline a new JATP tour of Europe, but gradually club owners, who usually budgeted for one guest star at a time, baulked at paying for two big names within the same group (particularly when the unit wasn't breaking any box-office records). The two co-leaders then realized that they would be financially better off making the quintet bookings an occasional pleasure and this they did for many years.

The social relationship between these two jazz giants never developed beyond a certain point, even though their music-making suggested it was a very close partnership. They shared various interests, and both were, at this stage of their lives, capable of drinking a quantity of alcoholic beverage that would poleaxe an average human being. Both were adept at charming the ladies, each of them enjoyed preparing – and eating – good food. They both liked driving big, fast cars, and they enjoyed teasing each other, but above all they maintained a huge respect for each other's musical capabilities.

Roy Eldridge said:

> The old man knew so much music, nobody could ever catch him out. He knew just about every tune that had ever been written and he could play all of them in any key whatsoever, just like that, no hesitation. In all the years we worked together I never stopped being surprised by the things he could do. And he always kept his classy outlook on life; only the very best was good enough for him. If someone bought a good camera, he had to have a better one; if someone bought a fishing pole he had to go and buy a bigger one. He was like that about everything. He was so competitive. But it kept you on your toes; we'd play two sets and nothing much would be happening, then all of a sudden the thing would take off and we'd be playing as though our lives depended on it. But he never wanted to take the responsibility of

being leader, so if there was anything unpleasant to be said to the guys we were working with, it was always left to me. If the guy who owned the club had any complaints he'd come to me and Hawk would just look the other way, go to the bar, or look up at the ceiling, or just grin a little and not say a word. That used to burn me a little.

But I was always a real fan of his. I got my first job through learning his solo on Fletcher's record of 'Stampede', and I've still got records of his, going way back to when he was doing the slap-tonguing. I didn't get to know Coleman until he came back from Europe in 1939. He told me he'd heard my records and said he liked the way I phrased, legato. He didn't like things too staccato. I was at that jam session in 1939 when Lester and Hawk played together. I teamed up with Hawk and Charlie Shavers went on the stand with Lester, but if you had told me at that time that the session would have been written about forty years later I'd have laughed. I think people thought that we were closer buddies than we were, but Hawk, like Lester, was kind of difficult to get to know. We never had quarrels or things like that, but if we went out on the road he'd drive his Cadillac and I'd drive my Lincoln. We did some journeys, I'm telling you – from St Louis to Buffalo and then from Buffalo to Boston. We'd usually have a good time on the stand, making little cracks, but my friends weren't automatically his friends and vice versa.[14]

One subject that provided constant fuel for the Hawkins–Eldridge badinage concerned their ages. Each teased the other continually on this point, and Hawkins delighted in producing a photograph that had been taken of Roy Eldridge at the Three Deuces Club in Chicago during 1937; on it Hawk had written 'Roy Eldridge at the age of twenty-five, 1918'. When Hawkins's cabaret card was renewed (which allowed him to work in New York nightclubs serving liquor) it mistakenly denoted that he had been born in 1912, and he made sure that the first person to whom he showed the card was Roy Eldridge. Flourishing it with pride, he said, 'Damn it, I've always told you I'm younger than you are, and here's the proof.' Roy was actually born in 1911.

But, underneath all this horseplay, there was, on Hawk's part, a serious – almost morbid – concern about growing old; it was not difficult for him to become genuinely vexed if the teasing came from casual aquaintances. When Hawkins originally applied for a passport in 1934, his parents furnished the US government authorities with a copy of his birth certificate (born: 21 November 1904), together with a sworn statement from a public notary confirming its authenticity. Later, in April 1948, after this passport had expired, Hawkins reapplied for a new one, and in doing so he lopped five years from his true age, giving 21 November 1909 as his date of birth. This immediately brought a warning from R.B. Shipley, then Chief of the Passport Division at the Department of State, who wrote to Hawkins pointing out that he must adhere to his correct date of birth, 21 November 1904.[15]

Hawkins was forced to take notice of this official instruction, but there was nothing illegal in him reducing his age for publicity purposes and that was what he did. In interviews from 1953 onwards he began describing himself as 'born 1907'. Hawkins had always shown a certain reticence when being interviewed by journalists, but this attitude gradually tightened into a monosyllabic reserve when he was dealing with unfamiliar pressmen. Even those who were on affable terms with him sometimes found it difficult to get an interview going and *Down Beat*, in the early 1950s, said of him, 'He is an enigma to many people. Quiet, reserved, cynical, worldly, he is enormously different from the portrait of the average jazz musician.'[16]

One of Hawk's bookings in the spring of 1953 was at Cafe Society, a famous Greenwich Village nightspot, recently reopened. Hawkins shared the billing there with a couple of singers and a trio led by pianist Cy Coleman. Hawk's task was to compere the floorshow (not a chore he relished) and to play for dancing after the cabaret had finished. The trio that backed Hawk – Kenny Bryan (piano), Kenny Clarke (drums) and Curly Russell (bass) – also had the job of accompanying the singers.

Hawkins was visited at the Cafe Society by Leonard Feather, who could not help noticing that business was bad, the club almost deserted. Hawk joined Feather after he'd played his set and answered a question about whether his children were learning music; 'I don't care if they don't, I wouldn't ever want any child of mine to get into anything as rotten as this business. I hate the music business.' It was a theme to which Hawkins often returned in his later years. His determined, competitive qualities never left him, and colleagues rarely saw him despondent, but as he approached fifty he sometimes suffered moods of deep gloom. His melancholia was not helped when he observed half-empty clubs and heard people refer to him in a matter-of-fact way as 'the old man'. He could not have failed to notice that his old rival, Lester Young, was increasingly being talked of as the principal inspiration for most of the young modern tenor sax players who, because of their light tones and minimal use of vibrato, were referred to as being part of the 'cool school'.

Leonard Feather questioned Hawk about recent sylistic changes:

> I asked about his feelings toward the cool school, who have taken over domination of the polls. I wanted to know whether he had any preference among these youngsters.

'They all sound alike to me,' he answered with a smile.

'How about Paul Quinichette?' [a black Lester Young copyist].

'Still not robust enough for my taste.' Coleman excused himself, returned to the stand and started pouring those big, lush tones into 'Sophisticated Lady'. I wondered how a man who has meant so much to jazz could bear to go through the motions like this, playing a minor role in what is now a minor club. I thought of this year's *Down Beat* poll, where he trailed in fifth position after Getz, Flip Phillips, Lester Young and Charlie Ventura. Perhaps Coleman should go back to Europe. Here he's making a good living, but his prestige has slipped pitifully.[17]

This was certainly a low point in Hawk's career. The lack of acclaim was not due to bad performances; it was simply that his style of playing was out of fashion. The young stars of bebop had established themselves, and so too had the 'cool' jazzmen – who utilized the harmonic innovations of bop then deliberately took the heat out of its phrasing and the vigour from its rhythms. But, regardless of response, Hawkins didn't let his musical standards slip, and he remained determined not to take his style back into the past simply to win approval from old fans, most of whom never went to hear him anyway. Trombonist George Masso has vivid memories of working a four-day engagement at this time with Hawk at Diana's Sea Grill in Providence, Rhode Island (in a group led by pianist Joe Lombardo). 'We played three sets a night spread over a four-hour period; Hawk varied the tunes he played each night. He was really pleased when he found out I knew things of his like "Stuffy". He was sober throughout the entire booking, and always easy to talk with. He made a point of playing the whole of each set with the band.'[18]

During this period Hawkins existed between two stools. He was not interested in working only with veteran 'swing-style' players, but he was not part of the bop scene. Leonard Feather, in summarizing Hawk's playing at the Cafe Society gig said, 'There are traces of bop influence on Hawk's faster numbers, but his time was still close to the older dotted-eighth-and-sixteenth-note school.'[19] All the same, Hawkins always seemed to be stimulated when working with young jazz individualists. He particularly enjoyed a two-month season at the Bee Hive Lounge, 1503 East 55th Street, Chicago, where he worked with Julian 'Junior' Mance (piano), Buddy Smith (drums) and Israel Crosby (bass). Hawkins played magnificently throughout the run, and word of mouth brought the crowds flocking in. Hawkins had successfuly introduced himself to a new generation of Chicago club goers. During a follow-up residency at the Bee Hive Lounge in May 1954 Hawkins achieved an ambition by recording with a vocal choir. Unfortunately, the two titles, 'I'll Follow My Secret Heart' and 'What a Difference a Day Made', are a disappointment, the performance of the singers being as indifferent as the recording quality. These titles were part of a long session in which Hawk was accompanied by local musicians; the pianist followed a growing trend by doubling on organ.

By this time the microgroove era had begun. The first of the 33 rpm long-playing recordings were only ten inches in diameter, but their duration offered at least four times the time available on similar-sized 78 rpm recordings. Singles and extended-play discs were being issued on 45 rpm. For someone of Hawk's musical imagination and stamina the new process brought a welcome challenge. Atmospheric jam sessions, recorded in a way that allowed the soloists to stretch out, became an immediate success via the newly marketed recording process. Beginning in 1953, Columbia had commissioned Buck Clayton to organize and direct recorded studio jam sessions. They were eminently successful and led to a series. Beginning in August 1954, Coleman Hawkins was featured on several of them.

The British jazz writer Stanley Dance had first coined the term 'mainstream jazz' to describe the style of musicians who were neither part of the bop movement nor performers in the traditional-jazz mould. The description didn't apply only to the work of veterans, since relative newcomers to the profession, such as cornettist Ruby Braff, played in a way that was typically mainstream. Though musicians generally dislike the pigeon-hole system critics have devised for various nuances of jazz, the term mainstream became an acceptable marketing description. Various sessions in this genre (such as those organized by Buck Clayton) sold well and persuaded younger buyers to seek out earlier work by the musicians involved; they were thus introduced to a vast treasure trove of yesteryear's jazz.

For Hawkins, taking part in a mainstream jam session was not a difficult endeavour. This doesn't mean that he stinted his efforts or the flow of his ideas, but he had participated in so many jam sessions that involved cut-throat competition that the task seemed an easy one when everyone was working to achieve the same end: a tuneful, swinging album. Many of the solos on a Buck Clayton jam-session album are peppered with phrases that have been heard before, but the ideas are always projected with spirit and enthusiasm, and the recordings radiate a sense of relaxed enjoyment (a quality that was scarce on many of the contemporary-jazz recordings made in this period). Hawkins is usually given pride of place as the final soloist within the loosely arranged routines, as on 'Jumping at the Woodside', where he is allocated three choruses instead of the two given to the other soloists. He thrives on the prominence and blows some assured phrases, projected with an infectious swing. This particular track was one of the first jazz releases to be a spliced blend of two sessions. The recent introduction of recording tape meant that part of a Buck Clayton session held in March 1954 could be linked with segments from the August date.

The August session involved Hawkins recording 'Blue and Sentimental' as a tribute to the memory of one of his most devoted disciples, the late Herschel Evans. Jo Jones, the drummer on the original Count Basie recordings that featured Evans, was also part of the band that Buck Clayton assembled, and he recalled Hawkins saying, 'I would like to make the tune. Do you think it would be alright from a spiritual standpoint?' Hawkins then looked up at the ceiling of the studio (which was housed in a converted church on 30th Street, New York) and added, 'I want to make this and see whether he can hear me up there.'[20] Hawk certainly performed a worthy tribute, sounding warmly reverent in re-creating the original melody and inspiringly inventive in the climactic phrases that lead into his opulent coda.

Three days after the August 1954 session with Clayton, Hawkins took part in a similarly styled recording organized by his former pianist Sir Charles Thompson. This was for a smaller unit than the Clayton ensemble but, like the bigger group, this octet also featured a rhythm guitarist (an instrumental sound bop groups had dispensed with long ago). A succession of well-crafted solos flow effortlessly from Bennie Morton (trombone), Earle Warren (alto sax), Emmett Berry (trumpet), Hawkins and the leader on piano. The up-tempo originals (two created on standard thirty-two-bar sequences, and one on a twelve-bar blues) are performed with neatness and filled with expressive improvisations, but the music takes on a new dimension when Hawkins is featured on the ballads: 'Under the Sweetheart Tree' (a Thompson composition) and 'It's the Talk of the Town'. This latter number had been one of Hawk's biggest recorded successes with Fletcher Henderson, but this version is a much more accomplished performance. The ornamentation of the 1933 recording is discarded and in its place there are ideas that seem the perfect liaison between harmonic adventurousness and rhythmic poise. The relaxed phrasing zooms effortlessly into double time to stress a build-up of musical tension during the second chorus. The track would automatically gain a place in a listing of Hawk's best performances in the 1950s, but unfortunately his conception of the final eight bars doesn't bring the piece to the climax it deserves.

So, after a period of relative inactivity as far as recordings were concerned, Hawkins was featured, at length, on two sessions within a week. This didn't make him change his hardening views on the profession he was in, however, and in a *Down Beat* feature from this period he said:

> The state of the music business now is just as bad as, or even worse, than it's ever been. The musicians today are fine, the music today is great, but I don't think we have a listening public. And the situation is sadder here than in any other place in the world. I remember when people were really listening here, before jazz became popular in foreign countries. Today they don't listen. They might make a noise at one of the jazz concerts, but they don't listen. Today they want a vocal. This started right after the war. All through the war people were very attentive, but when the war ended the trend started changing. So the problem today is the public, not the music.

Hawkins then put in a point about mainstream performers:

> There are still a lot of musicians who are just as good as they ever were. I don't see the point of anyone putting down older musicians. Don't forget that Dizzy Gillespie used to copy Roy Eldridge. He used to sound just like Roy. I'm told there are some listeners who say that jazz stopped with Johnny Dodds, and there are others who think that jazz started with Stan Kenton. People who don't listen to what's in the middle are people who have no sense of rhythm.[21]

Hawkins may have been looking through an engagement book that was far from full when he made these remarks, but the fact that he had some vacant dates during the autumn of 1954 helped him to secure a place on a lucrative tour of Europe that was being organized by tenor saxist Illinois Jacquet and the former trumpeter George Treadwell, now a booking agent. The package, which featured Jacquet's band and Sarah Vaughan (then Treadwell's wife), was originally scheduled to include Charlie Parker, but shortly before the tour set out, Parker attempted suicide. Hawkins was called in to take Parker's place in the show, which went under the name of the Jazz Parade.

Illinois Jacquet said:

> I was so pleased and relieved that Hawk could make the trip, but he was booked at such short notice that years later someone showed me a poster they'd saved from a Geneva concert and Charlie Parker was billed as being part of the show. Hawk was

fine with me and, as we were going to places I'd never seen before that Hawk knew well from his previous visits, he showed me around. He walked me all over the place, and it was very interesting. He was a gem all the way and the show was a smash wherever we went. Hawk was such a master of his instrument. He didn't need any gimmicks. In all the time I knew him he always played a Selmer tenor, with a 'Hawkins Special' Otto Link Five Star mouthpiece, which he'd had opened a little more than the standard model. He usually used a three or three and a half Rico reed, not too hard. People who say he blew a hard reed don't know what they're talking about. But of course when he'd had a few drinks it wouldn't matter what reed was in any horn, he'd just storm ahead.[22]

19
Renaissance

The Jazz Parade package flew into London for a brief airport stopover then left for Sweden, where they opened their tour at Stockholm's Konserthuset on 2 October 1954. From there they went, during the three-week tour, to Denmark, Germany, Holland, Belgium and France, concluding their itinerary by returning to England to play at the US service bases in Lakenheath, Suffolk and Sculthorpe, Norfolk. These final performances were restricted to US military personnel, the British general public not being admitted, though a few devoted musicians managed to gain entry. The *Melody Maker* report of the event made tantalizing reading for British jazz lovers, deprived of live American jazz for many years.

Throughout the tour, Jacquet's rhythm section: Adriano Acea (piano), Al Lucas (bass) and Osie Johnson (drums), backed Hawkins, whose feature spot was usually in the first half of the show. He played four numbers, which were most often 'Lady Be Good', 'Disorder at the Border', 'Body and Soul' and 'Stuffy'; he was then joined on stage by Illinois Jacquet for a tenor duet on 'Bean and the Boys (Lover Come Back to Me)'. Sometimes, Jacquet's entire front line, consisting of Russell Jacquet (trumpet), Matthew Gee (trombone) and Sahib Shihab (baritone sax), joined the two tenor stars, and very occasionally Sarah Vaughan and her trio (Jimmy Jones, piano; Joe Benjamin, bass and Roy Haynes, drums) took part in a jammed finale on 'Perdido'.

Hawkins was in a jovial, teasing mood for most of the trip, and took delight in ribbing Illinois Jacquet, then a keen golfer, about his own prowess on the links. British journalist Max Jones overheard this routine and asked Hawkins how long he took over a round of golf. Hawk's answer was nonchalant: 'Not long. I don't study holes like other people. I've got my own method and I don't need but three clubs.'[1] But apparently Hawk was always missing when his challenge games with Jacquet were due to be played.

The two tenor players were certainly stimulated by each other's musical presence on that tour. A version of 'Bean and the Boys' recorded live at a European concert has each of them playing long, challenging solos. Jacquet goes first, articulating a stream of swinging phrases in a way that highlighted his skill at applying telling accents to his lines, then Hawkins counters strongly with a formidable display of speed and ingenuity.

The tour certainly bucked up Hawkins's spirits; it also revitalized his prestige. He had taken Charlie Parker's place and had triumphed, satisfying every audience. American bookers and recording managers were rarely swayed by reports of sensational tours of Europe, but the emphatic praise accorded to Hawkins made its mark back home, and proved to doubters that there was great deal of life still left in the Hawk. His first task back in the USA, however, was to play gigs he had contracted before leaving for Europe, and this involved some uneventful, but successful dates at Scaler's House of Jazz in Milwaukee. Hawk then returned to New York to be featured on a recording session for the Jazztone label.

Trombonist Eddie Bert has vivid memories of this November 1954 date:

> When I recorded with him, Billy Taylor, Milt Hinton, Jo Jones and Emmett Berry, he had just gotten off a plane and his horn had come through baggage. So we were forty-five minutes into the date and he was still oiling his horn. We had no music and the producer got nervous. Well, we did the whole date with head arrangements – and finished on time. My feet were tingling. My wife took my temperature when I got home; it was 104 degrees. I wasn't going to give up that date, temperature or not.[2]

Hawk's 'comeback' gathered momentum; he continued to play a number of small, unglamorous club dates, but record sessions and broadcasts came in thick and fast. He was even invited to appear occasionally on television. Hawk was heavily featured on a session issued as by Cozy Cole's Big Seven, which also starred Rex Stewart and Tyree Glenn. These two horn players held the fort by recording a version of 'Caravan' while awaiting Hawk's arrival; true to form, he was late getting to the studio. He soon made his presence felt, however, blowing a gruff 'Sweethearts on Parade' over a medium-tempo shuffle rhythm. He sounds smoother and more inventive on 'My Blue Heaven', where he alternates betwen ultra-relaxed phrases and wailing one-liners. The worst number is a rock-and-roll pastiche of 'Organ Grinder's Swing', where Hawkins sounds bored and liverish, but this mood had passed by the time the band got around to recording 'Perdido'. Hawk must have ridden that old warhorse on countless occasions but this didn't stop him reaching a whole series of new ideas. Capricious Rex Stewart displays the worst and best of his puckish talent within his two-chorus outing.

Another Buck Clayton jam session showed Hawk in a powerful light, blowing eagerly on standard sequences. But as with the previous date, familiarity didn't breed a lacklustre performance and his solos on two versions of 'Out of Nowhere' are both ingeniously different, one of them complete with the most penetrating banshee-like reed squeak ever recorded. In May 1955 Hawkins played on another record date with Eddie Bert, this time with Ernie Royal on trumpet. He is again a model of enthusiasm, and seems particularly stimulated by the natty arrangement of 'Blue Room', creating a jaunty, rollicking solo. Pianist Earl Knight moves on to a shrill-sounding pipe organ for 'When Your Lover Has Gone', but even this doesn't diminish Hawk's zest and he constructs a solo that opens reflectively and develops into a series of swaggering, double-time phrases; in turn these are succeeded by the dramatic high-note motifs that round off his chorus. The other track utilizing the organ, 'What's New', has a brief solo from Coleman, but on several numbers (accompanied by the four-piece rhythm section) he is heavily featured, producing two superior ballad performances on 'I'll Never Be the Same' and 'I'll String Along with You'. Hawk's only 'ordinary' moments occur on 'My Own Blues'. Just as it was possible to hear faint echoes of Don Byas's style in Hawk's solos in 1944, after the two men had worked regularly together, so it seemed (in this period) there were traces of Illinois Jacquet's work in Hawk's improvisation, particularly on the ballads. They were probably the residue of ideas the men shared during their recently concluded European tour.

A concert recording from November 1955 produced an unusual incident. Al 'Jazzbo' Collins, compering the show at the Pythian Temple in New York, said to Hawkins on stage, 'When you're limbering up the saxophone and there's nobody around, just an empty room, and you're sitting on the edge of the bed looking out the window, playing a few things, thinking about nothing in particular, making a few runs on the saxophone . . . Would you do that for us?'

Hawkins was slightly taken aback but asked, 'Just make the runs?'

'Yeah,' said Collins, 'just sit right down here.' He then said to the audience, 'I want you to hear the tone of this saxophone with nothing else, just Coleman Hawkins.'

Hawkins dutifully obliged by launching into a minute and a quarter of beautifully conceived phrases, all projected in his broad, handsome tone.

The audience were delighted, but they were even more impressed by the subsequent rendering of 'The Man I Love'. Hawkins creates wave after wave of brilliant ideas, stimulated by the invigorating swing engendered by a fine rhythm section consisting of Hank Jones, Shadow Wilson and Wendell Marshall.

Though Hawk was now turned fifty, his stamina and breath control remained awesome. He was living proof of his own theories:

> Good phrasing is dependent on good breath control, but perhaps more than that it's the way you think. Actual playing on the job is the best way to learn to think. Improvising is playing with a lot of thought behind it, but none of the hard work that goes into thinking should show up in your playing. Too often improvising is really copying. To really improvise, a musician needs to know everything, not only his instrument, but harmony, composition, theory, the whole works.[3]

Hawkins had bounced back to confound those jazz administrators, journalists and fans who had written him off. Very few musicians ever ignored or derided Hawkins, since they recognized that he had, over the years, consistently transcended styles and jazz fashions. British bandleader John Dankworth, on a visit to New York, noticed how attentively Miles Davis had listened to Hawkins playing at the Bohemia Club. Davis had never wavered in his admiration of Hawk's playing. He said in 1955, 'Coleman Hawkins plays just as well as anybody you can name. Why, I learned how to play ballads by listening to Coleman. I saw Stan Getz making fun of Hawkins one night and I said to Getz, "If it weren't for Hawkins you probably wouldn't be playing as you are." I don't go for putting down a man just because he's older.'[4]

Hawk was gradually changing his work schedule; instead of moving away from New York to play a week or a fortnight's residency in another city, he took to playing weekend dates at clubs close to Manhattan, such as the Cork 'n' Bib in Westbury, Long Island. He found that by cutting down on overheads, such as hotel expenses and restaurant charges, he was almost as well-off working three nights close to home as he was playing a week out of town. Sometimes a single concert date, such as playing the Tanglewood Music Festival, brought in nearly as much net cash as six nights in a dowdy club. An appearance at the Berkshire Music Barn in Lenox, Massachusetts (with Paul Chambers, bass; Art Taylor, drums and Freddie Redd on piano) was another prestigious and lucrative engagement that Hawkins played that summer. In July Hawk and Roy Eldridge (now doubling on flugelhorn) played a lively set on the opening night of the second annual Newport Jazz Festival, supported by Nat Pierce (piano), John Beal (bass) and Jo Jones (drums). Singer Joe Turner joined the group for a spirited finale.

Hawk explained his change of tactics:

> I keep busy right around New York, don't have to go no place. You go to another town; in two days you're sick of it, knowing you've got to be another five days there . . . paying double expenses, commissions, transportation, taxes and so forth. When you get through you come home and what have you got? Nothing. You say to yourself I've been away from home for a week and what have I got? I could have done a gig over in Jersey City last week and had more than this.[5]

Not that there was any need for Hawk to plan a stringent budget; he had amassed a lot of money over the years. He did have a growing family, however, and he also did his best to support his mother and his grandmother (until her death in 1954), both still resident in St Joseph, Missouri. He tended to quote double union scale for any record date (though this was open to negotiation) but he rarely haggled with clubowners; if they didn't want to pay his price then he'd sooner not work. Sometimes Hawk looked back, somewhat ruefully, to the long residencies he'd played at Kelly's and at the Spotlite during the 1940s. He felt it was mutually beneficial for a club to hire the same musicians for long bookings:

> Engagements used to be much longer, and then you had a chance to build up a following. You don't get to know the people now and they don't get to know you. They may like what you're doing but when they come back they find a totally different group and music. The combo would be identified with the place and the place with the combo.[6]

But despite the supposed rigidity of his quotations to clubowners, if Hawk like the atmosphere of a venue he could be flexible about his fee, as he was for a series of dates he played at Lou Terrazzi's at 254 West 47th Street. During the mid-1950s if Hawk felt short of 'match practice' he arranged to be added to the line-ups that played at the various two-dollar-admission jam sessions organized by Bob Maltz in New York. At one of these, held at the Stuyvesant Casino, he locked horns with Ben Webster on a number that lasted for twenty minutes, giving youngsters in the audience an indication of what the pre-war musical battles had been like. Hawk thrived in this sort of situation; the only bringdown for him was participating in the massed version of 'When the Saints Go Marching In' which always seemed to conclude this series of bashes. Hawk also occasionally played at sessions Maltz organized at Child's Paramount on Second Avenue. One of these (held in late 1956) featured an impressive and unusual line-up, consisting of Bobby Hackett, Buck Clayton, Hawkins, Tony Sbarbaro and Sonny Greer on drums, plus two famous jazzwomen: trombonist Melba Liston and pianist Lil Armstrong Hardin.

These get-togethers, and similar ones held at the Central Plaza, weren't strictly jam sessions, they were organized assemblies in which jazz musicians were booked (and paid) to appear. Gone were the days when musicians could casually drop into any number of New York venues and sit in with a resident band. Some clubowners had taken advantage of that situation by just booking a pianist, knowing that visiting jazzmen would soon provide him with a free band; the musicians' union put an end to that practice. Although he didn't go in for jamming often, Hawkins regretted its demise, but nothing like as much as Roy Eldridge did, who said ruefully in 1956, 'For people like me and Coleman there are no places for jamming these days.'[7]

Hawkins continued to go out to listen to other jazz musicians on his nights off. He also maintained his movie-going habit, but most often he'd sit at home listening to classical music selected from his vast library of recordings. He wasn't a regular member of any social club, though he was a long-time Mason and sometimes visited the Masonic Temple on 155th Street. On one occasion he met up with his old friend, Albert 'Happy' Caldwell, there. In the ensuing conversation Hawkins raised the subject of another saxophonist of the 1920s, Paul 'Stump' Evans, saying, 'I never heard Stump but I heard him on records. What sort of fellow was he?' Caldwell said he replied, 'Hawk, if he'd have come here to New York, like we asked him to, he'd have upset everybody.'[8]

In 1956, when Hawkins was asked whether he was interested in forming his own permanent group, he said:

> Would I get a group together to travel? I wouldn't be too eager unless I was very highly paid. I average two to five or six gigs a week staying home, plus record dates, and I go down to Child's on Saturday nights if I'm not booked somewhere else. What would I travel with if there were no financial restrictions? What I'd want nobody could afford. I would want to travel with a lot of strings, a lot of brass, a lot of reeds and a lot of woodwinds – and definitely a harp. I don't want an old-time band like seven or eight brass and four or five reeds.[9]

Hawkins was never over-sentimental, but in that same interview he commented on the recent death of trumpeter Clifford Brown, who had been killed in a car crash, 'He was going to develop into something. He was a heck of a trumpet player,' but, as usual, Hawkins remained candid: 'He could fly all over the horn. He could make a million notes but you'd heard those notes already. Years and experience would have given him a distinctive thing of his own.'[10]

Hawk had never been very keen to give press interviews, but during the 1950s (and 1960s) he became positively reluctant to get involved in question-and-answer sessions with journalists. It was therefore something of a coup when Riverside got him to agree to take part in series called 'Spoken Word Recordings'. His vanity may have been stroked by the fact that some of the other contributors to this series included Eleanor Roosevelt and Henry Miller. Whatever the reason, Hawk dutifully appeared one 1956 summer night at Bill Grauer's apartment at 490 West End Avenue, New York, to be interviewed by Grauer and Paul Bacon, both of them long-time jazz record collectors.

Though Paul Bacon now modestly feels the interviewers were 'awestruck and inept', they did a considerable service for jazz lovers in getting as much information as they did from Hawkins who, in keeping with his nature, was often playfully evasive during the interrogation. Looking back thirty years Bacon said:

> I remember Hawkins's impressing presence and steady consumption of Scotch. He was quite at ease and befittingly regal in style. He seemed amused by the whole thing, as he might – given the bumblers confronting him. He seemed sensitive only in one area, and that was age; he didn't want to discuss Mamie Smith or anything much before Henderson. I remember that he seemed tired in the beginning, much less as we went on, but that's a classic response to alcohol. The outstanding thing in the whole interview in my opinion was his admiration for, and closeness to, Jack Teagarden.[11]

For the cover of the 'Spoken Word' album, Riverside commissioned a photo session at Paul Weller's studio on East 67th Street. Riverside's Harris Lewine attended the studio and remembers Hawkins arriving promptly at 3 p.m., wearing an iridescent grey-blue shantung suit:

> Hawk was intimidating in this suit in his quiet way. I had seen Mafia Dons at a hangout in Italian Harlem wearing the same sort of suit. It probably came from Phil Kronfeld; hip, but fine tailoring and workmanship. Probably a $150–200 suit in 1957. At the end of the photo session a chauffeur from the garage below came into the studio to ask Paul Weller something; he wasn't a jazz fan and didn't care, but he

> was introduced to Hawk. Slowly, amid pleasantries, Hawk began to work on him. Although the chauffeur was an obvious racist, Hawk's demeanour, dress, power and stance seemed to affect this chauffeur in a trancelike way. Before long he was Hawk's chauffeur and literally gave Hawk a ride (out of his way and time) to either Hawk's home on Central Park West or up to Harlem to some appointment. Hawk never really asked for a ride but this chauffeur was Svengalied.[12]

In July 1956 Hawkins played at the third annual presentation of the Newport Jazz Festival, which was establishing itself as the most prestigious event in the jazz world's calendar. On a damp summer evening Hawk, Buck Clayton and J.J. Johnson combined to create a flexible front line that delighted the 8,000 crowd. The band (billed as the Buck Clayton All Stars) had three of their numbers subsequently issued on a composite album. Each of the front line blow well-shaped solos without seeming to exert themselves unduly, though Hawk moves close to a stomping mood on a twelve-bar blues entitled 'Newport Jump'. The style of the band is non-denominational, with Clayton establishing the melody of 'You Can Depend on Me' and 'In a Mellotone' while his two colleagues noodle in the background. So as to avoid any on-stage confusion the soloists play in the same order on each offering: Hawk, Buck, J.J.; they are then followed by pianist Dick Katz, whose work is full of neat, swinging ideas.

This stellar group was something of a *hors d'ouevre* for the crowd eagerly awaiting the appearance of the Louis Armstrong All Stars, but *Down Beat* reported that Hawk's playing drew 'the first concerted applause of the evening'. The success of Newport gradually spawned numerous similar (but smaller) enterprises on the East Coast and from that summer onwards Hawk took part in many of these *alfresco* events. Writer Dan Morgenstern was on hand when Louis Armstrong and Coleman Hawkins ran into each other at Newport: 'They greeted each other warmly; a tremendous rainstorm started and Louis and Hawk ran off to Louis's bandbus which was nearby. I saw them sitting there together, both smoking, obviously having a great time, laughing together. It was plain to see that it was a warm meeting.'[13] But this sort of social contact didn't stop Hawk from giving an honest evaluation of Louis's work to Leonard Feather: 'Now he's playing just like he did when he was twenty years old; he isn't going any place musically. So sometimes you may say to yourself, "Why beat your head against the wall?", because as far as commercial value goes he's bigger than he ever was, and after all, there will never be anything to compare with Louis.'[14]

There was a rich contrast in the sounds of the groups with whom Hawk recorded in 1956. In January he had begun a series of dates for RCA Victor, on three of which he was accompanied by Billy Byers and his Orchestra (two of these session featured string sections). Released as *Coleman Hawkins in Hi Fi*, the recordings were widely praised, justifiably so because Hawkins's tone is captured at its majestic best. In July Hawk did a series of follow-up dates with Manny Albam, who was employed as leader and arranger, and two of these sessions also utilized strings. The Albam sessions used either songs written in, or concerning, France. Hawkins makes the most of some exquisitely melodic themes, and the lush backgrounds highlight the power and vibrancy of his playing. Again sales were encouraging and by the end of the year Hawk had begun work on another series of string dates; this time the musical director was Glenn Osser.

These svelte sounds were in marked contrast to the robust jazz created on the series that Buck Clayton made for Columbia during this period. A rival company, Capitol, decided that they too would like to issue an all-star, jam session album, and Hawk was also featured on this (released as *Session at Riverside*). Hawk is a model of vigour on both dates but gets closest to an inspired mood of relaxed invention on the Capitol version of 'Out of Nowhere', which featured a three-piece front line consisting of himself, trumpeter Billy Butterfield and trombonist Lou McGarity. It seemed almost impossible for Hawk to be anything but marvellously creative when playing solos on 'Out of Nowhere'. A month after the Capitol date Hawk was part of an all-star date assembled by cornettist Ruby Braff. Most of Hawk's solos here are brief and variable; he sounds desultory on 'You're Lucky to Me' but near-sublime on 'Just One More Chance'.

In November 1956 Hawkins (and Roy Eldridge) took part in recordings made at a concert in Carnegie Hall, at which they worked with Billie Holiday. This show was held to coincide with the publication of Billie's autobiography *Lady Sings the Blues*, parts of which were read to the audience by Gilbert Millstein. Billie made no secret of the fact that she preferred Lester Young's tenor-saxophone playing to Hawk's work, but for part of the 1950s her friendship with Lester temporarily ceased to exist. Hawkins accepted the concert gig without any deliberation. He and Billie had never been close friends, but they had worked together amicably many times on 52nd Street.

Hawk probably realized that deep down Billie would still have preferred to have worked with Lester on the show, but a job was a job. He had nothing against Lester socially, but (as in the case of his recent assessment of Louis Armstrong's playing) he didn't soft-pedal when asked about Young's present-day work in 1956: 'I first heard Lester Young way back in Kansas City. He sounded then just the way he does now, or rather he sounded better, because I don't think he's too interested in his music anymore. He can't even play on the beat anymore, doesn't have any beat at all, he just slurs, never tongues anything.'[15] In private Hawk could be more vindictive about his old rival, as he showed in his comments to Bud Freeman: 'That Lester Young, how does he get away with it? He's stoned half the time – he's always late and he can't play.'[16]

In late 1956 Hawkins began establishing close links with a venue that was to provide him with many subsequent engagements. The place was the Metropole, a large bar on Seventh Avenue, near Times Square. The place had formerly featured 'Gay '90s' music, but during the mid-1950s it began presenting live jazz from 1.30 p.m. until 7.30 p.m., and then again from around 8 p.m. until 3 a.m. (4 a.m. on Fridays). Usually bands alternated every hour (on the half-hour mark), but in order to make the changeover as smooth as possible they often combined for a jam-session number.

Several small groups were needed to fulfil this rigorous schedule, but instead of hiring workaday musicians to play during the normally quiet periods of trade, the owner, Ben Harriman, decided to book a large team of jazz greats who, he surmised would attract enough customers to keep the tills permanently busy. His strategy worked for a long time and many veteran jazz fans and interested newcomers took to visiting the Metropole at all hours to enjoy a drink and some lively music. With the doors left wide-open the amplified sound from the bandstand flooded out on to Broadway, attracting many casual listeners.

The biggest snag for the performing musicians was caused by the position of the elevated bandstand, which was up behind the bar. Floorspace was at such a premium the jazzman had to work on an elongated stage so narrow it forced the horns and the rhythm section to play in a spread-out, single line. The musicians, however, put up with this inconvenience because of the regularity of the bookings. The gigs at the Metropole were not the best paid in town, but they were very plentiful and the management didn't expect to have an exclusive call on any particular player, so if a musician went off to play out-of-town dates, or even overseas tours, they didn't raise any violent objections.

During the late 1950s many famous jazz musicians worked at the Metropole, including Henry 'Red' Allen (who led his own resident group there for years), Lionel Hampton, Illinois Jacquet, Gene Krupa, Charlie Shavers and Claude Hopkins. Coleman Hawkins and Roy Eldridge played there on countless occasions, in tandem and as soloists. They were backed by a variety of rhythm men including drummers Mickey Sheen, Cozy Cole and Buzzy Drootin, and pianists Andre Persiany (temporarily working in the USA), Al Williams and Marty Napoleon. For a long period Hawk and Roy worked regularly at the Metropole on Sunday matinees and on Monday and Tuesday evenings; they also swopped duties with other resident musicians and filled in on other nights.

A reporter commenting on a 1957 visit to the Metropole wrote, 'The Hawk still plays excellent driving tenor and even managed to look as though he was enjoying himself in that deafening beer joint.'[17] The smile gradually wore off as Hawkins reacted to the seldom varying routine, and to a vociferous crowd of regulars who were particularly impressed by vocals, drum solos and ultra-fast flag-waving numbers. Hawk refused to sing 'The Saints', and ignored any inane requests bellowed up at the bandstand. In general Hawk did not hold his listeners in any high esteem. He said in 1956, 'The audiences don't know anything. You can break it up with an audience, make them think you're the greatest thing ever was, with a little trick.'[18]

He stuck it out at the Metropole because he realized that the job kept him in good playing shape for record dates and special occasions. He knew that if he wasn't working regularly he'd never get around to practising for even a tenth of the time that he spent on the Metropole bandstand, and he enjoyed some parts of the routine, particularly the intermissions. During these intervals Hawk usually crossed the street to patronize the Copper Rail, a bar that functioned on the other side of Seventh Avenue, situated between 47th and 48th Streets. The drinks were cheaper than in the Metropole, and the soul food served there was as good as any in town.

The Metropole sessions served to reunite Hawk with several musicians with whom he'd worked in Fletcher Henderson's band, including Henry Allen, Buster Bailey and J.C. Higginbotham. RCA Victor decided to feature these four men on an album to be issued as by Henry 'Red' Allen's All Stars. These recordings served to introduce a 'new' husky-toned Red Allen to many listeners, the tracks showing that the trumpeter's sense of timing was more daring than ever and that he was constantly exploring the lowest notes on his trumpet in sudden, spectacular descents. Some of the musical fare on the album was as served at the Metropole, but the ballads were presented in a sophisticated way and mainly featured Allen and

Hawkins. 'I Cover the Waterfront', 'I've Got the World on a String' and 'Sweet Lorraine' all have admirable solos from the two veterans, with Red presenting the melody of each in his soft, wood-smoked phrases. His warm-sounding vocals, perfect in diction, are a delight throughout. Hawk sounds cheerfully interested in the proceedings and reverts to a former ploy by inverting the same basic idea through half a dozen chord changes.

The other two ex-Hendersonians, Bailey on clarinet and Higginbotham on trombone, do not recapture their former glory. The brash side of Higgy's playing is uppermost, and whereas he would, in his heyday, have followed an exciting brazen phrase with an engrossing idea, here he links his hollers with musical platitudes. Bailey's technique is still agile, but apart from some finely shaped phrases on 'St James Infirmary' and some relaxed legato work on 'Algiers Bounce', most of his efforts reek of over-ripe corn.

Marty Napoleon on piano is tasteful throughout and works well with bassist Lloyd Trotman, drummer Cozy Cole (energetic and inventive) and guitarist Everett Barksdale. Barksdale wisely doesn't adopt four-beats-in-a-bar patterns and instead plays a series of interjections and cues that suit Hawk's style of playing, allowing him to include (or hint at) substitute chords without feeling anchored to a preconceived harmonic plan. Red Allen blows thrilling trumpet on the up-tempo numbers, occasionally playing to an imaginary gallery, yet always sounding creative. It had been almost a quarter of a century since he and Hawkins had recorded together within a small group, but Red's esteem for the tenorist was undiminished. In his flamboyant vocal on the breakneck version of 'Ride Red Ride', Allen emphatically introduces Coleman as 'King Hawkins'.

Early in 1957, a sidekick of the mid-1940s, bassist Oscar Pettiford, gave his views of Hawk's stints at the Metropole: 'Coleman has always been further advanced musically than the other guys. Right now he's playing with the Dixieland guys and he hates it. But it's a matter of making a buck.'[19] Pettiford was one of Coleman Hawkins's All Stars on a March 1957 recording which created music that was a long way from Dixieland. On this album (issued as *The Hawk Flies High*) Hawkins shares front-line duties with trombonist J.J. Johnson and trumpeter Idrees Sulieman (who had formerly been known as Leonard Hawkins – no relation to Coleman). Not long before this recording date Hawk commented:

> There's a trumpet player who's not so well known, but who's developing his own way of playing and I'd like to bring him out. He's Idrees Sulieman. He plays an awful

lot of trumpet, but he plays too much at times. He needs somebody to say, 'Settle down – wait a minute.' He gets excited and off he goes. But he's young. Give him ten years.[20]

But despite the talented cast assembled for *The Hawk Flies High* there isn't an absorbing plot, and everyone on the date seems happy to remain within a comfortable groove. Creative striving wasn't the order of the day and one of the few solos from the date with a degree of abandon is by Sulieman on 'Sanctity'; it conveys a refreshing approach and some apt quotes. Hawk claimed this piece as a new composition, but it is nothing more than one of the riffs that he and Roy Eldridge used to play on 'Stompin' at the Savoy'. The theme is given new packaging, however, and delivered in a neo-Basie bag, but its attractiveness is marred by a long, silly bridge which was contrived to represent an atonal interlude. Even Hawkins, who devised the idea, seems to lose interest halfway through.

There are no fireworks from J.J. Johnson, who plays with relaxed aplomb, avoiding any machine-gun-like bursts of notes and keeping well within his immense talents. Sulieman keeps the ideas flowing but one of them is highly dubious: on 'Juicy Fruit' he seems to be attempting the world record for holding a long note in the trumpet's middle register. His marathon (lasting for almost a minute) has only the saving grace of being accompanied by a series of well-constructed climactic phrases from Hank Jones, supported by a rhythm section consisting of Barry Galbraith (guitar), Jo Jones (drums) and Oscar Pettiford (bass). The rhythm men get a cohesive impetus going on 'Chant', but on several tracks they seem less than unanimous as to where the beat is actually falling, which is surprising considering their individual skills and vast experience. Hawkins's best moments are the powerfully projected notes on the slow minor-keyed theme 'Think Deep', which compensates for the desultory version of 'Laura'.

In the period from October 1956 to February 1957 Hawkins did three recording sessions accompanied by Glenn Osser's Orchestra (strings, woodwinds and rhythm section). The resultant album, *The Gilded Hawk*, demonstrates Coleman's immense gift for phrasing time-honoured standards with authority and with a huge degree of feeling. There are no bold improvisations and the approach is almost gentle, but the artistry with which Hawk embellishes a series of fine tunes is an object-lesson. In place of elaborate codas there are brief sign-off phrases, yet each piece seems to culminate perfectly. John Green (who composed 'Body and Soul',

'Out of Nowhere', 'I Cover the Waterfront', amongst others, said after hearing *The Gilded Hawk*: 'If the improviser can improve on what the composer wrote instead of destroying it, more power to his embouchure.'[21]

20
Festivals Galore

The summer of 1957 was rich in jazz festivals, the most important and the most publicized of which was (as in previous years) the Newport, RI event. Hawkins and Eldridge again played on the festival's Friday-night session. For the 1957 event they had altoist Pete Brown with them in the front line, and backing was provided by a superb rhythm section consisting of Ray Bryant (piano), Al McKibbon (bass) and Jo Jones (drums). The group's set, part of which was subsequently issued on an album, had an uneven quality, with the cool night air playing havoc with Pete Brown's tuning. The crowd, though, were delighted when trumpeter Roy Eldridge borrowed a spare pair of Jo Jones's drumsticks and started a percussion duo on 'Sweet Georgia Brown'. Hawk sounds particularly rugged on his feature, 'Moonglow'.

Hawk opens his solo on 'I Can't Believe that You're in Love with Me' with a series of scintillating riff patterns, spurred on by McKibbon and Jones, but he fails to maintain this high level of inspiration during the latter stages of a lengthy solo. The entire performance is too long. Pete Brown sets out and plays five choruses, which inevitably meant that his colleagues would match this exposure, exemplifying an attitude often bred by the competitive atmosphere of the concert jam session ('He took five choruses, so I did the same'). A long solo is a wonderful thing when the musician is bursting with meaningful ideas but when the adrenalin isn't flowing more than one chorus of improvisation can invite boredom, even in a committed listener.

On the stage at Newport Hawkins couldn't suppress his laughter when Roy Eldridge shouted to him, 'Bet you never thought you'd be back playing carnivals again, did you Bean?' One of the musical highspots of that Newport weekend occurred after the Friday show ended when Norman Granz organized a party at the nearby Viking Hotel. Granz, visiting the festival as a listener, invited about a hundred people to call in, among them Hawkins, Eldridge, Pete Brown, Jo Jones, Gerry Mulligan, Specs Wright, Walter Page, Nat Pierce and Cannonball Adderley. The resultant jam session was described as the liveliest jazz event of the whole festival.

Later that same month (July 1957) Hawk took part in the three-day Great South Bay Festival held some fifty miles from Manhattan at Great River, Long Island. Hawk worked there with Rex Stewart's South Bay Seven (19 July) and with Roy Eldridge, Cutty Cutshall, Jimmy Rushing and Rex Stewart (21 July), but his main task was to star in the principal event of the weekend, a performance by the Fletcher Henderson Reunion Band, directed by Rex Stewart. Some of the participants in the big band (such as drummer Jimmy Crawford and baritone saxist Gerry Mulligan) were not Fletcher Henderson alumni, but most were. Rex Stewart went to a lot of trouble to ensure that the tribute was appropriate, both in the selection of the personnel and in the choice of the arrangements used (some of which were transcriptions of Henderson's original scores).

Apparently some tapes were made at the festival but a plan to issue them was dropped. Later in the year, however, Rex Stewart assembled a similar line-up (with some personnel changes) which recorded several of the numbers the band had played at the July concert. *The Big Reunion*, as the album was called, is a spirited tribute to an outstanding musical aggregation. A hit-or-miss mood affects the brass section but the individual members of it make amends by playing stylish solos. None of the reed players seems in top form, though Hawkins is generally authoritative, and on 'Sugar Foot Stomp' and 'Honeysuckle Rose' responds magnificently to the impetus of Jimmy Crawford's drumming, which sounds perfectly suited to Hawk's up-tempo playing. Hawk accords the melody of 'A Hundred Years from Today' due respect, but no great passion; in the latter stages of the piece he and Rex Stewart intertwine on a brief ride-out, with Stewart making up in spirit what his tiring chops failed to contribute. Hawk's dramatically conceived opening figure on 'Casey Stew' never quite blossoms and his solo on 'The Way She Walks' (a pretty Rex Stewart tune, poorly arranged) sounds slightly nebulous.

The most fascinating aspect of the album is hearing Hawk and Ben Webster soloing together within the big-band format (on 'Sugar Foot Stomp', 'Honeysuckle Rose', 'Wrappin' It Up' and 'King Porter Stomp'). Ben sounds less adventurous than Hawkins throughout the session; it was a day on which his ideas weren't really flowing and when he attempts to force the pace the effect is melodramatic. Ben was as sensitive as he was tough and he probably let Hawkins's presence rattle him. Garvin Bushell, who played in the reed section at the festival and on the album said:

> There was a lot of jealousy between them. More so on the part of Ben, who was fearful of Hawk. They played back to back and wouldn't look at each other. Hawk didn't bother about anybody, because he knew he could blow. He also knew how limited Ben was – how little harmony and theory he knew. Hawk blew Ben out of the studio that day.[1]

Hawkins discussed Rex Stewart's playing with Bushell, saying that although Rex still played out of tune because of his incorrect fingering he also created many original phrases in his solos. So it seems that Hawk had finally mellowed in his views about Stewart's cornet work.

But the Henderson tribute recordings did not measure up to another 1957 album that Rex Stewart organized. This was *The Big Challenge*, an apt title for the inspired duelling that went on between Rex Stewart and Cootie Williams, trombonists Lawrence Brown and J.C. Higginbotham, and Hawkins and Bud Freeman on tenor saxophones. A fine rhythm section, Hank Jones (piano), Billy Bauer (guitar), Milt Hinton (bass) and Gus Johnson (drums), ensured that inspiration rarely flagged, and the sparse but ingenious arrangements (by Ernie Wilkins and Joe Thomas) are highly stimulating.

The supreme individualism of each of the front-line soloists is apparent on every track, and the deep contrasts between the styles of Hawkins and Freeman (relating to tonal differences, dissimilarity of phrasing and contrasting approaches to harmony) produce showers of interestingly patterned sparks as the two flinty veterans duel. In the issue of *Down Beat* that went on sale just before this session took place, Hawkins said some candid things about his rival. Having already identified Bud Freeman's playing on a recording of 'Perdido', he went on to say, 'Do I like that tenor style? Well, no, not exactly.' This comment may have added extra zip to Freeman's challenges. On 'Alphonse and Gaston' there's an interesting moment when Hawkins appears to be aping Freeman's phrasing; it could have been deliberate or it might have been another example of Hawkins dropping into a riff pattern before launching a series of more complex phrases. Each track is full of musical grandeur and the two released takes of 'Walkin' My Baby Back Home' show that no one was relying on set solos; the album remains one of the best mainstream recordings ever made.

Another reunion, this time with a colleague from the 1940s, took place when Hawk recorded as part of a septet led by pianist Thelonious Monk (for the Riverside label) in June 1957. Among the stellar players Monk assembled for the date was the brilliant young tenor saxist John Coltrane, destined to become a major influence on a whole generation of jazz players. Coltrane was thrilled to work alongside Hawkins and cast his mind back to his formative years: 'I went through Lester Young and on to Charlie Parker, but after that I listened to Bean and realized what a great influence he was on the people I'd been listening to.'[2]

The highlight of an intriguing session is 'Well You Didn't', on which all of the soloists are in good form. After Art Blakey's scintillating drum solo Hawkins enters cagily, backed only by bass and drums. Hawks' reticence is caused by a degree of confusion between Blakey and bassist Wilbur Ware as to the exact plan of action, but he is soon spurred on by Blakey's deftly accented off-beat patterns and begins to swing easily. Throughout the date it's obvious that Hawk is intent on showing Monk (whose work he still greatly admired) that he was not feeling at all out of place among the young talents. The rhythm section settle down to give Hawk just the kind of firm (but not heavy) support on which he thrived.

Hawk and Monk provide a fine example of mutual admiration in their quartet version of 'Ruby'. There are no gushing displays by either musician, but Hawk shapes his lines and sings out his notes in an effectively bitter-sweet way, indicating the stimulation he felt at being backed by Monk's ingenious and highly individualistic keyboard voicings. On the witty 'Off Minor' Hawk is bold and challenging, but his solo on 'Epistrophy' sounds overweight, whereas Coltrane's improvisations seem lithe and almost feverishly exploratory. Hawk didn't solo on 'Abide With Me' (where the front line's unaccompanied harmonies sound like a supercharged harmonium) or on Monk's inimitable tune 'Crepuscule with Nellie'.

Monk was ill on the first part of the session and plays no part in 'Blues for Tomorrow', a hastily contrived anachronism that sounds similar to themes Johnny Hodges used to compose for his small groups. Hawkins is rather slow to begin unfurling his ideas, but eventually settles on some energetic but familiar swinglike riff patterns. Coltrane underlines the contrast between the two men by swirling through intricate runs, using his awesome technique to shape a series of what sound like stream-of-consciousness phrases. After a bass-and-drums duet, the front line engage in six choruses of four-bar chases, but unfortunately the running order never allows Hawkins and Coltrane to vie directly with each other.

On that same day (26 June 1957) Hawk recorded as part of a JATP line-up whose studio task was to present the sort of programme they might have done in concert, namely two long numbers featuring all the horn players and two ballad medleys. Any comparison between Hawk's work here and his playing on the Monk date is invidious. His stamina certainly doesn't flag on this Verve session, but despite the muscle-flexing on 'Dizzy Atmosphere' most of the excitement in his solo sounds contrived, whereas Dizzy Gillespie's cup-muted solo is full of invention and genuine zest. Hawk plays a rather leaden version of 'September Song' as his ballad feature; his choice in the medium-tempo pot pourri is 'Stompin' at the Savoy', on which he disdainfully avoids playing the melody and instead issues two 'no news today' choruses. In contrast Paul Gonsalves tries hard, and succeeds, on his admirable version of 'Gone with the Wind'. The fourth member of the front line, Stan Getz, performs well throughout, but comes into his own on the fast version of 'The Way You Look Tonight', aided by the considerable swing of a fine rhythm section consisting of Wynton Kelly (piano), Wendell Marshall (bass) and J.C. Heard (drums). Playing in front of this same trio, Hawkins seems to be straining at the leash and pulling them into a fragmented formation.

In truth, Hawkins was being over-recorded. His output during 1957 was too high for him to maintain his own remarkable standards of creativity. Within a twelve-month span he made over 125 sides, spending even more time in the studios than he had done during his hectic freelancing heyday back in 1944. Most of his greatest recordings, notably 'Body and Soul' and 'The Man I Love', contained the distillation of thousands of ideas he had previously played on those tunes. But many of his recorded solos in 1957 were little more than blueprints, some of them indicating potentially great designs, others just a representation of undeveloped ideas. Hawk's immeasurable musicianship enabled him to grasp the intricacies of any chord sequence he was called on to deal with, and his technique allowed him to play at the fastest tempos, but no artist, however talented, has an unlimited supply of inspiration. In 1957, Hawk's hectic self-imposed schedule proved that even someone with his gifts could not always bring forth epic improvisations. However, he continued to take part in as many sessions as he could; as a result there were many uneven moments during solos he recorded during the coming decade.

The most disappointing recordings from 1957 are the reunion sessions between Hawkins and his old Henderson band colleague, Don Redman; many of the titles were for a series of Sesac transcriptions featuring an all-star big band playing Redman's arrangements. Unfortunately most of the tunes are pot-boilers, and the scores are bitty and synthetic. Hawkins, Charles Shavers and Hank Jones are accorded brief solos, but these fleeting moments of artistry don't compensate for the twee arrangements. Hawk plays relaxedly on 'Last Night in Town', 'Christmas in the Valley' and 'Star Dreams', but more inspiringly on 'Ain't Gonna Get Fooled Again' and 'Free and Easy'. He does his best on 'You Turned the Tables on Me', but the chosen tempo is almost fast enough to be funny. A small band plays 'Coffee Light' (which features a duet between Hawk's sax and Redman's whistling); the rest of the tenor-sax solos on the big-band sessions are taken by Al Cohn and Seldon Powell.

But the muse hadn't deserted Hawkins and among the variable dates of 1957 there occurred a marvellously productive recorded confrontation featuring him and Ben Webster accompanied by Oscar Peterson (piano), Herb Ellis (guitar), Ray Brown (bass) and Alvin Stoller (drums). The two tenorists' gargantuan tones produce as rich a musical brew as was ever created by saxophone duettists. Playing through a selection consisting mainly of fertile standards, the two jazz heavyweights produced cascades of fascinating ideas, all of them delivered with zest and passion. Oscar Peterson told Peter Clayton in a BBC radio interview: 'The session with Coleman Hawkins and Ben Webster was of monumental importance to me, not only as a person but as a player. I sat and watched these two behemoths of the music world jostling each other for position.'

Ben Webster had established his originality years before this record date, but he still insisted on acknowledging his initial debt to Hawkins, and often recounted how pianist Clyde Hart's sarcastic comments in the 1930s had caused him to seek his own style of playing. Hart had said, 'Well, Ben, you finally did it. You sound just like Hawk now.' The pianist's observation made Webster realize that he was being thought of simply as a Hawkins clone. 'I packed up the record player and took it to Kansas City for my folks. From then on I developed my own.'[3] Ben had first heard Hawkins live in the mid-1920s. Late in life he reflected on his hero's personality: 'I'd say that Coleman was hard to get close to. He didn't meet new people too fast, and he didn't buy too many drinks. We drank a lot of my bottles over the years.'[4] Tenorist Lew Tabackin highlighted the difference between the two men's music when he commented on 'Maria' (from the duet album): 'Hawkins is the intellectual, he's probing, very adventurous, he's always stretching. Ben Webster is beautifully rhapsodic, melodic, just so warm'.[5]

The sides with Ben Webster were made in California while Hawkins was out there with the eighteenth JATP national tour, which had begun on the East Coast on 14 September. It had been a long time since Hawk had been part of a Norman Granz package, a fact that Granz acknowledged in the announcement that introduces recordings made at the Chicago Opera House on 19 October. Granz added, 'When we first started out he was the first man I chose. He's probably one of the most important, or the most important musician in the history of the tenor saxophone.'

These Chicago recordings present the best sound picture ever made of Hawkins and Eldridge working together. Both men are in superb form, ceaselessly inspiring each other. They are backed by three quarters of the Modern Jazz Quartet – John Lewis (piano), Percy Heath (bass) and Connie Kay (drums) – a rhythm section that would not, on paper, seem to be totally appropriate for the virile music of Hawkins and Eldridge, but the results compensate for the brief moments that suggest a mismatch. Fortuitously, recordings were made of two shows that day, one in mono and one in stereo. As an almost identical programme was played, there is a fascinating opportunity to hear how these top-flight jazz musicians reshaped their ideas (consciously or subconsciously) during the periods between the two shows. The only change of tune concerned one of Eldridge's ballad performances: in one show it was 'I Can't Get Started'; in the other 'Blue Moon'. Hawkins plays an enthusiastically received version of 'Cocktails for Two' in both concerts.

After creating lively, extended solos on 'Bean Stalkin' ' the two horns trade four-bar phrases, following this with two-bar exchanges and ending up blowing brief musical ripostes at each other in a penetrating example of spontaneous counterpoint. The second (stereo version) is more relaxed, with Hawkins hitting an empyrean patch as he enters his third chorus. Hawkins and Eldridge share the verse of 'Tea for Two' four bars each; they then launch into a variation of Vincent Youman's melody that Hawk had recorded as 'Bean Soup' back in 1946. Again the stereo version depicts a more relaxed take of some marvellously combative soloing. 'Kerry' (a twist on 'Sweet Georgia Brown') ends in a spirited chase, but the solos are less well wrought than the other tracks though Eldridge digs out some splendid phrases that first appeared on his 1943 recording 'The Gasser'. Hawkins's boldest look at the sequence occurs on the stereo version.

Hawk's performances on the two versions of his feature 'Time On My Hands' are both noble achievements. The presentation is brief, covering a single chorus and cadenzas, but within that span there are improvisational differences too numerous to count. In the hours between concerts Hawk's imagination had conceived a whole new set of fascinating variations. Varied improvisations also enrich 'The Walker' (a workout on 'Stompin' at the Savoy'); here Hawk's instrumental strength and Eldridge's fiery concepts lift the performance to a remarkable height. This is the only number that features a solo by the accompanists: an eight-bar drum bridge from Connie Kay. John Lewis provides the horns with some inviting introductions, but occasionally the symmetry of his chordal comping adds a quaint feeling to the proceedings. The results, though, prove that neither Hawkins nor Eldridge found this off-putting. The men are in irrepressible form on a jam-session version of 'Stuffy', which also features J.J. Johnson and Stan Getz. Hawk takes six choruses and sounds full of gusto and invention throughout.

A few days later, during a return to California, Hawkins did a quintet session accompanied by the same men who had backed the reunion with Ben Webster: Peterson, Ellis, Brown and Stoller. Hawk's playing is never less than excellent on this album, but he sounds as though he is not extending himself unduly, except perhaps on 'In a Mellow Tone'. Even so, there is no suggestion of a mechanical performance. Most tracks have a three-chorus routine, with the melody stressed emphatically during the opening section. There is a welter of familiar Hawkins phrases, but then quite suddenly a completely new idea emerges, as in the second chorus of 'Like Someone in Love'. Hawk seems to be treating himself to a joke on 'How Long Has This been Going On?' (which Ben Webster regularly featured in his repertoire). For the first two choruses Hawkins comes on like Webster, before moving into his own faster-flowing ideas. This number also has an absorbing duet between Hawkins and Oscar Peterson; elsewhere, except for guitar or piano introductions, Hawk's is the only solo voice on the album.

The most prestigious event in Hawk's year was yet to come. This was his appearance, along with a multitude of other jazz greats, in a CBS television show entitled 'The Sound of Jazz'. The participants included Count Basie, Henry Allen, Vic Dickenson, Roy Eldridge, Harry Carney, Lester Young, Pee Wee Russell, Gerry Mulligan and Billie Holiday. Both the rehearsal on 5 December and the live show on 8 December have appeared on albums. They show that despite the pressures of having to improvise jazz on cue, and in front of a camera, the players give an awesome demonstration of their musical powers and individuality.

Hawkins, behatted alongside Lester Young and Ben Webster, seemed, on the television show, to be no more concerned than if he had been playing a club date. He was affable throughout the proceedings and let out a bellow of his deep-chested laughter when Billie Holiday (during a rehearsal) made a wisecrack about the difference between suntan and shuntan. Sadly this was to be one of the last big occasions in Lester Young's career; he was on the verge of a nervous breakdown and soon after the show was transmitted he entered the King's County Hospital in Brooklyn. He recovered and subsequently made a trip to Europe, but his days were numbered.

One of Hawk's more unusual gigs during this period was guesting with the bright-sounding, adventurous group Bobby Hackett was leading at the Henry Hudson Hotel on New York's 57th Street. His recording schedule also continued to place him in widely varying company. On one date he worked with a large string-laden orchestra backing vocalist Tina Louise. The fare is ballads, and Hawk is featured on the introductions and codas of several of them; he also plays occasional fill-ins and short solos. His tantalizingly brief effort on 'Embraceable You' (a tune he rarely played) is absolutely ravishing, mellow in tone and rich in ideas. In utter contrast Hawk (as part of Jimmy McPartland's All Stars) played on a *Music Man Goes Dixieland* album. Interspersed throughout the dialogue there are interludes containing a fair smattering of high-class jazz. Hawkins pops in and out of the action by improvising sixteen-bar solos on three of the numbers.

The bulk of Hawk's dates in the latter part of 1957 were at the Metropole (from where he occasionally played on live broadcasts). He came to regard the tavern as a regular part of his life and used it as a base for storing his tenor saxophone. Hawkins was inclined to be as careless about his instrument as he was diligent about his performances. Even as a young man with Mamie Smith's troupe, he had never really looked after his horns, and he maintained the same attitude during his travels in Europe, often leaving his sax at a club if he was playing there on the following night, saving himself the trouble of carrying it back to his hotel or apartment. At Kelly's Stable he even tipped someone to pack the horn away at night and get it out ready for the next night's performance, so that he only had to pick it up off the bandstand. If he was doing a series of dates in different New York clubs he couldn't be bothered to take his horn up to his apartment; bassist Red Callender, recalling the 1930s, said, 'In New York we used to hover around his big Chrysler parked near his apartment on St Nicholas Terrace. His horn and music would be lying on the back seat and no one ever touched it. Try that now!'[6]

On tour in America Hawk was notably careless about his instrument and this eventually resulted in his Selmer saxophone being stolen during a booking he did in Boston (this tenor – model number 27666 – had been presented to him in Paris in the 1930s). Hawk simply replaced the lost sax by buying another balanced-action Selmer, collecting it only after the dealer had carried out his instructions to have the instrument gold-plated three times over. This replating was an expensive procedure, but even the big outlay didn't make Hawkins, usually so thrifty, any more careful about his instrument.

When Hawkins worked for two consecutive days at the Metropole he invariably put his instrument in a room that was upstairs in the club and left it overnight, but he did this once too often and was again the victim of a thief. Another Selmer was purchased and triple-plated, but much more serious than the loss of the saxophone was the disappearance of the mouthpiece, almost impossible to duplicate. It had started life as a normal Otto Link model but, over the years, it had been altered in several small but important ways. After his 1957 loss Hawkins spent months experimenting with various replacement Otto Link mouthpieces, adjusting and paring them in an attempt to duplicate the previous specifications, but none of them felt comfortable. Hawk decided to try the work of a different manufacturer, and began using a Berg Larsen mouthpiece, gradually making his own adjustments to that model.

Hawk's schedule at the Metropole allowed him plenty of time to call into other New York clubs to listen to the playing of younger tenor saxists. He rarely missed any newcomers to the city, but made a particular point of hearing Sonny Rollins regularly. Consciously or unconsciously, Hawk adopted some of the younger star's concepts, a fact that writer Martin Williams noted in his review of an album that Hawkins made with guitarist Tiny Grimes. One of the tracks, 'Marchin' Along' (a twelve-bar blues) evoked a lot of comment because Hawkins seemed out to show the young players that he had the stamina and energy to enter their pastures and thrive. He made his message clear almost to the point of brutalism by wailing out an overlong solo. Tiny Grimes follows with an equally unappealing marathon and it is left to pianist Ray Bryant to redress the balance by playing some swinging, unstrained blues choruses that seem to blossom from sturdy gospel roots. 'Soul Station' has flautist Musa Kaleem joining a less frantic blues workout; Grimes again overstates his case but gets closer to his true form on a relaxed 'Blues Wail'. Hawk's playing on this track is also more thoughtful. 'April in Paris' is devoid of spring, being a ramshackle succession of modulations from which only Hawkins emerges with credit. 'A Smooth One' is simply a run-of-the-mill track-filler.

In February 1958 Hawk and Roy Eldridge did a studio session that enabled them to record extended versions of two of the tunes they regularly featured at the Metropole: 'Sunday' and 'Hanid' (Dinah spelt backwards). Perhaps because they were determined not to take any of the Metropole's slightly frenzied atmosphere into the studio the date has an urbane, almost polite edge. Honours here are taken by Roy Eldridge, whose playing, whether muted or open, has a biting lyricism. On 'Sunday' Eldridge blows his first chorus muted then creates an explosive effect by dramatically removing his mute in mid-phrase, allowing his robust tone to burst open the second chorus. This was not a celebrated session for Hawk; he sounds uninspired and often gets himself caught in similar rhythmic patterns, like a speaker who keeps inadvertently lapsing back into the same subject. After punching out some attention-catching low notes to open his solo on 'Hanid' Hawk starts spinning out skeins of phrasing that are reminiscent of a Scottish reel: the first stanza is no more dramatic than the last, they simply go round and round without developing any sort of climax.

Pianist Hank Jones is a model of delicate inventiveness throughout, and George Duvivier plays several excellent walking bass solos; both men are well featured on a slow Hawkins composition, 'Honey Flower'. On this, Hawk again starts to regurgitate, whereas Eldridge projects an invigorating forcefulness in his muted solo. The final chorus is a model of ineffective scoring. Hawkins starts to move towards a purposeful mood on 'Nabob' but just as his adrenalin begins flowing the arrangement brings this unalluring theme (another Hawkins composition) to a close.

Hawkins, Hank Jones and drummer Micky Sheen took part in another quintet session that same month, this time with Ray Brown on bass and Buck Clayton on trumpet. This *High and Mighty Hawk* date is as lively as the 'Nabob' session was mundane. A sense of swinging urgency propels the fast numbers and a mellow warmth fills the ballads. The session was produced by the jazz critic and writer Stanley Dance, who had been commissioned by British Decca to make a series of recordings featuring mainstream jazz musicians to be issued on the Felsted Label. Dance recalled:

> All the Felsted albums were made on a limited budget, so that overtime had its terrors. Hawkins arrived twenty minutes late for this date, with a large roast-beef

> sandwich that took him another twenty minutes to eat and wash down. When the session finally began, after a good deal of leisurely repartee, I soon discovered that there was no need to watch the clock with *these* professionals. In fact we ended up with more time than could legally go on the record and this accounted for a tape cut that amazed and delighted Hawkins. 'How in the world I played that. I'll never know,' he told me years later.[7]

'Bird of Prey Blues' is a milestone in the latter part of Hawk's career. It swings from the opening notes of Hank Jones's two scene-setting choruses. After sharing a rather hackneyed blues riff with trumpeter Clayton, Hawk stealthily begins his monumental seventeen-chorus solo. His ideas surge out but he paces them admirably, interspersing them in a way that allows a different motif to buttress each twelve-bar section. Hank Jones picks up Hawk's concluding phrase and begins to build his own edifice; Clayton follows and he too successfully assembles a hugely impressive musical framework, beginning in the low register and climbing surefootedly to his high notes.

Buck Clayton takes the longest solo on Hawk's tune 'Oh Wee Miss G.P.' (the G.P. here standing for Good Pussy), but plays only brief, muted interludes within the ballads 'My One and Only Love' – which receives a mature and caring Hawkins performance – and 'You've Changed', taken very slowly and benefiting from Ray Brown's long sonorous bowed notes. Brown's lines throughout the album are models of musical expertise, and Sheen's neat brushwork blends nicely with Jones's graceful touch. Playing the high-rising melody of 'Get Set' would test the cup-mute technique of any trumpeter in the world, but Buck Clayton triumphs. He goes on, still muted, to play a magnificent solo which even Hawk's competitiveness cannot top. The only indifferent moments from Hawkins occur on 'Vignette', where he enters with such a swagger he can't seem to stop himself from rolling into the same sort of rhythmic stanzas that marred his work on 'Hanid'. Instead of swinging along with the rhythm team he seems to be keel-hauling it.

On the last days of a productive month Hawk played in the saxophone section of an all-star band assembled to back the sturdy voice of Jimmy Rushing. The results, issued as *Jimmy Rushing and the Big Brass*, can be considered as the most joyous album that talented singer ever made. The section work is not unblemished but the spirit and warmth that the swinging band engenders, particularly on the up-tempo numbers, more than compensates.

The assembled jazz giants play brief but eloquent solos, stimulated by arrangements written by Buck Clayton, Jimmy Mundy and Nat Pierce. Hawkins sounds reflective during his sixteen bars on 'Trav'lin' Light', bustling in his eight bars on 'It's a Sin to Tell a Lie', bombastic on the pacy 'Somebody Stole My Gal' and full of bravura on 'When You're Smiling' (doubtless energized by Buddy Tate's fine preceding tenor-sax solo). Hawk's most substantial contribution is on 'Rosalie', where he steams into his second chorus with all the power of a freight train. Buddy Tate, who had first heard Hawkins almost thirty years earlier, summarized his thoughts on the man: 'Hawk was a very nice cat. He didn't talk too much about music, but when he did he was warm and encouraging, never on an ego trip. He could be very humorous at times. Sometimes he didn't talk at all, but there were other days when you couldn't stop him talking.'[8]

21
New Era for Big-toned Tenors

In May 1958 Hawkins again returned to Europe, this time as a member of a newly-organized JATP package. Somewhat to the surprise of most European critics Hawk and Roy Eldridge were cast as show openers. They played a brief opening set backed by Lou Levy (piano), Gus Johnson (drums), Herb Ellis (guitar) and Max Bennett (bass), after which they had a good deal of backstage waiting while Dizzy Gillespie, Sonny Stitt, Stan Getz, Oscar Peterson, Ray Brown and other jazz luminaries played their feature spots. Hawk and Roy returned to the stage to take part in the concluding jam session.

After playing on the Continent the package travelled around Britain for sixteen days, playing major concert halls in various cities. This first-ever JATP tour of Britain (they had played one date in London in 1953 for a Flood Relief concert) found Hawkins in variable form. But the wide-ranging trip allowed him to meet up with lots of his pre-war British friends; he seemed undismayed that he was being written of as simply a 'curtain raiser'. Whatever his position on the bill, however, he looked and acted like a star. Bassist Max Bennett was hugely impressed by Hawk's demeanour on-and-off stage during that tour: 'I recall that he was very professional, that he was very gentlemanly and that he was easy to work with.' Most of the troupe dressed in colourful casual clothes and sports shirts when they travelled, but Hawkins 'always wore a suit and a tie.'[1] Hawkins did not approve of all of Norman Granz's tactics but he wholeheartedly endorsed the impresario's insistence that musicians were to wear evening dress for concert appearances. Hawk told Dan Morgenstern, 'Norman has class; making the musicians wear tuxedos is the right thing to do'.

Neville Skrimshire, the EMI record-company representative with the tour, observed several of the JATP stars indulging in high jinks at a little village some ten miles from Manchester. Norman Granz and Dizzy

Gillespie decided they wanted to have a sprinting race. Sonny Stitt became interested in the idea and said he'd act as pacemaker. Oscar Peterson asked Hawkins if he was going to bet on the outcome and was suitably amused when the saxist replied, 'No. I was thinking of running.' Stitt set off at a fast clip and continued to set the pace from first to last, finishing ahead of the two contestants.

Sonny Stitt, when he had a few drinks under his belt, could be just as much of a teaser as Coleman Hawkins. Writer Steve Voce overheard some of Stitt's tangy jocularity when the JATP show played Liverpool.

> Stitt said to Hawkins, 'Is that right when you were with Fletcher Henderson's band, Louis Armstrong used to call you "Mister Hawkins"?'
>
> 'Yeah, that's right,' came the reply.
>
> 'And is that right that they only called the oldest guy in the band "Mister"?'
>
> 'No, that's wrong. I'm much younger than Louis.' By this time Hawk was getting agitated and Stitt concluded his fun by saying, 'Ah, don't give me that Hawk. I got a record of you playing tenor in 1904.'[2]

But this teasing covered Stitt's deep respect for Hawk's part in pioneering modern jazz; he freely admitted, 'Bean set the stage for all of us.'[3]

For all Hawkins's touchiness on the subject of age, he devoutly believed that maturity was an important factor when it came to playing top-class jazz. On one occasion he said, with some emphasis:

> I'll tell you something about the young players. It takes everyone age and experience to find themselves on their horns. Take Dizzy Gillespie. To me he plays 100 per cent better today than he did ten years ago. He's had all that experience. There's a certain amount of wildness in a young player but they eventually get down to precision, to real artistry.[4]

The JATP package next played a series of concerts in Europe; after working in Italy they journeyed to Knokke-Le-Zoute in Belgium for festival dates on 5 and 6 July. For Hawkins it was a nostalgic return to another of his pre-war havens. He soon made his way to a familiar cafe on the seafront, ordered himself an ice-cold beer and sat there for an hour gazing out to sea, perhaps contemplating the many changes that had been wrought on himself, and on the town, since he had last sat there.

Hawkins was so intent on reliving his past in Knokke that he missed the plane ferrying most of the JATP troupe on to the Cannes Festival. Much as it pained him, he was forced to hire a plane and a pilot at a cost of $500. He flew to Geneva in the hired aircraft and from there picked up a scheduled flight to Cannes, arriving just in time for the opening concert (with Roy Eldridge on 8 July). Hawk returned to play in Knokke on 11 July, then flew back to Cannes for that festival's closing concert, part of which featured a conclave of tenor saxists; Hawkins, Stan Getz, Don Byas and the two French stars Guy Lafitte and Barney Wilen. Guy Lafitte recalls, 'Stan Getz was made the "master of ceremonies" and he decided to ask Hawkins to play the final solo, which I think was very respectful of him.'[5] An eight-minute version of the tenorists' version of 'Indiana' was eventually issued on record.

Back in New York, Hawkins slipped comfortably into his routine at the Metropole, but soon took time off, along with Red Allen, Buster Bailey, Cozy Cole, Claude Hopkins, and J.C. Higginbotham, to play in Canada at the Stratford, Ontario, Shakespearean Festival held in late July. That same month Hawk was featured at the Stonybrook (New York) Musical Festival, as part of drummer Micky Sheen's All Stars.

In August 1958 Hawkins did another studio session with his Metropole confrere Henry Allen. In contrast to their March 1957 session this was a restrained affair, with Red Allen deliberately playing a subdued role. As if to prove something, he plays without vibrato on several of the slow ballads, which gives his solos a mannered air, but even at his most restrained Allen remained an adventurous player, and his idiosyncratic shaping of the melody of 'Sleepytime Gal' is inimitable. Alto-sax specialist Earle Warren plays only clarinet on this date, and does so with warm-toned competence. Pianist Marty Napoleon is elegantly reliable and the ex-Woody Herman star Chubby Jackson plays some interesting bass solos, particularly on 'Lonesome Road'. The excellent drummer, George Wettling, exhibits strength and subtlety but somehow the three rhythm men do not blend into a highly cohesive section. Hawkins takes sixteen-bar solos on most of the numbers and plays the opening melody of 'All of Me' in a booming, authoritative way. Even more appealing is his chorus on 'Tea for Two', which opens with some acrobatic phrases and swings from first to last. This number was one of the few Red Allen recordings on which the trumpeter remains muted throughout.

This was one of Red Allen's own favourite sessions; he obviously enjoyed the opportunity to blow softly and with finesse, but there was little chance of musical understatement on another date that Allen and Hawkins also did for the Soundcraft Tape company (both sessions were later issued in album form). The restrained mood of the first Soundcraft date was abandoned for the December 1957 follow-up, the recordings from which were of tunes that were favourites with the Metropole customers. J.C. Higginbotham is on trombone, and Sol Yaged on clarinet. Yaged shakes off the Benny Goodman *doppelgänger* role and creates some mellow solos, notably on 'South'. Stridency is the name of the game for this session's ensembles, and during the frantic final choruses Hawkins determindedly keeps a low profile, emerging, however, in all his glory for a stomping solo on 'Maryland'; his brief outing on 'Battle Hymn of the Republic' is also a gem.

During 1958 Hawkins (and some of his Metropole colleagues) took part in a series of programmes organized by a director of the television station WNTA, former disc-jockey Art Ford. These shows (Art Ford's Jazz Party) were transmitted live from Newark, New Jersey on Thursday evenings; they were also broadcast simultaneously on AM and FM radio. Almost a hundred famous jazz players were featured between May and December 1958. Most of the music was created in the jam-session format but star guests were given their own feature numbers. Hawkins took a two-chorus rove through 'Body and Soul' on one show, and on another he calmly played through an 'Indian Summer', despite having to contend with some unseasonal accompaniment from pianist Willie 'The Lion' Smith. There are some uneasy moments, harmonically and rhythmically, during this version of the Victor Herbert composition, but a feeling of unity is reached in the final bars.

Some of the jammed numbers on the shows, 'Air Mail Special' for instance, veer dangerously towards the chaotic, but here, and on a scrambled 'Bugle Call Rag', Hawk keeps his head while others flounder and manages to produce some stately solos. On one programme (25 September 1958), Hawkins and Lester Young were featured together. The two veterans unexpectedly engage in a three-chorus chase on 'Jumpin' with Symphony Sid', but no shots are fired in anger during the 'duel'; the exchanges take the form of affable, middle-register salutations.

Hawk's recording schedule as a leader in 1958 involved him in the making of several albums, none of which was a notably big seller. With hindsight it's easy to see that he had flooded the market. The record racks were full of his work, and even though there wasn't a truly bad record among this plethora, his strategy of playing on as many sessions as people would pay him to make had caused a glut. For all his years in the music business there were times when Hawkins would have benefited from the services of a shrewd personal manager. During the late 1950s and 1960s he tended to shun the use of agents and managers whenever he could.

Occasionally individuals attempted to look after Hawk's business affairs, but they were usually given short shrift. Sometimes he gave these temporary managers impossibly high quotes for club dates, knowing that there was a good chance that the club's owner would get back to him direct.

But Hawkins remained in demand as a sideman, and he was regularly booked to appear on other people's recording dates. One hesitates to say that Hawkins took to churning out records during this period because a supreme example of his skills could suddenly surface in the midst of an 'ordinary' date, but consistent inspiration became rarer. *Bean Bags*, an album made with Milt Jackson in September 1958, has the entire sextet: Hawkins, Jackson (vibraharp), Tommy Flanagan (piano), Kenny Burrell (guitar), Eddie Jones (bass) and Connie Kay (drums) playing as though they were working a dull club date on top of a draughty bandstand. The rhythm section achieve a relaxed feel on 'Close Your Eyes' but on all the up-tempo numbers they sound decidedly unsettled. Tommy Flanagan's ingenious use of substitute harmonies on the bridge of 'Get Happy' fails to inspire any special response from Hawkins, who is notably inventive only on a brief sixteen-bar outing on 'Don't Take Your Love from Me', a number that also has a subtle, highly rhythmic solo from Milt Jackson. The session suffers from a grievous lack of planning; solos fall into the same order on most tracks and both 'Sandra's' in the minor and 'Indian' in the major sound almost trite.

A better-planned and more estimable date was the 1958 session on which Hawk joined forces with Count Basie's saxophone team: Marshall Royal, Frank Wess, Frank Foster and Charlie Fowlkes, supported by a rhythm section in which Nat Pierce played the Count's role. Billy Van Planck's arrangements are well thought out but Basie's saxophonists seem to miss the competitive zip of the Count's brass team. Even so, Hawkins plays his role admirably and sounds convincingly involved on 'I've Grown Accustomed to Her Face', which has a Marshall Royal alto solo that contains a dash of Benny Carter mixed with a lot of pleasing originality. The best music occurs on the slow blues 'An Evening at Papa Joe's', where Frank Foster's bold blowing stirs Hawkins into a higher stratum.

Hawk had driven arranger Billy Van Planck out to Rudy Van Gelder's New Jersey studio in his Chrysler, and en route the two men became involved in a deep discussion about harmony. Van Planck still recalls with admiration the depth and wisdom of Hawk's words on the subject, but the session itself, despite lasting for nine hours, was generally a light-hearted affair. A slice of the good humour comes through on the record: following Marshall Royal's praise of Ben Webster's skill at sight-reading some Basie band arrangements, Hawkins asks, with a chuckle, 'Are you sure he wasn't taking them home?'[6]

In October 1958 Hawk guested for two numbers on a Tony Scott recording session, playing the first sixteen bars of 'Body and Soul' before handing over the release to Tony Scott's unpredictably brilliant clarinet playing. Tommy Flanagan makes his artistry felt in a brief solo then Scott again underlines his individuality by producing jazz that is both wistful and determined; Hawk returns to take the final solo and the concluding cadenzas. The adept trombonist Jimmy Knepper is added for a unison romp through 'Ornithology' 's theme; the front line then take turns to create brisk, lively solos before blowing another unison chorus of this bop anthem.

One session from this period (with Claude Hopkins' All Stars) must have reminded Hawkins of his days on the road with Mamie Smith during the early 1920s. This was the album that featured the fine blues-and-burlesque vocals of Juanita Hall. Some of the tunes have skeletal arrangements but most often the accompanying sextet's front line (Hawkins, Doc Cheatham on trumpet and Buster Bailey on clarinet) have to implement their quick-wittedness in backing a selection that relies heavily on the Bessie Smith repertoire. This tactic usually works smoothly, except in the case of 'Gimme a Pigfoot', where all three horn players sound in doubt. This is one of Buster Bailey's best latter-day recordings and Doc Cheatham is as reliable as ever. The failure of the album lies in the choice of tempos; almost everything is medium-slow. Hawkins plays solos on four tracks, blowing his best efforts – a relaxed, sonorous chorus – on 'Nobody Knows You when You're Down and Out'.

One of Hawk's own dates (in November 1958 for Prestige) was a particularly informal affair. As often happened, Hawk arrived at the studio without having made any elaborate plans about what he was going to record. This strategy could – and sometimes did – engender some relaxed and free-blowing dates, but often it produced hastily conceived, skimpy arrangements. During the 1950s countless tenor-sax-plus-rhythm-section recordings were made by modernists and by mainstreamers. A euphemism came into being that labelled many of these as 'blowing' dates, which usually meant that planning was at a minimum and a long blues (or two) was used to fill up time – and to gain the leader a good slice of composer royalties. 'Soul Blues' from Hawk's November date is a typical example of that genre; it curls its uninspired form across nine minutes of playing time.

During this session Hawkins heard Ray Bryant casually playing the old English air 'Greensleeves' on the piano and sauntering over, learnt the melody and its harmonies in an inkling and promptly recorded it. It was a mark of Hawk's musicianship, and supreme confidence, that he could greet new material and record it minutes later. Unfortunately his version of 'Greensleeves' is disappointing. Waltz time has sparked many fine jazz performances, but here it produces the sort of weary sounds that usually fill the tail-end of a sedate ballroom dance. One critic wrote that Hawkins played the tune as though 'he wanted to beat it to death', but nothing in the performance seems lively enough to convey a feeling of intended mayhem. Hawk, as usual, raises listening interests dramatically by playing a ballad, 'Until the Real Thing Comes Along', but even then the emotion is ladled out sparingly.

During this era several television producers attempted to convey the excitement of a live jam session to viewers, but their schemes almost always failed, either because the musicians were intimidated by the studio atmosphere or because their inspiration was blunted during countless rehearsals – for lighting, for sound, for camera angles and so on. The 'Timex' show of December 1957 had been a glorious exception, but one of that company's subsequent shows, in January 1959, produced what *Metronome* described as a monstrous version of 'Perdido', featuring Dizzy Gillespie, Roy Eldridge, Louis Armstrong, Vic Dickenson, Milt Hinton, Jo Jones, Marty Napoloen and Coleman Hawkins together with the entire Duke Ellington Orchestra (with Paul Gonsalves out front). Preceding that number was an up-tempo version of 'Body and Soul' in which Hawkins took the first sixteen bars, Eldridge, Gillespie and Dickenson are allocated morsels before Hawk creates a slow ending that salvages something from the disaster.

Neither Lester Young nor Billie Holiday (both of whom had starred in the 1957 show) were in the January 1959 production. They were in poor health; both died before the year had ended. In Lester Young's final interview he said, 'I think Coleman Hawkins was the President first. When I first heard him I thought, "That was some great jazz." As for myself, I think I'm the second one. If a guy plays tenor he's got to sound like Hawk or like Lester.'[7]

Hawkins didn't utter any public tributes at the time of Lester Young's death – in not making a valediction he was simply following his usual practice – but some while later he reflected, 'I liked Lester Young the first time I ever heard him, and I always got along very well with him. We were on a lot of tours together and I spent a lot of time with him, talking and drinking in hotel rooms and places like that.'[8]

Playing at the Metropole on Sundays, Mondays and Tuesdays must have occasionally blunted Hawk's enthusiasm, despite the high-class musicianship of his accompanists. His backing group underwent many changes, due to people getting better offers or going away on tour, and players who worked with Hawk at the Metropole included Al Wiliams, Ronnie Ball (pianists), Arvell Shaw and Peter Ind (bassists), Gus Johnson, Harold Austin, Nat Ray and Jackie Williams (drummers). Although the sign outside the Metropole said Dixieland in big letters, the music that Hawkins played there with his own rhythm section was definitely not of that ilk, but when working with pick-up backings he settled for a programme of well-worn standards. Happily he began to use a regular trio consisting of Joe Knight (piano), Francesco Skeets (bass) and J.C. Heard (drums), and this allowed him to play a lot of unfamiliar, intricate tunes.

Pianist Joe Knight worked regularly at the Metropole during the late 1950s:

> I got the job there through working with tenor saxist Hal Singer; previously I'd worked with John Coltrane in Earl Bostic's band, and actually there wasn't any huge differences in backing Coltrane or Hawkins. There was a musical universality that linked their styles. Hawkins had a huge knowledge of harmony – I would say a truly academic knowledge – and he knew a greal deal about the piano, he could demonstrate some very interesting inversions at the keyboard. The piano at the Metropole was a good upright, backed up to the wall, so that the pianist had his back to the audience. Hawk would look across and take an interest in how I was voicing a particular chord.
>
> I would describe Hawkins as pensive, but not broodingly so. He wasn't a brooder, but he could be a closed-mouth sort of guy. He maintained a detached, professional attitude at the Metropole, but this disappeared when he was with his friends in the Copper Rail. He didn't kid at all in the Metropole, but when he got in the Copper Rail he'd rib J.C. Heard, and especially someone like Buster Bailey, whom he'd known for years. But this was only with friends. It was interesting to see the difference between Hawk and Red Allen. Lots of old fans of Red Allen's turned up at the Metropole, those who'd bought his records years ago, and he used to be surrounded by these people. When he crossed to the Copper Rail he'd take them across Seventh Avenue all in tow, but Hawk wouldn't dream of doing that. He might exchange a few words with someone in the Metropole, but he felt his intermissions were a time to relax among friends, so he never left the Metropole in a crowd.[9]

Stanley Dance, a frequent visitor to the Metropole, observed, 'Coleman Hawkins seemed to stand aloof, like an aristocrat.'[10]

But the convivial atmosphere of the Copper Rail didn't make Hawkins throw caution to the wind when it came to buying a round of drinks; he retained his habitually tight grip on a dollar. There was one memorable occasion, however, when Hawk bought writer Dan Morgenstern a drink. Onlookers were astounded, and a few with superior memories were able to cite a similar incident that had occurred some years earlier when Hawk had treated his old friend Happy Caldwell to a bourbon in the White Rose bar. Tony Scott recalls, 'Hawk knew exactly when to be taciturn. He wouldn't buy anyone a drink in the Copper Rail; even if people, fans, bought him several, he'd never say "What are you drinking?" '[11]

Jazz-loving celebrities often dropped into the Metropole to catch a set or two, some of them making a night of it. One of these was the British actor Trevor Howard, who became friends with some of the musicians who worked there: 'I was always there at three in the morning and then used to go with them up to Harlem.' Howard often chatted to Hawkins and recalled an occasion when the saxophonist (who was still something of a film buff) thought the actor had walked out on him: 'We'd had a drink first, he knew I was there, and then when he looked to see me I'd moved seats. He was so upset I had to say, "I'm still here, fellow." '[12]

Drummer J.C. Heard said, 'The Metropole was the damndest place to play. Nobody made any money, but the cats just wanted to blow with each other. We'd go across the street to the Copper Rail or to Beefsteak Charlie's and everybody was lying and drinking. Oh, those were the good old days.[13] Hawkins invariably relaxed as soon as he entered the Copper Rail, and usually joined in the banter and jovial boasting that went on there. The bulk of the clientele were musicians, and many tales were told of yesteryear's escapades. Details of past hell-raising on tour were fondly recalled, memories of shared girlfriends were mulled over, and the aphrodisiac merits of various health-food products seriously debated. All this helped stoke the 'macho' atmosphere. None of the fifty-year-olds wanted to be thought of as ancient, and there was still a good deal of hinting about recent sexual conquests. Topics such as the latest sports results entered the conversations, as did comments on the latest automobiles. Serious talk about jazz was not exactly forbidden, but neither was it encouraged. Quite a few journalists found that it was not the ideal place to conduct an interview.

Dan Morgenstern recalled the lively atmosphere of the Copper Rail.

'Even when they were three-deep at the bar you could hear Hawk's laughter, or his voice emphasizing a point, from anywhere in the house. Though he was not a large man, his voice had a presence remarkably similar to his saxophone sound.'[14] Often the ambience stimulated Hawkins into re-creating the mischievousness that had been part of his persona during the years with Fletcher Henderson. One night in the Copper Rail he decided to wind up Roy Eldridge and Henry 'Red' Allen, both proud men who tended to look at fellow trumpeters with a quizzical and combative eye. Hawkins could not resist making some capital out of their attitudes. Buck Clayton witnessed the build up:

> One day I saw Red Allen and Roy Eldridge almost ready to have a fight. And all because Coleman Hawkins liked to play a kind of little practical joke. He goes up to Red, says something like, 'Red, I heard Roy say you couldn't even blow your nose if you had to.' Then he goes right along to Roy and tells him, 'Red says you must be slipping because he hears you're having trouble keeping up the payments on your car.' So both of them get to needling at each other and in the end there's the two of them wanting to take their coats off and fight, while Coleman gets off in a corner and laughs like hell.[15]

If, as sometimes happened, a musician working at the Metropole entered the Copper Rail with a woman at his side, winks and nudges were likely to be shared by his friends already seated at a bar, which displayed a sign saying 'Ladies will not be served without Escort'. Hawkins was far happier spending his intermission time talking to a beautiful woman than being pestered about recordings that he had forgotten making, so he rarely failed to provide a ready answer to any questions he received from these female visitors, often beaming at them as if to prove that he was still capable of producing a sudden, brilliant smile. One night at the Metropole Hawkins met a young woman, twenty years his junior, who became a very close friend. Roy Eldridge recalled, 'I introduced Heidi to Hawk. She came from Switzerland; that's where I met her originally. She turned up at the Metropole and I introduced them to each other; they clicked straight away.'[16]

During the late 1950s Roy Eldridge was often absent from the Metropole, particularly during the periods that he toured as an accompanist to Ella Fitzgerald. During Roy's absence Hawk worked alongside various trumpeters at the club, including Johnny Letman, Emmett Berry, Howard McGhee and Charlie Shavers. Shavers's effervescent style bubbled attractively on an album he made as a member of

Coleman Hawkins's Sextet in April 1959. The four-piece rhythm section (Ray Bryant, George Duvivier, Osie Johnson and Tiny Grimes) combine well, with guitarist Grimes also functioning as a soloist, creating some twangy but individual improvisations. 'Hawk Eyes' is a catchy thirty-two bar theme that shows Hawk in a harsh, driving mood, but despite expressing pleasure at working with Shavers he never hits top form. The slow blues 'C'Mon In' sets out promisingly with a Hawkins-Duvivier duet, but it soon degenerates into a sprawl, and the fade-out ending comes as something of a relief.

'Through for the Night' is a remake of the fine theme that Hawkins had recorded in 1944. Ray Bryant streamlines the 'Honeysuckle Rose' chord changes for this version. The call-and-answer interlude between Hawkins and Shavers promises much, but proves tantalizingly brief, and on 'I Never Knew' the piece ends just as Hawkins seems to be moving into a high gear. Shavers is nonchalantly daring for most of the album but shows his finesse during the harmon-muted solos. The most impressive item is 'La Rosita' (complete with verse), with Hawk achieving an interesting, ruminative mood. Ray Bryant on piano is tasteful and supportive throughout the date, but excels himself on this track.

Bryant, who had not long been in New York, had a style that was highly compatible both with modern and mainstream players. On one occasion he wryly made the point that the two styles were closer than most people acknowledged: 'In the afternoons I'd play at the Metropole with Roy Eldridge and Coleman Hawkins, and with Charlie Shavers, and at night-time I'd be down playing at the Five Spot with Benny Golson. I found that the same C chord I played at the Metropole worked down at the Five Spot at night.'[17] Bryant's versatility was tested on the *Stasch* album he made with Coleman Hawkins (in February 1959). Four of the six tracks are twelve-bar blues in various tempi, and since Bryant was notably good at playing the blues this in itself presented no problems, but the group was billed as the Prestige Blues-Swingers and so they set out to play a series of arrangements crammed full of stock riffs. In doing so they create a half-hearted, unappealing brand of rock and roll. The whole date sounds under-rehearsed and at times the front line is not quite in tune. There are some good solo spots, notably from trumpeter Idrees Sulieman on 'Roll 'em', where his chops are not at their best but he plays some idiosyncratic, original ideas. Jerome Richardson's alto sax sounds first-rate on the series of choruses he alternates with Hawkins on 'Stasch'. Richardson plays flute on the ballad 'Trust in Me', which contains the best Hawkins of the date (some breathtaking double-time improvisations). The rhythm section stick to their task of simply swinging, and make no attempt to parody poor music.

Recordings issued under the album title *Very Saxy* feature a summit meeting (held in April 1959) of four big-toned tenor saxists: Hawkins, Lockjaw Davis, Buddy Tate and Arnett Cobb. The electric organ was still enjoying its jazz vogue and Shirley Scott makes the most of it by playing swinging solos and good staccato backing figures, but the squeaky sound captured on record almost invalidates her good work. George Duvivier on bass and Arthur Edgehill on drums combine well to complete the rhythm team. The title track (based on the records of 'Sweet Georgia Brown') has all of the tenorists opening with a cagey chorus and then systematically building from there. All the phrases are energetic, but the effect is of a tag-wrestling match between lifelong friends. An air of synthetic liveliness also fills 'Lester Leaps In', but the solos on the various medium-tempo blues that make up the album are a good deal more satisfying and Hawk's solo on 'Foot Pattin'' is a feature of the album.

In that same month Hawk took part in another gathering of eminent jazz tenor saxists, this time sharing a recording with Ben Webster and Budd Johnson. Roy Eldridge was the solitary brass player and the four-piece rhythm section consisted of Jimmy Jones (piano), Ray Brown (bass), Les Spann (guitar) and Jo Jones (drums). The session, issued as by Ben Webster and Associates, typifies the lack of preliminary planning that debilitated so many mainstream sessions. Ben Webster's three blues compositions, 'Budd Johnson', 'De-Dah' and 'Young Bean' sound disappointingly makeshift, and their triteness is magnified by the obvious lack of thought concerning the routines; two of these blues use the same solo order: Johnson, Eldridge, Hawkins, drum breaks, Webster. All of the musicians involved were top-class jazzmen so no one disgraces himself, but inspiration is sadly lacking. Johnson and Eldridge play thoughtfully and enthusiastically on 'De-Dah', but Hawkins seems to chug his way through 'Young Bean' and 'Budd Johnson'. His playing is more exploratory on the slow (too slow) version of 'In a Mellow Tone', but his delivery has a troubled quality and the solo eventually trails away. Ben Webster himself sounds really happy only on his solo feature 'Time After Time'.

Hawk's schedule at the Metropole allowed him to work at various festivals during the summer of 1959. He played Newport in July, where he and Roy Eldridge were backed by Ray Bryant, brother Tommy Bryant on bass and Oliver Jackson on drums; for the finale the group was joined by vocalist Helen Humes. Later that same month Hawk visited Canada to appear at the Toronto Jazz Festival in a 'Seven Ages of Jazz' presentation devised by Leonard Feather; Hawk shared the stand with Buck Clayton, Tyree Glenn, George Auld, Terry Gibbs, Milt Hinton, Dick Hyman and Don Lamond. For the evening show (on 25 July) Hawk and Roy worked with George Wein on piano and three local musicians.

A memento of the 'Seven Ages of Jazz' presentations had been recorded the previous September during a concert held in Wallington, New York. The format was that of an organized jam session, with the front line of Hawkins, Clayton and Glenn producing some eminently satisfying interplay. The group was augmented by George Auld (playing tenor and baritone saxes) and Don Elliott (vibes and mellophone). None of the routines allows long solos, and this keeps everyone on their toes; they respond with concise but well-rounded improvisations. 'It Don't Mean a Thing' is particularly refreshing, and well received by the audience; it's obvious that Hawk's playing enraptured the crowd that day. His tone sounds particularly full on his feature 'If I Could Be with You One Hour', but he seems determined not to become involved in romanticism and takes a growling, almost aggressive run at the ballad. He is noticeably emphatic on a slow version of 'Stuffy' and exudes an even more formidable presence than usual on 'Indian Summer', which was his contribution to a ballad medley.

Hawkins and Eldridge were well used to taking their chances in working with local rhythm sections, but on one occasion during that summer of 1959 they found a highly compatible team at the Bayou Club in Washington, DC. Everything fell nicely into place and recordings issued from the engagement show the two visitors in superb form. Hawkins enjoyed the stimulating competition that Eldridge never failed to offer and, during 1959, even went as far as to admit, 'Roy and I get that good feeling going when we play together.'[18]

On 9 August 1959 Hawk went to Chicago to appear in the Playboy Jazz Festival held at the Chicago Stadium. He had to follow Ella Fitzgerald, who had received the only standing ovation of the festival, but (backed by Eddie Higgins on piano, Bob Cranshaw on bass and Walter Jenkins on drums) Hawk was reported by *Down Beat* to have survived creditably. Indeed, after a tumultuous welcome Hawk settles into a compelling version of 'All the Things You Are', swinging cohesively with the rhythm section, and not attempting to pull them this way or that. He hits a rocking groove on a medium blues, 'Centerpiece', which lasts for nine minutes, following this with a version of 'Body and Soul' on which he does a great deal more than go through the motions. His 'Just You Just Me' is less inspired but performed with considerable sustained energy. If Hawkins ever got stage fright, nobody – backstage or front – was ever aware of it; he still exuded a musical presence that automatically drew an audience's attention. Tenorist Johnny Griffin referred to this quality when he said, 'You can sense Coleman's personality and his character when he plays.'[19]

But Hawk was still having technical problems connected with his change of mouthpiece. He often made minor adjustments during this period, producing an uneven quality in his tone. His awesome confidence was not affected, but sometimes the mouthpiece didn't 'speak' properly, and this caused some of Hawk's high notes to sound empty. This is noticeable on two September 1959 sessions that Hawk did with vocalist Joe Turner (as part of an octet). The lack of instrumental response is apparent on 'Time After Time' and 'When I Was Young', and produces a harsh solo on 'Rebecca', but on the credit side Hawk plays some interesting substitute blues changes on 'Switchin' in the Kitchen' and delivers a fascinating solo on 'Until the Real Thing Comes Along'. Joe Turner's ballad singing could sometimes be a little eccentric, but here he observes the composers' lines rewardingly. The fine rhythm section of Jimmy Jones (piano), Jim Hall (guitar), Charlie Persip (drums) and Doug Watkins (bass) are good throughout, but hit a golden patch on 'Rebecca', where Watkins's playing is inspirational.

Hawkins and Eldridge travelled out to California to take part in the opening concert of the October 1959 Monterey Festival, where they shared the bandstand with Woody Herman, Urbie Green and the Earl Hines Trio. This all-star group was joined on stage by vocalist Jimmy Witherspoon for a set that thrilled the 6,000 in the open-air audience; five of Witherspoon's numbers were later issued on an album. Ben Webster is in the musical foreground with breathy solos on 'Good Rockin' Tonight' and 'Tain't Nobody's Business', and Roy Eldridge and Woody Herman take four rousing choruses apiece on 'Big Fine Girl' (backed by surging drumming from Mel Lewis). For most of this set Hawk's part was subsidiary, consisting of occasional background phrases, but on the slow blues 'When I been Drinkin'' his unexpectedly spartan solo is highly effective. Hawk opens up his two chorus innings by belting out some down-home phrases in the manner of a keen, if unsophisticated rhythm-and-blues saxist. It's a tongue-in-cheek ploy to get the audience cheering and it succeeds. Hawk keeps up the bombardment for most of the solo but adds a few elegant touches to what was one of his rawest efforts on record. Also in California, Hawk and Roy took part in what was billed as the first Los Angeles Jazz Festival, playing to a near-capacity crowd at the Hollywood Bowl. For this booking they were part of the Swing Era Sextet, which consisted of Hawk, Roy, Ben Webster, Pete Jolly (piano), Curtis Counce (bass) and Frank Butler (drums). Again *Down Beat* noted the triumph. 'They only did two numbers but the audience was yelling for more.'[20]

The only restriction imposed by most concert promoters relates to the amount of time a performer spends on stage; overrunning can create overtime bills and causes backstage friction. But one impresario for whom Hawkins worked in the late 1950s put an embargo on ballads. This was like asking George Burns to go on stage without a cigar, but even so Hawkins went ahead and did a fine job, revelling in the swinging accompaniment that pianist Red Garland provided. This was something of a reunion since Hawk had worked with Red Garland at the Down Beat club in Philadelphia during the mid-1940s.

Eventually, in August 1959, Hawkins recorded with Red Garland's trio (Doug Watkins, bass and Specs Wright, drums). The results are disappointing, considering the brilliance of this well-integrated rhythm section. Hawk sounds musically at ease, but physically uncomfortable, as though his new mouthpiece was cutting into his lip. Garland's skilful comping on 'Blues for Ron' almost sets things alight, but Hawk's efforts sound willing but weary. The iron control he usually maintained over his intonation is missing and his tone sounds astringent on 'I Want to be Loved'. Garland is his usual supple self (both as a soloist and accompanist) but, as on some other quartet sides from this era, Hawk seems ever so slightly out of synch with the rhythmic pulse that the trio is establishing. This nagging discrepancy always seems more obvious as the long saxophone solos develop, but a searing burst of four-bar chases between Hawkins and drummer Wright makes 'It's a Blue World' into an outstanding track.

22
A Jazz Doyen

In 1959 Hawkins took a sabbatical from the Metropole. Writing for *Jazz Journal*, Dan Morgenstern detailed the multifarious gigs and brief residencies with which Hawk filled his datebook during this period. Morgenstern listed a weekend booking in Pennsylvania on which Hawkins used trumpeter Booker Little, bassist Paul Chambers and drummer J.C. Heard. He also mentioned a residency in Chicago where the tenor saxist had been accompanied by a trio led by pianist Gene Harris. Hawk flew back from this residency on Monday 26 October 1959 and played that night at New York's Five Spot club in a session with pianist Randy Weston, recorded for United Artists. The assembly of the group used on this date depended on the co-ordination of various musicians' travel plans. Hawk came in from Chicago, bassist Wilbur Little from Washington, DC and drummer Roy Haynes from Boston. The arrangements came by air from Melba Liston, hospitalized in California.

Hawkins, Weston, Little and trumpeter Kenny Dorham assembled at 9.30 pm and were joined by drummer Clifford Jarvis, who temporarily took Roy Haynes's place. Without having any rehearsal the group buckled down and began recording the newly-arrived arrangements in front of the assembled audience – a tremendous test of musicianship. Hawk's deliberately harsh tone and Dorham's mellow sound make an effective contrast, and Weston's strong, two-handed playing gives the group a full, robust sound.

All of the solos are interesting without being sensational. Weston takes the main honours on 'Spot Five Blues' with a display of energetic inventiveness that causes the combative Hawkins to impart a sense of urgency to his opening phrases, but this solo never develops fully. Hawkins is featured on Billy Strayhorn's ballad 'Star Crossed Lovers' and creates one of his most tender latterday recordings; if the session had taken place in a studio the A & R man would have called for another take to eliminate the slight intonation problems that Hawk experiences in his high register, but even so the performance has a good deal of poignancy. Both Hawkins and Dorham are in good form on Brock Peters's dramatic vocal feature 'Where', and Roy Haynes (who ended up sharing drum duties with Clifford Jarvis) plays a lively solo on the jazz waltz 'Lisa Lovely'. Randy Weston was pleased and relieved that the session had gone so smoothly, since he had always had the highest regard for Hawk's work; 'I was a tremendous Coleman Hawkins fan. I discovered Monk from my love of Hawkins. The first time I heard Monk he was playing with Coleman Hawkins.'[1]

In his survey of Hawk's work schedule Morgenstern saved his longest description for a weekend booking at the Cork'n'Bib Club in Westbury, Long Island, on which Hawk used Eddie Costa on piano, Henry Grimes on bass and Paul Motian on drums. It was one of those occasions on which Hawkins chose to move into top gear. Morgenstern wrote:

> On Saturday night a lukewarm audience had gotten under Hawk's skin and since he felt like playing he decided to show them a thing or two. Working through a program of standards (mostly things he had recorded) Hawkins produced extraordinary versions of 'Out of Nowhere', 'Body and Soul', 'All the Things You are' and 'I Hadn't Anyone 'til You'. Hawkins, the master professional, had chosen the sort of tunes that he knew would delight the weekend crowd. In between his two sets there was some steady drinking by Hawkins but much of the energy came from the huge intake of spaghetti, and some of his delight from the company of a beautiful young woman . . . The sermon that Coleman Hawkins preached that night covered a lot of ground. It was one of those things that happen once in a while and which help keep the faith. Faith in the enduring strength and beauty of the music we call jazz, and in the greatness of that handful of men, Coleman Hawkins among them, who embody its spirits or rather its soul. Coleman Hawkins, whose playing constantly renews itself without ever losing its essence, is one of those who merit the title of genius.'[2]

Hawk's 1960 recording schedule began with a mainstream date involving trumpeter Joe Thomas and trombonist Vic Dickenson. The rhythm section of Tommy Flanagan, Osie Johnson and Wendell Marshall set up a kicking, swinging beat throughout, and the two brassmen solo in their inimitable ways, Dickenson rasping his way humorously through phrases that are much more complex than they sound, and Thomas constructing fat-toned, economical lines that show his enormous admiration for Louis Armstrong. Hawkins seems determined not to be lured into an easy-blowing mood and from the first notes of 'You Blew out the Flame' takes an obviously adventurous look at the tune's standard chord sequence. His five blues choruses on 'More Bounce to the Vonce' are full of pithy quips but, as usual, when playing a medium-tempo blues Hawk chose not to carry over his ideas into the next choruses, instead beginning each twelve-bar segment with a newly-minted phrase.

A Charleston beat launches Hawk's rendering of 'I'm Beginning to See the Light', then the rhythm section drop into a lively four-in-the-bar pattern for Hawk's three matter-of-fact choruses, followed by Joe Thomas's concise but highly satisfying efforts. Thomas's cup-muted solo also enhances the pedestrian 'Cool Blue' theme, which is also graced by Flanagan's piano solo (an attractive blend of clever ideas and quiet daring). Hawk sounds uninspired on that track, and doesn't manage to impart any real zest into his long solo on 'Some Stretching'. What set out to be a lively date for Hawkins thus subsided into little more than a sparring session for him.

Reflecting on various sessions he had shared with Hawkins (whom he greatly admired) Vic Dickenson recalled the bizarre start to one studio date.

> Hawk wasn't late but long after we'd unpacked our horns he sat in the corner listening to something on a small radio that he carried. I think it was a sports quiz; he kept shaking his head and nodding at what he was hearing through his tiny earphones. The producer knew Hawk of old; this was just as well because time was ticking away. We discussed our routines and blew some riffs and tunes and still Hawk hadn't even unpacked his tenor. Just as things were coming to a head the radio program ended and Hawk unpacked his tenor, and to my surprise he blew everything we'd been rehearsing, note-perfect. I'd seen some things in my time but this was it. He couldn't have known what we were going to do on the head arrangements we'd worked out, but he'd been listening to his radio and to us, and he was such a musician he caught up with what we'd taken an hour to think about in one minute.[3]

Hawk rarely became perturbed in a recording studio. On a Bob Prince session he arrived to discover that due to a misunderstood telephone conversation between himself and Prince an arrangement had been made of 'The Gypsy' that had a middle section that was sixteen bars long, instead of eight. Hawk simply grinned and said, 'Sounds great, and I like to do things that are different.' The piece was recorded in one take.[4]

Three weeks after Hawk's mainstream date with Thomas and Dickenson he returned to the studio with the same rhythm section but minus the two horns. All the tunes recorded were established standards (such as 'Poor Butterfly' and 'I'll Get By') in contrast to another 1960 Hawkins date on which only tunes written by the participants were used.

These recordings feature Hawkins with one of his favourite trumpeters, Thad Jones (Hawk also admired the playing of Thad's brothers, Hank and Elvin). Thad Jones was one of the most graceful of jazz trumpeters, his ample technique allowing him to distil and renovate ideas from many sources, and this is apparent on the free-flowing 'Cloudy', which features a lively chase between Thad and Hawk. The two men also present some effective contrapuntal ideas on 'Bean in Orbit'. Hawk is superb on 'After Midnight', where his 'new' tone conveys consummate experience without sounding world-weary. A bridge passage on 'Stalking' brings back vivid memories of Hawk's 1933 tune 'Queer Notions', and also allows the tenor saxist to develop a series of atonal runs. On 'Moodesville' the group dress up a twelve-bar blues by extending the dominant seventh section into six bars (thus making the chorus sixteen bars long). The main disappointment concerns the ordinary quality of most of the compositions, the slow 'Shadows' (with Nat Pierce on piano and Eddie Costa on vibes) being a notable exception.

Several items from these recordings bear the imprint of the recently established vogue for soul music and hard bop. The jazz dial had swung round and big, guttural tenor-sax tones were back in fashion. Instead of jazz being crowded out with Lester Young copyists using light tones and minimal vibratoes (relying mainly on linear improvisations), it became inundated with heavy-toned, fast technicians who flamboyantly explored the upper limits of extended arpeggios. Hawk was often referred to (not to his displeasure) as the direct instigator of this new movement, and was hailed by its leading practitioners as their doyen. His star again ascended but, as with the advent of bebop, Hawk chose to move alongside the hard boppers rather than become enmeshed in their stylistic quirks.

On an April 1960 live recording Hawk proved that his playing was timeless. The occasion was a concert at the vast Grugashalle in Essen, Germany, where he was featured with three seminal figures from the original bebop era: pianist Bud Powell, bassist Oscar Pettiford and drummer Kenny Clarke. Hawk is in superb form, producing a version of 'All the Things You Are' packed with new ideas, including some strong-jawed slurring patterns. Though Bud Powell was past his best, Hawk appears stimulated by the pianist's ingenious, if unpredictable chordings, and blows a magnificent 'Yesterdays' (which contains one of the most powerful reed squeaks ever recorded). There is none of the uninteresting 'chugging' that sometimes marred Hawk's work in the late 1950s and

1960s (particularly when he tackled up-tempo material) and 'Stuffy' is full of terse, swinging phrases.

Hawk moved from Germany into Holland, where he had a reunion with one of his most ardent pre-war fans, Pete Felleman, who recalls:

> Hawk, Kenny Clarke and Oscar Pettiford played at the Concertgebouw in Amsterdam, second on the bill to Dave Brubeck's quartet. These three had been working in Essen with Bud Powell, but the Dutch promoter had experienced previous problems with Powell so the group worked in Amsterdam as a trio. I knew Kenny Clarke well and he greeted me warmly when I entered the dressing room. Hawk didn't recognize me; he had seen me at seventeen and now I was thirty-eight. However, after I started talking about the Palace in 1937 and 1938 and reminding him of his long versions of things like 'Bei Mir Bist Du Schoen' he smiled and said to Kenny, 'This cat is a real old-timer.' He told me that he had just sent a telegram to Freddy Johnson, telling him that he was back in Amsterdam. He was friendly, more mellow than he had been in pre-war days, less aggressive.[5]

Hawk's spirited inventiveness made itself obvious on an octet session he did with Jimmy Rushing back in New York during the summer of 1960. Most of the backings are arranged but there are some fine moments of ad-libbing and Hawk makes a wonderful job of the sixteen bars he is allocated on 'Trouble in Mind'. On the fast version of 'Muddy Water' Hawkins for once fails to interpret the harmonic twists of an unexpectedly interesting sequence, but still manages to deliver his phrases with considerably panache, doubtless stirred by the exciting drum work of Jimmy Crawford.

The festival circuit kept Hawkins occupied for a good part of the summer of 1960, but he didn't take part in that year's Newport Jazz Festival, choosing instead to play (in July) at the rival Cliff Walk Manor Festival, held close to the Newport site and organized by bassist Charles Mingus and drummer Max Roach. Hawk revisited the Hollywood Bowl to play a concert on 18 June, this time as part of a front line featuring Roy Eldridge, Ben Webster, Benny Carter and Rex Stewart.

Hawk journeyed a lot further west in October 1960 when, as a member of a star-studded jazz package, he went to Australia. The troupe were booked to appear in what was billed as Australia's first International Jazz Festival (organized by promoter Lee Gordon) and were scheduled to play dates in Adelaide, Melbourne, Brisbane and Sydney. The American contingent in the show consisted of Hawkins, Dizzy Gillespie, Al Hibbler, Sarah Vaughan, Dakota Staton, Gene McDaniels and the Teddy Wilson Trio (Wilson, Arvell Shaw on bass and Bert Dahlander on drums). Hawk usually did his sets backed by Dahlander, bassist Freddie Logan and pianist John Griffiths. Travelling vast distances meant nothing to Hawkins; on one occasion he said, 'I'd play in Timbuktu if they paid me.'[6] The show's itinerary turned out to be less extensive than Lee Gordon had originally envisaged so he decided to fulfil his commitments to the American musicians by having them work at his Pigalle Club in Centennial Park, Sydney. The Australian multi-instrumentalist John Sangster recalled the situation:

> I guess Lee's planned concert tour had gone 'arsa peak' so we wound up in the same dressing rooms as Teddy Wilson and Coleman Hawkins and the like. Dressing rooms? The two bands and the waitresses and the lady strippers and all shared this World War I dugout under the stage. Anyhow, there was Coleman Hawkins doing two shows a night with the American band. Used to drink a bottle of sweet sherry in two gulps before going up the stairs on to the stage. Each show. And that's after huge eight-paper joints had been passing round. I asked Mr Hawkins how he managed to keep up the pace. He told me, 'I'm a working man; my work is playing the jazz saxophone, and it's hard work. Half an hour on stage and I sweat it all out.'[7]

Hawkins finished his stint in Sydney and flew back to New York.

The JATP package that Norman Granz took to Europe in November 1960 consisted of Cannonball Adderley's group, plus Dizzy Gillespie, J.J. Johnson, Jo Jones, Benny Carter, Roy Eldridge, Lalo Schifrin, Art Davis and Coleman Hawkins; Don Byas joined up with the show when they reached Europe. The itinerary was a daunting one, covering Holland, Germany, Sweden, France and England. The only sprinting undertaken on this trip was from one aeroplane to another. Hawkins slept while less experienced travellers in the party tried to get a glimpse of famous landmarks. To the amusement of some of the younger tourists, Hawk slept solidly through one beautiful vista after another, unaware that Nat Adderley and vocalist John Hendricks were taking a series of photographs of him. Hawk's ability to take catnaps on the bumpiest of journeys led Jo Jones to bestow on him the nickname 'Snooze'.

But, like a hibernating bear, Hawkins could quickly move back into action, as he demonstrated when the JATP show flew into Sweden on 21 November 1960. Hawk was met at Stockholm Airport and driven straight to the Metronome recording studio, where (accompanied by Harry Arnold's Swedish Radio Studio Orchestra) he recorded an outstanding version of 'On the Sunnyside of the Street' and a commendable 'Tea for Two'. Playing these ultra-familiar standards, backed by a sixteen-piece band, full of highly competent sidemen, was an easy task for Hawkins, but he didn't rest on his laurels and instead played with a lot of spirit and flair. 'Sunny Side' is full of interestingly developed ideas, robustly blown and climaxed in a remarkable series of candenzas. On 'Tea for Two' Hawk unleashes some thrustful phrases that almost get the band swinging. After an eight-bar solo from pianist Rune Ovferman, Hawk re-emerges, sounding as fresh as a daisy despite his already gruelling day.

Anyone who attended shows on this tour must have been struck by the fact that on some performances Hawkins was lackadaisical throughout yet, on the very next night, inspiration took over and he blew solos that eclipsed the efforts of everyone in the esteemed cast. Max Harrison wrote about one of the indifferent nights in a *Jazz News* report: 'Hawkins appeared little interested in the proceedings and played far below his best. The wonderful tone and control were obvious, yet they were used to little real purpose. Hawkins was badly cut by Don Byas, whose long European exile from good American rhythm sections has not weakened his powers in the least.'[8]

Don Byas was a skilful and consistent performer who was never reluctant to discuss his own talent; he said: 'There have never been but three schools of tenor; the first was Coleman Hawkins, the second Lester Young and the third was me. You see I was the only one of that sort of Hawkins school who had modern ideas with it.'[9] It was true that Byas had inspired a number of younger tenor saxists, including Benny Golson, who said, 'Don Byas is the one that set me back on my heels when I first heard him in person,'[10] and reed-player Roland Kirk, who affirmed, 'To me Don Byas had it all; I think he had it over them all, even Hawkins.'[11]

Don Byas was not in the least afraid to mix it with Hawkins on the bandstand, but he always paid homage to Hawkins's influence and cited him as his original inspiration: 'That sound always stayed with me and never got away. Hawkins and Benny Carter – though Art Tatum influenced me more than any horn player.'[12] After that 1960 JATP tour had ended Byas said philosophically, 'I always had the dream to be the world's greatest tenor player. I doubt if I ever will make it now. I have no regrets.'[13]

That 1960 JATP gathering gave Byas the opportunity to share numbers with Hawkins and Carter, and recordings made at the Konserthuset in Stockholm on 22 November produced some interesting combats. On 'Take the A Train' Carter's solo eclipses the efforts of both tenor players. After making a quiet entry Hawkins begins exploring but somehow seems shackled whereas Carter's lines have a carefree quality, and he successfully introduces some unexpected 'jump' phrases that add an air of freshness. Byas shows some ingenious touches and uses the soulful sound of his high register to advantage but doesn't succeed in stringing his ideas together in good formation. Carter is again superb on 'Indiana', sounding as though he were enjoying himself; Hawk is more adventurous here and Byas's technique creates some spectactular runs. Roy Eldridge takes two husky middle-register choruses then moves upwards to evoke excitement. During the rhythm section's solos Lalo Schifrin's polished piano phrases epitomize his lithe touch, Art Davis plucks and bows with skill and spirit and Jo Jones takes a long, impressively ambidextrous drum feature.

Hawkins's infallible ballad skills make his version of 'These Foolish Things' the most superior aspect of a four-part medley. He begins casting elaborate variations from the off, adorning the tune with harmonies and ideas that are more advanced than anything his confreres on the platform were creating. Byas's 'Yesterdays' (strange that he chose a celebrated Hawkins feature) is full of superbly developed melodic twists, but it is much less forward-looking than Hawk's preceding achievement. All the septet are featured on a blues entitled 'Jazz Portrait of Brigitte Bardot', within which Hawk constructs a long, impressive solo. The denouement is complicated, with a near light-hearted section in which Hawk quips his brief phrases, but he soon becomes sterner and, backed by some insistent chording from Schifrin, produces climactic figures that seem to indicate that an epoch-making conclusion is in the pipeline. Instead, Hawkins winds down calmly and hands over to Benny Carter. Don Byas does his utmost to top Hawk's efforts but doesn't succeed and eventually runs out of steam, not before blowing (with an air of desperation) some shrill high notes that must have caused Hawkins to smile inwardly. The 'All the Things You Are', with Stan Getz added, is something of a disappointment. Getz produces a thousand and one elegant ideas but all of them are delivered with the same emotional content. Hawkins and Byas fail to hit top form and the long series of four-bar chases involving the three tenor saxists never takes off.

Don Byas had once told Eddie 'Lockjaw' Davis, 'Coleman Hawkins could never play really fast; his tone was just too big.'[14] Soon after returning from his European confrontations with Byas, Hawkins had occasion to make an album with Lockjaw (on 30 December 1960). It's an interesting pairing, one that seems to have stimulated both tenor players, who were aided by an inspiring rhythm section consisting of Tommy

Flanagan on piano, Ron Carter on bass and Gus Johnson on drums. Lockjaw, an intriguing mixture of Hawkins, Webster and his own individuality, shows that he was a swifter player than Hawkins, but Hawk's ideas are more intricate and his sense of thematic development more acute than the younger man's. On the eight-bar 'Nighthawk' theme Hawkins seems determined to show that his tone was even broader than Lockjaw's formidable sound, but Davis evens things up by playing 'In a Mellow Tone' with a defter touch; the horns play a simple unison version of Duke Ellington's tune, and this unelaborate exposition is beautifully bordered by Tommy Flanagan's ingenious use of substitute chords. Lockjaw's solo is full of bustling ideas that seem to fly from his fingers, whereas Hawk sounds as though he had played the sequence too often that week.

The twelve-bar blues 'Pedalin'' shows Hawkins much more in command, producing a spate of rich ideas in his concluding chorus. On 'Lover' Davis takes the honours in a generally undistinguished version, but Hawkins has the edge on a superb 'There is No Greater Love', where he creates a memorable counterpoint to Davis's melody lead. Throughout the song the old master sounds relaxed and eager to communicate a vast array of ideas, the best of which he saves for the closing bars of his third and final chorus. Lockjaw gives chase and blows clusters of intensely played sixteenth notes; his third chorus is full of lusty challenges but none of them supplants the memory of Hawk's earlier solo. Both tenor saxists play gloriously on 'Don't Take Your Love from Me' but Hawkins's reflective almost gentle exposition is the more convincing.

Hawkins was in variable form on tracks recorded in April 1961 with an all-star nine-piece band which included trumpeter Joe Newman and clarinettist Jimmy Hamilton (who did the arrangements). On 'Spring's Swing', Hawk, following Newman's mellow solo, enters with all the energy of a young lion and all the skills of an old champion. The tenor saxist is allocated two choruses, whereas all the other soloists are granted only one. Guitarist Tiny Grimes's novel chorded solo isn't offensive; Jimmy Hamilton remains, as usual, a model of precision, Hilton Jefferson plays warm-toned and tidy alto-sax phrases, but J.C. Higginbotham is unfortunately only a shadow of his former self. A series of four-bar chases are disappointingly uneventful but the rhythm section of Claude Hopkins (piano), Wendell Marshall (bass) and Bill English (drums) maintain a light, bright beat, though elsewhere on the album they are less spry. A medium-tempo blues, 'Jammin' in Swingville', has Hawk trotting out four urbane choruses; his colleagues follow suit and only Joe Newman attempts to stir up excitement. Here, Higginbotham sounds more in command, but Hopkins's piano solo is prim and restricted. 'Cool Sunrise', a meandering twenty-bar composition, has another batch of innocuous solos. Hawkins bustles in as though intent on cutting away the layers of sleekness but he is soon nudged into the pervading mood by uneventful rhythmic support. 'Love Me or Leave Me' also has a series of lyrical, undramatic performances, but Hawk's artistry triumphs. He adopts a poetic approach devoid of harshness, creating a series of glowing horizontal phrases.

Norman Granz's tours still regularly visited Europe, but there had been no JATP travels in the USA since 1957. Few promoters were prepared to take the financial risks involved in organizing tours of star jazz musicians within America, but occasionally various entrepreneurs other than Granz formed a concert unit for an overseas trip. Impresario-producer Monte Kay organized an impressive American Jazz unit for a three-week tour of South America in July 1961. The show, which was compered by Willis Conover (of Voice of America fame), featured Coleman Hawkins, Roy Eldridge, Zoot Sims, Al Cohn, Kenny Dorham, Curtis Fuller, Ahmed Abdul Malik, Ronnie Ball, Dave Bailey, Chris Connor, Tommy Flanagan and Jo Jones.

For tenorist Al Cohn it was a chance to work in close proximity to one of his early heroes.

> I first saw Coleman Hawkins on 52nd Street. I was a youngster learning my instrument and I was tremendously impressed not only by Hawkins's music but also by his sophistication and his manner. He was an aristocrat, and so sharply dressed. Beautiful women were always with him. Later, on the tour of South America, most of us shared a large dressing room and it was there that I realized how witty Hawkins was; he said some shrewd things about many subjects. He and Roy Eldridge used to start talking and saying amusing things; it was very entertaining and enlightening. The rest of us sat around enjoying every word.[15]

Jo Jones, Tommy Flanagan and Ahmed Abdul Malik were the accompanying trio for Hawkins and Eldridge on the South American trip. Jones, who had known Hawkins for years, kept up a running gag about Hawk's vast wealth throughout a tour that took the musicians through Brazil, the Argentine, Uruguay and Chile. Jones found Hawkins to be a fount of knowledge about an unexpected subject: 'Coleman Hawkins was crazy about plants. We went off to South America and Hawk was telling me all about these plants. He had one plant and said, "I'm giving my plant some gin. I drink it, so can my plant." '[16] After returning home Hawkins continued to buy dozens of species of exotic indoor plants, but the craze soon subsided. Hawkins had previously gone through bouts of avid collecting, accumulating stamps, cameras, electric trains, tropical fish and model cars, but their appeal was transient.

Much more permanent was Hawk's love of kidding. On the South American trip the musicians got involved in a long discussion about various countries in the world and bassist Ahmed Abdul Malik said how much he would like to visit Ethiopia. Hawk snorted and said, 'Man, I've been there.' Malik, hoping to hear a first-hand account of life within that fascinating ancient kingdom, plied Hawk with questions. The veteran listened solemnly for some minutes and then offered a solitary pronouncement, 'Couldn't eat a thing there.' Recordings taken from a concert on the South American tour, however, confirm that whatever the circumstances Hawk never let frivolity play any part in his music. The tracks show that the quintet had soon achieved a robust, stimulating blend. Unfortunately the recording quality is disappointingly variable, but Hawk's 'Body and Soul' feature sounds fresh and full of invention.

Altogether, 1961 was a successful and lucrative year for Hawkins. He was featured at several festivals in the USA and also played many casual dates on the East Coast: at rotary clubs, at night clubs and again at the Metropole. British bassist Peter Ind, who lived and worked in the USA for most of the 1950s and early 1960s, played regularly with Hawkins during this period:

> I played some gigs with Roy Eldridge during the 1950s, and everything went fine, so he introduced me into the quintet. I worked with Roy and Hawk for about eighteen months on and off. They were a great team musically, but they were entirely different people; I think you could almost say there was a love-hate relationship between them. We not only worked at the Metropole, we did gigs out on Long Island, various festivals, Tanglewood, Mass, etc. On one 'society' gig out at Southampton, Long Island (I think pianist Marty Napoleon was with us on that one), the woman running the gig said to Hawk, 'How nicely you play. I feel that you've been a musician for quite a while. What is your name?' With a smile Hawk replied, 'Coleman' and the woman said, 'Well, Mr Coleman let me say how delighted we are that you are here.' It gave me an insight into the fact that, although every jazz musician in the world revered Coleman Hawkins, few of the American general public had any idea who he was.
>
> Hawk had a dry sense of humour; some of it could be a bit acidic. He came to my recording studio on the Lower East Side to take part in an album with Max Roach,

> and he spotted the ten-inch reflector telescope I kept there. Hawk questioned me about it and when I began telling him how interested I was in astrology and cosmology he laughed and said, 'Don't give me that old shit, the only reason anyone would want a telescope that big would be to see the girls in Brooklyn undressing. Hey, let me try and see what's happening in those apartments!'[17]

The Max Roach recording was of the *Freedom Now* suite; Hawk appeared on only one track, playing the role of the principal soloist on 'Driva' Man'. On this Hawk creates some highly atmospheric phrases against the deliberately stark backgrounds scored by Roach. His strongly conceived solo was marked by a couple of reed squeaks but Hawk was prepared to let them remain on the record, saying, 'No, don't splice. When it's all perfect, especially in a piece like this, there's something very wrong.'[18]

Hawkins was also briefly featured in the presentation of the suite (early in 1961) at the Village Gate club in New York, where the production was sponsored by the Council of Racial Equality. For Hawk this was simply a case of fulfilling a booking to work alongside Max Roach, whom he admired. He steadfastly refused to become actively involved in any overt political activities. When asked about the Black Muslims and segregation, he replied:

> I know it's around me but I don't know anything about that stuff. I'm a musician, I play music. That's my job. There is a 'Back to Africa' movement now. People wearing robes, cutting their hair, playing African rhythms in their music and all that. I mind my own business. Some musicians say, 'I won't play white men's music'. Why, that's ridiculous. I play white men's music – they wrote some beautiful things. Playing African music in America is like Africans playing jazz. It just can't be done right.[19]

In April 1961 Hawkins took a restrained role in a recording session organized to create a comeback album for the veteran blues singer Ida Cox, then seventy-two years old. The vocalist had retained her gift for delivering lyrics admirably, but her once magnificent voice had lost most of its flexibility. Roy Eldridge puts effort and feeling into his solos and is near brilliant on 'Lawdy Lawdy', but Hawkins often sounds subdued in attempting, it seems, to simplify his ideas to fit the circumstances. At times he sounds out of place, as though he were inhibited by pianist Sammy Price's authoritative (and apt) blues phrases. On 'Hard Times' the saxophonist gets some spoken encouragement from Ida Cox, but elsewhere his instrumental answers to her vocal lines sound peremptory. One novelty is the series of four-bar chases between Eldridge and Hawkins on 'Fogyism'; they rarely used this tactic when they performed a slow twelve-bar blues.

Hawk guested on a Sol Yaged session recorded live at the Metropole in May 1961, his efforts grafted into a group modelled on the Benny Goodman Quintet. The leader's clarinet and Harry Sheppard's vibes are heavily featured, but Hawk plays some robust solos, urged on by the crowd. He moves imperiously through the gears for a compelling version of 'I Can't Get Started', which contains many ingeniously connected musical asides.

But despite all his freelance recording activities, Hawkins did only one session under his own name in 1961. This was in February, when he was backed by a four-piece rhythm section consisting of Ronnell Bright (piano), Kenny Burrell (guitar), Ron Carter (bass) and Andrew Cyrille (drums). The album was appropriately called *Hawk Relaxes*; five of the seven selections are ultra-slow ballads. Hawk deliberately (and smoothly) stresses the melody on a series of evergreen standards, relying heavily on legato phrasing but at no stage becoming maudlin, and on 'Just a Gigolo' he takes a wry, sardonic approach to the tune. Burrell's guitar playing fortifies Hawk's mood and when he and Ron Carter play as a duo behind Hawkins on 'When Day is Done' the effect is elating. Bright's chording is effective and his solos neat, and the unconventional punctuations from Cyrille preclude any displays of lethargy. The two non-slow American numbers, 'Moonglow' (taken at a jog) and 'Speak Low' (with a Latin American beat), are the least successful on the album.

Soon after their return from South America, Hawkins and Roy Eldridge began playing a series of occasional dates at the Museum of Modern Art on West 53rd Street, New York. The two of them also took part in a short film that purported to be an after-hours session in a 52nd Street club (it was actually shot in Leon and Eddie's shuttered nightspot, in front of professional extras). The film, intended to be the pilot for a television series, featured Hawkins, Eldridge, Barry Galbraith, Milt Hinton, Cozy Cole, Johnny Guarneri and vocalist Carol Stevens. A behatted Hawkins, smartly dressed in a dark suit, joins the supposed late-night jam session and plays a resourceful 'Lover Man' which starts relaxedly but builds up to an impressive, passionate finale. Roy Eldridge bursts into the club, trumpet in hand, and creates a fiery version of 'Sunday', in which Hawk is the bit player. The two giants share a version of 'Taking a Chance on Love' then reprise the same tune to back Carol Stevens's vocal. The set ends with

'Just You Just Me' in which Eldridge and Carol Stevens swop bursts of scat-singing. The atmosphere of the film is contrived but what is genuine enough is the fervour of Hawkins's tight-eyed performance on 'Lover Man'.

Also in 1961, Hawkins, Eldridge (and Jo Jones) were seen in the television drama series *Route 66*. The episode, entitled 'Goodnight Sweet Blues', featured veteran singer-actress Ethel Waters. Roy Eldridge thrived on the occasion, particularly as he was cast as a drummer (Jo Jones was depicted as a trumpeter); each of these two musicians were given lines to speak, but not Hawkins. This suited Hawk fine. At the rehearsals Eldridge examined his script, to discover that Hawk's only verbal contribution to the drama was to say 'Uh-huh'. He asked Hawkins, 'Is uh-huh all you have to say?' Naturally, Hawkins replied, 'Uh-huh'.[20]

During the 1960s Hawk's former colleague, cornettist Rex Stewart, developed a well-deserved reputation as a journalist. During the course of one of his features for *Down Beat* magazine he wrote of Hawkins's taciturn qualities: 'Both in print and in recorded interview he seldom has a good word for his peers. You may question Hawk for an opinion about anyone from Duke Ellington to Louis Armstrong, and the best you can expect is some kind of derogatory remark or grunt, which may indicate anything or nothing. Then later he has been heard gleefully telling how he fooled someone again.'

Yet some young musicians, such as bassist Larry Ridley, who got to know Hawkins during the early 1960s, found him to be friendly and loquacious. Ridly recalls:

> I first saw Hawk in the early 1960s, but my first jobs with him were at Pio's Lodge in Providence, Rhode Island. I think it was a two-week stay and I think we flew up there. I was on bass, Clifford Jarvis on drums and Paul Neves on piano. We had some great times up there. After the gig we'd sometimes sit and talk until the sun was coming up. Hawk told me that listening to European classical music gave him lots of ideas and encouraged him to take a different approach to improvising. He was very much into new ideas and liked to encourage young musicians to describe how a piece of music affected them. It was easy to see how he had taken to Monk and to Oscar Pettiford. I called him 'Bean'. One day I said to him, 'How come you have such a big tone; it seems to come up from the tip of your toes,' and he laughed and laughed. In the whole history of jazz I think only Sonny Rollins had that same sort of fullness as Hawk. He'd talk about his early days with Fletcher Henderson and his travels. He loved to talk about trains and when he found out that I was from Indianapolis, Indiana (which was a railroad hub for many areas) he told me about various journeys he made through Indianapolis years and years before. He talked about the vast

circuits they used to play, the country dances, and gigs through so many Mid-western towns. But he also spoke about later days and laughingly told me how one of the trios he'd used on tour got themselves into a problem that involved the local police. Bean was a Mason and he had to use this as leverage in getting the young musicians out of trouble.[21]

For Hawk's long-time fans the most intriguing recording date of 1961 was a session organized and supervised by Nat Hentoff which reunited Hawkins with Pee Wee Russell. It was the first time the two stalwarts had made a studio recording together since the 1929 Mound City Blue Blowers' date (though they had shared radio and television gigs). A fine band consisting of Emmett Berry (trumpet), Bob Brookmeyer (valve trombone), Jo Jones (drums), Milt Hinton (bass) and Nat Pierce (piano) was assembled but the vibrant atmosphere of the earlier encounter wasn't recaptured. It was not meant to be a re-creation session, but the success of the original meeting led fans to develop sentimental hopes about the reunion.

Comparisons between the magic abandon displayed on the 1929 'One Hour' and this group's 'If I Could Be With You One Hour Tonight' are inevitable, considering that both tunes share the same sequence. In fact, to all intents and purposes they are the same tune, but after someone pointed out to Hawkins that his 1929 'One Hour' recording had not been entered as the James P. Johnson classic, he decided (after some prodding) to claim composership and made (with Bob Thiele's help) a successful application to ASCAP (The American Society of Composers, Authors and Publishers). On the 1961 session the tune is positively listed as written by James P. Johnson and Henry Creamer. It sets out interestingly with Emmett Berry's acrid-sounding harmon-muted trumpet playing and Russell's astringent clarinet tone sharing the melody. Hawkins enters by playing a swaggeringly impressive break and begins what promises to be a masterful solo, but the fingers aren't locked into the flow of his ideas and there are several minor fluffs. To his credit Hawkins makes no attempt to revisit Memory Lane and the last bars of his first chorus are boldly contemporary. His second chorus is cohesive and embossed with crisply played double-tempo runs but the solo never begins to suggest the deep passions displayed on the original.

Soon after the album was issued writer George T. Simon asked Hawkins about the stylistic changes in his playing during the long period that had elapsed between the two dates. Hawk replied, 'I didn't change consciously. All I can tell you is I always play the way I feel – it can be this sort of mood or that sort of mood, but I'm not interested in trying to please other musicians. I just want to please myself . . . and the public too.'[22]

Leaving comparisons aside, there are many enjoyable moments on the 1961 date, but a more extended session might have eased out some of the stiffness that mars the playing of the rather bitty arrangements. Bob Brookmeyer's particular brand of eclectic inventiveness is perfect for this group, and all of his solos – dainty and vigorous – come off successfully, particularly on 'All Too Soon' (where the rhythm section's co-ordination is superfine). On this number Hawkins's second eight bars contain a gorgeous flow of melody, but in the last section of his solo on the quirky '28th and 8th' blues he and Jo Jones play a fidgety duet in which the tempo only just manages to survive, making the closing theme lurch to a conclusion.

When the session ended, Nat Pierce commented on Pee Wee Russell's inventiveness, and Brookmeyer followed up by praising the clarinettist's daring. Hawkins joined in and said, 'I know, I know. For thirty years I've been listening to him play those funny notes. He used to think they were wrong, but they weren't. He's always been way out, but they didn't have a name for it then.'[23] But Pee Wee Russell's own modest account of the exchanges was interestingly different; he recalled, 'Brookmeyer came up and said, "I didn't know you could play modern, Pee Wee." Bean broke in and said, "Pee Wee was playing like that thirty years ago. He doesn't know what he's doing, but he's doing it and that's the way he feels." '[24]

Down Beat published a nice vignette of the session's aftermath. As usual, as at almost every recording session he ever made, Hawkins had found his way to the piano keyboard:

> Hawkins sat at the piano and worked over the chords of a sentimental melody – the kind he calls 'a tear-jerker'. 'I'm going to record that some day,' he said, 'I've been working on it for a little while.'
>
> 'Maybe like forty-five years,' Nat Pierce said.
>
> 'Ha! You like it then,' said Hawkins. 'You know, I've been making records with Max Roach and Eric Dolphy and them cats lately. Here Berry [trumpeter Emmett Berry], listen to this. You hear this chord. That's what those kids are doing. They hit this chord and all the time they got this other thing going down here. You hear it? Then they say, "Go, you got it, Bean." But it's interesting. That's what music's all about anyway – finding those things; the adventure. You know, the young ones get confused about me being able to play with them. What they don't know is that I got tired of this chord, this one and that one by the time I was thirteen. Hell, I was listening to Stravinsky when I was a kid. You've got it. It's not a question of being modern. It's just music – adventure – Pablo Casals – my he can play. But he's all the

time playing those Bach things now. He's through with the adventure. Hell, he must be ninety years old. You know, you start off with those Bach things. You get to be his age, you end with them. In between is the adventure. Now it's over for him. Maybe that's what I'll do when I get that old.'[25]

During the early 1960s the tides of inspiration might not have flowed as often for Hawkins as they had done in the past, but he was still as serious about, and as involved with, his music-making. He told Stanley Dance:

I think a solo should tell a story, but to most people that's as much a matter of shape as of what the story is about. Romanticism and sorrow and greed – they can all be put into music. I can definitely recognize greed. I know when a man is playing for money. And, good gracious, there's plenty of that going on right now![26]

A few months after the recording session with Pee Wee Russell, Hawkins took part in another reunion album called *Further Definitions*, sharing top billing with Benny Carter, who arranged eight numbers for a four-sax line-up. They included two tunes he and Hawkins had recorded (with Alix Combelle and André Ekyan) in Paris during April 1937. This time Hawkins's and Carter's front-line partners were Phil Woods on alto and Charlie Rouse on tenor. To strengthen the links with the earlier date, a guitarist (John Collins) was used; Django Reinhardt had been on the original session. Working with Collins were Dick Katz (piano), Jo Jones (drums) and Jimmy Garrison (bass).

The individuality of all four saxophonists leaves no room for doubt as to the order of the soloists. Charlie Rouse's phrases suggest a laidback attitude but all his lines are thoughtful and resilient, and it is he who takes top honors on 'Doozy', an ingenious Carter blues. Phil Woods plays solos full of vitality and ingenuity on 'Honeysuckle Rose' and 'Crazy Rhythm'; without sacrificing his originality he captures the mood of the date to perfection. After a long period in which he devoted his time to composing and arranging, Benny Carter had resumed playing saxophone regularly. Though his performances here are impeccable, an air of hauteur pervades most of his solos on the date, but his scoring for the saxophones is lyrical and imaginative. Within the section, the four saxophonists submerge their individuality to form an impressively integrated unit. As a young man, Hawkins often seemed powerfully conspicuous in a sax team, but in later years he learnt to harness his musical strength and to divert it into his solos. This gave him the ability to blend more easily with his section colleagues, as he does so admirably here.

Surrounded by skilful, competitive soloists Hawkins seeks and finds new ideas: the middle section of his solo on 'Cottontail' has a novel twist and he successfully experiments with alternate fingerings on 'Midnight Sun'. All of Hawk's solos on this album are full of power, and bestowed with a confidence that borders on nonchalance. He shows superb instrumental control by skimming effortlessly through glissandos whose starting and finishing points are octaves apart, and he produces cascades of notes so complexly linked that they appear to defy the bar lines. The adventurousness is not always attractive, however, and though he is stimulated by some emendations to the chords of 'Body and Soul' his tone takes on a yelling quality that negates the appeal of his phrases.

23
Global Gigs

In October 1961, when Hawkins and Eldridge settled in for another series of regular bookings at the Metropole, things there were not quite the same as before. The bar had dropped its afternoon sessions in order to concentrate on drawing in the evening crowds. Another change – a welcome one – was that Hawk and Roy were backed by a more or less permanent rhythm section, consisting of Eddie Locke on drums, Tommy Flanagan on piano and Major Holley on bass.

The accord that this rhythm section possessed developed further when they were added to a JATP tour of Europe, which began in the following February. Hawkins and Eldridge had specifically asked that they be allowed to work with their own regular accompanists and Norman Granz had agreed. The tour package was smaller than usual, consisting of Ella Fitzgerald accompanied by the Paul Smith Trio – Paul Smith (piano), Wilfred Middlebrooks (bass) and Stan Levey (drums) – plus the Hawkins–Eldridge Quintet. The quintet opened the show by playing a forty-five-minute set, usually containing six tunes, mostly old favourites such as 'Disorder at the Border' and 'Hollywood Stampede'; Hawk's usual ballad feature was 'If I Had You'.

Hawkins still made it his business to improvise freely on concert appearances, rather than relying on set solos that could have been crafted to excite or impress an audience. But in taking that sort of chance the veteran Hawkins left himself at the mercy of his muse and despite his unfaltering musicianship there were times on this tour (and on later ones) when his lines sounded forced and jagged. This led someone to write, 'All Hawkins cares about are the answer to three questions: "What's the bread?", "Where's my horn?" and "Which way is the audience?"'[1] No sooner had a bad review been printed, however, than Hawkins roared into a startling display of creativity.

Tommy Flanagan had worked on the South American trip with Hawk and Roy but, as this JATP trip involved a smaller touring party, he was able to get to know Hawk a little better:

> I think the first dates we ever played together were at the Metropole, which was kind of a hard place to work because everybody was in a line. But I was happy to be working with Coleman Hawkins. I was kind of in awe of the man and it took a while to relax in his company, but I warmed to him and I think he did to me. We did a lot of dates around New York, places like Newburgh etc. In the days that I worked with him he was very punctual, and sometimes we got to the gig an hour before we need have done. But then he had a little peculiar habit: about ten minutes before hit-time he'd say, 'Let's go out for a drink,' and this meant we'd be five or so minutes behind time getting on the bandstand, but the clubowner knew we'd play a full set so there were no problems.
>
> He didn't talk much about other musicians; occasionally he'd mention other pianists, but only in passing. When you sat down after a gig the subject of music rarely came up because Coleman's range of conversation was so wide. I really learnt a lot from him, on many subjects. I found him to be a pretty gracious kind of man, a good friend. Most people didn't realize that he was a very humorous man; he could tell some funny stories, but he was also a select man, and not too many people were part of his circle. He seldom wrote out any music (or any chord changes) except for a recording session, and then he'd rarely ever play the tunes again after we'd recorded them. He mostly played standards, or tunes based on standards.[2]

In January 1962, not long before the JATP package left the States, Hawkins and the rhythm section recorded for the Moodsville label; this was the first of three albums that the quartet did for that company during the course of a year. The internal dynamics of the quartet are impressive, and Flanagan's voicing of accompanying chords is, as ever, a joy to hear, but the slant of the albums is towards a subdued, albeit top-class, sort of dinner music. Locke and Holley swing smoothly in tandem, and all the material is interesting, but a sense of restraint is always close at hand. Hawk plays admirably and provides brief rainbows of inspired extemporization, but the sound engineers can't seem to avoid the temptation to supplement his tone with a touch of echo, a distracting and superfluous tactic. On some numbers, such as 'Smoke Gets in Your Eyes', there is an impression that something memorable is in the offing, but although Hawk's performances never sag below a highly commendable level, the presentation of the numbers precludes the possibility of any new masterpieces.

The most relaxed performances from Hawkins during this period occur on the Impulse album *Today and Now* (recorded in September 1962); the quartet share an identical mood and Tommy Flanagan follows every nuance of Hawk's flowing improvisations to perfection. Hawk's tone is as cavernous as ever, but there isn't a dreg of harshness in his delivery on this album, and the ballads 'Quintessence' and 'Don't Love Me' contain superior performances. Hawkins projects the haunting and sophisticated theme of 'Love Song from Apache' superbly, making it the outstanding track. The faster tunes are swinging versions of old 'sing-along' numbers. Hawk's technique seems at its most effortless on 'Don't Sit Under the Apple Tree', and his long, involved phrases sound seamless, but 'Swingin' Scotch' (a workout on 'Loch Lomond') seems a little contrived and the rocking send-off for 'Put on Your Old Grey Bonnet' gradually palls during the overlong (ten minutes) version. This was an album that Hawkins enjoyed making and, for years afterwards, he cited it as one of his favourite latterday recordings.

The quartet played a series of residencies at New York's Village Gate during the summer of 1962 (working at various times opposite groups led by Horace Silver, Thelonious Monk and Eric Dolphy). Hawk occasionally left New York to play solo dates, though, and one of these involved him in a brief visit to the Belgian town of Dinant (birthplace of Charles and Adolphe Sax). Hawk went there to take part in a June festival that honoured the memory of the inventor of the saxophone. It was fitting that Hawkins, who had done so much to reveal the enormous potential of the instrument, should have been asked to perform in Dinant; his concert at the Theatre du Casino was a huge success. His accompanists there were the French pianist Georges Arvanitas and two American musicians, drummer Kansas Fields and bassist Jimmy Woode. These three, plus American guitarist Mickey Baker, also backed Hawkins in a thirty-one-minute film (directed by the Belgian writer, Yannick Bruynoghe) made in a Brussels studio during the brief visit.

Back home, one of Hawk's 1962 summer dates provoked a good deal of teasing from his sidekick Roy Eldridge. On Friday 6 July Hawk was due to appear with Roy at the opening evening of the Newport Jazz Festival, backed by Bill Rubenstein (piano), Jo Jones (drums), and Jim Neves (bass). When the time came for the group to go on stage there was no sign of Hawkins, and Eldridge had to do the first set in a quartet. Hawk appeared just as the set was ending, saying he'd run into unavoidable traffic problems. Roy playfully suggested that he'd done this on purpose, knowing that Eldridge was going to spring something new on him. This produced a gale of laughter all round, then trumpeter Harry Edison chipped in and said that Hawk was too old to make these sort of journeys.

Hawk insisted that road conditions were bad, and Eldridge, sensing more fun, said, 'Only when you get to your age.' Edison followed on by saying, 'People come in using wheelchairs and they always ask for Coleman Hawkins'. Hawk paused and said with mock scorn, 'You're the only trumpeter I know who still carries the number-one-method book for trumpet in his case.[3] This rejoinder ended the discussion. Hawk made up for lost time by guesting with the Gerry Mulligan–Bob Brookmeyer Quartet.

During yet another return booking at the Village Gate Hawk's quartet made a live recording for the Verve label (in a session organized by Creed Taylor). Here the quartet achieve a relaxed swinging sound, more sanguine in quality than their previous studio recordings. Hawk's opening chorus on 'All the Things You Are' is superbly conceived but 'Joshua Fit the Battle' has a contrived air. A brisk 'Mack the Knife' demonstrates the admirable rapport that existed between Flanagan and Hawkins. Hawk then announces 'a very pretty, old ballad which you don't hear too much anymore' and goes on to play a jagged but absorbing version of 'It's the Talk of the Town'. The group's version of 'Bean and the Boys' sounds a shade too fast for Hawk's fingers at that particular part of the session.

The remainder of the album was completed two days later at another live session that had Roy Eldridge and Johnny Hodges guesting with the group. Eldridge's tightly muted, economical solo on 'Satin Doll' leads into a restrained chorus from Hodges and some flowing ideas from Flanagan. Hawkins sweeps into action and produces some bold, angular phrases that form the best solo of the set. Some high-class, albeit tight-reined efforts emerge on 'Perdido', but even the challenge of a series of eight-bar chases can't persuade any of the distinguished improvisers to throw caution to the winds. Johnny Hodges shows superfine skills on a slow blues, 'A Rabbit in Jazz', Roy Eldridge follows on with some dramatic and wonderfully effective high-note playing, but Hawkins eschews poignancy and chooses to arpeggio his way through a series of somewhat detached substitute chords, saving his expressiveness for the quartet version of 'If I Had You' which ended the session. When the session was over Hodges said of Hawkins, 'The older he gets the better he gets. If ever you think he's through you find he's gone right ahead again.'[4]

Among those who visited the Village Gate during the course of the recordings were Miles Davis and arranger Gil Evans. Davis had retained an affable relationship with Hawkins and most of their conversations were embroidered with banter. On one occasion Hawkins had gently chided

Davis for his latterday habit of turning his back on the audience, but Davis quickly made the jocular point that when he'd worked for Hawkins the audience was lucky if the bandleader got on stage at all some nights. Underlying all this was Davis's respect and affection for Hawkins; recalling earlier days, he said, 'He would buy a coat for $300 and sell it to me for $15.'[5]

In 1962, producer Bob Thiele successfully organized a recording session that reunited Hawkins with drummer Shelly Manne; the two principals flew to the New York City date, Manne from California and Hawkins from Schenectady. The session was fairly informal and allowed the participants to demonstrate their amazingly swift musical reflexes on long versions of 'Take the A Train' and 'Cherokee'. At 3 a.m. pianist Hank Jones and bassist George Duvivier left to catch up with some sleep and Hawkins was persuaded to record on piano, the only time he did so. The debut takes the form of a duet with Shelly Manne. Hawk seems content to play 'arranger's piano', voicing a series of block chords while Manne offers polyrhythmic support. The results have only a novelty value; Hawk himself later described the exercise as 'some foolishness'.[6] The contest evens up when Hawkins leaves the keyboard and blows some fiery tenor-sax phrases. Hank Jones wasn't present on the second part of the session, and his place at the piano was taken by Eddie Costa. After creating some incisive, exciting keyboard work, Costa moved on to vibes and played some admirable improvisations on 'The Sicks of Us'.

Hawkins was given a burst of national publicity via a feature on him in *Time* magazine, 31 August 1962. In it he was quoted as saying, 'Good playing, precise playing has no date. It goes on and on. There has been no evolution in jazz; it's the same old stuff, reinterpreted and played differently.' Hawk, as ever, was refusing to be impressed simply because some aspect of jazz was being hailed as new. His old values were unchanged, and during this period he told Stanley Dance that he would love to record an album of Bach's compositions; unfortunately this wish was never fulfilled. Stanley Dance was on hand, however, to see Hawkins achieve his ambition of recording with Duke Ellington. Hawkins said, 'Duke Ellington came to me twenty years ago, or perhaps it was nineteen, eighteen or seventeen, and said, "You know, I want you to make a record with me and I'm going to write a number especially for you."

"Fine," I said, "I'm for it."

But we never did make it, although we sometimes spoke of it when we ran into one another.'

It needed Bob Thiele's enterprise finally to get the two men into the recording studio together. The pre-planning for the session was carried out swiftly, but with more secrecy than was usual with a jazz recording, simply because it was felt that too many well-wishers would want to be present at the historic occasion and their presence might well have hampered the proceedings. Besides Hawk and Duke, the rest of the group were Ellington sidemen: Ray Nance on cornet and violin, Lawrence Brown on trombone, Johnny Hodges on alto sax, Harry Carney on baritone sax and bass-clarinet, Aaron Bell on bass and Sam Woodyard on drums. They assembled in Rudy Van Gelder's New Jersey studio on the afternoon of 18 August 1962.

All of the musicians involved were hard-bitten veterans who had made thousands of recordings between them, but this day seemed special. Hawkins arrived at the studio punctually and found Ellington and his men already there. Stanley Dance, who wrote the original sleevenote, described it as 'an informal yet thoroughly professional date'. Over the years Ellington had produced masterpieces out of ideas developed at similar informal recordings, but nothing monumental came from his pen on this occasion. This session could have been one of the most sublime of all jazz occasions had more pre-planning gone into the material to be used. Hawkins made no complaint – it seems he was genuinely thrilled to be on the date – but since he had waited for most of his adult life for the chance to be showcased in the manner of a 'classical' musician being featured in a concerto, he perhaps had hoped that Ellington was going to present him with something on which he could display his full powers of thematic development. The session produced several superb tracks and one near masterpiece, but Ellington did not fully utilize his own incomparable talents by composing sufficient new material for his enormously gifted guest.

The outstanding track, 'Self Portrait (of the Bean)' – originally called 'Hawk' – was written only on the morning of the session. Composers (like journalists) can often write at their best when threatened with a deadline, but often lack of time causes fine ideas to float away undeveloped. Duke just hadn't allowed himself enough time and decided he'd have to sketch out the rest of the material in the studio, so to this end he asked his resident copyist Tom Whaley to come to the recording to act as an amanuensis. But Whaley could not make the first part of the date, so Ellington's gifted reed player Jimmy Hamilton went to the studio to write what was dictated (or sketched) by Ellington.

Hawkins sounds magnificent playing the slow thirty-two bar theme of 'Self Portrait', (a collaboration between Ellington and Billy Strayhorn); his tone is captured in all its richness, and he hits his lowest notes with an impressive profundity. Intentionally, he doesn't re-create the ravishing sound he used in the late 1930s; instead he blows with an opulence that reflects the vast gamut of his experience and the mezzo-staccato cadenza seems to show how much he cared about this session. 'Mood Indigo' also has moments of enormous merit. After a soft rendering of the melody by Hodges, Brown and Carney (on bass clarinet), Hawkins drifts in and pays court to the tune by offering elegant variations that develop through three choruses. He makes the developments so logically that his concluding fourth chorus, full of spiral effects, seems the only way possible for him to provide the links for a reprise of the softly played melody. This is one of his finest recorded moments during the 1960s, and it might have been his apotheosis had he not created several phrases of similar rhythmic patterns, but the pros heavily outweigh the cons in Hawk's one and only recorded rendering of an everlasting jazz theme.

'Wanderlust' was originally recorded by an Ellington small group in 1938. It was used as a filler on this session, its inclusion being so impromptu that no one in the studio could remember its title. It's a typical Ellington–Hodges blues collaboration, and all of the front line solo, with Ray Nance outstanding. Rarely has his gift for playing stark phrases, full of emotion, been better displayed. A slightly subdued Hawkins also plays superbly; even his reticence exudes a powerful majesty. The ascending motif of 'You Dirty Dog' invokes a nimble-fingered solo from Hawkins, but here he is repetitive, and it is Hodges, with a sublimely rounded show of improvisations, who takes the honours.

'Limbo' was created there and then in the studio. What the group took to be a rehearsal take was so full of atmosphere – and effective solos – it became the master recording. Nance's economical phrasing, couched in his expressive hoarse tone, creates a wondrous effect. Hawkins tiptoes in and takes a more legato approach than is usual, but he gradually brings his big guns into play, egged on by some vocal interjections from drummer Sam Woodyard. Woodyard drops into a shuffle rhythm in the closing stages but soon proves this was a mistake. Strangely enough, he uses the same ineffective ploy on 'Ray Charles Place'. Ellington himself takes a brief eight-bar solo here, but for much of the date he concentrates on accompanying and directing.

Each member of this stellar front line takes choruses on a head arrangement of 'The Jeep is Jumping', taken too fast for the comfort of all concerned. Hodges manages to keep his poise, but has to drop back on his own licks to do so; Nance, by using well-placed gaps, gets his message across, but Carney and Brown sound unrelaxed. Hawkins, usually so mobile and inventive at swift tempo, sounds a shade too determined to appear daring on the whirling roundabout, but this time Woodyard's rocking off-beat strokes enhance the placement of Hawk's phrases.

Carney, Hodges and Brown left the studio, so the final part of the session featured a front line consisting of Hawkins and Ray Nance on violin. This smaller group recorded a version of 'Solitude' that begins with a series of piano chords from Ellington, suggesting sombre reflectiveness. Nance plays a chorus of the melody eloquently, producing a tone that sounds almost like a viola, his relaxed lines bordered by Ellington's attentive accompaniment. Hawk enters, seemingly determined not to disturb the plaintive mood; his tone (deliberately subdued) has an almost *sotto voce* quality, slightly nasal but not at all unattractive. Hawk glides into a second chorus; alongside his improvisations Nance reintroduces the melody but allows Hawkins to take a majestic approach to the middle eight. The method of ending the piece had not been emphatically pre-planned, but sheer professionalism allows the musicians to extricate themselves from a possible tangle and, almost without blinking, they produce a unified conclusion.

Ellington's quippy Latin American theme 'The Ricitic' (premiered that day) has some fascinating moments. Woodyard is superb on brushes and his shared introduction with Aaron Bell creates an inviting carpet for Nance to create some atmospheric violin playing. Hawk's opening phrases are brilliantly abstract, and he follows them with some familiar double-time flourishes that are technically impressive but nothing like as interesting as his opening gambit. Duke supplies the soloists with sporadic chords but in the latter stages adds a series of flamboyant ostinato phrases and these sounds end the session.

The performers seemed satisfied with the five hours they had spent at their task. Hawk said, 'After four hundred years, we made it!' and Ellington, with typically wry humour, replied, 'You don't think it was too soon?' Hawk then got into his Chrysler and drove off into the evening sunshine to begin the next stage of that day's work by playing the first set of his booking at the Village Gate.

Later in the year the Village Gate became the site for a benefit in aid of dependants of Eddie Costa, who had often worked with Hawkins during the early 1960s. Costa, who had been killed in a car-crash on New York's West Side highway in July 1962, left a wife and four children. Hawkins rarely played benefits, and when he did he usually made only a token appearance, but he was genuinely saddened by Costa's untimely end (he was only thirty-six years old) and did his utmost to make the benefit night a big success. Two recordings from the seven-hour event were issued; a sextet version of 'Just You, Just Me' (with Urbie Green on trombone and Markie Makowitz on trumpet), which contains fifteen minutes of affable, adept improvisations; and a quartet (Hawkins and rhythm section) playing three choruses of 'I'm Confessin'' to end the show at four in the morning. There isn't a trace of weariness in Hawk's playing of three choruses of the old ballad; his performance, full of absorbing ideas, sounds magnificently inspired.

Hawk's willingness to try new ventures led him into making *Desafinado*, an album of bossa novas and jazz sambas. On this session pianist Tommy Flanagan played claves in the percussion section along with Eddie Locke and Willie Rodriguez. The piano wasn't used – in its place were two guitarists (Barry Galbraith and Howard Collins) – and Major Holley was on bass. Hawkins was obviously well aware of the success of Stan Getz's recordings in the same idiom and takes a much gentler approach than usual, resting lightly on the quasi-Brazilian beat. In doing so he creates some highly melodic solos; his tone, devoid of aggression, is faithfully captured throughout. The most enticing track is 'One Note Samba', but there are interesting elements within the exotically clad jazz sequences: 'Samba Para Bean (There Will Never be Another You)', 'O Pato (Take the A Train)', and 'Stumpy Bossa Nova (Whispering)'. Within that same month (September 1962), Hawkins, Locke, Holley and Flanagan (this time on piano) took part in a similar enterprise under guitarist Kenny Burrell's name; additional percussion was provided by Ray Baretto on bongoes. If anything, the mood is even gentler than on the *Desafinado* session. A lilting elegance marks 'Tres Palabras', both Burrell and Flanagan exemplify this feeling in their solos and Hawkins underlines it, reflectively strolling through the changes, emitting vast-toned thoughts. The outstanding track is 'I Thought About You', which is taken at a very slow tempo. Hawkins, virtually using a sub-tone, blows some wonderfully sensitive answers to Burrell's melody line. Least successful is the twelve-bar blues 'It's Getting Dark'; here the chugging beat sets up a net of lethargy that seems to ensnare everyone.

On tour, Hawkins continued occasionally to guest with local rhythm sections (such as his October–November 1962 booking at the Friar's Tavern in Toronto, Canada) but whenever possible he used his own team of Flanagan, Locke and Holley. The trio gradually got to know their leader's idiosyncrasies but this didn't diminish their respect for him. Major Holley recalled:

I first met Coleman Hawkins when I was in the navy. He came to play a gig at the San Diego base in California back in 1945. I was hugely impressed by Hawk's performance and also the way that Oscar Pettiford played. The other musicians on the base with me, guys like altoist Johnny Board and a trumpeter called Moses, talked about the visit for weeks afterwards. I got my nickname 'Mule' in the navy because I used to carry so many guys' instruments back from the mess hall. Well, Hawk liked to take it a stage further, so he called me 'The Donkey', always in rebuttal. He liked to keep you on your toes by not quite telling you what was happening. He'd say quite casually, 'Well, sir, I think we're going to Chicago', and then he'd walk away, and that's all he'd say about it until we were on the bandstand, then I'd be right in the middle of my bass solo and he'd finish the sentence by saying, 'So, it's ten o'clock tomorrow morning at the station.' This used to throw me, but if you complained he'd carry on all the more. He knew that he'd got me when I was playing a bass solo – it was like the dentist asking you a question.

He was a deep man, but he had a big effect on me in straightening out my thinking. And he could be very subtle. When I was drinking more than was good for me he'd phone me up, wouldn't say a word but he'd just shake the ice in his glass over the telephone. His musical evenings at home were something to remember. He'd invite a few musicians to his apartment, and he would cook and serve all the drinks anyone could want. His cooking was excellent, more in the European style, whole vegetables etc. Jazz was hardly mentioned at these gatherings; he'd mostly play albums of classical piano solos, or he'd put on a recording of the Brandenburg Concerto, and when it was finished he'd question everyone there on how the piece had affected them. He'd sit at the piano in his home and he'd play something a little wrong, deliberately, and Roland Hanna would always rise to the bait and go over and play the piece correctly and Hawk would sit back contentedly in his chair and listen.

Hawk wouldn't take any shit from anyone. I've seen some musicians who were supposed to be tough but they would bend a little when things got awkward, but not Hawk, and no one could make him hurry if he didn't want to. I only ever saw him run once and that was one winter when we were in Schenectady, New York. We'd finished our gig and we got to the station to go back to New York City. The train pulled in and it was piled high with ice, even the engine was a mass of ice, so that was that, it couldn't go any further, so we had to go back to the hotel. It was bitterly cold and Hawk actually started to run to keep warm. It seemed totally out of character to see him do this. When we were in upstate New York we'd often do Sunday gigs for various unions (electricians etc) who might be putting on a club night; these jobs often finished early and then Hawk used to like to play cards way into the night. I didn't join in but Hawk enjoyed playing 'tonk' with Johnson Flanagan (Tommy's brother) and somehow Hawk always beat him. After a while Johnson got mad and

> one night he went out at 2 a.m. to buy a new deck of cards; he wasn't satisfied with the ones they were using. Well, this was a very quiet part of theworld, a town where everything closed early, but somehow Johnson managed to get a new deck, and this really amused Hawk. It was the sort of thing that could keep him chuckling for days.[7]

Major Holley saw Hawkins lose his temper only twice. The first occasion was during JATP's 1962 tour of Europe when Hawk and Roy Eldridge had a disagreement, the basis of which remained a mystery to the rest of the group. The second was on a December 1962 recording session (*Back in Bean's Bag*) when he became upset over a choice of drummers. It wasn't that Hawkins disliked Dave Bailey's work, but his presence meant that the regular Flanagan/Holley/Locke trio was minus one member: drummer Eddie Locke. This greatly irritated Hawkins and Major Holley considers it amazing that none of Hawk's angry whispers and vehement curses was audible on the issued tracks. In fact Hawk's grumbling didn't reach the control booth because Mike Berniker, the record's producer, seemed totally surprised when he learnt of the saxophonist's anger some years later. He gave his views on the situation:

> I wanted to use Dave Bailey because he had done a great job on several previous albums for me; he was the tastiest drummer around at that time. He was a friend of mine, and of Clark Terry's, who did the fixing for the date. The subject of Eddie Locke didn't come up, but if Hawkins was mad about this he must have kept all his anger internally. My main impression was of him wanting to get on with things. I think he was late arriving for the date, which was at the old CBS studios, 799th Seventh Avenue.[8]

A session with such an acrimonious pedigree could have been disastrous, but it wasn't; irritation brought forth some spiky, laconic playing from Hawkins. On 'A Tune for the Tutor', Hawk's rendering of the unison melody is slightly desultory, but his terse solo, slightly rougher-toned than usual, has a charm of its own, and Clark Terry and Tommy Flanagan chip in with some purposeful solos. Hawk's work on 'Feeding the Bean' (the Count Basie riff Hawkins had first recorded in 1941) does sound fragmentary, but Clark Terry is in superb form, playing episodic ideas that develop beautifully as he moves effortlessly through the twelve-bar format. Terry's feature 'Don't Worry 'Bout Me' allows him to exhibit his amazing breath control and on 'Squeeze Me' he demonstrates his stratospheric range but still manages to remain tastefully creative. Here Hawk's curmudgeonly output of notes is effective during his solos, but the final ensemble is informal to the point of scrappiness. 'Just Squeeze Me' has bassist Holley taking the lead by using his singing-and-bowing technique simultaneously; Hawkins and Terry supply the harmony parts, creating an unusual blend of tone colours. Flanagan demonstrates his harmonic ingenuity in a block-chorded solo and then Hawkins follows on with some more truncated offerings; unfortunately his fingers fail to formulate what he conceived and during the concluding bars of his solo he groans in despair.

Mike Berniker candidly admitted, 'The album could have been better, and I kind of wince at some of Hawk's playing; his attack wasn't what it should have been and his phrasing was loose. He was not in very good shape, and he was drinking a lot.'[9] Hawk's finest moments on the album occur during his ballad feature 'Michelle'. His tone retains an attractive burr and he phrases Clark Terry's thoughtful composition admirably, resting his lines on the rich harmonies and gliding neatly to an unelaborate ending.

The Hawkins–Eldridge Quintet occasionally reassembled, but less so after their 1962 tour of Europe with JATP. One cause of irritation to Eldridge was Hawkins's manner of quoting a fee; bassist Bill Crow overheard Eldridge say, with some irritation, that the only figure that Hawk knew was a thousand dollars. Asking for that sort of money made some of the bookings offered to the quintet unfeasible; if a thousand was taken out of the fee there was very little left for anyone else. However, Hawk maintained that he could easily get a thousand dollars a week for himself in Europe, and as if to make his point he flew across the Atlantic in January 1963 to play a series of dates in Scandinavia. He arrived in Norway on 26 January and played a concert that evening at Oslo University accompanied by Jarle Krogstad (bass), Ole Jacob Hansen (drums) and Swedish pianist Goran Lindberg. Hawk then left for Sweden, where he played for a week at the Golden Circle in Stockholm.

He returned to Norway after his Swedish bookings ended and played for six days (until 9 February) at the Metropol Jazz Club in Oslo, backed by Hansen, Krogstad and pianist Einar Iversen. The American author H.O. Brunn (who wrote*The Story of the Original Dixieland Jazz Band*) called in to the Metropol and asked, with a certain misguided boldness, 'When are you going to start to play jazz again, Mr Hawkins?' Hawk treated this inane statement with humour, saying, 'According to you I must have stopped playing jazz forty years ago!' The Norwegian jazz historian, Johs Bergh, who overheard that exchange, recalled other details of Hawk's visit:

> When I picked him up at the airport on 26 January it was the worst of weather. Around zero, cold, wet, lousy weather. At the hotel he had to show his passport. On the birthdate it said 1904, but he had scratched with ink over the zero, so it was mistaken for 1914. He settled in his room (at the Hotel Viking) and unpacked a little bag which contained one bottle of whisky (J & B) and two plastic glasses, one yellow, one green. I thought 'great', I really could use a drink. So Hawk filled one glass with whisky, one glass with water and started refreshing himself; nothing for me. Later he moved into the Hotel Bristol which he remembered from his visit in 1935, much more expensive than the Hotel Viking. He was very hard on money. His salary for the week at the Metropol was a thousand US dollars. On Friday the eighth I gave him the money, 7,000 Norwegian crowns, a very good salary at that time. Next day he was on me. I had cheated him! He had checked with the bank and since the rate was 7,011 he should have 7,011 crowns . . . which he got.[10]

From Norway Hawkins went back to one of his favourite countries, Denmark, where he did club gigs and radio and television shows. On 17 February he crossed into Sweden to play a date at the Club Celeste in Malmö (accompanied by a trio led by Danish pianist Jorgen Steen). The other band at the club was a mainstream group led by Danish trumpeter Arnvid Meyer, who recalls:

> This was one of those days when Hawkins's zeal to play was insatiable and he wanted to join in with my band during the following set. When asked what he wanted to play Hawk said, 'I don't care. Anything goes.' Our piano player got a little anxious, but this was just Hawk's comments; he didn't mean that he wanted to play tunes of those titles and readily agreed to do 'Honeysuckle Rose', 'Foolin' Myself' and 'Undecided' from our book. He sounded in extremely good shape to me.[11]

Meyer's appraisal is borne out by a private recording made at the gig. Hawk's enthusiasm and spirited inventions gleam brightly through the low-fi sounds.

In the USA Hawk's inflated quotations often prevented him from taking his own rhythm section with him for out-of-town engagements; this suited most clubowners, who were happy to have Hawkins work with their own resident musicians. During the early 1960s Hawk played many such dates throughout New England, often driving up from Manhattan and returning the next day. At one such date in New Haven, Connecticut, he was interviewed (by Jim Delahunt) for *Rhythm and Blues* magazine. Hawk took the opportunity to speak about his method of working: 'If I hear something I like I don't go home and get out my horn and try to play it. I just incorporate it in the things I play already, in my own style. I don't believe in just getting a record and practising from it. That's why so many of these boys now sound alike.'[12]

Hawk misjudged his journey time for this gig and was half an hour late arriving at the club. The house trio played the first set then, after being announced as 'a real, classy old man', Hawkins smiled wanly and stepped on stage to keen applause. The set over, Hawk went to his 'dressing room', a sparse cellar furnished with a wooden chair and lit by a bare electric lightbulb. Delahunt resumed his interview by asking about the past; Hawkins reacted testily:

> For God's sake, everybody wants to know about my past. Now tell me, what good does that do for me? People talk about me like I'm dead. Write about now. Write about today and tomorrow. Everything has been said already about what's happened. It's all been written down. History doesn't help me play any better. You have to do new things. What I did is old news. Now you asked about Charlie Parker. Sure I knew him. I played with them all. Now what good will it do Charlie Parker if I tell you about him?[13]

By the end of the evening Hawkins had mellowed and invited the local tenor player Houston Person up to play duets. Jim Delahunt left as the waiter was turning the lights out, but Hawkins was still on stage humming phrases to organist Ray Jackson.

At the 1963 Newport Jazz Festival Hawkins played in an all-star 'house band' consisting of Zoot Sims, Howard McGhee, Clark Terry, Wendell Marshall (bass), Roy Haynes (drums) and Joe Zawinul (piano). A good-humoured version of 'Undecided', featuring substantial solos from all of the front line (plus Zawinul and Hayes) was recorded, as was an exploratory rendering of 'These Foolish Things' by Hawkins; here Zawinul's chordal voicings seem to stimulate a spate of new ideas from the tenorist. 'Sweet Georgia Brown' offers a chance to compare the contrasting work of Clark Terry, (effervescent) and Howard McGhee (febrile). A long duet version of 'What Is This Thing Called Love?' featuring Hawkins and Sims (neither at their best) was taken from the 4 July concert, although it remained unreleased until twenty years later.

On the following evening, this illustrious front line's duties included playing a series of written arrangements to accompany singer Joe Williams, most of which had only brief solo interludes.

Hawkins is heard for eight bars on 'Gravy Waltz', and takes a long rugged solo on the 'Some of This' blues, but his main feature is on 'April in Paris', where his thirty-two bar outing starts in great style but then seems to lose direction. Some of the pieces, such as 'Wayfaring Stranger', are entirely orchestrated; others like 'Every Day' are presented as head arrangements. The most curious item is 'Do You Wanna Jump', where Hawkins sounds more like Ben Webster than at any time in his career. Zoot Sims takes a poetic solo on 'In the Evenin'' and pianist Junior Mance shows his blues-playing skill, ably backed by Bob Cranshaw on bass and Mickey Roker on drums. Hawkins and Clark Terry joined the Gildo Mahones Trio to accompany vocal trio Lambert, Hendricks and Bavan (Dave Lambert, Jon Hendricks and Yolande Bavan). Hawkins takes two choruses on 'Watermelon Man', the first of which is much more interesting than the second, and this same lack of continuity mars his four choruses on 'Walkin' '. The latter part of these solos is no less energetic than the beginning but at a certain stage one senses that Hawkins begins to ask himself, 'What am I doing here?' He was too much of a pro to throw away the rest of his solo, but it sounds as though his heart wasn't in what he was doing. It's a trait that gradually becomes more noticeable in his work from this point on; his paramount skills had not gone rusty, but they needed stimulation and coaxing before they were brought fully into action.

On the Saturday-night session at Newport (6 July) Hawkins guested with a quartet led by tenorist Sonny Rollins. This Rollins–Hawkins set was a fascinating meeting of two huge-toned tenor saxists who, despite being from different eras, were sometimes described (too conveniently) as having a similar approach to improvising. Both relied heavily on form and connecting ideas, but their method of implementing their musical thoughts was usually quite dissimilar. There is no doubt that Rollins had a deep admiration for Hawkins's work and regarded him as an influence.

> It was about 1946 that I got my first tenor, but I wanted to play tenor for quite a few years before that because of Hawkins. When I heard Hawkins play it seemed to me that he was very erudite and sophisticated musically. I became enamoured of Coleman Hawkins; there was really so much music in the way he played. To me it was a real intellectual experience listening to him. It would be hard to say who influenced me most: Charlie Parker or Coleman Hawkins. With Hawkins's playing I was impressed by the intellectual concept that he had. I mean he played all of the chords like a virtuoso.[14]

Rollins very much wanted the Newport session to be a triumph and Hawkins, who regarded Rollins as one of the leading young jazz players in the world, also looked forward eagerly to the meeting. But things did not gel musically on the bandstand; one report suggested that this was because Hawkins sounded 'uncomfortable' with Rollins's rhythm section (Paul Bley, piano, Henry Grimes, bass, and Roy McCurdy, drums).[15] Ira Gitler, writing in *Down Beat*, felt that trouble with the microphones ruined the set; he praised Hawk's contribution to 'All the Things You are' but felt the veteran was defeated by the speedy version of 'The Way You Look Tonight'. Record producer George Avakian, however, was encouraged enough by what he heard to book Hawkins and Rollins for a shared studio session later that same month. He said, 'At Newport the session did not come up to potential simply because they had no opportunity to blow together before they went on stage. So he went in to the studio the following week and did it right. Almost everything was done in one take, and on "Summertime" we used a rehearsal.'[16]

The recordings, spread over two days, featured the same pianist and drummer that Rollins had used at Newport; Bob Cranshaw played bass on the first three titles recorded but Grimes returned to complete the album. Neither Rollins nor Hawkins reached new heights on these recordings, but some fascinating things emerged from their co-ordinated efforts. After an emphatic introduction from Rollins, Hawkins gives an elegant rendering of 'Yesterdays', adding deft trills to his ornamentations. Rollins's lines are much more angular; the craggily hewn notes seem to burst out of his saxophone, his trills seem to be deliberately strident and his tone sounds even heavier than Hawk's. The ending of the Jerome Kern melody is beautifully conceived with Rollins spinning out clusters of bitter-sweet high notes. Hawk's opening chorus on 'All the Things You Are' is full of thematic variations, but he seems gradually to lose rapport with the rhythm section. Paul Bley creates a highly individualistic solo that is full of contrived abstruseness, though his improvisations on the same number at Newport seemed propelled by inspiration. Rollins's opening is certainly more unconventional than his Newport effort on the same sequence; here, using a combination of tonal, chordal and rhythmic explorations, he produces a barrage of ideas. Hawkins re-enters the arena and the two front-line players switch and swop melody and counterpoint through to a fade-out ending.

On 'Lover Man', Rollins and Hawkins amply prove that their approaches to improvising differed in many aspects. Each is assigned alternate eight-bar sections of the first chorus; Hawkins chooses to ornament the composer's lines whereas Rollins (not always successfully) attempts to construct a meaningful new melody. The ending of the piece is spectacular, with Rollins making high excursions into the whistling zone; Hawkins looks on and decides to play some languid phrases that move logically towards a low-note finale. Rollins engenders an atmospheric mood in playing the theme of 'Summertime'; Hawkins takes over and again displays his trilling prowess, and after an agile bass solo Rollins re-enters and plays an almost orthodox hard-bop solo. Hawkins ends the piece by playing a dramatic low note that buzzes into silence. As the album progresses the differences between the two men become more obvious than the similarities. Hawkins usually embroiders his phrases with a design that consisted basically of dotted eighth notes, phrased in a way that highlights the accompanying chord changes. But Rollins sets out to superimpose rather than to decorate, stamping out phrases which, by the certainty of his note placements, set up a stirring rhythmic impetus. Whereas Hawkins circles and settles on the choicest branches Rollins skilfully hacks his way through a dense musical undergrowth. Each man reaches his destination but their respective goals were farther apart than either realized.

'Just Friends' serves to illustrate the tonal differences. Hawk's tone is big and rich with spiky, harsh undertones but Rollins's huge sound is sinewy, like that of a vast oboe. On this title the two men come closest to establishing orthodox jazz-duo lines. The mutual respect is obvious, but even here there is no overt blending and the effect is that of two Harold Pinter characters talking earnestly and simultaneously on different subjects. When this track was played to Stan Getz, as part of a Blindfold Test, he said, 'It sounds like a couple of high-school players.'[17] Bob Dawbarn, in an incisive *Melody Maker* review of the album, called the two tenor saxists 'very uneasy partners', adding, 'like kippers and steak I prefer my Hawkins and Rollins separately'.[18] Twenty-five years later, producer George Avakian looked back on the pairing and said, 'A mix which failed, but with better preparation could have been better; Sonny's awe and warm respect for Hawk never quite let either man loosen up.'[19]

24
Penthouse Patriarch

As in previous years Hawkins played a summer residency at the Village Gate, New York (from 13 August until 4 September 1963). One night, after finishing his sets there, Hawk got his car and took his sidemen Eddie Locke, Major Holley and Roland Hanna over to the Half Note to hear Ben Webster. Hawkins sat contentedly at the bar listening carefully to Ben's quartet, which featured the bass virtuoso Richard Davis. Hawk couldn't resist having fun at the expense of his own bassist and called out to Major Holley, 'Mule, is he mad at you about something?'

A few nights later Webster repaid the compliment and went to hear Hawkins at the Village Gate, and that same night Eddie 'Lockjaw' Davis dropped in to listen to Hawk. Davis's relationship with Hawkins was slightly different from Webster's. Ben shared jokes with Hawk, and never hesitated to tease him about his age, but on all things musical he was always ultra-respectful towards his original idol. Lockjaw also revered Hawk's talents but he was prepared to trade jocular insults on any subject. One night he called in to hear Hawkins and told him, 'Bean, you're the last of the great honkers.' It was meant as a rough compliment and Hawkins took it with a grin. Davis had purchased a new mouthpiece but found it impossible to blow; he mentioned this to Hawkins, who said, 'Bring it on down.' Davis did so and Hawkins blew it with the utmost ease. During this period of his life Lockjaw developed the habit of drinking a tall glass of milk with one measure of spirits in it ('The whisky is for me, the milk's for my ulcer,' he'd say). He persuaded Hawkins that it would also benefit his health if he did the same so, for a brief while Hawk tried the mixture, then gradually began ordering the milk and whisky separately. He subsequently cut out the milk.

Over the years Hawkins often smoked marijuana, rarely buying any but seldom declining the invitation to sample any that was proffered. He ignored hard drugs, neither chiding nor showing interest if users were close at hand. The only exception was when he asked his old friend Count Basie, a long-time devotee of cocaine, how much he spent a year on his habit. When Basie gave him a rough estimate Bean almost keeled over with surprise but ended up chuckling and said, 'Goodness gracious Basie, for that sort of money I could afford the Queen of England's Rolls-Royce and her chauffeur.'

Soon after his stay at the Village Gate ended Hawkins flew out to California. The main purpose of his visit was a possible appearance on the Steve Allen television show, but in order to make the long journey worthwhile a booking was arranged at the Hideaway club in Los Angeles. The engagement there was a disaster, because neither the local jazz fans nor the Californian musicians turned out to hear Hawkins. This was in stark contrast to the situation that had occurred two decades earlier when hundreds had waited in line for the chance to hear him play at Billy Berg's club. The bassist in the accompanying group at the Hideaway was Herbert 'Herbie' Lewis, then only just turned twenty. He recalled with pleasure working with the veteran saxist:

> I remember performing with Brother Hawkins at the Hideaway, learning and studying his popular-music vehicle 'Body and Soul'. I remember thinking to myself how easy it was to create and play with Coleman because of his harmonic togetherness, his unwavering sense of tempo and his *time* when he improvised. No one came out from the music community of Los Angeles to hear his performances.[1]

After two nights of bad business the clubowners cancelled the contract and Hawkins made his way back to New York.

But this cancellation enabled Hawkins to take advantage of a sudden offer to play in Canada, replacing Oscar Brown, Jr who had pulled out of a two-week booking at the Friar's Tavern on Yonge Street, Toronto. Hawk did fair business at the club during the two-week engagement (which began on 28 October 1963), but the Canadian magazine *Coda* carried an item expressing dismay at what it saw as a mismatch between Hawkins and his accompanists. It said of the locally-recruited unit: 'Coleman Hawkins's music was beyond their grasp. This practice of supplying visiting musicians with local rhythm sections of incompatible styles is a major bane to the jazz listener in Toronto.'[2]

Indubitably, Hawkins was less worried about the 'modern' aspects of his accompanists than the critics, or the listeners. His musical tastes were as catholic as ever, a fact that was confirmed to Charles Graham when he visited Hawk's apartment for the purpose of writing an article on the tenorist's hi-fi equipment. Hawkins told him, 'I like all good music, classical, jazz, everything.' Graham wrote, 'He has often singled out Bach as one of his special favorites. The shelves over his high-fidelity system hold many hundreds of LPs, mostly complete operas, chamber music, and symphonic works. His jazz listening he prefers to do in person.' The article duly appeared in *Jazz* magazine. Graham listed Hawk's expensive JBL speaker set-up, which was linked with a Tandberg microphone (then retailing at $498) and Koss professional model headphones. His Olympus cabinet alone cost $700. Graham, a high-fidelity expert, was clearly impressed by Hawkins's comprehensive knowledge and wrote, 'During our discussions and comparison listening tests he came up with several numbers even new to me.'

In his later years Hawkins was always more willing to talk about classical music than about jazz. He said, 'I don't listen to too much jazz. I'm a classics man, but then I started like that. That's where I got myself from, and I keep it up.'[3] In a talk with Stanley Dance, Coleman discussed his tastes further: 'I love all the operas. I like Stravinsky when I'm listening to Stravinsky, Bach when I'm listening to Bach and Beethoven when I'm listening to Beethoven. I have no prejudices. I think Tchaikovsky was a great composer, but I guess his music became too popular to be chic.'[4] Hawkins had some shrewd views, however, on the merits of writing out jazz solos. He told Nat Hentoff:

> I think it's fine for ensembles, but it's hard to appreciate a fellow having a solo all written out for him. When you stop and think about it, maybe in a hundred years jazz will be like that, like classical music. But if it turns out that way you'll have taken the basic effect of jazz away. Improvisation is the key. Jazz would lose all its originality without it. That's why jazz is a different kind of music from classical. But it's also true that if classical music were written like it used to be, a couple of centuries ago, there'd be a lot of improvising in it too.[5]

By 1963 Hawkins had moved out of the family home at 445 West 133rd Street, which he had shared with his wife Dolores and their three children (all now in their teens). He took a spacious penthouse apartment at 372 Central Park West in which he regularly held musical soirees for his close friends; invariably an 'evening' meeting stretched through until dawn. Pianist Roland Hanna, who had joined Hawk's quartet when Tommy Flanagan left to work as Ella Fitzgerald's accompanist, attended a number of these gatherings:

We spent many hours at his apartment, sometimes talking throughout the night. This happened so regularly that I had to convince my wife that all we did was talk about music and play music on records. She needed to be reassurred and she actually came along once to see for herself. Hawkins would pour the Cognac liberally, and then discussion would be under way. If there was a point of argument Hawk always said, 'Let's check this out,' and he'd go over and look through *Grove's Dictionary of Music* to settle the point. He had a huge library of musical scores of Bach, Beethoven, Mozart, Mahler, Ravel, Debussy, Richard Strauss and so on. He had shelves of books on composers and their works; I was fascinated by the extent of his library. He loved Dinu Lipatti and the Robert Schumann Trios. He was always particularly interested in the cello and revered Pablo Casals. I had studied cello for many years and he was pleased to know that I had played for Casals in Puerto Rico in 1958. One evening when Major Holley was there I brought along a cello to his apartment and Coleman astonished us by playing it well, despite the fact that he hadn't played cello for many years. He'd listen enraptured to the Bach Cello Sonatas, but he was just as knowledgable about Bartók; his tastes were wide. He was a peerless musician.

He bought a Steinway Console grand piano for his apartment and he often sat at the keyboard and played things like Chopin waltzes, or his particular favorite Liebersfreund by Schumann. I felt a great deal of sympathy with him because he too loved classical music. I wrote 'After Paris' as a tribute to him; it was inspired by seeing Hawk looking at the big map of Paris that hung on the wall of his apartment. I got the impression that he felt warmest towards that city. I first worked with Coleman on Art Ford's Jazz Party, this would be about 1958–59; we went out to a television studio in New Jersey to do the show. But I didn't work with him regularly until the 1960s, I was one of a line of Detroit pianists who worked with Hawk. He said he loved the work of Detroit pianists, including early guys like Willie Anderson and Art Woodley.

We played many dates in the New York area, and in other parts of the country, including a residency at the Executive House in Chicago. At this time he never played 'Body and Soul'. He'd take his material from many sources, such as 'I Hear a Rhapsody', 'Yours is My Heart' (by Franz Lehar), 'Lost in the Stars' (Kurt Weill) and a J.J. Johnson tune called 'Lament', which Hawk was particularly fond of. He'd often play things in A major. I always felt he had perfect pitch because he could play anything he heard instantly. He was the complete musician; he could improvise at any tempo, in any key, and he could read anything. During the 1960s he liked the work of pianist Howard Reynolds and he's say to me, 'Come on, let's go and hear Howard Reynolds at the Surf Maid Club.' Sometimes we'd have evenings only attended by pianists and I can remember one where Joe Zawinul played classical pieces so beautifully you could have cried.[6]

Austrian-born pianist Joe Zawinul, then working in Cannonball Adderley's quintet, lived at 382 Central Park West, and was thus a neighbour of Hawkins. He reminisced:

Ben Webster shared my apartment for a couple of months. We'd play together when I was home from the road. Coleman Hawkins lived next door, so the three of us played together. I learned so much from those two old guys. We never made a tape though. And those guys cut each other up, man. I went down with Coleman in the elevator and I said, 'You know Ben is hot on those ballads.'

Hawkins said, 'Let's get together, you and me, and learn some of those quick and fast changes and I can burn on him.'

It's like a competition they had. They had the greatest respect for one another but they had this competitiveness.[7]

Tenor saxist Zoot Sims was occasionally invited to visit Hawkins at home. This friendship meant a lot to Sims because Hawkins had been one of his original sources of inspiration (along with Lester Young). Sims, who had a large framed photograph of Hawkins on the wall of his 69th Street apartment, always listened attentively when Hawkins offered advice. Hawk respected Sims's playing, and often said he preferred it to Stan Getz's work, but he wasn't one of Hawk's favourite players, despite being one of Hawk's favourite people. The veteran showed his affection obliquely by teasing Sims, particularly about his choice of automobile: a small European car. Hawkins (who always set store by big, sturdy, expensive vehicles) often asked Zoot when was he going to buy something decent, adding, 'Why are you driving around in that itty-bitty tin can?' Sims used to grin and say he was well satisfied, but early one summer's morning as Sims left Hawk's apartment after a night's carousing he attempted to get into his car but accidentally pulled the handle off the door. Drummer Eddie Locke witnessed the incident and relayed the information back to Hawkins who laughed so much that he had to sit down in order to get his breath back.

Younger musicians like Sims found Hawkins an easy companion. Writer Dan Morgenstern felt that at this stage of his life Hawk didn't like being with old people; 'He was still extremely careful about his appearance and spent a lot of money on clothes. Everything he wore looked expensive. He'd buy his shirts at Sulka's or at Brooks Brothers, and he'd spend a lot on accessories such as an alligator-skin belt.'[8] Hawkins still regularly visited the New York clubs to hear young players but became increasingly exasperated by what he heard, feeling that too many musicians were being praised for ignoring harmonies and playing with bad tones. Lack of originality was also a theme that Hawkins often dwelt on; he said:

Jam sessions used to be valuable for exchanging ideas. Today with many fellows it seems to be records. A fellow will steal a whole chorus off a record and go out and play it. Perhaps it may be partially from not jamming that so many younger musicians lack originality. I heard a thousand players today and they all sound alike. I guess maybe they're just satisfied with copying.[9]

In 1964 Hawkins often had free nights in which to visit the clubs, since work was not as plentiful for him as it had been in previous years. Hawkins didn't believe in working simply for the sake of working any more, and often declined jobs rather than reduce the price he'd quoted, but clubowners offered a price that they thought was a realistic indication of Hawk's crowd-pulling power (which was diminishing). The young avant-garde players were attracting publicity and big audiences – their records were well displayed in the store racks. Hawkins increasingly took to saying that if he liked the sound of a gig he'd be willing to lower his price. He was by no means desperately short of work, but during the whole of 1964 he didn't make a single recording session under his own name. Producer George Avakian recalls, 'I tried to interest three major labels in recording Hawk then, but nobody cared – "he's over-exposed", "too late, his best days are past" and "but what would you do with him?".'[10]

Early in 1964 Hawk returned to the Friar's Tavern in Toronto to work with Jimmy Dale's Trio; he returned there in the late summer, this time accompanied by Les McCann's group. Another summer booking in Canada was at the Muskoka Sands Inn, Cravenhurst, Ontario, where Hawkins worked with Hugh Clairmont's Trio. During the interim he appeared with Orchestra USA (organized by pianist John Lewis) at the Brooklyn Academy of Music. Hawk recorded two pieces with his large ensemble: a seven-minute version of Benny Golson's composition 'Portrait of Coleman Hawkins' (which had originally been premiered at the October 1959 Monterey Jazz Festival) and a long, somewhat throw-away feature on Arif Mardin's 'Duke Bey'. Hawk's playing of Golson's slow theme is effective enough but his subsequent improvisations have a taut edge, with clipped, discontinuous phrases abounding. A move into a faster tempo opens promisingly but the soloist's eloquence evaporates long before the piece reverts to its opening format.

In April 1964, Hawk and Ben Webster (backed by Eddie Locke, Major Holley and Paul Neves) shared the stage at New York's Little Theatre, taking part in a series of weekend concerts entitled 'Jazz on Broadway'. Holley, Neves and drummer Oliver Jackson played some weekend dates with Hawk at the Village Gate and at a club called the Gold Bug. By this time the Metropole had dropped its jazz policy and was now a 'girlie' bar, so the source of many of Hawk's gigs no longer existed. Norman Granz chose not to tour America with his JATP presentations. However, a jazz package featuring Coleman Hawkins, Harry Edison, Sir Charles Thompson and Jo Jones flew to Europe in October. They linked up with bassist Jimmy Woode (resident in Europe) and played a number of concerts in various countries, including Germany, Denmark, Spain, France and Great Britain.

In Paris, Hawk was interviewed by journalist Mike Hennessey, backstage at the Salle Pleyel. The questioning got off to an uneasy start when an emphatic gesture from Hawkins accidentally knocked over, and smashed, a bottle of whisky. When asked, 'What advice would you give to a young musician taking up the tenor?' Hawk's peremptory reply was, 'Learn to play.' He became more expansive when questioned about the jazz avant-gardists' 'New Thing'. 'They're playing "Freedom" and they're playing "Extensions", whatever these things are. Man, I don't know what they are. These guys are looking for a gimmick, a short cut. There is no short cut. All I know is that I'm still learning the instrument. I can be busy practicing and playing.'

Hennessy asked, 'What do you do when you're not practising and playing?'

'Drink Scotch,' replied Hawkins, then, after reflecting for a moment, he added, 'and drink Scotch.'

When asked about writing and composing Hawkins agreed that he liked to write and arrange but admitted, 'I am a bit lazy now. I hate to pick up a pen to sign my name, what I hate to do is endorse a cheque. Man, am I in bad shape!'[11]

It was another tongue-in-cheek answer session for Hawkins, but beams of truth shone through his foggy rejoinders. For the first time in his life he had lost interest in the work of most of the younger jazz musicians. 'Free-form' playing was anathema to him, and the deliberate shunning of harmony in favour of undisciplined displays of energy seemed sacrilegious. His statement about drinking also had the ring of truth; by now he was exceeding the formidable quantity of spirits that had been his regular intake for years. His comments about composing and arranging also offered clues to reality. He had always procrastinated about arranging, even though it was obvious he was a gifted orchestrator, but even when he had time on his hands he chose not to complete any scores. The same situation applied to his composing; he could think up a new tune (particularly one based on a standard chord sequence) with the minimum of effort, yet he did so only when one was needed for a recording session. He understood all of the classical forms completely, but shunned the idea of writing any extended works; in later years he didn't even bother to keep manuscript paper handy: 'I can only write when I feel like it,' he said.[12] On one occasion when Roy Eldridge asked him to write out 'I Mean You', a theme he had recorded in 1946 with Fats Navarro, Hawkins had to go out and buy some manuscript paper in order to fulfil the task. He joked about the situation but said it was a fortuitous piece of shopping because while he was in music store he bought the music of 'Deux Arabesques', which he liked to play on the piano and on the saxophone.

The pattern of Hawkins's life changed dramatically when he moved out of the family apartment, though he still visited his wife and children there, and Major Holley occasionally saw him helping to carry in the groceries, but for much of the time he spent in his Central Park West flat in 1964 he was alone. He had parted from his Swiss girlfriend, Heidi, a development that didn't greatly surprise the musicians who worked with him regularly. There had been some acrimonious exchanges in public between the couple, most of them (so it seemed to bystanders) ignited by Hawk's unreasoning jealousy; if this particular girl showed even the smallest degree of friendliness towards any other man Hawkins became angry.

The musician who was closest to Hawkins during this period was drummer Eddie Locke. Locke (born 1930 in Detroit, Michigan) originally came to New York in a dancing and drumming duo (with Oliver Jackson). After Bop and Locke had worked the Apollo in 1954 and toured Canada, they decided to stay in New York, where both became highly regarded drummers. Locke had occasionally worked with Roy Eldridge at the Metropole but his first gig with Coleman Hawkins was a one-night stand out at Fire Island in a group that also featured Roy Eldridge, Dickie Wells and Ray Bryant. Both Hawkins and Eldridge were impressed by the swing and power of Locke's drumming, and by his enthusiasm; he began working regularly in their quintet. During the first series of dates Locke noticed Hawkins listening to him very carefully while he backed Eldridge's solo, then he walked across and said, 'Are you playing like that for me?' Locke assured Hawkins that he was and from then on the two men's friendship gradually developed, with Hawk adopting a warm, patriarchal approach to the young drummer:

> Coleman could sometimes be withdrawn, but I rarely saw him get mad with anyone. Only two instances spring to mind: once an A & R man at Prestige kept clipping in with advice on this and that, and Hawk boomed at him, 'Let me play my horn, and

you sit in there and do your business.' Another time in Philadelphia he became angry with a young journalist who came up and asked a lot of things without doing any homework, so Hawk bristled and said, 'Why the hell do you guys always ask me the same damn questions? I've answered them a thousand times and it's all in print, but still I get asked. Just sit and listen to our music tonight and write about that, not about something I did twenty or thirty years ago.' Yet with younger musicians he could be a model of patience, carefully explaining some point about theory. He was the one who encouraged me to learn something about the piano, he'd say, 'Locke, why don't you study the piano? Learn to play a few pieces, no matter how simple they are they will give you a broader understanding of all music.' And he was delighted when I started playing the piano for my own pleasure. He'd say, 'We'll scare these pianists when we sit down and play,' and then he'd let out a deep chuckle. There was a warm side to his personality and he was deeply touched when I took one of my young sons around to him on Easter Sunday so that the kid could give him an Easter egg. And it wasn't unusual to see him brushing away the tears from his eyes when he was listening to a classical aria or a piano soloist.

When I first knew him he loved to cook, and he'd invite us around for a meal, elaborate stuff, beautifully prepared. He appreciated good food and loved to visit Zutty Singleton's home because Zutty used to make a special gumbo for him. Hawk said his mother was a good cook – I never met her, but I heard Hawk talking on the telephone to her and I could tell by his answers that his mother still thought of him as her young son. Coleman didn't talk too much about his childhood, but he did tell me that his grandfather bought him a baby bear as a present, but that the creature grew too quickly and practically clawed the house down. I joked with him and said, 'So that's where you get your deep-down voice, imitating your playmate.'

He was never a drunk, he could always hold his drink, even though he used to put a lot away. On one of my first gigs with him he drank a half a gallon of gin, and allowing for the fact that it was a very hot night I was still amazed. But no matter how much he drank he always seemed in command of his instrument. I went with him out to a date he did at the Brooklyn Academy of Music; there was a lot of waiting about and Hawk was, in truth, loaded, but he walked over to the music stand and looked at the orchestration that was spread over five pages and he sightread it all perfectly. Mostly he drank J & B whisky or Hennessey Cognac. He smoked at least a couple of packs of Salem cigarettes a day. I never heard him talk politics, but he loved to discuss baseball, and always watched it on television. If there was a good game on he'd phone me up and tell me. His particular favorite was the pitcher Sandy Colefax; in fact he liked individuals more than teams, more interested in so and so doing well than a particular team. He took some interest in basketball; one of the star players, Will Chamberlain, was a fan of Hawk's, and Hawk could talk knowledgeably with him, but he much preferred baseball.

Hawk didn't dwell on the 'old days' and if the subject of Fletcher Henderson came up Hawk always said the same thing: 'Biggest mistake Fletcher ever made was in letting Cootie Williams go: he would have been a great asset, as it was he used Russell Smith, and that was no jazz lead.' I must have heard him say that a dozen times or more, but beyond that, very little. If ever he had anything to say about a musician it was usually very brief and to the point; once in the Metropole he said to Eric Dolphy at the bar, 'I can out-melody you.' John Coltrane used to call in to hear Hawk, and I wish I had the beautiful letter that Coltrane wrote to Hawkins; it was a wonderful tribute.

It's true that Hawk and Ben Webster were competitive. On one of the Little Theatre dates we did in 1964, Ben warily asked Hawk, 'What do you want to play?

Hawk said nonchalantly, 'Let's do "Out of Nowhere".'

Then Ben got defensive and said, 'You ain't gonna play none of your crips on me,' so they played something else.

Hawk wasn't naturally an awkward person, but if he held a certain point of view he could be stubborn. When he cared to, Hawk could sum up exactly what an audience needed. I remember when we played a gig out at a black club in Brooklyn. Well, at that time we were used to playing sophisticated rooms mostly and this was a real 'down home' place. Hawk said to me, 'I've got to find something to get them with,' and the tune he chose was 'Joshua Fit the Battle of Jericho'; that was the first time we ever played it together, from then on it became part of our program wherever we played.[13]

Hawkins and Locke enjoyed each other's company, and for a time the younger man acted as chauffeur, as he told Stanley Dance:

Bean had lost his license so many times that I ended up as his driver as well as his drummer. He sold his car and then one day he came out from his place and couldn't get a cab for a long time. When he finally got one he told the guy to drive him right to the showroom, where he bought his last car, the Imperial. Because he had no license, I was the only person to drive it. The furthest it ever went was one weekend in the summer when he had a job at Canaan, near Pittsfield, Mass. He had that car two years but I don't suppose it had a thousand miles on the clock.[14]

By early 1965 Eddie Locke was the only survivor of the original quartet: Barry Harris (yet another Detroiter) had replaced Roland Hanna on piano, and Buddy Catlett had taken Major Holley's place on bass. This was the rhythm section that backed Hawk for the January and February residency that he played at New York's Five Spot (a club on the eastern edge of Greenwich Village). When Eddie Locke briefly worked elsewhere his place was temporarily taken by Bill English. Locke soon returned and, with the rest of the trio, formed part of a six-piece band with which Hawk recorded an album for Impulse. Joining Hawk in the front line were Urbie Green on trombone, and Bill Berry and Snooky Young, who alternated trumpet duties. The role of these illustrious brass players was limited to reading some unelaborate arrangements written by Manny Albam.

Hawk takes the brunt of the solos but Barry Harris's pithy, spry piano playing is also featured, and his playing on the title track 'Wrapped Tight' (a medium-paced twelve-bar blues) fits Hawk's phrases like a glove. But throughout most of the date Hawkins seems lethargic, and even his seven well-formed choruses on 'Wrapped Tight' fail to climax satisfactorily. Some of the numbers are accompanied only by the rhythm section, and on one of these, 'Out of Nowhere', Hawk tries to circumnavigate staleness by playing a series of striking vertical phrases in place of the opening theme, but this brief display of fireworks soon gives way to a succession of familiar patterns.

On 'Indian Summer' Hawkins creates a burring sub-tone effect not dissimilar to the sound that Lester Young tended to produce during the late stages of his career, but Hawk's forceful tonguing is still well in evidence, even though his fingers sound stiff-jointed and his ideas desultory. On 'Red Roses for a Blue Lady' he sounds almost dismissive and 'She's Fit' is nothing more than a filler. 'Intermezzo' has a more pleasing mellowness and the slow ballad 'And I Still Love You' shows that Hawk was still capable of being highly expressive. The outstanding track, however, is 'Beautiful Girl'. This wouldn't find a place in the best fifty of Hawk's ballad recordings but it is still a mightily impressive performance, one that caused Urbie Green and Snooky Young to applaud the old master in the studio.

Soon after that album was recorded, producer Bob Thiele gave his views on the date:

> I think this is the beginning of a slightly new way of playing for Coleman. I think you're going to be hearing more and more rapid phrases, particularly on the up-tempo things. Hawk's breath control is probably not the same as when he was a younger man. The time when he used to play those long, long sweeping phrases has gone, so he has now altered his methods somewhat to suit his present physical condition. Of course it is still pretty exciting the way he plays; his creative energies are as wonderful as ever.[15]

Thiele, who had long championed Hawk's talents, remained a lifelong devotee of Coleman's work. Looking back, he said:

> I first met Coleman Hawkins in the early 1940s, he was playing at Kelly's Stables. 'Bean' was an extremely warm and friendly individual – no ceremony – if he felt one was sincere and appreciative of his playing a strong friendship would build up. Coleman just wanted to enjoy life. He was uncomplicated, trusted people and wanted them to trust him. He wasn't too serious about his personal/financial affairs. He drove a car without a license. I personally obtained membership for him in ASCAP so he could get royalties on songs that he wrote in the early 1920s and 1930s, such as 'One Hour' with the Mound City Blue Blowers. A simple basic approach to life, except when he put the tenor to his lips.[16]

Like Thiele, pianist Barry Harris was a devoted admirer of Hawkins's playing:

> My first direct experience of Coleman Hawkins occurred when I sat in with him. He called an old standard, and although I wasn't entirely familiar with it I'd got to know it by the end of the first chorus, so we got along fine and he said, 'Ah, you Detroits – I've added another Detroit pianist to my collection.' I moved to New York in 1960 and later began working with Hawk regularly. I was then a sort of Bud Powell/Bird disciple, but this old man was my awakening. It's difficult to explain, but my attitude changed almost magically one night when Hawk was playing 'All the Things You are'. What he did on that tune gave me a huge, instant insight into music as a whole. I'd idolized Parker, but in that moment Coleman sort of knocked Bird off the pedestal I'd always kept him on. Coleman didn't play chords, he played movements, and that concept has always stayed with me. His musical ideas were ageless and he had such knowledge he could be like a chameleon; if he was playing with one set of musicians he'd fit in perfectly, but then he'd play something with guys from a totally different era of music and it would sound just as right.[17]

The Hawkins quartet clicked at the Five Spot, and it seemed as if they had no sooner finished a two-week residency than they were rebooked for another stay. Roy Eldridge came to sit in with the group and made such an impression that he was booked to bring in his own quartet to work opposite Hawk's group. In March 1965, during a week's gap in bookings, Hawkins moved across town to guest with Earl Hines's trio (Hines piano, George Tucker bass and Oliver Jackson drums) at the Village Vanguard. These four musicians also spent a day at New York's Video Tape Center filming a pilot for a proposed television series. The film (directed by Karl Genus) included three numbers featuring Hawkins: 'Just One More Chance' (which Hawk and Hines had recorded on their only previous studio date together, back in 1944), 'Crazy Rhythm' and 'Lady Be Good'. A take of 'Indian Summer' was edited from the final version of the film, which failed to become part of an intended series; happily all the numbers were issued on a Pumpkin album.

The quartet filmed until 10.30 p.m. and then made their way to the Village Vanguard to play a full night's work; at 3 a.m. they were rocking their way into the final number of their long stint: 'I'll See You in My Dreams'. Later on in Hines's stay at the Village Vanguard, Hawkins and Roy Eldridge joined Earl's trio for a recording session at the club which produced a disappointing batch of standard tunes. The audience sounds lively enough, but there is scant joy for those who have the music on record, for the album is a muddled, below-par session that is not very clearly recorded. With no routines mapped out on 'C Jam Blues', confusion wins the day, but minor hitches within a jam session can be part of the fun; what is not expected is to hear Hawkins in difficulties with the constantly shifting patterns in Earl Hines's accompaniment. In response to some heavy bass-register work from the pianist Hawkins eventually starts to rock vigorously, but another kaleidoscope of sounds from the keyboard seems to unbalance the saxist and he drops into a series of unthrilling riffs. Hawk sounds equally fidgety on 'Take the A Train'.

The quartet sides (with Hawkins and the rhythm section) are just as unattractive. Hawk starts 'Rosetta' at exactly the tempo he wanted but his playing soon becomes an exercise in fits and starts. The pianist-composer is in fine, flamboyant form, and only his quick thinking (and the swift reactions of his rhythm-section partners) prevents 'Sweet Georgia Brown' from degenerating into disaster. After a businesslike start Hawk takes a breather, allowing Hines to fashion a highly adventurous solo, then the tenorist re-enters in a way that suggests he had lost full command of his fingers. He produces an approximate version of his 'Hollywood Stampede' riffs, missing notes haphazardly and sounding befuddled. In an attempt to clear a musical pathway, Hawk attempts some wild arpeggios but the misshapen phrases send a red alert to his accompanists who wisely lasso the sequence to bring the proceedings to an end. It is to be hoped the date left Hawkins with nothing more than a hangover, for the resultant recordings are among the worst he ever made, but they are challenged by his contribution to a live session recorded a fortnight later at a Charlie Parker Memorial Concert held at Carnegie Hall (10 April). Here Hawk shared front-line duties with Roy Eldridge and J.J. Johnson in a brisk 'Now is the Time' (backed by Billy Taylor, Tommy Potter and Roy Haynes). Hawkins takes ten consecutive choruses, and none of them is worthy of him; only an occasional phrase reminds us of his past glories.

Alcohol was gradually beginning to stalk Hawkins, but he was not totally surprised by the way the recordings with Hines turned out. On his way to the studios to film the television show Hawk shared a taxi with Dan Morgenstern who asked, 'How do you enjoy working with Earl?' There was a pause, then Hawkins answered weightily, 'I like to listen to him but I ain't particular about playing with him.'[18] Yet socially Hines and Hawkins got on well; the only frisson of ill will during the Village Vanguard dates came from another great musician, Charles Mingus, whose group was playing opposite the Hines–Hawkins unit. Hawkins, who was talking loudly with a friend during one of Mingus's sets, was publicly rebuked by the bassist-leader. Hawk's reaction was simply to throw up his hands in mock horror.[19]

During this period Hawkins again recorded with a large orchestra, this time conducted (and arranged for) by Frank Hunter. It's a disappointing collection; Hawk is not treated too kindly by the recording balance, but even so it is obvious that he was not filling the saxophone as he once did. His fingers are nimble enough here, but the bravura that such an album demands is rarely in evidence. The rhapsodic Hawkins of earlier years would have delivered a feast of rich sounds on this succession of ballads. The young Hawk would have triumphed majestically over the shortcomings of the shrill violins, his bold vibrato of yester-year might have stirred the ensemble, and his enthusiasm might have linked the efforts of the jazz rhythm section with their turgid 'straight' colleagues. The two excursions into the classical repertoire (Schumann's Traumarei and Brahms's Lullaby) are nothing more than quaint; Traumarei is taken too fast and the Lullaby is presented as a slow, smoochy foxtrot. Both pieces were long-time favourites of Hawkins, but his treatment of them gives no indication of this.

The best number from the date is Hawk's own composition 'Lazy Butterfly', an attractive slow theme, beautiful more than pretty. Its release on *The Hawk and the Hunter* album solved a riddle for trombonist Eddie Bert:

> In 1940 I had a Wilcox-Fay recorder (it made acetates), so I used to take broadcasts off the air. One night I caught Hawk's big band from the Savoy Ballroom and recorded his theme song. Next time I saw him I asked him whose song it was – he said he didn't know. I asked him the title and he said he didn't know. Years later I found a record he did with strings and there was that tune. The title was 'Lazy Butterfly'.[20]

25
A Finale of Despair

During one of his residencies at the Five Spot Hawkins was interviewed by the *New York Daily News* and asked to give advice to young musicians. He had this to say:

> If they think they are doing something new they ought to do what I do every day. I spend at least two hours every day listening to Johann Sebastian Bach, and man, it's all there. If they want to learn how to improvise around a theme, which is the essence of jazz (adding blue notes), they should learn from the master. He never wastes a note, and he knows where every note is going and when to bring it back. Some of these cats go way out and forget where they began or what they started to do. Bach will clear it up for them.[1]

Again and again throughout the years, Hawk referred to Bach's greatness; on another occasion he said, 'Those quartets and things that call themselves "modern" jazz quartets, all they're doing is trying to play Bach; they're playing Bach and Handel, that's all it is. They aren't playing modern classics because the jazz ear couldn't stand a modern classic.'[2] Hawkins was never a slavish copier of anyone's work, but it is fascinating to compare his method of thematic development and the form of Bach's writings for unaccompanied violin.

Hawk's first big date of 1966 was a prestigious concert held at the Lincoln Center, New York, on 19 February. It was billed as 'Tenor Titans' and featured Hawkins, John Coltrane, Zoot Sims and Sonny Rollins; Rollins, of his own volition, invited Yusef Lateef to perform in the show. From the galaxy of jazz that was heard it was impossible to say who was the most 'modern' player on the stage, but it was clear that Hawkins could still rise to a challenging situation, even though his solo spot was limited to one number. But the main talking point after the show was not about Hawk's performance but about his appearance. He had lost a lot of weight and was not immaculately dressed; *Down Beat* described him as 'looking like the picture of a jazz patriarch with his flowing full grizzled beard'.

During the last part of 1965 Hawkins had spent a lot of time alone in his apartment, and in doing so had let a few of his old routines slip away, including his habit of shaving regularly. In the past he often called in to a barber for a shave when time was short, but now he no longer even bothered about getting his hair cut; it seemed as though he had ceased to care how he looked. Yet, only months earlier at the filming with Earl Hines, he had been described as 'the arbiter of elegance, immaculate in a charcoal-grey suit, white shirt and sober tie'.[3] There was no question of Hawkins 'dropping out' – he was still intent on working – and by late February he began the first of a series of residencies (with his own group) at the Village Vanguard, run by veteran impresario Max Gordon.

Hawkins soon established himself as one of Gordon's favourite musicians, and what began as a trial residency (from 25 February until 6 March 1966) turned into the first of seven bookings the group played there during the following ten months. Hawk was working with a familiar team of accompanists; Eddie Locke, Barry Harris and, temporarily back in the quartet, Major Holley. Barry Harris recalled these bookings:

> Hawk's sound was still incredible and this was brought home to me at the Village Vanguard. The trio used to start out, and we'd play a few numbers before he came on stage. He'd walk into the club then go out the back to warm up behind closed doors, but the old man was so powerful that even in his warm-ups he was as loud as the trio combined and he'd be way out the back. His practise runs filled the club before he'd even got on to the stand.[4]

During their first residency at the Vanguard, Hawk's group worked opposite Thelonious Monk's quartet, which allowed Eddie Locke the opportunity to observe the relationship between Hawkins and his former associate:

> Monk was always on his best behavior when Hawk was around, whether at the Vanguard or the Five Spot. He'd play little things in his solos that Hawk recognized from arrangements they'd played years before. Hawk would listen and laugh and say to me, 'Listen to that, he's trying to tempt me to get up on the bandstand and blow with him.' Monk came to one of Hawk's birthday parties – I think it was 1965 or 1966. He came to the apartment and it was obvious that he paid great attention to everything Hawk said. Monk never did anything eccentric when Hawk was around, no silly stuff at all. That year, for a joke, somebody (I think maybe one of Hawk's children) put a figurine of the Beatles on his birthday cake; Hawk laughed like hell at it.[5]

Hawkins rarely mentioned rock music, but he did say on one occasion, 'You know . . . rock and roll has a lot of old music behind it. Don Redman could make some very good "gutbucket" arrangements. We used to call it "gutbucket", that's another name for rock and roll.'[6] When asked to comment on avant-garde saxophonists who deliberately distorted the tone of their instruments, Hawk said, 'Compared to this, rock and roll sounds like Beethoven.'[7]

Another booking at the Village Vanguard led to Hawkins sharing the billing with John Coltrane's quartet, and at a later date Hawk's quartet worked opposite the Bill Evans Trio. Hawk's personnel remained virtually constant, though Al Dailey came in briefly on piano. In between his engagements at the Vanguard Hawkins played brief residences in Philadelphia and in Providence, Rhode Island; he also guested with bassist Wendell Marshall's trio in Irvington, New Jersey. During the late spring of 1966 Hawk was featured at a jazz festival in Austin, Texas (organized by George Wein), where he was accompanied by Toshiko Akiyoshi on piano. At the Austin festival, George Wein, usually a shrewd alchemist when it came to blending pick-up groups, decided to have Hawkins, Stan Getz and Bud Freemen on stage together. He suggested they all solo on 'Body and Soul'. All three nodded agreement but Hawkins was determined to take the lion's share of the song with which he was so closely associated. After the theme he launched into what *Down Beat* described as 'three unbelievably wonderful choruses'. His would-be adversaries decided that this was not the time to issue challenges and the piece ended with a cascade of notes from Hawkins.

Hawk had proved yet again that he was still highly competitive, a point that Sonny Stitt made in the mid-1960s when he said, 'Coleman Hawkins isn't young anymore, but buddy, you get on the bandstand with him and you've got your hands full.' On the flight to Austin, Hawk and Bobby Hackett travelled together. Hackett recalled the trip in an interview he did with Max Jones:

> We're sitting next to each other and the stewardess comes over and I said to her, 'Miss, I want you to know that this gentleman is the world's greatest saxophonist; if there's anything he wants, see to it that he gets it.' He had a brandy every fifteen minutes. I don't know how he ever managed it, because he'd stay on his feet. He was killing himself but he did what he wanted to.[8]

In the autumn of 1966, Hawk's quartet played a weekend at the Madison Club in Baltimore (using Ron Carter on bass instead of Major

Holley). They also did a residency at Lennie's-on-the-Turnpike in Boston, Mass. But the biggest event of the year for Hawkins occurred in late November when he left the USA for Europe as part of a Jazz at the Philharmonic package. Norman Granz had decided it was time to resume touring with an all-star troupe, and his 1966 line-up consisted of Hawkins, James Moody, Benny Carter, Dizzy Gillespie, Clark Terry, Zoot Sims, Teddy Wilson, Louie Bellson and Bob Cranshaw plus blues singer/guitarist T-Bone Walker.

In the concert held at London's Festival Hall Hawkins had a triumph; though his set was relatively brief, covering three numbers ('Lover Come Back to Me', 'September Song' and 'Body and Soul') he won considerable praise from local critics. Bob Dawbarn wrote, 'It was Hawkins's night. I don't know which local brew he'd been sampling but he should carry a barrel of it around with him.' The *Melody Maker*'s editor, Jack Hutton, added, 'Hawk groped his way on stage after Norman Granz had called "His Majesty" looking as though he'd wakened from a deep sleep. But he didn't sound sleepy. He blew like a dream with Benny Carter who sounded curiously dated compared to the older fellah.'

But, as had happened in America, audiences familiar with Hawkins's barrel-chested walk were astonished to see a frail figure shuffle to the centre of the stage. The beard was unkempt, the trousers creased and the shirt collar wildly askew. Those who heard several of the shows on that tour were also struck by Hawk's inconsistency. He often had to rely on his colleagues to prompt him if there were any alterations to the programme; this became apparent in a show the troupe did for British television. An obviously confused Hawkins asked Benny Carter, 'What are we playing?' as Teddy Wilson created the piano introduction of 'Blue Lou'. Yet, if Hawkins was in the right mood, having shared good pre-concert company (and providing he had taken just the right quantity of spirits on board before he went on stage), he could blow magnificently. He retained his strategy of answering a bad review with a fine performance but those familiar with his latter day work found something vaguely ominous in the stark way that Hawkins delivered his unaccompanied version of 'September Song'.

The JATP tour visited Denmark in November, which allowed the Danish television producer Sten Bramsen (a devoted jazz lover) the opportunity to reunite Ben Webster – then living in Denmark – with Hawkins for a televised version of one of their album duets, 'You'd Be So Nice to Come Home to'. However, Bramsen was bemused temporarily by the musicians' response to his request that they perform that number. Hawkins said, 'Don't know it'; Webster asked, 'Could you please whistle the tune?' and Teddy Wilson added, 'I'm not familiar with the changes.' Bramsen's enthusiasm eventually won the day and the group ended up playing a highly satisfactory version of the old standard.[9]

Hawkins was choosy about whom he spoke to during that European trip, but he was still warm and lucid with old friends and on the occasions that he agreed to give interviews he had some incisive things to say:

> On the saxophone, sound is *it*. The whole thing is sound. I didn't have to work on it – the sound just came. You take a lot of boys over in New York, those that do all this playing – and the crazy ones that do all the crazy playing. They can't get my sound. That's what bugs them – so they have to get into these other things. Even people like Sonny Rollins ain't got my sound. And they never will.

He then added a comment about his old rival: 'Lester Young didn't change any conception of tenor playing. It was his *sound*, that's all.'[10]

James Moody, one of Hawk's co-tenorists on that tour, confirms that Hawk was still blowing with a huge sound. The trip brought back memories of his European tour with Hawkins in 1949:

> In those intervening years the physical change in Hawk was greater than the musical change; he had changed from a powerful figure into a frail slow-walking old man. He was playing OK, but you could tell he wasn't strong, and whenever I could I carried his tenor case for him. He was drinking two fifths of Courvoisier a day and this wasn't helping. I think Norman Granz said, 'You've got to cut down,' and I think he did – to a fifth a day. He was only eating a tiny amount each day and he complained of being terribly constipated. Finally he went to doctor on the tour and that problem was overcome.

Writer Steve Voce, recalling Hawkins on that tour, said:

> He told me that he had no interest in anything, and when pushed said that he had no remaining pride in his own achievements. He had done everything he wanted to do musically many years before and heard nothing now in either jazz, classical or any other kind of music that stimulated any kind of interest. He went on to talk about his belief in ghosts and I didn't know what to say to him.

The conversation took a lighter turn and Hawkins said, 'What I like to do is sit at home and take things easy, maybe go out for some Chinese food because it's bulky and stretches the stomach, because I don't eat much and

I like to have a taste. But what I really like to do is sit home and do nothing. What I like best is doing nothing.'[11]

An upright 'practice' piano was available in most of the dressing rooms on that concert tour; Hawkins usually made a beeline for it and began amusing himself by playing various classical pieces, much as he would have done in his New York apartment. Backstage, Hawk and Dizzy Gillespie sometimes whiled away time by playing a tenor-sax-and-trumpet version of works for two violins that they had memorized, but often Hawk sat by himself and sank into a gloomy mood. His old friend from Belgium, Albert Bettonville, observed this melancholic attitude when he visited Hawk at what turned out to be his last ever date in Brussels:

> He was extremely tired of everything and just stared absently. 'Sure I recognize you and your wife,' he said. He was sitting in a corner of the dressing room, looking at the floor. I showed him photos I had taken of him, ten years ago, twenty years ago, none of which he had ever seen. I asked him to take any he liked as a gift. He refused them all, didn't even look at them. 'Time is passed and gone,' he said.[12]

Hawk's Dutch friend Pete Felleman was apalled at his old hero's appearance as he emerged on to the stage of the Concertgebouw in Amsterdam:

> I could have cried; he looked a hundred, he was a shrunken man. He looked very sick and when he wasn't playing he stood there letting his lower jaw wobble from side to side. It was so sad and I felt Benny Carter really helped him through the performance. Afterwards I started to go upstairs to the dressing room but an ex-drummer, Hank Van Leer, said, 'I really wouldn't go in there. Hawk is in very bad shape,' so I turned back, reluctantly, but I've always regretted not going in to see him for the last time.[13]

Hawkins's comments to Steve Voce about his food intake highlighted a big change in the saxophonist's daily habits. He had always been a trencherman, able to tackle huge meals at any time of day – or night. It was not unknown for him to have a late breakfast consisting of eight fried eggs; even in the late 1950s he could demolish two full Chinese meals at a 3 a.m. sitting. Eating triple portions of his favourite dishes was a regular ritual in the 1920s and he maintained this champion appetite through to his middle age. Roy Eldridge recalled Hawkins being aghast when he learnt that Lester Young was going for days without food on a JATP tour.

> Hawk and me sat up for hours one night in Saint Louis, trying to get him interested in eating something, and Hawk kept saying, 'If you drink you gotta eat – that's the

> rule'. Well, years passed and what did I see but Hawk going just the same way. It was like a bad movie. We used to spend so much time talking about food when we worked together; people used to wonder what we were chuckling about on the bandstand, usually it was talk about some special food or other. When he cut right down on his eating I took to phoning him and telling him about a particular dish we were having at home and he'd say, 'Yeah, I'm going to cook that,' but you knew he never would.

Sonny Stitt was another who could scarcely believe Hawk's changed attitude towards food, recalling how, in earlier years, Hawkins had stressed the importance of eating regularly: 'He used to make me put my bottle down and take me to eat fish.'[14] Ben Webster solemnly said that Hawk's frailty was due to him losing his love of pork: 'Bean was always a great one for the hog, but now he won't hardly touch it. Fancy that, got all them pressure cookers and things and no inclination to cook himself even an egg.'[15]

Hawk's style of tenor-sax playing needed to call on huge resources of stamina; to compensate for his minimal intake of food he drank more and more brandy, a disastrous course to take. His debilitated frame shrank even further. The first signs that something was seriously wrong occurred in February 1967 during a booking in Toronto, Canada. Hawkins had journeyed there to play a residency at the Colonial Tavern, accompanied by Wynton Kelly (piano), Jimmy Cobb (drums) and Larry Ridley (bass). Ridley recalls the unhappy occasion:

> Bean was going through a rough period; he wasn't too vocal about what was happening, but he looked very remorseful and went on long binges. On the opening night at the Tavern he was on his second number when he lurched badly then crumpled up, regurgitating as he did so. I think it was Jimmy Cobb who got to him first and propped his head up.[16]

A uniformed policeman arrived at the club after an emergency call had been made, but by this time Hawkins was sitting up and told him, 'Don't worry about me. All I need is a good steak and a couple of brandies – I'll be alright.' It transpired that Hawk hadn't eaten anything since leaving Baltimore some days earlier, and immediately on his arrival at the Tavern he had been informed of the deaths of two old colleagues, Edmond Hall and Muggsy Spanier. This had set him off on a heavy drinking bout. After his fall he was helped upstairs and a taxi came to take him to St Michael's Hospital. When the cab got to the hospital, however, Hawkins refused to get out and demanded to be taken to his hotel. A hospital attendant couldn't persuade him to change his mind so the taxi driver duly took him to the Lord Simcoe Hotel. Next morning he announced he was feeling better and that he would be able to play that night, which he did. His only complaint was that he had twisted his knee.

When he next saw Wynton Kelly he asked, 'What happened to me?'

The pianist replied, 'You just fell down.'

'Oh, that's normal,' said Hawkins, 'Nothing to worry about at all.'[17]

Hawkins finished his booking in Toronto without further mishap, but his comment about falls being the normal state of affairs was proved to be all too true during the coming months. He returned to New York and rested up awhile, but was soon back on the road again as part of a new package Norman Granz had organized for a tour of North America. Several of the same faces who had been on the recent JATP tour of Europe were in the troupe, including Clark Terry, Zoot Sims, Benny Carter and Hawkins. They were joined by Ella Fitzgerald (with the Jimmy Jones Trio) and the Oscar Peterson Trio (Peterson; Sam Jones, bass; and Louis Hayes, drums). Throughout the long tour various star attractions were added for specific concerts, including a Carnegie Hall date in April.

All in all the tour spanned thirteen weeks, from 25 March until 1 July, playing major cities from coast to coast and travelling into Canada. The package played Montreal on 2 April then moved to Toronto to play a concert at the Massey Hall on the following night. Canadian jazz fans, having read about Hawkins's recent local calamity in their newspapers, anxiously awaited his entry on stage. Don Brown, reviewing the JATP concert for *Coda*, summed up this anxiety:

> A shrunken figure wearing a full, grizzled grey beard shuffled stiffly on stage carrying a tenor saxophone. My God! Coleman Hawkins! Hawk blinked a few times, put his horn to his lips and attempted manfully to summon up his once majestic tone. The audience seemed to sense that something was amiss, and Peterson and his sidemen were visibly embarrassed for the grand old man. I think everyone was relieved when he finally made it through to the end of the piece. Strangely enough he had better luck with a faster number 'Stuffy' but this was still only a pale reminder of the great Coleman Hawkins.[18]

This was not the pattern of the entire tour. If Hawkins had rest and food he could manage the schedule and perform satisfactorily, even when the itinerary called for two concerts a day, as at the Civic Opera House in Chicago on 14 April (where the entire Duke Ellington Orchestra were added to the bill). But the problem was persuading Hawkins to eat. Oscar

Peterson managed to cajole him into taking a snack here and there but, left to his own devices, Hawk would go for days without eating anything, all the while sipping from a brandy bottle. This regime was courting disaster, and in Oakland, California on 30 June (one of the last dates of the tour) the inevitable happened. Hawkins staggered on stage and appeared incapable of blowing his horn. Saxophonist Jerry Vejmola has vivid memories of the spectacle: 'I realized that something was badly wrong, that Hawkins was ill or something, but a lot of the audience felt mad and there was quite a lot of booing.'[19]

Reviewer Phillip Jacka painted a grim picture of the sequence of events:

> In the early moments of 'September Song' the saxophonist groped for a low-register note and drew only air. Half a dozen hissing attempts underlined the artist's desperation. Drunk, I thought. So why not? Who does not know that the Hawk drinks to excess? Finally the man turned and shuffled toward the nearest object of familiarity – a microphone. Norman Granz emerged from beyond the focus of the floodlights; at the same moment Oscar Peterson grimly abandoned the changes of 'September Song' to converge on the fallen figure. I was told Coleman Hawkins was hospitalized in Los Angeles the next day. It is possible he will never play another note.[20]

Others heard the same rumour, including the respected writer Ralph J. Gleason, who passed it on to his readers via a syndicated column. In turn the story was picked up by an international news agency and telexed around the world. It was as though Hawkins had played his last note. This was not the case, and the first to make this point emphatically in print was Don Morgenstern in *Down Beat*, who took Ralph Gleason to task for suggesting such a thing, and for making the supposition that Hawkins had a 'death wish'. Morgenstern wrote: 'Hawkins was not hospitalized. Quite to the contrary, the great tenor saxophonist played the following night at the Hollywood Bowl in Los Angeles and performed brilliantly.' Morgenstern went on to include an open letter to Ralph Gleason which the Baroness Pannonica Koenigswarter had written and sent to *Down Beat*; it read:

> Dear Mr Gleason,
>
> Have you ever had the privilege of hearing the great Coleman Hawkins laugh? There is no laugh like it in the world. It comes from *wa-a-ay* down and is as gigantic and all-encompassing as the sound of his horn! Not a trace of a 'death wish' in it, Mr Gleason . . . You see, I happened to be with him Tuesday night (10 July) when your quasi-obituary appeared in the *New York Post*. We were having dinner at Art

> D'Lugoff's Village Gate when somebody showed it to him, and when he got to the part following his supposed incarceration in a Los Angeles hospital where you said, 'and we don't know if he'll ever play again', the Coleman Hawkins roar of laughter rang out, and almost stopped the show! Because right after the incident you described in such dramatic terms, vast audiences were giving him standing ovations at the Carter-Barron Amphitheatre in Washington for seven nights in a row! Coleman Hawkins is in the best of health and he was not hospitalized in Los Angeles or anywhere else. If he had a momentary indisposition during an exceedingly strenuous tour, that is all it was: a momentary indisposition. Driving around the town in his brand-new Chrysler Imperial or relaxing in his beautiful penthouse overlooking Central Park, Coleman Hawkins shows no signs of suffering from frustration or from a hostile society. And indeed, why should he? He is as great a giant today as he always has been. He is still blowing everyone off the scene.

When the news of the original report reached England, Hawk's old friends Renée and Leslie Diamond immediately wrote a letter of commiseration to him. Hawk replied (on 17 August 1967): 'We have some fools over here writing for the papers; they write anything. I haven't been ill, and I haven't been in hospital. This nut was talking about me in the hospital in Los Angeles when I was at the Carter-Barron Amphitheatre in Washington, DC.' This wasn't simply a case of Hawk putting on a brave face about an impending tragedy; fortified by a few drinks he genuinely believed that he was in reasonable shape. And friends like the Baroness 'Nica' and other people close to Hawkins, including his family, had failed to observe how drastically he had changed during the previous eighteen months. But a quiet voice made itself heard via the correspondence column of *Down Beat*, and it indicated that things were far from satisfactory with Hawkins's health.

Sigmund Shapiro from Baltimore had been at one of the JATP concerts in Washington DC. After pointing out that he had long regarded Hawkins as a jazz giant, Shapiro commented, with genuine poignancy, on the performance at the Carter-Barron Amphitheatre:

> It consisted of three tunes. Each tune was attacked in the same way – little two-and-a-half-measure phrases, evenly spaced as if he were trying to feel his way. He was backed by Oscar Peterson's trio and the real pro was Peterson, who did his best to cover up Bean's seeming inability to perform. I thought at first it was a put-on; it was a rainy, muggy night and audiences, instruments and performers were quite soggy. We were halfway back in the stands but even at that distance I could see a somewhat bewildered or 'out of it' look on Hawkins's face. He received no standing ovation, but a smattering of puzzled applause. It was a very unhappy night for me.

In his letter to Renée and Leslie Diamond, Hawkins mentioned that he had been booked by Norman Granz to tour Europe with Oscar Peterson's trio in October; in retrospect this seems to have been a fine gesture on Granz's part to show Hawkins that he still had the utmost faith in his musical abilities. Hawk realized that the tour would be a big test and became determined both to make the trip and to quash the rumours about his poor health. He told Leonard Feather in a telephoned interview:

> I'm feeling just fine, I've been staying home listening to records, and keeping busy eating up a storm. I'm making myself a steak right now. Have I put on weight? You better believe it. There's nothing much happening in New York at present – but when the concert tour played a week at the Carter-Barron in Washington, you should have seen the crowds! They were sitting out there in the rain all through the show.

Feather asked, 'Have you heard any good young tenor players lately?' and Hawkins replied, 'No, but I hear from the tenor players. Sonny Rollins just called. No, we didn't talk music, we talked fruit. We're both on a big health kick, eating lots of fruit.'[21]

As much by determination as by diet, Hawkins managed to make the tour of Europe in late 1967. The first round of dates was a series of concerts with the Oscar Peterson Trio (Sam Jones, bass and Bobby Durham, drums). Hawk was not in a robust mood for any of the shows, but he was generally in command of his saxophone. When he couldn't get what he termed 'the right kind of food' he went without, and inevitably this produced some uneven performances. In Spain, at the Palau de la Musica Catalana, Barcelona, on 11 November, Hawkins was booed by a number of people in the audience, but his two concerts at the Queen Elizabeth Hall in London were generally well received. After playing dates on the Continent, Hawk returned to Britain for a series of one-night stands, on most of which he was accompanied by London-based musicians.

Jimmy Parsons, an employee at Ronnie Scott's club, acted as road manager on most of these engagements:

> On one date I had to take Hawk up to Newcastle. I think he played that date with a local rhythm section. I called for him at the Piccadilly Hotel at about 8.30 in the morning so that we could catch a train. His first words were, 'Where can I buy some liquor?' I took him to an Oddbins shop nearby and he tottered in and bought some Rémy Martin – five-star – the best; this was for the journey. He kept the bottle wrapped in brown paper but before we got on to the train he transferred the contents to an elegant silver decanter and he sat there sipping the Cognac throughout the

journey. It was shortly after his birthday and to mark the occasion the clubowner in Newcastle insisted on buying Hawkins another bottle of Cognac, and that was downed too. We got back to the luxury hotel and Bean ordered some more Cognac, but by then I'd developed a splitting headache so I went off to bed. I was in the next hotel room to him and I heard him enter his room, pick up the telephone and ask room service to bring him another bottle of Rémy Martin and a pitcher of iced water, as a chaser. This was around 2 a.m., and I think he stayed up drinking by himself for most of the night.[22]

After the tour ended at Manchester on 26 November, Hawkins began a month's residency at Ronnie Scott's club in Frith Street, London. Just before he began working at Ronnie Scott's, Hawk played a date in West Hampstead, London. He was late arriving for this gig; so much so, that a feeling of agitation – and anxiety – grew within the crowded club, but all was forgiven and forgotten the moment Hawk began to play. It was immediately obvious that he was in top form, and playing much better than he had done on his previous few visits to London. It was an example of his sudden, mysteriously unpredictable bursts of inspiration. He appeared to be a dynamo of energy, one that only needed a few seconds' rest to recharge itself; that night he granted only the briefest of solos to his accompanists, Mike Carr (organ), Dave Green (bass) and Tony Crombie (drums). The views I expressed at that club were quoted in the next issue of the *Melody Maker*; I said: 'No tenor player in the world could stand on that stage with the old man tonight,' and though over twenty years have passed I still feel that Hawkins created one of the most remarkable jazz performances that I ever witnessed.

Some of Hawk's performances at Ronnie Scott's club were almost as lively. It was as if Hawk's lengthiest stay in Europe for many years had rekindled some of his prowess and vigour of earlier times. But the transformation hadn't caused Hawk to resume his gargantuan eating habits. Pete King, co-owner of Scott's club, almost had to force Hawkins to eat; he recalls, 'He was such a frail old man by this time, we considered it an achievement if we were able to get one cup of soup in him.'[23] Even so, Hawkins somehow summoned up enough energy to blow some powerful music, backed by Carr, Green and Crombie. These three did most of the dates with Hawkins, though occasionally Dave Holland and Ken Baldock deputized for Green on bass.

Critic Val Wilmer, reviewing Hawkins's stay at Scott's for *Down Beat*, gave the veteran such ecstatic praise that the magazine put his photograph on their cover with a headline COLEMAN HAWKINS GASSES LONDON. Wilmer wrote:

> He has perhaps weathered age less gracefully than some other Grand Old Men of Jazz, but what counts is the mountain of music that still tumbles nightly from his beautiful horn. The verb 'to coast', so familiar to most of his generation, has no place in the Hawkins book. Of course he's not the Hawkins of 'Body and Soul', but is Gillespie the Dizzy of 'Groovin' High'? No one puts Dizzy down, but people do change with the years. But just by virtue of that huge monolithic sound, you know that Hawk could still give the youngsters a hard time they wouldn't forget.[24]

Hawkins's stay at Scott's club was generally a happy one. Ben Webster, who had moved to Europe in 1964, was visiting London and called in to hear Hawkins, hoping to be asked to sit in. Ronnie Scott recalled, 'When Ben played at the club he'd often invite musicians he knew up on to the bandstand to sit in, but Hawk never did. Dennis Rose asked Hawk why he didn't do the same as Webster, and Hawk replied, 'Ben needs 'em – I don't.' Hawk had a tremendous ego, but in him it was really great.'[25] At Scott's club, the British bandleader Humphrey Lyttelton had an opportunity to see Hawkins at his most taciturn.

> I was sitting with Ben Webster when Hawkins came up to join us . . . The two men sat exchanging badinage until an aristocratic-looking Englishman approached, elegant wife in tow. The man introduced himself as Lord Someone-or-other, presented his wife and reminded Ben that they had met fleetingly before. 'I wonder,' he said, 'if you would do us the great honour of introducing us to Mr Hawkins.' Ben Webster duly obliged, the couple sat down next to Hawkins, and there descended upon the little group a fathomless and seemingly eternal silence.[26]

Lyttelton had previous experience of Hawkins being determinedly mute: 'On the one occasion when I had the perilous task of interviewing him backstage before a concert, he responded to my enquiry as to whether he remembered various friends from the London visits in the thirties with a flat "No", and then stared at me unwaveringly as if to savour my confusion.'[27]

Recalling Hawk's tour and his stay at Scott's club, Jimmy Parsons said:

> He didn't go in for long conversations with anyone, and hardly seemed to take any interest in anything that was going on around him, but he got a lot of pleasure out of people coming up to him to pay homage. He sat there like the Pope, he didn't say much to these well-wishers but he was pleased that they wanted to pay him respect. He seemed so even-tempered; I didn't see him get upset about anything. One night at

Ronnie's exemplified this. Ben Webster came into the dressing room and kept talking non-stop to Bean. Bean was pleased to see Ben but only kept saying, 'Yep, yep, uh-huh' by way of an answer. But suddenly the atmosphere changed; Stan Getz walked in and Ben Webster immediately became uptight. He bristled at the sight of Getz and became openly hostile, saying, 'You insulted a great friend of mine.' Next thing Ben leapt at him and pinned him to the wall. We had to call two guys in to separate them, and throughout all this commotion Hawkins just sat there quietly supping his bowl of soup.[28]

Ronnie Scott was also present at the fracas, which was apparently caused by Webster believing that Getz had insulted Clark Terry, something that Getz emphatically denied: 'Usually there was a great atmosphere when Webster and Hawkins were together,' said Scott, 'and I'd make it my business to get into the dressing room to hear them trading jocular insults. Ben would say, "My daddy used to take me to hear you play"; Hawk would look up and growl, "Ben, you're older than shit."'[29]

After Hawk's stint at Scott's club had ended it was arranged that he would play a further series of one-night stands. Jimmy Parsons recalls:

The tour went smoothly until we went to Reading University. This was a special night [17 January 1968] because Hawk was sharing the session with Ben Webster. Everyone was really looking forward to it, but when I went to collect Hawk from his hotel, around 4 or 5 p.m., he was ill in bed. He was having difficulty in breathing and I said, 'I'll get a doctor.'

'No, don't do that, I don't want a doctor. Let's go and do the gig.' He was very insistent and got up, put his clothes on and was ready to leave.

Every few miles of our ride out to Reading I had to stop the car so that Hawk could throw up the phlegm that was on his chest. I got him to the dressing room at Reading, but I could see he was worse. I called the organizer of the concert and explained the position, then I phoned Pete King to let him know what was happening. The organizer called a doctor, who examined Bean thoroughly and then said, 'This man has pneumonia. You must take him home.' But Bean insisted on going on stage. Ben Webster went out first and played a few numbers, then I made an announcement explaining that Hawkins was ill, but that he had asked to come on stage and play. Bean came out and played no more than a couple of choruses then Jeff Ellison and I had to carry him off. We got him back to London and I called out Dr Sidney Gottlieb who confirmed that Bean had pneumonia, so we cancelled the rest of the tour.[30]

Hawkins rested up briefly then, defying all medical advice, he set out for Scandinavia to play a tour. On 13 February 1968 he opened at the Old Jazzhus Montmartre, Copenhagan, working there for three days with a trio consisting of Lou Bennett, Paul Weeden and Al Heath. For the next series of engagements he was reunited with his former sideman, pianist Kenny Drew, who recalls:

It was obvious that he was very ill when he came to Denmark, but we went on a tour and we played dates at the Old Montmartre Club. We (my former wife and myself) thought it would be good for Hawk to have dinner and relax at our apartment. We lived on the top floor and he managed the five flights of stairs OK, but then he just sat and looked at all the good food and didn't eat one thing, he just sipped his Cognac, couldn't even manage one mouthful.[31]

For the tour dates Kenny Drew (who was resident in Denmark) became part of trumpeter Arnvid Meyer's Orchestra, who had accompanied Hawk on a previous visit to Scandinavia in February 1963. Meyer has vivid memories of Hawk's 1968 visit:

Coleman Hawkins stayed at the Tre Falke Hotel. Tenor saxist Jesper Thilo, drummer Hans Nymand and I went there to collect Hawk and were greeted by the sight of him nicely dressed in dove-blue pyjamas. He looked at us in astonishment and said, 'I'm not ready yet.'

Though Hawk had been informed that part of his tour would involve travelling he was absolutely not prepared to go on the road, or even leave his room. We lost hours trying to persuade him, missing ferry after ferry (which meant my wife had to keep renewing our reservations). We were all on edge. Finally I said we must leave otherwise we would be late for the gig. Hawk replied with a hoarse laugh, 'I'm never late.' Jesper, our young Hawk disciple, was sent to get a paper bag for Hawk's toothbrush and hairbrush, which together with his saxophone was his only baggage for the trip. Once in the car he fell asleep for the four- or five-hour journey to Åbrenrå.

At the venue, Jesper unpacked Hawk's horn, looking in amazement at the awfully stiff reeds and wide mouthpiece opening. The mouthpiece was a specially-made Berg Larson No. 190 [most players used one around the 100 mark]. We Danes hurried on stage to compensate for our late arrival and to warm up the hall before the presentation of the star. After we had played a few numbers there seemed very little reaction from the audience. Something had to happen. Jesper found Hawk in the dressing room sitting exactly as we had left him. Did he understand what was going on at all? We had agreed beforehand that 'In a Mellotone' was to be Hawk's opener: a break on the last two bars of the chorus was to be the soloist's launching pad. No signs of him as we were approaching this break. But, by some wonder, he was there between trombonist John Darville and me exactly at the beginning of the break.

While we were holding our breath he very, very slowly moved one hand from his pocket, hung the sax on the hook, took the cap off the mouthpiece, put it in his pocket, licked the reed, and then, exactly at beat one of the first bar Hawk set off with an authoritative roar containing a world of music; off he flew! Instantaneously we we were struck with awe; his playing seemed to echo what he had said: 'I'm never late.' Hawkins made the whole night a ball.[32]

During the following week Hawk and Arnvid Meyer's Orchestra played in Odense, Holbaek, Korsør and Århus. Meyer comments:

> In Århus he pointed out the exact hotel where he had stayed thirty-three years before. As you know, Hawkins was not a wasteful man himself and he reminded our bass player, who brought his own beer to the gigs, 'Don't forget the empty bottles.' He didn't go in for long conversations; one of the first remarks he made to us was simply, 'I play no Dixieland.' Finding out that we didn't either he said some nice words, apologizing that his health prevented him from playing more with us. In fact his health seemed to improve a bit. As a supplement to his booze and vitamin pills John Darville succeeded in making him eat some food now and then – soup, eggs etc.
>
> At times he was so tired that only an impressive effort of self-preservation enabled him to play. His phrasing would then be somewhat slack, his figures short of breath, incoherent, fragmentary. But in the best moments and in spite of all the decay his music was still wild and grandiose. The overwhelming power, intensity, fierceness and rhythmic drive could still flare up.[33]

Despite Hawk's frailty he consented to record with Kenny Drew, bassist Neils-Henning Ørsted Pedersen and drummer Al Heath. The issued results were a moving version of 'Lover Man', on which Hawkins uses his valuable breath sparingly but to poignant effect, and an unexpectedly spirited 'Sweet Georgia Brown'. Amazingly his strategy of working off his illness succeeded and he slowly began to recover, so much so that *Down Beat* announced his return to the USA by saying, 'An early March arrival from across the Atlantic was Coleman Hawkins, looking hale and hearty after a lengthy stay in England and concerts in Copenhagen.' But the returned traveller realized that he'd been lucky to have survived his illness and those close to him felt that he never fully recovered from that winter trip to Europe.

Pianist Roland Hanna said, 'After that tour he was never again in full health, he was a little wheezy and sometimes lethargic, he couldn't shake off that cough.'[34] As in the previous winter, Hawkins spent a good deal of time alone in his apartment, but he still willed himself to go out and listen to what was happening in the clubs. Major Holley realized that Hawkins was full of despondency during this period of his life: 'I said to him, "Think of all your great achievements and all the things you have done in your life," but he just looked away, he wouldn't discuss it, couldn't bring himself to utter a word.'[35] Hawk's former vocalist, Thelma Carpenter said:

> In the last part of his life he looked a completely different man. I met him on 50th Street, between 7th and 8th, one morning, and he said, 'Come for a drink.' We went into one of the musicians' bars nearby and Coleman couldn't stop trembling. I didn't want a drink, it was too early, but he got a whisky and a glass of some sort of old ale and he drank them as chasers. He was in a bad state and you felt you could hear the drink hitting his stomach, *plop*; there was no food inside him. I thought, 'Oh shit,' remembering this man as a suave, sophisticated creature who radiated masculinity.[36]

But as the warmer weather came the old battler slowly prepared himself for action. Word of his physical instability and the resultant falls had discouraged festival organizers from booking him, but Max Gordon at the Village Vanguard offered Hawk some quartet dates, which led to him playing a brief season there in July 1968 (sharing the stand with the Sonny Rollins Quartet). After a brief lay-off Hawkins returned to the Vanguard in early August, this time working opposite Jimmy Witherspoon. For this booking Hawk's rhythm section – Barry Harris, Eddie Locke and bassist Herman Wright – backed both Hawkins and Witherspoon for their separate sets.

Hawk still looked frail but he kept to schedule for most of his stay at the club. Barry Harris recalled one alarming incident:

> One night at the Village Vanguard Hawkins fell down and as he did so he let out a huge gasp of breath, as though it were his last. But we couldn't get him to go to hospital, which was practically opposite the club. He had a dread of hospitals and said, 'Oh yeah. In the front door and out the back door.' But he had great recuperative powers, he'd eat a good meal and then come back strong.[37]

This fall and Hawk's general unsteadiness led Max Gordon, owner of the Village Vanguard, to the false conclusion that Hawkins was an epileptic, something that is vehemently denied by those close to the tenor saxist. Baroness 'Nica' felt so strongly about this issue (after reading Max Gordon's 1980 book *Live at the Village Vanguard*) that she wrote to *Jazz Spotlite News* putting the record straight:

> He (Gordon) claims that I told him the great Coleman Hawkins was 'epileptic'; that is going too far! Bean (whom I never referred to as 'the Hawk') was positively not epileptic! Nor did he have any need of me to install telephone extensions in his apartment (as Max also states). What is more, I not only loved Bean, I revered him and could never have spoken about him the way Max has it down.

Work became progressively scarcer for Hawkins but he kept in close touch with friends such as the Baroness, Barry Harris, Eddie Locke and Roland Hanna. Hanna, recalling this period, said:

> In 1968 he didn't get too many calls even though he was still as popular as ever with musicians. He came down to the Half Note sometime that year to see Roy Eldridge, who was working with Eddie Locke on drums, Buddy Catlett on bass and me. He seemed brighter then, but as the year went on he appeared to get weaker and he drank more for strength.[38]

But no one – friend or family – could get Hawkins to undergo a full medical check-up. He did agree to have some Vitamin B shots from Dr Robert Freymann to help disperse a scaly skin condition caused by diet deficiencies. Hawk's haphazard eating had also created a calcium shortage that had affected his joints, particularly his knees. He occasionally made a point of defrosting meat, but by the time it was ready to be cooked he had no appetite. Dan Morgenstern commented on the scene within Hawk's apartment: 'By then the expensive hi-fi equipment had fallen into disuse, the blinds were often drawn to shut out the view and the sound most frequently heard was that of the television – on around the clock to keep the insomniac company.'[39]

But when the mood was right Hawkins could still enjoy a night out on the town. The Dutch writer Jaap Ludeke, visiting the Village Vanguard on a chilly Monday night in the winter of 1968, sat next to Coleman, who was there listening to the music of the Thad Jones–Mel Lewis Orchestra:

> He was apparently in a very good mood and was accompanied by a young fellow whom he proudly called his son. Mister Hawkins told me on that special occasion, more than once, that they had enjoyed some lobsters and white wine for dinner. Judging from the state Bean was in I presumed that he had not restricted himself to one glass only. After some grunts and growls Mr Hawkins told me in his raspy voice that after leaving the restaurant his son had stopped in front of an automobile showroom on Broadway and talked Hawkins into buying him a huge new Detroiter.
>
> In the meantime Hawkins tried hard to concentrate on the sounds of the orchestra. It was right in the middle of a solo allotted to the frantic tenor player Eddie Daniels; Coleman Hawkins leaned over and whispered, 'I'm going home to get my horn and be mean to that motherfucker.'[40]

Not long before Christmas 1968 Hawk attended two birthday parties held at the Playhouse (the new name for Minton's Playhouse). One party was for the Baroness 'Nica', at which Charlie McPherson's quartet played; the other was for Barry Harris, and on that occasion Hawk sat happily among a whole team of his friends, including Eddie Locke and Tommy Flanagan. Thereafter, however, his late-night ventures became fewer and fewer; he amused himself by buying a new stereo cassette player but his tenor saxophone rarely left its case. As Hawk faced the New Year the downward spiral of his moods was hastened by the news that his mother, Cordelia, had died in St Joseph on 9 January, at the age of ninety-six. He was too poorly to attend the funeral, and he would no doubt have reflected that circumstances had prevented him from attending the burial of both his parents. Perhaps the reflections of his father's tragic end came back into focus as he pondered that he was now older than his father had ever been. The onset of Hawkins's unpredictable melancholia and the loss of interest in his own appearance had occurred at the age at which his father had taken those drastic steps that had caused his own death. Bean laughed (and others scoffed with him) when journalists suggested a lurking 'death wish', but despite the vigour of Hawk's laughter who is to say what sombre thoughts lurked within his mind?

Early in 1969 his old friend and devotee, Big Nick Nicholas, telephoned Hawkins: 'I said, "I heard you've been sick, and I thought I'd ask how you were." He laughed and said, "They should have told you I'm still blowing." '[41]

Hawk had no plans to become a total recluse, but he had to be tempted out. On 24 February 1969 the Duke Ellington Jazz Society persuaded Hawkins to address them. Unfortunately the hospitality they showed him before the meeting got under way was a little too generous, and the net result was a befuddled guest speaker. The answers to some of the questions took a great deal of time to emerge, and several enquiries irked him by alluding to his early days as a professional. He said, quite testily, 'I don't know nothing about Mamie Smith's Jazz Hounds,' and to someone asking about when he first worked with Fletcher Henderson, he replied, 'About 1950.' He did, however, make a few observations about his former bandleader: 'Oh, Fletcher was alright, quite alright, nice fellow. Fletcher used to take all the head arrangements and write them down on paper. All that stuff he sold to Benny Goodman.'

Hawk seemed happier talking about his later days and cited the album *Today and Now* as one of his own favourites from recent times. He also said, 'I just did a couple of numbers with Hack Hanna the other day.' This comment referred to recordings that he had done with Roland Hanna, Eddie Locke, Buddy Catlett and (from Duke Ellington's Orchestra) reed player Norris Turney. This session was speculatively organized by a friend of Roland Hanna's in the hope that a recording company would buy the tapes, but so far they remain unissued.

On 16 March 1969 Hawk led his own quartet for a Sunday gig at Filmore Street East, New York. His performance received a glowing review in the *Village Voice*:

> Here at the close of the 1960s was a first opportunity to witness jazz at its three-score-and-ten, almost completely embodied in Coleman Hawkins. His high point – and one of the extraordinary moments in jazz history – was his solo on 'Yesterdays'. With his eyes closed he savored his tenor sax as if it were a fine cigar. For a while he stuck close to the melody. Then he began to sigh out little snatches of improvisation, unhurried, selected out of decades of creativity, adjusted to the consideration of old age.[42]

Hawk's appearance continued to startle those who remembered him as a strong, dapper figure. Trumpeter Billy Butterfield recalled:

> I went to the Filmore Street East club with Jack Lesberg. It seemed as though everyone there was smoking pot, and out of the haze I saw an old man with a beard nearly down to his waist, using a stick to walk with. He looked so out of place I said to Jack, 'Who is that for Christ's sake?' and he said, 'Coleman Hawkins.' I was totally amazed. I had worked with the man but there had been such a change I just didn't recognize him. He had just let himself go.[43]

But despite Hawk's relative inactivity he was not forgotten by his devotees. One of them, Dan Morgenstern (then editor of *Down Beat*) decided to involve the tenor saxist in a new project. Morgenstern supplies the details:

> I moved to Chicago in the early summer of 1967, so this meant I hadn't seen Coleman for a while. Early in 1969 I became involved, with co-director Bob Kaiser, in plans for a jazz television series at WTTW in Chicago. It was scheduled that Coleman Hawkins and Roy Eldridge would come from New York to do a pilot show, which it was hoped would become the first of the series.
>
> So I telephoned Roy Eldridge and said, 'Do you think Hawk will be well enough for the trip?'
>
> He said, 'I guess so, call him.'
>
> So I called Coleman about six weeks before the date of the show and he sounded great on the telephone, that deep voice of his sounded full of strength; he said, 'Sure, I'd love to do it, Dan.' So April approached and I finalized the plans, but just to be sure I got a friend of mine, Cyra Greene, to help Hawk get ready for the morning flight to Chicago. Well, she went to his apartment and found him in bad shape. She called me and I said, 'Please help him dress and make sure he's on the plane and I'll meet him at the other end.' I went along to pick him up with two guys from the Jazz

Institute of Chicago. We went to the gate and waited but there was no sign of Hawk. Finally he came through the gate, supported by a stewardess. I was absolutely shocked by his appearance; he looked in terrible shape, as though he had aged twenty years since I last saw him, and he was too weak to carry his horn. I almost cried. Someone suggested we get a wheelchair, but Hawk wouldn't have that at all. So I took one arm and someone else took the other and we got him downstairs. One of the guys went to get the car and I went off to phone Bob Kaiser to acquaint him with the situation. One of the institute people stayed with Hawk.

I could only have been gone three minutes, but when I returned Hawk was down on the ground, stretched out and surrounded by firemen. He was flat on his back, but conscious, and he said, 'I'm OK, I'm OK.' The firemen had been called to help him as an emergency case and by regulations they in turn had called an ambulance. The ambulance arrived and I went in it with Hawk to the hospital. He was carried in on a stretcher and given a little oxygen. At the hospital the doctor examined him and said, 'This man is suffering from malnutrition, but his heart is good.' Meanwhile Coleman kept saying, 'Danny, get me out of here.' I told him to stop worrying and I explained that he would be paid for the show and his expenses no matter what happened. But he insisted on getting out of the hospital and signed a release form. Then we went to a hotel in downtown Chicago and got him to his room. I wanted him to lie down but he wouldn't do that, but I did manage to get him to eat something – just chicken soup and crackers – which he ate very slowly and methodically. Then he started to revive and said, 'The Cubs are playing today,' remembering that the Cubs were the only ball team that played afternoon games. Then he said, 'Let's do the show at 4 p.m.'

It was about an hour's drive to the television station and by the time he got into the car he was joking, but he kept the window open for fresh air even though it was chilly. We got to WTTW at about 3.30 and everyone was delighted to see him; they'd all been on stand-by – Roy Eldridge was there, and Barry Harris and the rhythm section. All of the camera crew were jazz-orientated so everyone greeted Hawk warmly. He slowly unpacked his horn and then blew, but no sound came out. But then he set about warming up with real determination. We kept our fingers crossed and worked out the program. Hawk and Roy did a feature each and then played a number together. Roy was emceeing and got things slightly wrong, just title details, but Hawk corrected him, and this reassured Roy and made him happy that Hawk was OK and his mind alert and bright. Hawk remained seated. His 'Yesterdays' was very moving and although people said afterwards that we should not have shown it, others were full of praise. We took him back to his hotel and he was worn out, but next afternoon he and Roy played a prearranged session at the North Park Hotel for the Jazz Institute of Chicago. Hawk was surrounded by well-wishers who were literally kneeling all around him. He sat there smoking a cigarette, and he said, 'Dan, get me a Scotch please.' He hadn't had a drink at all during the previous day's traumas.[44]

At the North Park Hotel session on Sunday 20 April 1969 Hawk and Roy were backed by the same team who had worked with them on the television show – Barry Harris on piano, Truck Parham on bass and Bob Cousins on drums – plus pianist Richard Abrams and bassist Malachi Favors. Many of those present who had known Hawk in earlier times could not reconcile themselves to his appearance. Chicago drummer Wayne Jones wrote, 'With his long unkempt hair and beard he resembled the Maharishi – from the neck up. His old robust figure had shrunk; he looked as though he weighed a hundred pounds and his clothing drooped. It was odd: Hawk sounded like Lester Young in his last days.' Quite independently Roy Eldridge, who knew Hawkins's playing so well, said to Dan Morgenstern how eerie it was that Hawk was sounding so similar to Young on his final sessions.

Larry Kart of *Down Beat* drove Hawkins back to the airport. There, one of the redcap luggage handlers recognized the saxophonist and made a fuss of him, which pleased Hawkins. Kart recalls:

> There was time to kill so we went to the airport bar for a drink. I asked him what he was having and his voice boomed out: 'Courvoisier' – only the best. He had a first-class ticket but when we got to the gate they said there were no vacancies. I'm normally diffident about challenging officialdom but I was determined to get the point across that here was a great musician who had a first-class ticket, and they were looking at him as though he was going to be a nuisance to them. I'm pleased to say my words had an effect and Hawk was given his first-class place. He was in bad way – a giant on his last legs – but he looked at me with a gaze of appreciation as he went aboard.[45]

Next day Barry Harris decided that it would not be wise to let Hawkins attempt to fend for himself:

> After that television show in Chicago it was obvious that he was really sick. I sort of moved in with him and tried to get him to eat a little. He could get to the bathroom, but he was too weak to walk back and I had to help him. I had a concert to do in Detroit that Hawk was supposed to do with me, but he was too ill for that so I got Sonny Red to do it. We were rehearsing and I called his apartment to see how he was, but there was no reply. Well, I went through that rehearsal with the phone at my ear and there still wasn't any reply. I decided to call Coleman's wife, and she got the guard at the apartments to break the door in, and they found Hawk sitting there in a chair and he'd been sitting there listening to the phone ring for about two hours, too ill to move. Well it was decided that we'd get him into hospital, but naturally he didn't want to go, but he was very, very sick. I've often thought about what we did in getting him into a hospital, but it was the only answer.[46]

At the Wickersham Hospital on New York's 58th Street, it was diagnosed that Coleman Hawkins had bronchial pneumonia. He was too weak to rally, or to respond to treatment. It was obvious that the end was near; his immediate family were called, and those who were part of his close circle, including Thelonious Monk, Eddie Locke, Baroness 'Nica' and Barry Harris came to visit Hawk. The Reverend John Garcia Gensel, known as the pastor of the New York jazz community, sat by the bedside for a while. Hawkins was fading but still lucid and said, with wry humour, to Barry Harris, 'When I get well I'm going to do some practice.' But the horn was silenced for ever; Hawk died in the early hours of Monday 19 May 1969.

Jazz fans throughout the world had been aware that Hawkins's battle for health was a desperate one. In London, Renée Diamond learnt that things had taken a turn for the worse and telephoned Hawk's apartment for news. As she did so she remembered what Coleman had told her during their last meeting (which had taken place in London the previous year). Renée had asked if Hawk would mind if she telephoned occasionally to see if he was all right, and he'd replied in a deliberately measured tone, 'Sure you can, but if a lady answers you'll know that there's no more me.' When Hawk's daughter answered Renée's call she had no need to be told that it was all over.

Hawk's funeral took place on Friday 23 May at the Woodlawn Cemetery in the Bronx, New York. Eddie Locke was consulted by Hawk's family as to who should serve as honorary pallbearers alongside him, and as a result Zutty Singleton, Zoot Sims, Major Holley, George 'Big Nick' Nicholas and Roy Eldridge were chosen. A vast array of jazz stars, including Dizzy Gillespie, Johnny Hodges, Illinois Jacquet, Yusef Lateef, Charles Mingus, Ornette Coleman, Horace Silver, Jackie McLean, Barry Harris, J.C. Higginbotham, Charlie Shavers, Junior Mance and Clifford Jordan joined Mrs Dolores Hawkins, her son Rene and daughters Mimi (by this time Mrs Melvin Wright) and Colette at the memorial service held at St Peter's Lutheran Church in Manhattan. There the Reverend Gensel conducted the service, which included a poem, 'Hold Out Your Hand' by Sandy McGhee (wife of Howard McGhee). Roland Hanna played one of Hawk's favourite pieces, Schumann's Traumerei, following it with his own composition 'After Paris'. Thad Jones on flugelhorn played his own 'Say It Softly' then, prior to the benediction, Ray Nance played 'Body and Soul' on violin. Hundreds of devoted fans packed into the church and hundreds more, who couldn't be fitted into the building, stood in reverence outside in Lexington Avenue.

Subsequently, the Missouri House of Representatives passed a resolution expressing their sadness at Coleman Hawkins's death, and honouring him as 'one of Missouri's most famous and best-loved natives'.[47]

Unlike so many other veteran jazz musicians, Hawkins was a wealthy man at the time of his death. He had worked virtually non-stop throughout four decades and had known periods of musical inactivity only during his final years. Rex Stewart had once prophesied: 'There will never have to be a benefit given for Coleman Hawkins,'[48] a forecast that happily proved to be accurate.

On Sunday 25 May 1969 the television show that Hawkins had latterly recorded in Chicago was transmitted locally. It was later re-edited and shown nationally in July, with added contributions from Dan Morgenstern, Roy Eldridge, Barry Harris, Truck Parham and Bob Cousins. On this programme Eddie Jefferson sang the lyrics he had written to fit Hawk's solo on 'Body and Soul'; thus people were reminded of Hawkins's most famous recording, one that he had created at the peak of his inventiveness. The frail old man on the television screen had, in his golden days, thrilled countless listeners with his passionate artistry. Almost all of the recordings he made throughout a forty-five-year period were outstanding examples of improvisation, but among them were masterpieces by which all jazz tenor-saxophone solos will forever be judged.

References

Chapter 1 Missouri Breaks (pp. 1–20)

1 Riverside albums RLP 12-117/118
2 Shapiro & Hentoff: *The Jazz Makers* (New York: Rinehart, 1957)
3 Quoted from an address made by Hawkins to the Duke Ellington Society, New York, 24 February 1969
4 Ibid
5 Riverside op cit
6 *Down Beat*, 1 February 1962
7 Riverside op cit
8 State of Missouri Bureau of Vital Statistics, Form VS No.1
9 Letter to the author, 12 June 1987
10 Riverside op cit
11 Conversation with the author, 6 August 1988
12 Jazz Archive, Tulane University: Preston Jackson interview, 2 June 1958
13 Shapiro & Hentoff op cit, p. 166
14 *Down Beat*, 2 May 1957
15 Riverside op cit
16 Conversation with the author, 12 March 1987
17 Rutgers Jazz Archive: Albert 'Happy' Caldwell interview, May 1976
18 Rutgers Jazz Archive: Walter 'Foots' Thomas interview, 1981
19 Bushell & Tucker: *Jazz from the Beginning* (Ann Arbor: University of Michigan Press, 1988)
20 *Chicago Defender*, 27 May 1922
21 *New York Amsterdam News*, 17 February 1940
22 *New York Amsterdam News*, 2 March 1940
23 *Down Beat*, 14 November 1956
24 *Down Beat*, 5 October 1957

25 Conversation with the author, summer 1986
26 Shapiro & Hentoff: *Hear Me Talkin' to Ya* (London: Peter Davies, 1955), p. 162
27 Bushell & Tucker op cit
28 *Jazz Review*, February 1959

Chapter 2 The Young Star in New York (pp.21–36)

1 Schuller: *Early Jazz* (New York: OUP, 1968)
2 *Melody Maker*, 28 April 1934
3 *Record Changer*, May 1944
4 *Melody Maker*, 14 April 1934
5 Rutgers Jazz Archive: Howard Scott interview, 8 March 1979
6 Ibid
7 *Down Beat*, 19 March 1966
8 Ibid
9 Allen: *Hendersonia* (Highland Park, New Jersey, 1973), p.93
10 Allen op cit, p.113
11 Shapiro & Hentoff: *The Jazz Makers* (New York: Rinehart, 1957), p. 166
12 Armstrong & Gerlach: *Swing that Music* (London, Peter Davies, 1936), p. 80
13 Allen op cit, p. 124
14 *Jazz Journal* August 1958
15 *Storyville*, issue 71
16 *Record Changer*, July 1950
17 Allen op cit
18 Shapiro & Hentoff: *Hear Me Talkin' to Ya* (London: Peter Davies, 1955), p. 189
19 *Down Beat*, 5 October 1967
20 *Cadence*, December 1977
21 *Hot Record Society Rag*, January 1941
22 Rutgers Jazz Archive op cit

Chapter 3 Armstrong's Influence (pp.37–50)

1 Riverside albums 12-117/118

2 *Metronome*, November 1946
3 From notes prepared for Robert Goffin by Louis Armstrong, *c.* 1946
4 Shapiro & Hentoff: *Hear Me Talkin' to Ya* (London: Peter Davies, 1955)
5 *Down Beat*, 19 May 1966
6 Conversation with the author, 1974
7 Riverside op cit
8 *Melody Maker*, 21 April 1934
9 Ibid
10 Taylor: *Notes and Tones* (London: Quartet Books, 1983), p. 71
11 *Jazz Journal*, September 1984
12 *Down Beat*, 14 November 1956
13 *Storyville*, issue 71
14 *Down Beat*, 17 November 1954
15 Riverside op cit
16 Ellington: *Music is My Mistress* (London: Quartet Books, 1977), p. 49
17 WKCR broadcast, interviewer Phil Schaap, New York, 15 October 1975
18 *Storyville*, issue 55
19 *Down Beat*, 19 May 1966
20 Riverside op cit

Chapter 4 Fast Cars and Silk Suits (pp. 51–66)

1 Down Beat, 19 May 1966
2 *Down Beat*, 14 November 1956
3 *Down Beat*, 1 February 1962
4 *Down Beat*, 17 November 1954
5 Rutgers Jazz Archive: Horace Henderson interview, April 1975
6 *Melody Maker*, 13 November 1948
7 WKCR broadcast, interviewer Phil Schaap, New York, 15 October 1975
8 Conversation with the author, 9 April 1987
9 Dance: *The World of Swing* (New York: Scribner's, 1974), p. 120
10 Dance: *The World of Earl Hines* (New York: Scribner's, 1977), p. 209
11 WKCR broadcast, 30 March 1988

12 Riverside albums RLP 12-117/118
13 *Jazz*, June 1963
14 Riverside op cit
15 Shapiro & Hentoff: *Hear Me Talkin' to Ya* (London: Peter Davies, 1955), p. 193
16 *Hot Record Society Rag*, October 1940
17 *Down Beat*, 27 February 1964
18 Shapiro & Hentoff op cit, p. 201
19 Riverside op cit
20 Wells: *The Night People* (London: Robert Hale, 1971), p. 46
21 Dance: *The World of Swing* op cit, p. 73
22 *Jazz Review*, November 1959
23 Conversation with author, 30 January 1989
24 Rutgers Jazz Archive: Horace Henderson interview, April 1975
25 Wells op cit, p. 20
26 Rutgers Jazz Archive: Cootie Williams interview, May 1976
27 Rutgers Jazz Archive: Walter 'Foots' Thomas interview, 1981
28 Associated Press interview, 30 June 1983
29 *Down Beat*, 19 May 1966
30 *Down Beat*, August 1935
31 *New York Times*, 1 October 1961
32 *Australian Jazz Quarterly*, August 1946
33 Foster: *The Autobiography of Pops Foster* (University of California Press, 1971), p. 148
34 Allen: *Hendersonia* (Highland Park, New Jersey, 1973)

Chapter 5 The Emergence of Swing (pp. 67–78)

1 *Jazz Journal*, June 1961
2 Shapiro & Hentoff: *Hear Me Talkin' to Ya* (London, Peter Davies, 1955), p. 199
3 BBC radio interview with Charles Fox
4 BBC2 television interview, December 1967
5 *Chicago Defender*, 7 February 1931
6 *Melody Maker*, 9 December 1967
7 Conversation with the author, 1966
8 Rutgers Jazz Archive: Horace Henderson interview, April 1975
9 *Melody Maker*, 28 April 1934

10 Letter to the author, 14 December 1987
11 WKCR broadcast, 1975
12 *Jazz Journal*, April 1967
13 *Melody Maker*, October 1931
14 Rutgers Jazz Archive: J.C. Higginbotham interview
15 *Crescendo*, January 1967
16 WKCR broadcast and Hammond: *John Hammond on Record* (Harmondsworth: Penguin Books, 1977), p. 113
17 Hammond op cit, p. 70

Chapter 6 The First Rival (pp. 79–91)

1 *Melody Maker*, 3 January 1942
2 *Melody Maker*, 10 January 1942
3 *Swing Music*, November 1935
4 Ibid and Hughes: *Second Movement* (London: Museum Press, 1951), p. 267
5 *Jazz Journal*, September 1964
6 *Swing Music*, November 1935
7 Ibid
8 Hughes op cit, p. 271
9 Wells: *The Night People* (London: Robert Hale, 1971), p. 87
10 Conversation with the author, 1987
11 Conversation with the author, 1987
12 *Jazz Monthly*, June 1964
13 Hammond: *John Hammond on Record* (Harmondsworth: Penguin Books, 1977), p. 113
14 Rutgers Jazz Archive: Horace Henderson interview, April 1975
15 Shapiro & Hentoff: *The Jazz Makers* (New York: Rinehart, 1957)
16 *Melody Maker*, 1 May 1954
17 *Down Beat*, October 1988
18 Shapiro & Hentoff: *Hear Me Talkin' to Ya* (London: Peter Davies, 1955), p. 264

Chapter 7 British Adulation (pp. 92–119)

1 Hammond: *John Hammond on Record* (Harmondsworth: Penguin Books, 1977), p. 110

2 Riverside albums RLP 12-117/118
3 Conversation with the author, 16 January 1987
4 Shapiro & Hentoff: *The Jazz Makers* (New York: Rinehart, 1957), p. 167
5 *Rhythm*, May 1934
6 Conversation with the author, 16 January 1987
7 *Down Beat*, 1 February 1962
8 Riverside op cit
9 Conversation with the author, 16 January 1987
10 *Melody Maker*, 21 April 1934
11 Conversation with the author, 16 January 1987
12 *Melody Maker*, 7 July 1934
13 *Melody Maker*, 23 June 1934
14 Ibid
15 *Melody Maker* 14 July 1934
16 Ibid
17 Letter to the author, 12 June 1987
18 Conversation with the author, 19 January 1987
19 Conversation with the author, 4 November 1986
20 Conversation with the author, 15 November 1987

Chapter 8 Dutch Treats (pp. 110–24)

1 BBC TV: *Le Jazz Hot*, 9 January 1987
2 Delaunay: *Delaunay's Dilemma* (Mâcon: Editions W, 1985), p. 89
3 *Mississipi Rag*, October 1977
4 Letter to the author, 12 February 1988
5 *Mississippi Rag* op cit
6 Letter to the author, 22 November 1988
7 *Melody Maker*, 11 April 1936
8 *Mississippi Rag* op cit
9 *Down Beat*, 7 March 1956
10 *Down Beat*, 5 October 1955
11 *Coda*, April 1976
12 Delaunay op cit, p. 93
13 Henius: *Svend Asmussen* (Sweden: nd), p. 9
14 *Melody Maker*, 15 June 1935
15 *Melody Maker*, 7 December 1935

16 Letter to the author, 12 February 1988
17 Shapiro & Hentoff: *The Jazz Makers* (New York: Rinehart, 1957), p. 173

Chapter 9 Family Tragedy (pp. 125–44)

1 Bernhard Peritz, interviewed by Johnny Simmen, 2 June 1988
2 *Melody Maker*, 13 June 1936
3 State of Kansas Death Certificate 3.2176
4 Letter to the author, 18 November 1988
5 Panassié: *Douze Années de jazz* (Paris: Edition Corrêa, p. 200
6 Delaunay: *Django Reinhardt* (London: Cassell, 1961), p. 86
7 BBC TV: *Le Jazz Hot*, 9 January 1987
8 Ibid
9 Letter to the author, 18 November 1988
10 Letter to the author, 19 October 1988
11 Letter to the author, July 1987
12 Conversation with the author, 11 August 1988
13 Letter to the author, July 1987
14 Conversation with the author, 3 March 1987
15 BBC radio interview with Charles Fox
16 *Melody Maker*, 11 January 1964
17 Conversation with the author, 3 March 1987
18 *Storyville*, issue 95
19 Ibid
20 Conversation with Bryn Venus, 17 May 1987
21 *Melody Maker*, 11 December 1937
22 Conversations with the author, 16 August 1988 and 8 September 1988
23 *Storyville*, issue 55

Chapter 10 Home Again (pp. 145–60)

1 Conversation with the author, 11 August 1988
2 *Jazz Journal*, July 1957
3 Conversation with the author, 8 September 1988
4 Goddard: *Jazz Away from Home* (London: Paddington Press, 1979), p. 288

5 Letter to the author, July 1987
6 *Melody Maker*, 12 November 1938
7 Letter to the author, July 1987
8 Conversation with the author, April 1987
9 Conversation with the author, 8 September 1988
10 *Melody Maker*, 18 March 1939
11 Conversation with the author, 18 March 1987
12 BBC TV: *Le Jazz Hot*, 9 January 1987
13 *Coda*, issue 189, 1983
14 *Melody Maker*, 8 July 1939
15 *Down Beat*, September 1939
16 *Down Beat*, 2 November 1951
17 Conversation with the author, April 1987
18 Conversation with the author, April 1987
19 Letter to the author, 26 March 1987
20 *Jazz Hot*, issue 20, February 1948

Chapter 11 Body and Soul (pp. 161–74)

1 *Down Beat*, 12 January 1955 and Riverside albums RLP 12-117/118
2 *Mississippi Rag*, January 1983
3 *Down Beat* op cit
4 Riverside op cit
5 Ibid
6 *Down Beat*, 31 October 1957
7 *New York Times*, 28 June 1983
8 *Down Beat*, 29 September 1959
9 WKCR broadcast, October 1975
10 Ibid
11 Letter to the author, July 1987
12 *Bandwaggon*, 11 November 1939
13 Conversation with the author, 9 April 1987
14 Conversation with the author, 11 April 1987
15 Ibid
16 Conversation with the author, 9 April 1987
17 Conversation with the author, September 1985
18 Coleman: *Trumpet Story* (Paris: Editions Cana, 1981), p. 211
19 *Swing*, February 1940

20 *Melody Maker*, 29 June 1940
21 Feather: *The Jazz Years* (London: Quartet Books, 1986), p. 182

Chapter 12 The Rise and Fall of a Big Band (pp. 175–88)

1 *Bandwaggon*, July 1940
2 *Down Beat*, 1 June 1940
3 *Metronome*, June 1940
4 *Down Beat* op cit
5 Conversation with the author, April 1987
6 Conversation with the author, April 1987
7 *Mississippi Rag*, January 1983
8 Conversation with the author, April 1987
9 Conversation with the author, 15 June 1988
10 *Mississippi Rag*, January 1983
11 *Melody Maker*, 23 November 1940
12 Conversation with the author, 13 September 1987
13 *Storyville*, issue 116
14 *Jazz Journal*, February 1975 and WKCR broadcast, October 1975
15 Conversation with the author, 18 March 1987
16 WKCR op cit
17 Rutgers Jazz Archive and WKCR broadcast, interviewer Phil Schaap
18 Gillespie & Fraser: *To be or not to Bop* (London: W.H. Allen, 1980)
19 *Crescendo*, October 1973
20 *Coda*, October 1973

Chapter 13 Chicago Siesta (pp. 189–202)

1 *Down Beat*, 5 March 1941
2 Letter to the author, 1987
3 Conversation with the author, April 1987
4 Letter to the author, 20 August 1987
5 *Crescendo*, January 1963
6 *Metronome*, February 1942
7 *Music and Rhythm*, August 1941
8 Shapiro & Hentoff: *The Jazz Makers* (New York: Rinehart, 1957), p. 168

9 *Jazz Record*, July 1946
10 Shapiro & Hentoff: *Hear Me Talkin' to Ya* (London: Peter Davies, 1955), p. 278
11 Radio Free Jazz interview
12 *Down Beat*, 15 January 1942
13 *Time Life* Booklet STL JO 6
14 Travis: *An Autobiography of Black Jazz* (Chicago Urban Research Institute, 1983), p. 418
15 Travis op cit, p. 209
16 Letter to the author, 16 March 1987
17 Letter to the author, 4 June, 1987
18 Kleinhout & Van Eyle: *The Walter Bishop Story* (Holland: Micrography, 1981), p. 23
19 Cassette to the author, 1987
20 Ibid
21 *Jazz Hot*, Special Edition, 1950
22 *Jazz*, November–December 1962
23 Rutgers Jazz Archive: Budd Johnson interview, March 1975
24 Letter to the author, 15 May 1987
25 *Down Beat*, March 1985

Chapter 14 A Deluge of Discs (pp. 203–15)

1 Conversation with the author, April 1987
2 Rutgers Jazz Archive: Budd Johnson interview, March 1975
3 Gillespie & Fraser: *To Be or not to Bop* (London: W.H. Allen, 1980)
4 Ibid
5 *Down Beat*, 1 February 1962
6 *Metronome*, October 1961
7 WKCR broadcast, 18 September 1988
8 Lewine & Driggs: *Black Beauty, White Heat* (New York: Morrow, 1982), p. 321
9 *Down Beat*, 1 September 1944
10 *Village Voice*, 10 April 1957
11 Rutgers Jazz Archive op cit
12 *Melody Maker*, 18 March 1944
13 WKCR broadcast op cit
14 *Jazz Journal*, March 1972

15 *Down Beat*, 10 April 1951
16 Conversation with the author, April 1987
17 Riverside albums RLP 12-117/118
18 Travis: *An Autobiography of Black Jazz* (Chicago Urban Research Institute, 1983), p. 418
19 Cassette to the author, 1987
20 *Jazz Monthly*, September 1962
21 *Boston Traveler*, 2 February 1961

Chapter 15 Bean and Bop (pp. 216–30)

1 Riverside albums RLP 12-117/118
2 Shapiro & Hentoff: *Hear Me Talkin' to Ya* (London: Peter Davies, 1955), p. 323
3 Letter to the author, 19 June 1987
4 *Kansas City Jazz Magazine*, June 1978
5 Bergers & Patrick: *Benny Carter* (New Jersey: Scarecrow Press, 1982), p. 195)
6 BBC radio interview with Charles Fox
7 *Down Beat*, 25 July 1956
8 *Metronome*, October 1944
9 Rutgers Jazz Archive: Walter 'Foots' Thomas interview, 5 January 1981
10 Rutgers Jazz Archive
11 WKCR radio interview with Phil Schaap
12 Rutgers Jazz Archive
13 *Bandleaders*, September 1945
14 WKCR broadcast
15 Rutgers Jazz Archive
16 Letter to the author, 20 August 1987
17 Rutgers Jazz Archive
18 *Melody Maker*, 2 March 1946
19 Letter to the author, 20 August 1987
20 Rutgers Jazz Archive
21 Gitler: *Swing to Bop* (New York: OUP, 1985)
22 *Melody Maker*, 2 March 1946
23 Letter to the author, 20 August 1987
24 Ibid

25 WKCR broadcast and Rutgers Jazz Archive
26 Coleman: *Trumpet Story* (Paris, 1981), p. 251
27 WKCR broadcast

Chapter 16 Jazz at the Philharmonic (pp. 231–44)

1 *Cadence*, March 1987
2 Conversation with the author, April 1987
3 *Metronome*, January 1946
4 *Down Beat*, 14 November 1956
5 *Metronome*, November 1946
6 Conversation with the author, September 1987
7 *In the Groove*, December 1946
8 *Jazz Journal*, September 1982
9 *Metronome*, November 1946
10 *Metronome*, July 1946
11 *Metronome*, October 1955
12 Ibid
13 *Jazz Journal*, December 1974
14 Conversation with the author, July 1984
15 *Down Beat*, September 1986
16 *Jazz Record*, July 1946
17 WKCR broadcast, October 1975
18 *Cadence*, issue 181
19 Ibid
20 Conversation with the author, 24 December 1987
21 *Down Beat*, 20 October 1950
22 Barnet: *Those Swinging Years* (Louisiana State University Press, 1986), p. 71
23 *Crescendo*, September 1971

Chapter 17 Return to Paris (pp. 245–59)

1 Conversation with the author, April 1987
2 WKCR broadcast, 3 October 1988
3 *Down Beat*, 27 January 1966
4 Wilmer: *As Serious as Your Life* (London: Allison & Busby, 1977), p. 82

5 *Jazz News*, 5 September 1962
6 Conversation with the author, 12 April 1987
7 *Metronome*, December 1961
8 *Melody Maker*, 10 December 1949
9 *Melody Maker*, 13 June 1953
10 Conversation with the author, 25 October 1987
11 Conversation with the author, 14 May 1987
12 *Melody Maker*, 17 June 1950
13 BBC radio interview with Peter Clayton, 11 November 1974
14 *Melody Maker*, 17 December 1949
15 *Jazz Journal*, January 1950
16 *Melody Maker*, 24 December 1949
17 Riverside albums RLP 12-117/118
18 *Jazz Hot*, Special Edition, 1950

Chapter 18 A Dynamic Partner (pp. 260–74)

1 *Jazz Hot*, Special Edition, 1950
2 *Down Beat*, 8 September 1948
3 *Metronome*, May 1944
4 Coleman Hawkins addressing the Duke Ellington Society, 24 February 1969
5 *Down Beat*, 14 November 1956
6 Riverside albums RLP 12-117/118
7 *Down Beat*, 2 May 1957
8 Shapiro & Hentoff: *The Jazz Makers* (New York: Rinehart, 1957)
9 Conversation with the author, 7 December 1988
10 *Metronome*, March 1952
11 *Melody Maker*, 13 June 1953
12 *Jazz Journal*, October 1970
13 *Down Beat*, September 1987
14 Conversation with the author, 9 April 1987
15 Passport Division of the US Department of State: memo, 26 April 1948
16 *Down Beat*, 20 October 1950
17 *Melody Maker* op cit
18 Conversation with the author, October 1988
19 *Melody Maker* op cit

20 WKCR broadcast, August 1978
21 *Down Beat*, 17 November 1954
22 Conversation with the author, 12 April 1987

Chapter 19 Renaissance (pp. 275–88)

1 *Melody Maker*, 9 October 1954
2 Letter to the author, July 1987
3 *Music and Rhythm*, June 1941
4 *Down Beat*, 2 November 1955
5 Riverside albums RLP 12-117/118
6 *Down Beat*, 1 February 1962
7 *Down Beat*, 19 September 1956
8 Rutgers Jazz Archive
9 *Down Beat*, 14 November 1956
10 Ibid
11 Letter to the author, 14 October 1987
12 Letter to the author, 11 November 1987
13 Conversation with the author, April 1987
14 Shapiro & Hentoff: *The Jazz Makers* (New York: Rinehart, 1957), p. 171
15 Shapiro & Hentoff op cit, p. 172
16 Freeman: *You Don't Look Like a Musician* (Detroit: Balamp, 1974), p. 101
17 *Melody Maker*, 4 May 1957
18 Riverside op cit
19 *Down Beat*, 21 March 1957
20 *Down Beat*, 14 November 1956
21 *Down Beat*, 17 October 1957

Chapter 20 Festivals Galore (pp. 289–301)

1 Bushell & Tucker: *Jazz from the Beginning* (Ann Arbor: University of Michigan Press, 1988)
2 *Down Beat*, 19 February 1959
3 *Down Beat*, 26 June 1958
4 *Melody Maker*, 31 May 1969

5 *Down Beat*, October 1980
6 Callender & Cohen: *Unfinished Dream* (London: Quartet Books, 1985), p. 18
7 Master Jazz Records 8115
8 Conversation with the author, April 1987

Chapter 21 New Era for Big-toned Tenors (pp. 302–16)

1 Letter to the author, 18 December 1987
2 *Jazz Journal*, August 1958
3 *Down Beat*, 21 November 1974
4 *Down Beat*, 14 November 1956
5 Letter to the author, 22 August 1988
6 Savoy WL 70530
7 *Jazz Review*, January 1960
8 *Down Beat*, 1 February 1962
9 Conversation with the author, April 1987
10 *Jazz Journal*, May 1958
11 Conversation with the author, September 1987
12 Taped interview with Michael Pointon
13 *Jazz Journal*, November 1986
14 Milestone 47015
15 *Jazz Beat*, December 1964
16 Conversation with the author, April 1987
17 *Cadence*, August 1979
18 *Down Beat*, 19 March 1959
19 *Down Beat*, 29 May 1958
20 *Down Beat*, 12 November 1959

Chapter 22 A Jazz Doyen (pp. 317–34)

1 *Crescendo*, May 1976
2 *Jazz Journal*, January 1960
3 Conversation with the author, summer 1965
4 Warner Brothers 1336
5 Conversation with the author, 8 September 1988

6 *Rhythm and Blues*, October 1963
7 Sangster: *Seeing the Rafters* (Australia: Penguin Books, 1988), p. 121
8 *Jazz News*, 3 December 1960
9 *Melody Maker*, 21 August 1965
10 *Jazz Journal*, January 1983
11 *Jazz Journal*, January 1964
12 *Jazz News*, 20 December 1961
13 Ibid
14 *Jazz Journal*, July 1983
15 Conversation with the author, 14 May 1987
16 *Into Jazz*, March 1970
17 Conversation with the author, 24 August 1988
18 Candid 9002
19 *Rhythm and Blues* op cit
20 *Jazz Journal*, October 1961
21 Conversation with the author, April 1987
22 *New York Herald Tribune*, 1 October 1961
23 Candid 9020
24 *Melody Maker*, 15 April 1961
25 *Down Beat*, 13 April 1961
26 *Down Beat*, 1 February 1962

Chapter 23 Global Gigs (pp. 335–51)

1 *Down Beat*, 5 October 1967
2 Conversation with the author, 12 April 1987
3 *Down Beat*, 16 August 1962
4 *Down Beat*, 1 February 1962
5 Chambers: *Milestones I* (University of Toronto Press, 1983), p. 31
6 Coleman Hawkins addressing the Duke Ellington Society, 24 February 1969
7 Conversation with the author, April 1987
8 Conversation with the author, 25 April 1988
9 Ibid
10 Letter to the author, 13 May 1988
11 Letter to the author, 8 January 1989
12 *Rhythm and Blues*, October 1963
13 Ibid

14 *Crescendo*, April 1965 and *Jazz Journal*, April 1983
15 *Jazz*, September 1963
16 *Jazz*, October 1963
17 *Down Beat*, 27 February 1964
18 *Melody Maker*, 1 February 1964
19 Letter to the author, 4 December 1988

Chapter 24 Penthouse Patriarch (pp. 352–65)

1 Letter to the author, 1 August 1987
2 *Coda*, December 1963
3 *Melody Maker*, 9 December 1967
4 *Down Beat*, 1 February 1962
5 *Down Beat*, 14 November 1956
6 Conversation with the author, April 1987
7 *Down Beat*, August 1984
8 Conversation with the author, April 1987
9 *Down Beat*, 14 November 1956
10 Letter to the author, 4 December 1988
11 *Melody Maker*, 10 October 1964
12 *Melody Maker*, 24 February 1962
13 Conversation with the author, April 1987
14 Dance: *The World of Swing* (New York: Scribner's 1974), p. 159
15 *Jazz Journal*, February 1966
16 Letter to the author, 28 May 1987
17 Conversation with the author, April 1987
18 Conversation with the author, 7 April 1987
19 *Crescendo*, May 1965
20 Letter to the author, 2 July 1987

Chapter 25 A Finale of Despair (pp. 366–89)

1 *New York Daily News*, 25 March 1965
2 Shapiro & Hentoff: *The Jazz Makers* (New York: Rinehart, 1957), p. 171
3 *Down Beat*, 6 May 1965
4 Conversation with the author, April 1987

5 Ibid
6 Riverside albums RLP 12-117/118
7 *Melody Maker*, 16 September 1967
8 Jones: *Talking Jazz* (London: Macmillan, 1987), p. 123
9 Letter to the author, 6 January 1989
10 *Crescendo*, January 1967
11 *Jazz Journal*, January 1967 and letter to the author, 10 May 1987
12 Letter to the author, July 1987
13 Conversation with the author, 8 September 1988
14 *Down Beat*, 21 November 1974
15 Conversation with the author, 1967
16 Conversation with the author, April 1987
17 *Toronto Telegram*, 14 February 1967
18 *Coda*, July 1967
19 Conversation with the author, April 1987
20 *Coda*, September 1967
21 *Melody Maker*, 16 September 1967
22 Conversation with the author, January 1987
23 Conversation with the author, December 1987
24 *Down Beat*, 8 February 1968
25 Conversation with the author, January 1988
26 Lyttelton: *Take It from the Top* (London: Robson, 1975), p. 94
27 Lyttelton: *The Best of Jazz* (London: Robson, 1981), p. 88
28 Conversation with the author, January 1987
29 Conversation with the author, January 1988
30 Conversation with the author, December 1986
31 Conversation with the author, 7 December 1988
32 Letter to the author, 8 January 1989
33 Ibid
34 Conversation with the author, April 1987
35 Ibid
36 Ibid
37 Ibid
38 Ibid
39 Milestone 47015
40 Letter to the author, 25 May 1987
41 Conversation with the author, April 1987
42 *Village Voice*, 20 March 1969
43 Conversation with the author, 9 October 1986

44 Conversation with the author, April 1987
45 Conversation with the author, 10 May 1989
46 Conversation with the author, April 1987
47 *Down Beat*, 24 July 1967
48 *Down Beat*, 19 May 1966

Bibliography

Allen, Walter C	*Hendersonia: the Music of Fletcher Henderson and His Musicians: a Bio-discography* (Highland Park, NJ, 1973)
Balliett, Whitney	*Such Sweet Thunder* (London: MacDonald, 1968)
—	*Dinosaurs in the Morning* (London: Phoenix, 1964)
—	*Ecstasy at the Onion* (New York: Bobbs-Merrill, 1971)
Barnet, Charlie	*Those Swinging Years* (Baton Rouge, LA: Louisiana State University Press, 1984)
Basie, Count	*Good Morning Blues* (New York: Random House, 1985)
Berger, Morroe; Berger, Edward and Patrick, James	*Benny Carter: a Life in American Music* (Metuchen, NJ: Scarecrow Press, 1982)
Bernhardt, Clyde	*I Remember* (Philadelphia, PA: University of Pennsylvania Press, 1986)
Bushell, Garvin and Tucker, Mark:	*Jazz from the Beginning* (Ann Arbor, MI: University of Michigan, 1988)
Callender, Red and Cohen, Elaine:	*Unfinished Dream* (London: Quartet Books, 1985)
Chambers, Jack	*Milestones I (The Music and Times of Miles Davis to 1960)* (Toronto, Canada: University of Toronto Press, 1983)
Charters, Samuel B. and Kunstadt, Leonard:	*Jazz: a History of the New York Scene* (Garden City, NY, Doubleday, 1962)

Chilton, John — *McKinney's Music* (London; Jazz Book Service, 1978)

— *Sidney Bechet, the Wizard of Jazz* (London: Macmillan, 1987)

Clayton, Buck — *Buck Clayton's Jazz World* (London: Macmillan, 1986)

Dance, Stanley — *The World of Swing* (New York: Scribner's 1974)

— *The World of Earl Hines* (New York: Scribner's, 1977)

Delaunay, Charles — *Delaunay's Dilemma* (Mâcon, France: Editions W, 1985)

Dexter, Dave Jr — *Playback* (New York: Billboard Publications, 1976)

Ellington, Duke — *Music is My Mistress* (New York: Doubleday, 1973)

Evensmo, Jan — *The Tenor Saxophone of Coleman Hawkins 1929–1942* (Hosle, Norway: Evensmo, 1975)

Feather, Leonard — *The Jazz Years* (London: Quartet Books, 1986)

Freeman, Bud — *You Don't Look Like a Musician* (Detroit, Michigan: Balamp, 1974)

Gillespie, Dizzy — *To Be or not to Bop* (London: W.H. Allen, 1980)

Gitler, Ira — *Swing to Bop* (New York: Oxford University Press, 1985)

Godbolt, Jim — *A History of Jazz in Britain 1919–1950* (London: Quartet Books, 1984)

Goddard, Chris — *Jazz Away from Home* (London: Paddington Press, 1979)

Goldblatt, Burt — *Newport Jazz Festival* (New York: Dial Press, 1977)

Gordon, Max — *Live at the Village Vanguard* (New York: St Martin's Press, 1980)

Grime, Kitty — *Jazz at Ronnie Scott's* (London: Robert Hale, 1979)

Harrison, Max; Fox, Charles and Thacker, Eric — *The Essential Jazz Records (Ragtime to*

Swing) (London: Mansell Publishing, 1984)

Hammond, John — *John Hammond on Record* (New York: Ridge Press, 1977)

Hentoff, Nat — *Jazz is* (New York: Ridge Press, 1976)

Hodeir, André — *Jazz, Its Evolution and Essence* (New York: Grove Press, 1956)

— *Toward Jazz* (New York: Grove Press 1962)

Hughes, Spike — *Second Movement* (London: Museum Press, 1951)

James, Burnett — *Coleman Hawkins* (Tunbridge Wells, England: Spellmount, 1984)

Jones, Max — *Talking Jazz* (London: Macmillan, 1987)

Kleinhout, Henk and Van Eyle, Wim — *The Wallace Bishop Story* (Netherlands: Micrography, 1981)

Lord, Tom — *Clarence Williams* (Chigwell, England: Storyville, 1976)

Lyttelton, Humphrey — *The Best of Jazz – 2, Enter the Giants* (London: Robson, 1981)

— *Take It from the Top* (London: Cassell, 1975)

McCarthy, Albert — *Coleman Hawkins* (London: Cassell, 1963)

Panassié, Hugues — *Douze Années de Jazz (1927–1938)* (Paris: Edition Corrêa, 1946)

Porter, Lewis — *Lester Young* (London: Macmillan, 1985)

Sangster, John — *Seeing the Rafters* (Victoria, Australia: Penguin Books, 1988)

Schuller, Gunther — *Early Jazz: Its Roots and Musical Development* (New York: OUP, 1968)

— *The Swing Era: The Development of Jazz 1930–1945* (New York: OUP 1989)

Scott, Ronnie and Hennessy, Mike — *Some of My Best Friends Are Blues* (London: W.H. Allen, 1979)

Shapiro, Nat and Hentoff, Nat, eds — *Hear Me Talkin' to Ya; the Story of Jazz by the Men Who Made It* (London: Peter Davies, 1955)

Shapiro, Nat and Hentoff, Nat, eds — *The Jazz Makers* (New York: Rinehart, 1957)

Shaw, Arnold — *The Street that Never Slept* (New York: Coward, McCann and Geoghegan, 1971)

Simon, George — *Simon Says* (New York: Arlington House, 1971)

Stewart, Rex — *Jazz Masters of the Thirties* (New York: Macmillan, 1972)

Taylor, Arthur — *Notes and Tones* (Liege, Belgium: Taylor, 1977)

Travis, Dempsey — *An Autobiography of Black Jazz* (Chicago: Urban Research Institute, 1983)

Vian, Boris — *Round About Close to Midnight* (London: Quartet Books, 1988)

Villetard, Jean-Francois — *Coleman Hawkins Discography Volume 1 (1922–1944)* (Amsterdam: Micrography, 1984)

— *Coleman Hawkins Discography Volume II (1945–1957)* (Amsterdam: Micrography, 1985)

Wells, Dicky — *The Night People* (London: Robert Hale, 1971)

Wilber, Bob — *Music was not Enough* (London: Macmillan, 1987)

Williams, Martin, ed — *Jazz Panorama* (New York: Crowell-Collier, 1962)

Williams, Martin — *The Jazz Tradition* (New York: OUP, rev 1983)

Wilmer, Valerie — *As Serious as Your Life* (London: Allison & Busby, 1977)

The following magazines and periodicals were consulted

Great Britain — *Band Wagon, Crescendo, Hot News, Into Jazz, Jazz and Blues, Jazz Beat, Jazz Express, Jazz Forum, Jazz Journal, Jazz Monthly, Jazz News, Jazz Scene, Jazz Tempo, Jazz Today, Jazzology, Melody Maker, Pickup, Rhythm, Storyville, Swing Music, The Wire*

France	*Bulletin du Hot Club de France, Jazz Hot, Jazz Magazine, Jazz*
Holland	*Doctor Jazz, Jazz Wereld*
Eire	*Hot Notes, Jazz News*
Australia	*Jazz, Australian Jazz Quarterly, Jazz Notes, Music Maker*
Canada	*Coda, Toronto Daily Star*
USA	*Amsterdam News, Baltimore Afro-American, Bandleaders, Cadence, Capitol News, Chicago Defender, Clef, Down Beat, HRS Rag, IARJC Journal, In the Groove, Jazz, Jazz Finder, Jazz Information, Jazz Music, Jazz New England, Jazz Quarterly, Jazz Record, Jazz Review, Jazz Session, Jazz Spotlite News, Jazz Times, Jazz To-day, Jersey Jazz, Journal of Jazz Studies, Kansas City Jazz, Metronome, Mississippi Rag, Music and Rhythm, Music Dial, The Needle, New York Daily News, New York Times, New Yorker, Orchestra World, Radio Free Jazz, Record Changer, Record Research, Saint Joseph News Press, Sounds and Fury, Swing, Tempo*

Index